Piracy, Slavery, and Redemption

Piracy, Slavery, and Redemption

BARBARY CAPTIVITY NARRATIVES
FROM EARLY MODERN ENGLAND

Selected and edited by Daniel J. Vitkus

Introduced by Nabil Matar

COLUMBIA UNIVERSITY PRESS NEW YORK

Columbia University Press

Publishers Since 1893

New York   Chichester, West Sussex

Copyright © 2001 Columbia University Press

All rights reserved

Library of Congress Cataloging-in-Publication Data

Piracy, slavery, and redemption : Barbary captivity narratives

from early modern England / selected and edited by Daniel J. Vitkus;

introduced by Nabil Matar.

p. cm.

Includes bibliographical references.

ISBN 0–231–11904–6 (cloth) – ISBN 0–231–11905–4 (paper)

1. Slaves–Africa, North–Biography. 2. British–Africa, North–Biography.

3. Captivity narratives. 4. Slavery–Africa, North–History–16th century.

5. Slavery–Africa, North–History–17th century.

6. Pirates–Africa, North–History–16th century.

7. Pirates–Africa, North–History–17th century.

I. Vitkus, Daniel J. II. Matar, N. I. (Nabil I.), 1949–

HT1345 .P57   2001

306.3'62'0961–dc21   2001028215

Columbia University Press books are printed

on permanent and durable acid-free paper.

Printed in the United States of America

Designed by Audrey Smith

c 10 9 8 7 6 5 4 3 2 1

p 10 9 8 7 6 5 4 3 2 1

CONTENTS

_⌿_

ILLUSTRATIONS

Following page 52.

PREFACE

⟀

Throughout the Elizabethan period and during the seventeenth century, British seamen and traders, pirates and privateers, sailed to the Mediterranean and Atlantic coasts in search of markets, booty, and profitable relations with foreign allies. During their forays to the East, British vessels were sometimes seized by ships from North Africa, and their crews abducted and enslaved. Some of these British captives succeeded in returning to their homes, where they wrote accounts of their captivity. These narratives have remained in rare editions or manuscripts and are therefore inaccessible to the student of early modern history and literature.

The purpose of this book is to present seven complete captivity narratives from among the twenty-five or so extant accounts that are set in North Africa and were written between 1577, when John Fox escaped from his captivity in Egypt, and 1704, when Joseph Pitts's memoir of captivity and conversion to Islam was published (see the bibliography at the end of this volume). In recent years, there have been numerous studies and editions of the narratives that describe captivity among the North American Indians (in and after the late seventeenth century), and recently an edition of American Barbary captivity narratives was published, including nine texts about Americans who were captured by North Africans (these were originally printed between 1703 and 1904).[1] But very little has been available about the prototypical captivity narratives produced by early modern Englishmen who were enslaved or held for ransom in North Africa. This is a lacuna that this book hopes to fill.

NIM

DJV

NOTES

1. *White Slaves, African Masters: An Anthology of American Barbary Captivity Narratives*, ed. Paul Baepler (Chicago: University of Chicago Press, 1999).

ACKNOWLEDGMENTS

Many people have been helpful in making this book possible. In particular, we wish to thank Mrs. Marilyn Goravitch and Mrs. Sue Downing of the Humanities and Communication Department at Florida Tech for their careful typing and proofreading and Ms. Linda Khan and Ms. Victoria Smith at the Link Library for their assistance with microfilms and interlibrary loan material.

NIM
DJV

If there is one date on which this book could be said to have started, it is the evening of October 21, 1986, when I was released from captivity in Beirut, Lebanon. Ever since, and after my emigration to the United States, I have been reading about the history, interpretation, expression, motivation, and dynamics of captivity, both in the contemporary Middle East and in the early modern Mediterranean. Although I have become fascinated by accounts of Arab captives in early modern Europe—a topic I will examine in *In the Lands of Christians, 1611–1766* (forthcoming, 2002) and *Europe Through Arab Eyes, 1578–1727* (in progress)—the English experiences particularly struck me because they reveal some amazing similarities to my own experience, as well as, of course, vast differences. As a result, I perused those experiences with a vengeance, reading, compiling, copying, and photocopying every document I could get my hands on. Unfortunately, as I began rereading the material and working on the introduction to this project, the memories of May 7 through October 21, 1986, often returned. Time, it seems, does not heal.

But friends certainly help. Two friends I wish to mention with tremendous gratitude: my former department head at Florida Tech, Dr. Jane Patrick, and Dr. Rudolph Stoeckel, professor of English at that same institution. These colleagues had barely known me before I arrived in this country but had the sensitivity and depth to recognize the damage six months in solitary confinement had caused and to help me, with their humor and their willingness to read my memoirs, come to grips with an incomprehensible horror. To a disoriented immigrant, who had to leave his apartment and university at very short notice, these two friends made America gentle.

Many other people were also there for me, despite the distance: my supervisor at Cambridge, now retired, Dr. Dominic Baker-Smith, who always remembered me in his prayers; my friends Alex Baramki and Maya Yared, who flew to Cyprus as soon as I had landed there; my sister, Dr. Inaam Matar, who tried to help me via every contact she could establish in Jordan and Syria, from royalty to fortune-tellers; and, of course, my aging parents in Merritt Island, Florida, who prayed and prayed and prayed.

If there is one person to whom this research about captivity should be dedicated, however, it is my wife, Dina, who relentlessly pursued politicians and party leaders in Lebanon's vast spectrum of violence to gain my liberation from captivity. One day, when the ban is lifted, that captivity account will be published and dedicated to her.

My research on the English captives has chiefly been conducted at the British Library and the Public Record Office, in London. To the assistants and staff there, I am deeply grateful. I am also grateful to the librarians at the University Library, Cambridge University, and the Houghton Library, Harvard University, where over the years I have made many friends from among the staff. To all of them, I am thankful.

Readers and reviewers of this introduction have been numerous. I again wish to thank Dr. Jane Patrick, who always reads my work and comments helpfully; Mr. Alex Baramki, my long-distance reader and mentor; Dr. Mary C. Fuller, for a wonderful discussion at the Algiers restaurant in Cambridge, Massachusetts; Dr. David Brooks of London University, who discussed the text frequently with me; and Ms. Laura Baade, who helped me with Spanish texts. Finally, I wish to thank Dr. Daniel Vitkus, who read various drafts of the introduction and provided helpful observations and suggestions.

No changes have been made in spelling or punctuation in the introduction. Any shortcomings remain mine.

NIM

I am pleased to acknowledge the help and support of the many people who aided me, in one way or another, in the project of editing these texts. First and foremost, my thanks go out to my friends and teachers at Columbia University, who have patiently supported my career and given me so much encouragement in my work, including this particular task. I want to thank Jim Shapiro for his example as a scholar, his sagacious advice, and his spirit-lifting conversation. I owe a tremendous debt of gratitude to David Kastan for the inspiration, wit, and learning he has shared with me. And I cherish the unwavering support given to me by Jean Howard, someone who stands as a model of political commitment, intellectual achievement, and general decency. They are energetic, brilliant, and generous people, all three.

I am grateful to Jennifer Crewe, my editor at Columbia University Press, without whom this project would not have come about. I wish to thank the staff at the Folger Library for their aid: they have always made me feel welcome. Georgianna Ziegler was especially helpful with some of my specific queries. I am indebted to Beth McPherson of Bristol Mills, Maine, for her help with Latin and to Jeff Miller at SUNY, New Paltz, for assistance with Greek. Without the timely help of my computer-savvy colleague Martin Foys at FSU, there would be no map to accompany this text. I am very grateful for his assistance, which he lent on very short notice. I also want to acknowledge the labors of those at Florida Tech who have helped me in the preparation of this book: Marilyn Goravitch, Peggy Machado, Sue Downing, Suann Powell, and Victoria Smith. Most of all, I wish to recognize the generosity of my very learned former colleague at Florida Tech, Nabil Matar, who was a tremendous help in the selection of texts for this collection. His archival research at the British Library uncovered several of the documents that appear here in the appendices, and he very kindly provided them to me. For that, and for all his effort to make this anthology a success, I am grateful.

Finally, I wish to thank my wife and family for their support and understanding during all the late nights and weekends I spent away from them, with Turks and renegades. To my wife, Jane, I am always—and happily—obliged.

DJV

NOTE ON EDITORIAL METHOD

In all the early modern texts printed here, spelling, capitalization, and punctuation have been modernized. Foreign words that do not have a conventional spelling in English are an exception, and they have been kept in their original spelling (these include some proper names and place names), even when this is inconsistent within a single text. Foreign words (mostly from the Turkish or Arabic) that are not found in a standard college English dictionary have been left in their original form and italicized. Among the italicized words in the texts are those that make up the many passages of "phonetic," transliterated Arabic found in Pitts's narrative (Pitts's transliterations have been preserved in their original spellings). Ships' names are also italicized. Foreign words that are well known to English speakers (such as "imam" or "kaaba") are not italicized. Substantial emendations or editorial additions to the texts were rarely necessary, and when given they are indicated by brackets. Joseph Pitts's narrative includes a series of glosses that were set in separate, smaller print blocks of text, framed on three sides by the narrative proper. In this edition, the glosses have been placed in brackets at the points in the narrative where the interlaid blocks originally appeared. The texts of the captivity narratives printed here are taken either from the original copies found in the Folger Shakespeare Library (in the cases of Fox, Hasleton, Okeley, and Pitts) or (for the rest) from the texts reproduced in the Early English Books microfilm collections (*Early English Books, 1475–1640* [Ann Arbor: University Microfilms International, 1964] and *Early English Books, 1641–1700* [Ann Arbor: Michigan University Microfilms, 1967]).

Piracy, Slavery, and Redemption

Introduction: England and Mediterranean Captivity, 1577–1704

Nabil Matar

Until the seventeenth century, the peoples of the Far East, sub-Saharan Africa, and the New World remained shadowy figures with whom Britons had little contact. The Moors and Turks of the North African region were closer to home and better known.[1] From the Elizabethan period until the end of the seventeenth century, thousands of English, Scottish, Welsh, and Irish men and women interacted directly with the North Africans of the Barbary States as sailors, traders, soldiers, craftsmen, and artisans who either went to North Africa in search of work and opportunity or were seized by privateers and subsequently settled there. According to the Moroccan court scribe al-Fishtali (d. 1628), "craftsmen and experienced men from every land, including the lands of the Franks (*ifranj*)" worked in Marrakesh at the end of the sixteenth century. "Every day, large numbers of builders, skilled men, and those knowledgeable in decoration and construction from among the laborers and the captives, assembled together."[2] There were so many European emigrés in Algiers during the early seventeenth century that they constituted a "lobby," and before the beginning of the Great Migration to North America at the end of the 1620s, there were more Britons in North Africa than in North America, as men were drawn to the Barbary States in search of work, livelihood, and settlement.[3]

No Britons became better acquainted with the inhabitants of the Barbary Coast than the seamen, traders, travelers, and soldiers who were captured by the Barbary privateers and hauled to the slave markets located in a territory ranging from Alexandria to Sallee (Salé) and from Tunis to Meknes. Some of these captives never returned to their homes; instead, they converted to Islam and settled permanently in the Muslim world. At a time when "every major European town and city" had "thousands" of poor,[4] many viewed conversion to Islam and emigration to the Muslim dominions as the only way to start new lives. After learning of the large number of Christian converts who had risen in power and prominence in Algeria and Tunisia, Robert Burton concluded that the Christian who "will turn Turk . . . shall be entertained as a brother"; derisively, Samuel Hartlib confirmed in his "Remonstrance" of 1644 that poverty made "many that would live honestly to cheat, lie, steal, kill, turn Turk, or anything."[5] Whether because North Africa was underpopulated (after numerous bouts of plague), or because the converts to Islam practiced professions and crafts that were in high demand, or because the Qur'an urged Muslims to convert nonbelievers, Europeans converted to Islam in large numbers. In Cervantes' 1580 play *El Trato de Argel*, the captive Aurelio exclaims at the ease with which Islam prevailed over old and young Christians.[6] "A Turkish garment will become me as well as a Spanish petticoat," retorted a woman when she was reprimanded for converting to Islam.[7] In the period under study, the allure of Islam was powerful, and the borders between Christian Europe and Muslim North Africa were porous.

While some captives converted and settled among their North African coreligionists, others resisted and subsequently remained in captivity until they were ransomed or they escaped or died. Those who returned to their homes told and retold their stories in villages and marketplaces, discovering in the process that there would be a readership for their tales about the Islamic world. Until the publication of Richard Knolles's *History of the Turkes* in 1603, there was not a single original account written about Islam by an English writer; everything had either been translated or adapted from continental sources. Furthermore, while many travelers from the Elizabethan period on published descriptions of the Ottoman Levant, none had published descriptive accounts about the terrain, peoples, political organization, and customs of North Africa until after England came into possession of Tangier in 1661, and even then writers described the English rather than the Moors in the region. Very few publications about North Africa appeared in England before the second half of the seventeenth century, far fewer than the accounts of the Ottoman Empire by Moryson, Sanderson, Biddulph, Sandys, Lithgow, Blount, and others.[8] This lack of firsthand information about the Moors may explain why an account of captivity in North Africa was written in nearly every decade of the period under study. From 1577 until 1704, twenty-three captivity accounts were written by British captives (some with the help of editors or ghostwriters), but only two were published about captivity in the Ottoman Levant.[9] In texts produced for English readers, travelers described the Ottoman Levant, while captives described Tunisia, Algeria, and Morocco.

Many of the captivity accounts became popular and were reprinted: John Fox's account, for example, reappeared in an expanded version twenty years after its initial appearance in Hakluyt's 1589 edition of *Navigations*; Edward Webbe's appeared four times by 1600; Richard Hasleton's and Francis Knight's appeared twice in the year of their publication; William Okeley's twice in two years;[10] Joseph Pitts published a new edition in 1731 because pirated editions had appeared as a result of the "great" demand for his captivity account.[11] Some of the English accounts were published by friends who were eager to tell the captives' stories: after William Barley found Richard Hasleton's memoir of captivity among his papers, he promptly proceeded to publish it; A. Roberts published the "pleasant ADVENTURES" of T.S. (Thomas Smith) after the death of the author. Thomas Phelps wrote his account after friends importuned him to do so, and John Whitehead wrote his "relation of Barbary" in obedience to the "Commands" of his patron, "Mr. Hans Sloan Doctor of Physick."[12] Thomas Pellow's manuscript was published by an unknown "we" who thought it would provide an "agreeable Entertainment to the Publick."[13] So eager were Britons to read and learn about the Moors and their world that a number of additional accounts were translated from French into English.[14]

As the seven narratives included in this volume show, the writers insisted that their reports were "true." To support these claims, they repeatedly demonstrated their knowledge of Arabic or Turkish. "I having the language," wrote Thomas Sanders in 1584.[15] Thomas Smith learned Turkish, having served a Turkish master in Algiers (the Arabic transliterations he included indicate a very limited Arabic vocabulary); William Okeley assured his readers that he had "learnt" from other captives "a smattering of the Common Language"; and Edward Coxere frequently quoted Arabic or the "Lingofrank" (the latter was a mixture of the Arabic, Turkish, Greek, and Romance languages).[16] Francis Brooks could pass as a Maghrebi after mastering the dialect, and Joseph Pitts filled his text with transliterations of Turkish terms and Arabic-Qur'anic quotations and presented himself to the reader as a "historian" of the region. Although not all captives learned Arabic or Turkish, most became multilingual, and this helped them to become widely familiar with the lands and peoples of North Africa.

The captives were the first Englishmen to provide firsthand descriptions of the "customs and usages" of the Moors, unlike the dramatists who filled the English stage with types nearly always based on Spanish and Italian literary sources and never on actual familiarity with Muslims. From the *Battle of Alcazar* to *Othello* to *The Renegado*, English plays were all based on continental models and sources, and English playwrights, notwithstanding their imaginative brilliance, invented stage Muslims without any historical or religious verisimilitude. Like the Renaissance painters who depicted Jesus and the Apostles in contemporary Italian dress and manner or situated them in a Nazareth of Florentine architecture and topography, English playwrights depicted Moors through English modes of fabrication. Not a single Moor in Elizabethan drama ever reveals any knowledge of Islam; instead, the Moors on stage always appeal to classical deities. Captivity writers were not necessarily objective, since they were often encumbered with anti-Islamic prejudice, but at least they had experienced the world they described: they knew its geography, ethnography, political society, fauna, and flora better than any other British subjects. And despite the anti-Islamic lens through which they viewed Muslim religion and belief, they conveyed for the first time in English writing an extensive range of information about cities, distances, crops, military conflicts, religious practices, and social organization and behavior. The captives had lived in the households of their Moorish captors and had discovered many of the skeletons in the cultural cupboards; they had also heard the Moorish other "speak,"[17] and men such as Hasleton, Spratt, Smith, Okeley, Brooks, and Pitts partly based their accounts on the Islamic voices they had heard.

The importance of the writings of captives cannot be underestimated: in their political and commercial dealings with North African Muslims, traders, government officials, sailors, and others relied on the depositions and stories of the thousands of now forgotten Britons whose names have not even survived in ransom lists. There was so much interest in captives that in 1663 King Charles II went to Thomas Lurting's ship to hear from him the amazing story of how the Quaker and his English compatriots had been captured, how they had overpowered their Algerian captors, and how they then risked their lives to return those captors to their country, all without shedding a single drop of blood. So popular was the story that Lurting published it in 1680 and then prepared a longer version in 1709.[18] For decades, people talked about Okeley's escape from Algeria in 1644; the boat in which he and his companions had made their escape was even hung up as a monument near the central church in Majorca.[19] Meanwhile, from Hull to Plymouth and from Edinburgh to Cardiff, merchants and sailors, investors and bishops, royal courtiers and East India and Levant company stockholders all felt the impact of captivity: in sermons and homilies, during collections asking for charitable contributions to pay ransom,[20] and in tales told in public houses, Britons learned about the suffering of their countrymen in captivity.

There was such social anxiety about the captivity of large groups of men, especially seamen, that from the 1620s on thousands of destitute wives and dependents repeatedly took to the streets with petitions on behalf of their captured kinsmen.[21] In 1653 commercial and naval overseers unsuccessfully attempted to ransom all the captives in North Africa because "the country wants their services."[22] Other professions and crafts suffered, too: a 1694 list of ransomed captives from Algiers mentions carpenters, gunners, gunsmiths, coopers, sailmakers, and surgeons;[23] there were also cabinboys and "gromets" (youths ranking between adult seamen and cabinboys),[24] along with traders, fishermen, and priests. The historian al-Zayani (1734–1809) reported that the Moroccan ruler Mulay Ismail (r. 1672–1727) had "more than 25,000 captives from among the infidels, who served in building his palaces. Some were marble cutters, decorators, stone cutters, ironsmiths, builders, carpenters, architects, astrologers, doctors, and many others."[25] Ismail confirmed to the English ambassador on October 28, 1699, that some of the English captives "cutt marble, having none that cutt it but them, and they set up the pillars which none but them understand, and they serve in all the great works we have."[26] There were so many captives in Meknes, Ismail's capital, that the inner part of the city, al-Qunaytara, became their exclusive living quarters, with separate residences designated for the various nationalities—British, French, Portuguese, and Spanish—and for women, clergy, and the wealthy. Captivity brought about an intermixing of peoples, races, and religions that was rarely seen during this period of history. In cities such as Meknes and Marrakesh, Tunis and Algiers, captivity introduced a unique element of internationalism. The presence of peoples from outside the Mediterranean basin–Britons, Russians, Slavs, Poles, and Armenians–shows the diversity that prevailed among the captive population.

Captivity accounts reflect the social and religious challenge non-Christians and non-Europeans presented to early modern Britons. They also provide valuable information about Mediterranean trade, exchange, piracy, and cooperation, as well as about personal and sometimes intimate relations between Christians and Muslims, Britons and Moors. In early modern Britain, captivity had such wide national and international repercussions that, in addition to the accounts, vast numbers of letters, petitions, lists, reports, translations, treatises, depositions, proclamations, ordinances, ballads, and memorandums about captives have survived. There are also captivity manuscripts that until now have been ignored (such as John Whitehead's, at the British Library), along with hundreds of letters from North African factors and consuls about maritime conflict, captivity, negotiation, and ransom. Numerous references have also survived in Maghrebi Arabic sources, along with a large number of accounts, plays, poems, and treatises that appeared in France and Spain. Together, all this material, most of which has been hitherto ignored in English scholarship on Mediterranean captivity, shows that the *corpus captivitis* provides the most extensive description of England's early modern encounter with Islam and Muslims in North Africa.

The Barbary States

In the period under study, the North African part of the Ottoman Empire included three regencies: Algeria, Tunisia, and Tripoli. Though officially part of the Ottoman sultan's domain, these areas enjoyed a certain degree of political and commercial autonomy.[27] After the battle of Lepanto in 1571, the Ottomans' naval presence in the western Mediterranean diminished, allowing the regencies to set themselves apart from direct economic and political control by the Ottoman administration in Istanbul. Of the three regencies, Algeria was militarily the strongest. Algiers was its capital city, fortified and planned on the pattern of Istanbul. From 1587 until 1659, the period of the *bashawat*, Istanbul appointed a civilian *basha*, who was assisted by a group of advisers, the *diwan*, consisting of military representatives, sea captains, and sometimes the head of religious affairs, the *mufti*. Supporting the *basha* were the janissaries, who had their own commander, the *agha*, and the sea captains, the *ta'ifat riyyas al-bahr*, who were drawn chiefly from the local population. Despite rivalries among these elites, Algeria remained under effective Ottoman rule until 1711 and was to be titularly allied to the Porte until the French occupation in 1830.

The government the Ottomans established in Algeria served as a model for the other two regencies of Tunisia and Tripoli.[28] To the west of the three regencies, Morocco resisted Ottoman occupation and sometimes pursued politics that were anti-Ottoman. Ahmad al-Mansur (r. 1578–1603) unified Morocco and turned it into the land of "sugar and gold," as it came to be known to European traders. At the same time, he so intensified trade with England and Holland that throughout the Elizabethan period there was a kind of Anglo-Moroccan cooperation in military, commercial, and political affairs.[29] Many rulers in the Maghreb sought similar cooperation, and England signed numerous treaties with various Moroccan potentates in 1627, 1632, 1637, 1682, as well as with the regencies: Tunis in 1662; Algiers in 1664, 1672, and 1700; and Tripoli in 1676. As long as such treaties of cooperation existed, the seas were relatively safe, despite the inevitable breaches.

At the same time that friendly commercial exchanges were conducted, captive taking, slave trading, privateering, and piracy were carried out in the Mediterranean and Atlantic by Christians against Muslims, Muslims against Christians, and Christians against their Protestant or Catholic adversaries and even, among the undiscriminating English, against Orthodox Christians as well.[30] In order to join this international enterprise of privateering, Morocco and the three regencies developed fleets of varying size and effectiveness, the largest operating out of Algiers and Sallee and the smallest out of Tripoli. An unwritten agreement seems to have divided the spheres of operation: Tripolitanian privateers stayed close to home, attacking Maltese and Neapolitan ships, while Tunisian brigantines and galleys roved the eastern Mediterranean and particularly targeted trade in the Adriatic Sea. On the Atlantic coast of Morocco, Sallee grew as a privateering harbor soon after its settlement by embittered Moriscos, refugees from Hornachos in Spain, who arrived there in the early seventeenth century. With the help of English and Dutch converts, they turned Sallee into a kind of republic of privateers, independent of the central government in Marrakesh, with its own political goals and naval and military organization. From 1626 until 1668 the republic possessed over forty ships and a fort with sixty-eight cannons.[31]

Technically, there was no piracy among North Africans because the sailors and their captains always had the official support and cooperation of the *diwan* and the *basha*. All the ships, wrote Richard Blome in 1678, belonged "to private persons, Armed out as our Privateers are in England."[32] Although North Africans often operated without their rulers' authority, they were limited in their activities because of the unaccommodating nature of the Moroccan Atlantic coastline and the various Spanish and Portuguese presidios that had been established in Melilla, Tangier, Ceuta, Ma'moora, Ara'ish [Larache], and elsewhere that threatened Muslim ships. A typical privateer convoy consisted of the leader, *al-rais*, who had full authority over his three or four ships. He employed janissaries, whose role was to board the enemy ships (they possessed no navigational skills). His crews also included locals from the Arab and the Arab-Turkish population who were experienced at sea. During the preparation of the ships, the port was closed while ammunition, weapons, cannons, and food supplies (olives, vinegar, dried figs, rice, biscuit, and fruit collected from surrounding orchards) were taken aboard. A doctor accompanied the fleet, bringing enough bags of medicines and ointments to last the nearly fifty days of the journey. As the ships left the port, they saluted the ruler and the saints of the city with cannon shots.[33]

The North African attacks on Europeans extended from the Mediterranean to the Atlantic and the North Sea. The Algerian privateers reached as far north as Wales, Ireland, and Iceland; they also attacked the sea routes to New England, seizing ships that were either carrying colonists and traders from England to the New World or bringing back fishermen and unhappy settlers. "A List of what ships haue beene taken & destroyed by the argeyrons," prepared in the 1670s, confirmed that four ships (sailing "from Plym[outh] to Virginia . . . for Virginia . . . for New England . . . for Virginia") had been seized by the Algerians.[34] As Thomas Baker, the English factor in Tripoli, warned in September 1691, the "Turkes" ranged "the ocean from the Islands of Cape de Verd near the Coast of Guinny Euen as farr as Norway soe that . . . our Ships for Portugall Spayn, Madera, Canaryes & Westward Islands, New England Virginia & all the East & West Indies [are] obliged to furnish Themselves with such Papers" (passes) to protect themselves against attack.[35] Although they did not cross the ocean to the Americas, in 1585 the Algerians (under the Dutch convert Jan Jansen, or Murad Rais) sacked the town of Lanzarote in the Canary Islands, and in the next century there were some allusions to "Turks" reaching and harassing New England.[36]

As English, French, and Dutch pirates received letters of marque from their rulers, so the North Africans received authorization from theirs; and as Francis Drake and other European privateers shared their booty with their monarchs, so the Muslim privateers shared their gain with the *bey* or the *dey*, or "emperor." And, just as European rulers used the money to fill national coffers, so some North African rulers spent the income generated by priva-teers to effect social change and urban renewal. With the wealth that he received from Tunisian privateers, including the English and Dutch converts John Ward and Samson, "who were very fortunate and had a great reputa-tion at sea,"[37] Yusuf Dey went on a building spree: he built the Turks' market in Tunis, a mosque with a school attached to it, numerous inns, and a slave market (all of which can still be seen in the *Medina* of Tunis). He also brought potable water to the city and to roads used by travelers and left behind him, as the eighteenth-century historian al-Qadiri wrote, "great acts of charity."[38] His successor, Murad 'Alooj ("the convert"), closed down alco-hol-drinking places and cleaned up the seacoast by removing the heaps of garbage that had accumulated there.[39] Even the powerful Mulay Ismail relied on money generated not just from booty but from ransom, too: he "paid to the merchants silver which he had collected from the Christians for the redemption of their kin."[40] Given the need for European currency in North Africa, privateering became one of the chief means by which hard currencies, such as the dollar, the doubloon, and the pound, were earned and circulated in the region.[41] Privateering was an essential component of the maritime economy in both North Africa and Europe, and as historians such as Hebb and Pennell have shown, it brought in a substantial income to the state.[42]

Christian Piracy, Muslim Jihad

Although the North African privateers sought profit from capturing Britons and other Europeans, they also wished to retaliate against attacks on them by these same Europeans, whom they and their Muslim coreligionists had encountered as marauding crusaders and piratical *ifranj* since the medieval period.[43] In October 1584, for example, the Venetians captured a Tunisian galley on its way to Tripoli, killing all the crew: 50 Moors, 75 Turks, 174 Christian converts to Islam, and 45 women.[44] Thomas Sanders, an English-man who had been a captive in Tripoli the year before, thought the act God's just judgment on the infidels.[45] Throughout the sixteenth century, as they gained the technological edge over the North Africans, Spanish and Por-tuguese soldiers terrorized the African shores. They held thousands of Moors in their prisons and presidios, while thousands of others were enslaved, branded, and chained in Maltese, Italian, and French galleys. The Morisco writer Ahmad bin Qasim noted that in the first decade of the seventeenth century, there were over fifty-five hundred Muslim captives in Venice and Malta alone.[46] An English captive in Tunis, the Catholic Robert Ellyatt, even complained in 1612 about the depredations of his heretical (Protestant) compatriots,[47] while another captive, John Rawlins, admitted that the reason the Algerians maltreated the English captives was that the English fleet had tried to burn the Algerian harbor months earlier. The Algerian ruler explained to James I in October 1624: "Your Ma[jes]ties su[b]iects did take some moores, and Turkes; and now our Captaines did take certaine Englishmen, and sold them; which if your Ma[jest]tie shalbe pleased to send us the Moores, and the Turkes, Wee shall suddainly and out of hand putt the Christians att Liberty."[48] English aggression led to Algerian counteraggression. In the 1620s scores of Moors and Turks were held in English, Irish, and Welsh jails and later either sold as slaves in Spanish sea towns or executed as pirates.[49] It is not surprising that in many North African Arabic writings, whenever an author mentioned European Christians–*nasara*–the words that he invariably added afterward were *damarahum Al-lah* (may God destroy them).

In 1627 the inhabitants of Sallee wrote to King Charles I complaining about the depredations committed by the English captain Neaston; three years later, they complained again.[50] A few years after that, English ships attacked Algeria in an act of war that the English captive Francis Knight blamed squarely on his compatriots: "I am certaine that the last peace was broken by the English, by whom those of Argere received many injuries and long suffered them before they sought the least revenge."[51] During the Restoration, the English became so deeply involved in the owning and trading of Moorish slaves that the Algerian dey had to insist that if peace was to prevail, for which a treaty had been signed in 1662, the English should refrain from "carrying Turks or Mussulman slaves."[52] Sometimes, the English used brutal methods to intimidate the Barbary privateer communities. The commander of the British fleet in the Mediterranean, Sir Edward Spragg, described in May 1671 how his fireships put all the Algerian ships "in flame. . . . The castles and town [are] miserably torn, with an infinite number of inhabitants killed and wounded, and that which fell out very luckily to second this success was, that all their chirurgeons' chests were burnt on board their ships, that they have not the least medicine to dress a wound with."[53] Over ten years later, it was the French who devastated the city. The English consul Philip Rycault reported on August 16, 1683, that the French fleet launched "4000 Bombas out of ye 6000: they first brought with them and ye damage to this towne is about 800: houses & shops beat downe besides 4 ships 3 fettezes & one gally sunk."[54] The captive Joseph Pitts confirmed the destruction, saying that streets and neighborhoods could no longer be recognized after the bombardment. At the end of the century, Ibn Abi Dinar recalled how "Christians attacked with their ships and galleys and cut off the sea travellers and seized every ship against its will, thereby harming all Muslims."[55] Well into the nineteenth century, the destruction committed by *al-Ingleez* (the English) was still recalled as the comments of the Tunisian traveler Ahmad bin Abi Diyaf (1804–73) show: "In his days [Dey Mustapha Laz, ca. 1665], the ships of the English came to Ghar al-Milh and burnt a ship and bombarded the towers, whose ruins can still be seen."[56]

It is no wonder that in Arab-Islamic sources the Barbary privateers stand out as defenders of the community and the faith. The Arabic term used to describe the privateers was *al-ghuzat*, the same term that had been used to denote those who fought with the Prophet Muhammad or in Ottoman warfare. The term is connected with the early Islamic conquests when men fought for both faith and gain, or *ghaneema*, a term that harks back to the time when the Prophet divided the spoils of battle among his warriors. The term connotes a fair reward: a Muslim fighter was rewarded for his *ghazu* (raid) by the gain he might acquire from his enemies, a profit deemed honorable in the eyes of the Islamic community. The Barbary *ghuzat* therefore saw themselves as religious warriors. While among them were certainly some vagrants, social deviants, and mercenaries (as with the *hajee* described by Okeley), they also numbered men of moral and religious caliber who recognized a national cause in their *ghazu*. In 1577 Ibn Askar described how the jurist Abdallah al-Waryagli would teach in winter and spring but in summer and fall participate in *ghazu*; in the middle of the seventeenth century, Ali al-Nouri, a man of ascetic temperament, spent all his wealth on "*al-ghuzat* [who fought] at sea against the infidels. He launched ships, on which he spent money, to repel the attacks of the Christian corsairs." On Sunday, the sixth of Muharram, 1095 (1683), wrote al-Da'eef al-Rabati, jurists, *shareefs* (descendants of the Prophet), and *marabouts* (holy men) departed Fez intent on *jihad*.[57]

An important factor in the rise and empowerment of *al-ghuzat* was the hostility the Moriscos developed for European Christians after their expulsion from Spain. Hundreds of thousands of the expelled Moriscos settled in North African sea towns and turned their navigational skills against their former compatriots. "The Sultan of al-Maghreb al-Aqsa [of Morocco] employed many of them as soldiers," wrote the historian al-Maqiri (d. 1631). "They lived in Sallee and their sea-borne *jihad* is now famous. They fortified Sallee and built in it palaces, houses, and bathhouses."[58] Many who had been law-abiding subjects in Iberia turned into embittered sea rovers. After his expulsion, the Morisco Amurates Rayobi led ten ships with over four thousand fighters to harass the coast of Spain; Abul-Ali, who had sold coal in Osuna, turned into a terror of the Mediterranean after his expulsion.[59] The exiled Andalusians, confirmed an anonymous historian at the end of the seventeenth century, "sailed the seas of the Maghreb [out of Sallee and Arai'sh] and attacked the Christians, and gained much booty."[60] *Al-ghuzat* were only too happy to capture Spanish and other Christian ships and wreak vengeance on those who had persecuted them and their coreligionists. Many had experienced Christian violence firsthand as they fled from Spain and France to North Africa. Having been dispossessed of their property, separated from their children, and exiled from their homeland because of their religion, they felt that vengeance was their due. The literature of the Maghreb in the period under study resonates with the memory of Spanish-Portuguese-French enmity against the Arab Muslims of Europe and North Africa: in poems and in biographies, in song and in polemic, the exiled Andalusians perpetuated the memory of injustice and deprivation and sustained the desire for retaliation and compensation.

Notwithstanding these emotions, it is important to note that privateering did not exclude purely practical needs. The privateers of the Maghreb pursued European ships and captives because they sought *ghaneema*, which buttressed faltering national economies. Commerce in trade and booty was organized and coordinated in a very professional manner to bring in the highest possible revenue. As European trade with America gradually reduced the amount of commerce and exchange with the Maghreb, the privateers sought vengeance as well as hard currency and political leverage: the seizure of captives enabled Maghrebi countries to assume a role in inter-European Mediterranean rivalry because consuls and ambassadors had to court them not only to obtain the release of captives but to secure monopolies in trade, exclusive usage of ports, and access to supplies and munitions during times of war. In the Maghreb, privateering and captive taking were a response to declining trade.

The British Captives

In each successful raid directed at Britons, whether on land or at sea, North African privateers took anywhere from a handful of captives to a few hundred. Although they operated mainly on the high seas, they also seized fishermen near the coasts: many captives were taken in small boats carrying no more than half a dozen or a dozen men and boys. At other times, privateers went on land and with the help of sympathetic locals captured their victims asleep in their homes or hiding in their churches. As William Court, a freed captive, stated in his 1625 deposition, "the Englishe and Flemmishe runnegadoes often saie that they would fetch the Christians from the shore."[61] Other Britons were seized while conducting illegal trade in North Africa: the Moroccan ruler, Mulay al-Walid, complained to Charles I in December 1631 that English traders, unlike the French or the Dutch, had been supplying rebels with weapons and ammunition; in August 1634 he repeated his complaint after the king failed to control his subjects.[62] When those who helped the Moroccan rebels were caught, their captors viewed them as deserving of enslavement. Some captives were soldiers and mariners who were taken during military actions. Particularly during the war of liberation in Morocco under Mulay Ahmad and Mulay Ismail, many men (and sometimes women) were taken in battle or skirmishes. In March 1681, for example, "all the Christians [Spaniards in Ma'moora], along with their possessions, arms, and artillery, were taken as booty" to Ismail's capital in Meknes;[63] a year later, British soldiers (chiefly Irish and Scottish), who had been besieged in Tangier, were captured as they sortied in search of food.

It is important to recall that during this period large numbers of British seamen and soldiers were pressed into military service by force or trickery. Paid very low wages, if any, they were expected to loot and pillage in order to feed themselves and their families. Many who were taken captive had themselves taken others captive, and many who were robbed had been robbers themselves. As Joshua Gee admitted, "After that war was made with france we took many ships & did Recruit owr selvs with Cloathing when we had leave to goe one board the prises which was a favor shone us."[64] It was while committing these acts of violence against the French that Gee was taken captive and brought to North Africa. Thus, while there were many innocent villagers and harmless travelers and traders among the captives, there were also soldiers, pirates, and marauders, as they themselves admitted in song:

> To Tunis and to Argiers, boys,
> Great is our want, small be our joys;
> Let's then some voyage take in hand
> To get us means by Sea or Land.
>
> . . . .

Methinks, my boys, I see the store
Of precious gems and golden ore;
Arabian silks and sables pure
Would make an haggard stoop to th' lure.
Come follow me . . .[65]

For English sailors and seamen, the land of the Moors provided opportunity for conquest, loot, and golden "means."

It is impossible to calculate the exact number of Britons who were captured by the Barbary privateers during the period under study. While there are records of thousands of captives who were ransomed, innumerable others simply disappeared after being sold into slavery in the North African and Middle Eastern hinterlands. In 1577, after fourteen years in Alexandria, John Fox escaped, but only three of the Englishmen who had been captured with him in 1563 participated in the escape; whether the rest had died or joined Turko-Egyptian society by converting to Islam is not clear. In 1632 thirty-eight captives presented a petition (included here as appendix 4) to King Charles I; in it, some stated they had been held "20 yeares, some 16: some 12," while others had been forced to convert.[66] In 1631, months after an attack on Baltimore, Ireland, in which eighty-seven children and women and twenty men were carried captive to Algiers, the English representative there reported that there were only eighty-three captives "fit to be ransomed," implying that nearly 20 percent had either died or converted.[67] Thomas Smith, who was a captive in Algiers, mentioned how he had been sent with others to help the Algerian army and therefore had not been included in the head count of captives that was conducted when English middlemen arrived in North Africa to ransom their compatriots.

A list compiled on September 6, 1669, names 400 English captives held in Algiers, 348 who had been "brought new" and 52 "old slaves."[68] The list mentions the dates on which captives were seized, their names, and the ships on which they had been sailing. It further shows how, on many occasions, brothers and cousins were seized together on the same ship, how non-Britons were also seized (Italians, Flemings, and Hamburgers), and how some died after their capture. A year later, "A List of the English captives [seized by] the Pyrates of Argier, made Publick for the Benefit of those that have Relations there" was published in London and included the same names, ordered as they appear in the manuscript. The only difference, aside from the spelling of the names, is the omission of Richard Hoare, John Parkes, Abraham Harris, Joseph Galler, "David," and others. What had happened to them is not clear, but it was not uncommon for captives to be seized by one group and then sold to another, as was the case of the men whose capture is described in *Newes from Sally*. Keeping track of such transfers was not always possible, which explains why certain captives appear suddenly in the written records many years after their initial capture. In 1637, for example, Britons were released who had been in captivity for thirty years, and in 1668 a certain Captain Galilee was reported to have been a slave since 1652.[69]

Sometimes, whole families were taken together, the father then being allowed to return to England in order to raise the ransom for his captive family. In other cases, all the male adults of a small community would be seized; for example, a petition to the king in June 1670 mentioned the names of captives taken from Stepney, "amongst whom were the petitioners' husbands, sons, and relations."[70] Throughout, relatives as well as shipowners tried to keep the captives in the forefront of both public and government attention. In March 1676 a writer dedicated his "Journal" to the duke of York and included "A Liste of persons slaves in Tripoli wch must be redeemed according ye Articles of ye 5th of March 1675/6."[71] The "Names of Captives Redeemed out of Algier by Thomas Baker from May 1692 to 10th Decemb: 1694" listed 110 men and 1 woman and made reference to their professions.[72] "A List of Captives at Mequiness [Meknes] on Sept. 29th. 1719" mentions the date on which captives were taken and which of them had converted to Islam: "June 19th 1715 / Andrew Coke . . . / Wm. Johnson Turned Moor / Wm. Killeen Boy." This list includes a reference to "Tho: Pellow Boy Turnd Moore," the same Pellow who wrote the last account of English captivity in the early modern period. The list concludes with the following summary: "Living 188 / Dead 53 / Turnd Moor 16."[73] Such lists, of which there are dozens, served to keep a record for the authorities of captured, converted, or dead nationals.

Captives hailed from all over England, Wales, Scotland, and Ireland, but the majority came from the southern coastal region, as the extant lists reveal. The first list of captives published in England appeared in Hakluyt: in 1584 ships from Plymouth, Guernsey, Hampton, and London had been seized and the names of the captives given, but no information has survived about their backgrounds.[74] The list published by John Dunton in 1637 showed the geographical origin of captives: of 339 ransomed men, women, and children, the majority came from Plymouth (37), Dongervin (26), Dartmouth (23), London (22), and Apson (18), but there were also captives from all over Britain, from Hull to Jersey and from Dublin to Cardiff and Lyme.[75] Another list, published in 1646, mentions 246 men, women, and children who were ransomed by

Edmond Cason, "Agent for the Parliament."[76] This is the only list from this period to include the name, place of origin, and ransom amount for each captive. The vast majority came from London (70), while nearly all the others came from coastal towns in the south and the west—Plymouth (29), Dartmouth (19), Barnstable (18), Bristol (14), Weymouth (11), Yahall [Youghal] (11), Apson (8), Dover (8), and Foy (5)—a few more came from Poole, Liverpool, Southampton, Swansea, Falmouth, and Penzance; and a handful came from as far as Dundee, Edinburgh, Hull, Yarmouth, and Ipswich. When Cason first counted the captives, he mentioned "650 and upwards, besides above an 100 in the ships of this place, now at Candia in the service of the great Turk."[77] The names and information that have survived cover only one third of all the Britons who were held or enslaved. No information has survived about the others.

Captives met with rough treatment, particularly at the start, when they were being "broken." The privateers wanted captives to describe the ordeals they suffered to their kin and thereby hasten the ransom process. Some privateers tortured prisoners for information about wealthy passengers and hidden jewelry and merchandise; the Trinity House archives, for example, confirmed that Edmond Bostocke was beaten "unmercifully . . . to make him confesse what was in the ship."[78] Another Trinity House certificate stated in 1624 that Richard Morris was so brutally handled that "many small bones and splinters had to be taken from his head,"[79] while James Wadsworth wrote that after failing to do his chores, he was so flogged that, for a while, he lost the use of his left arm.[80]

The North Africans were not unlike the English, French, and Dutch pirates and privateers in the Caribbean who tortured Spanish captives for reasons similar to theirs. No Muslim privateer, however, is described in English sources as having resorted to the brutal methods employed by Morgan or L'Olonnais in the Caribbean, although there are some references in English sources to what appears to have been sadistic cruelty. In his letter from Sallee of June 7, 1625, William Leg wrote: "The cruelty used in cutting their ears, forcing them to eat them, burninge other, and almost starving others. The excessive ransoms: 1500, 1000, 800, 600; the meanest, 300 duckets. Diverse forced to turn Turks."[81]

Was this an accurate account, or was it inspired by a need to vilify the Muslims? Writers such as Pitts and Pellow gave lengthy descriptions of the torture of which their captors were capable in order to emphasize their own courage (and indirectly justify their conversion to Islam). But the overwhelming evidence shows that North African captors took care of their captives in order to use them for work or to collect their ransom.[82] Okeley understood that he was spared execution for having blasphemed against Islam because his owner knew that if Okeley died, the owner's son would lose his money. When Thomas Smith was first taken ashore in Algiers to be inspected and sold into slavery, the relatives of some of the Algerians slain when the English crew defended themselves called for revenge: "Had not our guardians protected us from their violence," wrote Smith, "I think we had been torn in pieces."[83] The business acumen of the captors prevailed, however, over their desire for personal vengeance. When 150 men were ransomed from Algiers in March 1675, it was observed that they were "stout and lusty."[84] Evidently, those captives had been well taken care of.

Upon returning to their home ports, captors customarily paraded their human commodities, who were chained and nearly naked, having been robbed of their clothes. The port population, along with the officials who had financed the privateers, came out to inspect the captives and the booty. The captives were then led before the local ruler (who was also the chief shareholder in all privateering ventures), and he usually chose the best for himself. (Thomas Smith and William Okeley both recalled how the Algerian *dey* squeezed the captives in order to judge their physical condition, looked at their teeth to verify their age, and examined their hands to see how much labor they had been used to.) The remaining captives were then led to the bagnios, the public bathhouses, which were used as holding pens for captives and slaves.[85] Similar in function to the forts that Britons were building in sub-Saharan western Africa to house slaves, bagnios were chosen because they were the most spacious and most easily guarded buildings available (no windows and only one entrance).

From the bagnios, of which there were dozens in North Africa, each with its own name and designation (Royal Bagnio, Ali Mami's Bagnio, Sidi Hassan's Bagnio, Lions' Bagnio, Ali Bichteen's Bagnio, St. Catherine's Bagnio, and others), the captives were then sold in open auctions into private slavery. Captives' prices at market were usually an estimate of both the ransoms they could command and, for men, their professional value. The first question that Richard Hasleton was asked by the "king" of Algiers after he was brought before him was about his profession, specifically whether he was a "Gunner," a profession in great demand in North Africa (indeed, numerous British soldiers served in the armies of Islam in the Elizabethan and Jacobean periods).[86] The English factor in Morocco, John Harrison, reported that when Abd al-Malek inherited the throne from his father, he released the captives from the "chaines both by the neck and legs" and "made them, his gunners, giuing them free leaue to goe vp and downe where they would at their pleasure, and doe almost what they would: and not a Moore that durst controll them, but rather stood in awe of them."[87] Other captives were put to work in household service, in farming, gardening, building, animal husbandry, or in business. We "were suffered to work upon any manner of trade or occupation wherein we were any way expert," wrote Edward Webbe in 1591, "and what we did or made, we sold to the Turks, and they gave us money for the same."[88] Robert Ellyatt continued to conduct business while in Tunisian captivity; in December 1612 he witnessed a document in which two captives, a Dutchman and an Englishman, granted power of attorney to Thomas Hout in Leghorn to try and effect their release.[89] William Okeley told how his patron gave him money to open a shop, how he established a partnership with two Englishmen, and how he was able to save a substantial sum of money that his fellow captive, the minister Devereux Spratt, smuggled out for him in a box with a false bottom.[90] John Hart, "an ingenious young man," was captured by the Algerians in 1667 and within a few months became "keeper of [the] treasure" for "Mustapha Homer, General of the camp of the Arabs."[91] Intelligent, engaging, and multilingual (he could speak Arabic, Turkish, Spanish, and some Italian), Hart quickly rose in status.

A report from Algiers in June 1675 confirmed that captives

> are imployed by theer severall Patrons, some in their Garden-houses, or sent to sea according to the professions and qualityes of ye Patrones, by whom for ye most part they are better trated then any slaves in all the grand Signors Dominions, haueing the benefitt to Keep shopps, Tauerns, to worke vpon their hand craft trade. . . . Many thousand Captiues obtayned their liberty by theer own Industry. They haue allsoe liberty to say & and hear mass euery places allowed for that Seruice. The protestants have allsoe a place to preache & pray in wch is performed in ye English Consull'e House by the seuerall nations, English, German, & Dutch.[92]

A few years later, John Pridaux wrote to his aunt about his cousin: "He was a slave in Sally; but being so very understanding above the rest of the captives, was sent to King Charles from the King of the Moors with letters, as an ambassador, to treat about the redemption of captives. Had not such a thing happened he would be a slave to this day."[93] Other captives also served as emissaries. In August 1689 Mulay Ismail of Morocco wrote to William of Orange that he was sending him "one of our slaves of the English Nation, whose name is James Hamel on purpose into England, that these Our Letters may be safely delivered to your Majesty."[94] "The Emperor," wrote the Moroccan ambassador Ali Benandala to Queen Anne after the death of her consort, "sent a letter . . . by the hands of a Captive Vassall of his Majesty of Great Brittain, in the company of Jones, and the said Jones being returned to these Dominons tells me that the letter was delivered."[95] The Spanish captive Joseph de Leon (a captive in Morocco between 1708 and 1728) stated that there were captives who worked in shops, as he did, and in steel and ammunition factories, while others opened taverns in which both captives and Moors congregated.[96] Captivity clearly varied in its conditions, from cruel enslavement to well-paying employment and from professional labor to ambassadorial opportunity.

When slaves with useful skills were put to work, they were allowed some latitude in their movements. Some took walks in the countryside, while others worshiped together in groups. William Okeley reported that he and other Christian slaves in Algiers were permitted to meet three times each week in a "cellar" he had rented from a Turk, where they heard Devereux Spratt preach "the Word of God."[97] Because he was a Protestant minister with no external evidence of his religious calling, unlike Catholic clergy and monks with their habits and tonsures, Spratt was forced to work as a servant in his Algerian owner's house. Later in the century, however, in Morocco, Mulay Ismail forbade captured Catholic priests from being put to labor, and after a Franciscan won permission from him to build a small chapel in Meknes, priests served the Catholic community as religious leaders and overseers of infirmaries and hospices. Often, priests led their coreligionist captives in processions to celebrate holy days and instructed them in literacy and the articles of faith.[98]

Many continental captives commented on the latitude shown to them by their captors, the like of which was never regularly shown to Muslim captives in England, Spain, or France. Cervantes, who had experienced captivity for five years (1575–80), wrote in *Los Baños De Argel* of how the Spanish captives had the opportunity to celebrate a "fiesta" that included a "comedia cautiva," which their captors attended; the Flemish captive D'Aranda wrote that in the bagnio, there was "une vraie kermesse de Flandre" every day; and the chevalier d'Arvieux, a French traveler, described the pomp and status the slave Don Manuel attained in Tunisia in the 1660s.[99] In the case of Britons, there are no references to festive communal activities, but there are allusions to moments when their masters expressed compassion and intimacy. Thomas Smith recalled his captivity in Algiers as "the happy time of my slavery"; Francis Knight had "an honest moral man" for a captor; William Okeley was tempted not to escape back to England, where there was civil unrest and poverty, but to stay among his captors, who had gainfully employed him; Adam Elliot used to get drunk with his captor and entertain him with popular London ballads; Francis Brooks escaped his captivity with the help of a Moor who was later executed for his kindness; Joshua Gee recalled the generosity of one captor who shared his food with him; Joseph Pitts was adopted by his last master, who treated him as his son. The prayer for the conversion of the Muslims at the end of Pitts's account reveals his deep connection to the religious community of his captor. Perhaps no captives fared better than Nash and Parker, two merchants who were captives in Sallee for four years, during which time they learned the language and trade of the country, and then "set up a House in Tetuan in the Year that the English quitted Tangier [1684], which House has continued ever since; and it is said those Gentlemen before they left Barbary got better Fortunes in it, than they lost by being taken."[100] All these positive anecdotes explain why the Algerian scholar Moulay Belhamissi has urged that the study of captivity accounts should discriminate between what is "histoire" and what is "hystérie," between what actually happened and what captives, their relatives, and modern historians have projected.[101]

While some of the land slaves fared relatively well, the galley slaves had a harsher time. The accounts by Thomas Sanders, Edward Webbe, Richard Hasleton, John Rawlins, Robert Ellyatt, and Francis Knight provide a glimpse of the grim life in the galleys: bread and water for sustenance, the brutal labor of rowing, and the despair of enslavement, conditions similar to those experienced by Arab galley slaves at the hands of Christian captors.[102] Slavery in the galleys, wrote Knight, "is most inhumane & diabolical," and an anonymous poet wrote in 1664:

> For those poor captives, that for many years,
> serv'd him [the Turk] 'gainst their will
> with sighs and tears,
> And in his galleys taken uncessant pains,
> Rowing along their coasts in iron chains,
> Enduring many a blow upon their back.
> When their sad hearts were ready for to crack;
> And with their bastinadoes on their feet,
> Blow after blow most cruelly doth meet.
> Their prayers and tears ere long will soar on high,
> To ruin him and his conspiracy.[103]

Despite such horrors, English writers and observers agree that enslavement on Muslim ships was better than on French, Italian, or Spanish galleys.[104] For one thing, when the *ghaneema* was divided, Christian galley slaves serving the Muslims received two shares, as much as "the gunroom crew and best soldiers"; Muslims also kept cleaner ships, as Samuel Pepys noted in 1683.[105] Some sailors, such as Webbe, Hasleton, and Coxere, experienced captivity at the hands of both Muslim and Christian slave masters and were able to compare treatment: they described by far more horrible treatment at the hands of Italian and Spanish captors than that received from North African privateers (see especially Hasleton's text, below). In 1635 Henry Kebell wrote that he and his companions would have preferred to "have fallen into the Turks' hands than into Frenchmen's, for they [the French] would have hoysed them overboard."[106] Forty years later, writers praised "Turkish" civility while denouncing Ostender and Portuguese roughness.[107] Perhaps one of the most moving accounts of English suffering during this period appears in the letters written by a group of Quaker men and women who were imprisoned on Malta by the Inquisition. Rather interestingly, one of the women sufferers later went to Istanbul and preached before the sultan, after which she was given help paying her way back to England. The Muslims had been kinder to the Quaker than the Catholics of Malta had been.[108]

Captors encouraged communication between captives and their kin and permitted descriptions of the conditions of enslavement in the hope of expediting the ransom process. Many illiterate captives dictated letters to compatriot scribes, whom captors then bribed to gain information about the contents of the letters: the social status of the captive, the financial situation, and the family or court connections. Perhaps because of this recourse to scribes, letters sometimes repeated stock phrases and sentences: in a certificate by Trinity House in 1624, Peter Matthew, who was a captive in Sallee, wrote how he was "forced to grinde in ye mill like a horse all ye day";[109] John Gwillym wrote to Charles II, using the same biblical image, that he was being made daily "to grind in a Mill as a horse with chaines upon legges."[110] Other letters described individual situations: "You wrote me of your good health & that you had a brisk girl blessed be God for it," wrote John Willdon to his wife from Meknes in June 1716.[111] "My last to my uncle," wrote a captive on March 4, 1717, "was of 20th of Decem in which I gave him acct [account] of our being put to hard labour."[112]

On some occasions, letters sent by the captives or by resident merchants were excerpted and circulated in London to mobilize support: "An Extract of a letter written from Barbary to Mr. Thomas Ferris written by his factor there" in July 1632 is in the same hand and uses nearly the same words as another "Extract" sent by William Bennett to William Clowberie in that same month; the captives are described as having been forced to convert to Islam and submit to circumcision.[113] Like Pitts, who included letters he had written to his parents in his published account, captives remained in contact with their relatives and countrymen, communicating with them about their plight or about the condition of their friends: "Dear Sir," wrote a captive from Meknes in April 1716, "I beg you at the sight of this [letter] to make me some speedy answer adviseing me how all things are at home. . . . Mr. Delbridge desires you to let his wife know of his being heer. Please to let Mr. Nicholas sister know the same for he Expects she will send him some money and if she desires you to forward it the quickest way you can."[114] Captives, captors, relatives, employers, and intermediaries were all eager for letters to be exchanged and information relayed to the proper destinations (see appendix 2 for three examples).

After the initial shock of finding themselves transformed from free men into slaves, captives tried to make the best of a bitter reality: they learned what social codes to follow, if only to reduce the possibility of harsh discipline at the hands of offended captors. They observed how Islam affected their masters' lives, in part because they sometimes had to take part in their masters' religious duties and festivities. During the celebration of the Prophet's birth in Morocco, for example, it was "state captives," according to al-Fishtali, who had to carry candles and tree branches in the procession.[115] Captives learned to adjust to an ethnic diversity that was quite different from the relatively closed and homogeneous society of England. There were Arabs, Moors, Turks, and Central and East Europeans among the converts to Islam. Jews often played an important role in the state economy and the arrangement of ransom, which may have been why Thomas Phelps was so hostile to them.[116] The climate was also different from Britain's, as was the terrain.

In captivity, Europeans learned about the social and private lives of Muslims in a manner no traveler could. While English dramatists and travel writers praised the Muslims for dominating and controlling their wives, the reality described by some captives, such as Hasleton, Thomas Smith, and others, as well as by North African writers, showed a different and less restricted side of Muslim marital and gender relations.[117] Some captives were granted access to women's quarters and learned about the hidden power of their Muslim patronesses. Cervantes noted in the "Captive's Tale" in *Don Quixote* (chapter 41) that Christian captives were allowed freedom of communication with women, even more than what was considered appropriate for other slaves from sub-Saharan Africa or from among captured enemy tribesmen. Hasleton wrote how the wife of the Algerian king repeatedly met with him to implore him to convert to Islam and remain in the service of her husband. Muslim women, claimed D'Aranda, "will take any occasion to fall into discourse with the Christians,"[118] while the Sieur Mouette reported, "My mistress often pressed me to turn renegado, that she might have it in her power to give me greater tokens of her affection."[119]

Captives were also able to see places that no European travelers or other outsiders could: Webbe traveled widely from Palestine to Persia and claimed that he had been taken to the land of Prester John. Robert Ellyatt gave the first description of the political and social organization of Tunisia by an Englishman, estimating the forces needed to conquer the kingdom, suggesting the means to protect Christendom against the Turks, and remarking on the abundance of fish and coral. Thomas Smith traveled with his master deep into North Africa. John Hart went with his captors to "Tittory, Constantine, Biscery (Biskara), where the dates come from, Mosobis . . . Soye . . . Tunidis (?Tenedos), Constantinople."[120] John Whitehead gave a careful description of the interior of Morocco and also detailed the customs and clothes of the inhabitants, which "much resemble that of the Ancient Irish."[121] Joseph Pitts was the first Englishman to write about the Muslim holy cities of Mecca and Medina.[122] These and other captives came to observe, and later to describe, for the first time in English history, the cultural complexity and geographic diversity of the Barbary States.

Liberation of Captives

Once captives were seized, there were numerous options for their liberation. First was the military option: the monarch could issue letters of marque or of reprisal to the merchants whose ships had been seized. In 1582 Robert Oliphant petitioned Queen Elizabeth for "assistance towards an expedition undertaken by himself and others for the relief of the Master of Oliphant and Master of Morton."[123] (There is no evidence, however, that the queen supported the enterprise.) Under James I, who reversed his predecessor's pro-Muslim policies, the military option became more acceptable, and the king received numerous requests for letters of marque from disgruntled merchants and shipowners. In September 1610 Hewitt Staper, a merchant, asked permission from the earl of Salisbury to "set fire to their [Algerian] ships as they lie in the road, where there are often 8 or 10 at the least."[124] Although the king did not always grant such letters, in 1621 he did authorize an attack on Algiers for the purpose of putting an end to the capture of British seamen and of obtaining the release of the hundreds who were held there.

Three years later, in 1624, Captain Thomas King petitioned the king to "take out two ships at his own charge to Sally, to revenge the seizure there of his factor and goods,"[125] and from 1632 on King Charles was encouraged to attack Algiers, Tunis, and Sallee so that the fleet could "take enough prisoners to redeem the slaves," since "it was both impossible and inconvenient to think of redeeming captives by collection, contribution or at all by ransom."[126] In 1637 the English fleet under Captain Rainsborough attacked Sallee to liberate English captives, and in January 1638 the captain addressed to the king a number of "propositions for redeminge the captives in Argeire" in which he urged that a small fleet be stationed in the Mediterranean to protect commercial shipping.[127] During the Commonwealth and Restoration periods, the English fleet attacked harbors in Tunisia, Algeria, and Libya, and in the mid-1670s it imposed peace treaties on their rulers. But despite these efforts and England's growing naval power, Britons continued to be seized by North Africans well into the eighteenth and early nineteenth centuries.

The other way to gain freedom was to pay the ransom demanded by the captors. Once the sum was known, collections were taken in the parishes, local communities and from the public at large. From the second half of the sixteenth century on, there were "charitable collections" during Easter "in every parish, in answer to the [Privy] council's letters concerning the captives taken in Turkey."[128] In 1579 the burgess of Aberdeen began collections for "the relief of the Scottismen prissoneris in Argier in Affrik, and utheris partis [other parts] within the Turkis boundis."[129] Four years later, the burgess and his son were still pursuing their goal, and King James of Scotland appointed a committee to oversee their activities, "his Majestie being credibillie informt of the deceis [decease] of the saidis captives for quhais [whose] releif the said almous [alms] was collectit." The king demanded that the surplus be used for effecting the release of one David Hume "presentlie captive in Burdeaulx" (Bordeaux) in France.[130]

On a limited scale, the Corporation of the Trinity House assisted captives and their families and served as one of the avenues they could use to seek the means for ransom. Established by Henry VIII to help sailors, travelers, and explorers, Trinity House documented the whereabouts of seamen and ships and collected information about families of captives and their conditions, as well as about the locations and ransom prices of the captives.[131] Trinity House also issued certificates to "collectors" to travel around the country in order to raise money to ransom Britons who were being held captive. These certificates testified to the good conduct of the captives (they had not been pirates) and described their suffering and the plight of their wives and families. In 1613, for example, one Mary Temple turned to the corporation for "a Patent for collection in divers parishes" for her husband, who had been taken captive by the Turks.[132] Trinity House issued hundreds of certificates for collectors, and since ransoms were always in the scores of pounds, collecting pennies and halfpennies to make up such sums must have required extensive travel. To raise money for John Temple in 1614, for instance, the collector was licensed to beg in the parish churches of London, Middlesex, Kent, Sussex, Surrey, Berkshire, Buckinghamshire, Hertfordshire, Westminster, Canterbury, and Chichester; to ransom Michael Fletcher in 1624, the petition for collection covered Kent, Essex, Suffolk, Norfolk, Middlesex, and the cities of London and Norwich.[133] These cities and counties constituted a large part of the most populated area of England then.

When a collector entered a village public house and church, he told tales of horror about the captors, thereby projecting a frightening image of the Turks and Moors. The certificates often included a formula warning people that unless they offered money, the captives would remain unransomed and would subsequently "turn Turk" and so be lost to their families and country. To villagers whose knowledge of the "Mahumetans" may have exclusively derived from wandering players or parish preachers, the collector provided what might have seemed as the most authentic description of Muslims: cruel infidels who compelled Christians, with torture and savagery, to renounce their much-loved God and monarch. Marcellus Laroon's engraving at the end of the seventeenth century, *Remember the Poor Prisoners* (see illustration 4), shows how familiar the figure of the collector was in England.

On many occasions, captives were freed by exchange. When there was no money available to pay ransom, the best alternative was to capture opponents and then exchange them for compatriots. Neither military commanders nor writers seemed to have had any moral or religious qualms about such actions. After Robert Ellyatt became the slave of Mustafa Agha in Tunis, he tried in January 1613 to arrange for Ramadan, a captive in Malta, to be exchanged for him.[134] In the 1621 expedition against Algiers, Sir Robert Mansel, who commanded the fleet, was commissioned to capture Muslims and "redeem them head for head by his Majesty's subjects captives in Tétouan; and, in case they could not be so redeemed, that, then, we should ransom them for money, and, with the money raised by that means, we should redeem, as far as the money would go, those of our nation captives."[135] Exchanges had been used to free Britons captured by their Christian enemies: now they were used to free Britons from Muslim captivity. In July 1621 John Duppa concluded with the *mokaddam* (chieftain) of Tétouan an exchange of the Muslims captured by Mansel for "eight English."[136] In 1631 King Charles proposed to Mulay al-Walid that Moroccan captives in Spain be ransomed and then exchanged for English captives in Morocco.[137] Exchange was repeatedly seen as the best way to free compatriots, so much so that the Mediterranean basin became a scene of extensive slave exchange throughout the early modern period. From Portugal to Egypt and from Italy to Greece and Morocco, slaves were bartered and exchanged, Christian "tête pour [Muslim] tête," (head for head), although on some occasions one Moor was exchanged for two Britons.[138] As late as 1714 English ships sailed to Spain to purchase Moors to exchange for English captives, "at very reasonable rates, such as are aged, blind or lame. Its no matter, all will pass, so they have life."[139]

Although money was frequently raised, not all of it was channeled toward the ransoming of the captives. Some of it went to pay for presents for the captors. "Certaine things bought for a Present for redemption of Captifs under the King of Morocco" included pistols, pikes, and other items, altogether worth 278 pounds, 12 shillings, and 6 pence. To deliver thirty-two French captives, the privateers expected ninety-eight barrels of powder as well as "A suite of Armour, An Emerald Ringe."[140] Bribes and presents were clearly necessary in transactions with captors; indeed, the many lists of gifts in the State Papers reveal how presents were not only offered to the ruler but to his spouse and other members of the household as well: "A Box containing Royall Apparrell for Her Majesty and his Royall Highness The Prince according to the African manner."[141] At the same time, English consuls were demanding 2 percent commissions—the "right of Consulage"—on the ransoms paid for the liberation of their conationals. When this "right" was contested, Philip Rycault, the consul in Algiers, protested that it was "reasonable, that he should reape some benefit from thence; as that he who serves at the Altar should live by the Altar."[142] Since his job was to negotiate and pay ransoms, then his income should come from the sums raised.

The ransoming of captives always involved three parties: captive, captor, and intermediary, the third being a conational of either the captive or the captor or an outsider. Some captors were also international intermediaries, as was the case with Luis Zapata; Mohammad Jayar; Assan, son of Salem

Valentiano; Ibrahim Musa; and the sheikh of the Andalusians, Mustafa de Cardenas.[143] These intermediaries had an inter-Mediterranean web of associates so that money for captives could be paid in different currencies and cities, from Genoa to Paris and from Zanthe to Leghorn and Cairo. Often money was paid in one city so that a captive in another could be released, in exchange for the release of the payee or his/her own kin. Much haggling took place over ransom prices: in 1658, for example, seventy-two Britons (including three women) were ransomed at a price that was brought down from an initial $30,000 to $11,250.[144]

Given the geographical breadth of the ransom enterprise, corruption and fraud were inevitable. In May 1618 one Edward Eastman was accused of having embezzled money that had been "intended for the redemption of certaine Christian captives taken by Turkish pirattes."[145] A few years later, John Harrison wrote to the Privy Council to plead the cause of captives in Morocco: money had been collected, he wrote, but it had been "wasted by those whose trade is the occasion of their captivitie."[146] Merchant companies skimmed money that had been collected to ransom their captured employees. In 1683 the English consul in Algiers, Lionell Croft, confirmed ransoming "a hundred English Captives . . . at unreasonable rates" only to find himself, a few days later, accused by John Neuell of cheating and of having claimed to have paid ransom for people who had already been ransomed.[147] It is no wonder that thousands of British captives languished in North African slavery. As D'Aranda noted, among all the captives in the bagnios, Britons were the least provided for.[148] Catholic Spain and France, which had dealt diplomatically and commercially with North Africans since the medieval period, had established religious orders that regularly negotiated for the release of captives. Britain, however, had no designated institution to oversee these affairs. Although Parliament formed a "Committee of Algiers" in 1640 to address the needs of captives, nearly all moneys raised for ransom in the period under study came from alms, an unreliable and uncertain source. In 1716 captives still lamented the absence of institutional help: "All Nations," wrote Mr. Meggison to his wife on September 18, "is provided for but the poore English have noe assistance from their Nation but a parcell of Lyes & storys to come to clear & none will come."[149]

While such "poore" men languished in slavery, others with court or commercial connections were speedily ransomed. Wealthy captives frequently negotiated their own ransoms and "avoid[ed] the hardships that others endure[d]": soon after their capture, the master and the owner of the ship on which John Fox served "were redeemed" by their friends, "the rest abiding still by the misery."[150] When the French merchant residing in Sallee learned that James Wadsworth was a relative of the English consul in St. Lucia, he immediately paid his ransom but was unwilling to do the same for Wadsworth's companions.[151] When Captain William Hawkerbridge was captured in 1633, he used his private income to pay his own ransom, but his thirty-two men remained in captivity.[152] After receiving petitions from the earl and countess of Inchiquin, one of the first things King Charles II did after his restoration in May 1660 was to write to Robert Brown requiring him to demand the release of his cousin, the earl, and his son, "alleging all those inducements wch you shall conceive proper to effect the same: wherein if the successe shall not answer our desire in obteyning their deliverance; our Pleasure is that you treate and compound their Ransome on as easy termes as may be."[153] Clearly, royal connections and wealth ensured a speedy ransom. In 1676 Captain Alexander Makennyie was captured and taken to Mulay Ismail where he negotiated his own ransom: "400 guns, each 7 spans long . . . for which the English merchants there are his security." Had he been a mere sailor, he would never have found such support from compatriot merchants.[154] There is a letter dated October 16, 1682, "from a Master of a shipp who redeemed himselfe out of Argeir."[155] "The Captives belonging to the Kings house," wrote Lionell Croft from Algiers in that same year, "are allwayes redeemed first, and that at unreasonable rates."[156] A captive with connections was sure of royal or ecclesiastical intervention.[157]

Relatives of less fortunate captives—among them, a carpenter, a man with one eye, and a "Scottishman"—often had to take to the streets demanding action on behalf of "husbandes and sonnes and servantes . . . detayned captives in Algier and other portes of Barbary."[158] In May 1653 "divers poor women" presented a petition to Cromwell and the council of state, asking for assistance in redeeming their husbands in Tripoli. They reported how for two years, money had been available for redemption but had been diverted for military use. Although it is not clear why the money had been diverted, the referral of the petition a few weeks later to the "Irish and Scotch Committee" may offer an explanation: the captives were not English, and thus their cases did not merit immediate action.[159] Less than half a century later, in 1693, Francis Brooks pleaded with the "Sacred Majesties, William and Mary" to have a care for the "miserable Condition, wherein many of Your Majesties Subjects, with other Christians, now live groaning in slavery." There were, he explained, 340 "English-men, Subjects of our Gracious King, in this sore Captivity," slaves for over a decade. Notwithstanding his plea, which was reprinted in 1700, no official action was taken on behalf of these men.[160] In

June 1716 the captive John Willdon complained to his wife that "all Christian people have forgotten us In England because they have not sent us any Releife never since we have been In slavery"; a month later, "Severall Gentlemen of Bradford," along with the father of captive John Stock, who was being held in Sallee, were still imploring the secretary of state for "Assistance to gett those Distrested Creatures Releife from their Slavery."[161] In 1721 John Windus came across "three hundred" Englishmen in Meknes, the same number Brooks had mentioned.[162] Without personal wealth or court connections, many English captives languished in North Africa.

This lack of help in England significantly differs from the generosity exhibited on the continent. In France and Spain, large processions were led by redemptionist priests to raise money for captives. On many occasions, captives were ransomed on the written understanding that they would participate in such processions "à la manière acoustumée" (in the accustomed manner).[163] In addition to the religious orders who negotiated on captives' behalf, a special redemptionist ship–the alms ship *La Merced*, as it is called in Cervantes's *Los Baños* and elsewhere–was designated for this function. French and Spanish kings and their subjects willingly offered contributions because they saw the captives as soldiers in the Christian war against Islam; this is why before captives were ransomed, they were tested to ensure that they had not been corrupted by either Islam or Protestantism.[164] No similar view of the captives prevailed in England: while Trinitarian and Mercedarian priests ransomed Catholic captives, it was company agents–factors–who negotiated on behalf of English captives. British captives were part of the commercial enterprise in the Mediterranean, and neither the monarchy nor the Privy Council felt under any moral or religious obligation to extend financial help to the captured employees of the Levant and East India companies. Indeed, the Levellers, who championed the cause of prisoners of debt, petitioned Parliament in 1646 to help those "men, born free, Christians" who were in debtors' prisons rather than collect money for captives in North Africa: "Your zeal makes a noise as far as Algiers, to deliver those captived Christians at the charge of others, but those whom your own unjust laws hold captive in your own prisons; these are too near you to think of."[165]

Although the Levellers did not participate in overseas ventures, many Civil War Parliamentarians and Restoration nonconformists did. Such was the case with the Society of Friends. As a small and persecuted religious community, the Quakers knew that the monarchy would not ransom their coreligionists from captivity. In 1679, after a shipful of Quakers was seized while returning from Virginia, the Meeting for Sufferings in London sent appeals to all the quarterly meetings around the country and elsewhere for contributions. Support for captives, which sometimes came from as far away as Ireland, Jamaica, and Barbados, helped consolidate Quaker religious commitment. The Quakers collected "supplies for food" for the Algiers captives and kept close count of the number of Friends who were captured and the sums needed for their release. So effective was their commitment that in May 1688 one Roger Udy reported that after being held captive for seven years, he had finally accepted the "Truth" of Quakerism. Perhaps despairing of any other chance of ransom and noting how the Quakers helped each other, Udy decided to give the "Truth" a try. If some Englishmen were willing to convert to Islam to gain their freedom, accepting the doctrines of George Fox was surely a less opprobrious option.[166]

In some cases, a sea captain would arrive in a North African harbor, negotiate the ransom of captives, pay the captors, and then ask the captives who did not have money for bonds and letters of intent. The "Acc[oun]t of the Redemption of Captiues att Argiere" in 1644, effected by an English sea captain, lists the names of thirty captives and the amounts they owed. The captain meticulously wrote down the "debtts pendinge outt which by Reason of the pouerty off the Captiues cannott bee payed": Ann Parsons, the only woman on the list, owed him the whole ransom amount, while Edward Sanderson gave him a bond for the amount, and Bowden owed him one pound. All in all, the captain paid 2107 pounds, 17 shillings, and 9 pence to the captors, of which 920 pounds, 16 shillings, and 11 pence were owed to him by the captives.[167] A list similarly prepared by a merchant at the end of the 1680s shows the "Debts oweing to ye said Wm Bowtell on ye Captives Accot."[168] Many captains and even consuls found a lucrative source of income in lending money to desperate captives, regardless of nationality. The English consul in Tunis in 1695, Thomas Goodwin, lent the Frenchman Girolamo Gaglio the sum of 392 pieces of eight, which the latter promised to reimburse within twenty days of his arrival in Marseille.[169] Many captives thus returned to their homes burdened by debt. Not only did they have to repay their ransoms, they also had to cover the currency exchange fee, which sometimes could be as high as 25 percent of the ransom sum. Captives who did not find anybody from whom to borrow resorted to begging "of other Christian slaves," with dubious results.

There were many dangers on the return journey: some of the most unlucky captives were those who were captured again before they were able to pay back their first ransom.[170] Okeley was nearly captured again by the Algerians as he and his fellow escapees were sailing back to England. Many lists survive showing the names of ransomed captives who were transported by English sea captains, along with "the prouisions for each, Six weekes, sea allowances in ord and to there passing, which I oblige, my selfe to put on shore, in England, mortallity, the daenger of ye seaes, and forceable escapes, excepted."[171] Captains also carried with them certificates of release from the ruler. One certificate (in Spanish) carried from Sallee by Robert Denis and his nephew Mark in August 1653 bears the release statement of twenty-two English slaves and the signature of Hamad Benali; attached to it is a certificate signed by John Ware and four others that attests to the genuineness of the certificate.[172]

The most effective protection against attacks by the privateers, be they North African or French, Sicilian or Spanish, were the passes captains carried with them to ensure the safety of their crews as well as their ransomed captives (see appendix 7). Unfortunately, passes were often forged, and this problem necessitated continual confirmation and approval of the form of pass by the North African rulers. In January 1680 the English fleet admiral was sent to Algiers to provide the *deys* with a copy of the official pass—the same used in Tunis and Tripoli—because there were "slanderous reports of our [English] Negligence in committing to others the care & Trust reposed in us & expected from us by the Argereenes." The "Negligence" was actually a breach of trust, as English captains sometimes deceived the privateers by carrying more than one pass from more than one government (Spanish and British) and transporting passengers and cargo that belonged to nations with whom the privateers were at war. When more than three-quarters of the sailors and passengers on a ship were not English, the privateers complained that the English were "selling" their passes to other nations, which they felt entitled them to seize the ship and all it carried.[173]

British captives knew how many obstacles made their ransom improbable or impossible and therefore may have felt more desperate about their circumstances than did other European captives. Such desperation led them to attempt escape. Fox plotted his flight while roaming the city of Alexandria, and Knight and Okeley managed to build boats in secret. Four captives who were held in Sallee in 1642 reported how a Portuguese slave had "assured them that, if they could conveniently get out of the town," they could escape to Ma'moora, which they did. Gilbert Young was captured with his shipmates in November 1669 and marched to Tétouan; there, he "purchased an all Hague [a gown] a Cap and a Moorish shirt next morning tooke leave of his Consorts before day and marched towards the Seaside and about five days saw Arzille, and that Night saw Arab Army horse and foote on the side of a hill and then the next day gott under Cape Spartoll & marched by the Sea-side all day, and about ten at night came to whitly, and there they lett him in."[174] When three British ships came near Algiers in August 1671, they picked up "three Englishmen in the Bay that escaped in two bullock hides sewn together and bound to an oblong of spar wood, like a picture frame, having four barrel board paddles and one to steer with."[175] Thomas Phelps managed to escape with his fellow captives from Meknes, not a small achievement given the distance they had to traverse between that city and the Atlantic coast (around one hundred miles according to his calculations).

All but one of the accounts printed below describe escape. For each account that survives of a successful escape, however, there must have been numerous unsuccessful attempts. Equally numerous must have been the escapees who drowned or were lost at sea. While there were hundreds of ran-somed captives, there were thousands who died or who converted to Islam and "emigrated," leaving behind them confused, destitute, and traumatized families.

Captivity Accounts

Upon returning home, captives gave depositions about their ordeals. From the many that have survived (see appendix 3 for some examples), it is obvi-ous that their purpose was to provide the government with information about maritime affairs, geography, and naval danger. Captives were asked not about their suffering and circumstances but about the names of ships that had been seized, the number of their conationals held with them (with an important distinction being made among English, Scottish, and Irish cap-tives), the ransoms that were demanded, which of the captives had colluded with the enemy and which had converted to Islam, and, finally, about the mil-itary preparedness of the Barbary corsairs. In March 1626 Trinity House sent a letter to the Privy Council informing them that officials at Trinity House had interviewed three men returned from Sallee who had confirmed that the information gathered from earlier captives was correct: there were twelve to fourteen hundred English captives in that harbor town.[176] A list of ships seized by the Algerians was prepared in "Argeyr December from a Captive," and after his escape, Okeley was questioned by the Majorcans about the naval strength of the Algerians.[177] Such information helped determine whether a ship had sunk or been captured, whether sailors had drowned or been enslaved, whether merchandise had been lost or seized. Also specified were the nationality of the captors and whether sailors had fought them off, or simply deserted ship, or agreed to hand over the cargo in return for their freedom.[178] Depositions thus provided the London merchant companies and the admiralty with reliable information about the situation in the Mediterranean and on the Atlantic coasts of North Africa.

After giving depositions, a few of the captives went on to write their personal accounts. Adam Elliot explained that he wrote his in order to defend himself against the aspersions of the notorious Titus Oates. He used to tell his story of captivity to anyone who was willing to listen. "I have always freely comply'd with any handsome invitation to relate it," he wrote, and often, while riding in a coach, he recounted his story to his fellow passengers, some of whom, unfortunately, later distorted and misrepresented it.[179] While he and one other captive were clergymen, all the other captives-cum-writers were men of the middle or lower classes: traders, sailors, and soldiers. All but one wrote in English. Robert Ellyatt wrote in Italian and was, incidentally, the only Catholic; the rest were Protestants: Anglicans, Presbyterians, and Quakers. Indeed, the corpus of writings about captivity that survives in English is exclusively about British Protestants: "This book is Protestant," declared Okeley in the prefatory poem to his captivity account. Catholics are not present because they were ransomed by continental coreligionists in the same way that French Huguenots were ransomed by the English Protestants.[180] The captivity accounts thus tell the story of the first British Protestants to enter the world of North African Islam. For many readers who eagerly sought out these sensationalist narratives about life among the Moors, the texts served as the only source of information about the strange new world in the Mediterranean, the world where a "false" religion prevailed but where cheap food, clean cities, personal hygiene, employment opportunities, and social advancement abounded.

Some captives described their experience of capture, enslavement, escape, and return as an entire unit (for example, Rawlins, Okeley, and Pitts). Others, such as Wadsworth, Spratt, Coxere, and Browne, included captivity in their autobiographies or in their accounts of wider travels. "A True relation of an escape made out of Argier the fourth of July 1640," by George Penticost, John Butler and others, is a one-page report to Parliament about the escape of fifteen Englishmen from Algeria to Majorca,[181] while Brooks's and Whitehead's accounts are as much narratives about captivity as they are treatises on Morocco. The latter described the land, the flora, the lack of water, city locations (Meknes "lys in the latitude 33 Deg. 30 Min"), and the food (locusts "tasted, as seem'd to me, somewhat of fish"). Surprisingly, very few writers described the journey home after their escape or ransom; of all the writers included below, only Pitts described his dangerous twelve-month journey from Algiers to Smyrna to Leghorn to Frankfurt and finally to Exeter. Thomas Pellow was the only writer to describe the return to his community and the reunion with his parents.

Some accounts were written in the first person, others in the third, the choice suggesting differing authorial strategies and goals. Literary critics have been eager to treat all the captivity accounts together in order to arrive at some generic framework that can contain them all, claiming that they were the precursors of the novel, as G. A. Starr declared, or that they were early models for later "orientalist" writings, as Joe Snader stated.[182] But such for-mulizing ignores the differences in narrative voices, the uncertainty and multiplicity of authorship (is the author the captive himself or the editor/publisher?), and various modes of publication (did the captive oversee the publication of the account or was it left to a publisher who changed, added, or deleted as he saw fit?). As Okeley admitted in his preface, the "stuff" was his own, but the "trimming and form" was another's. Is the erudition of the Okeley text, with its Latin and French quotations and the politically sensitive lines from George Herbert, his own?[183] Furthermore, captives frequently told and retold their tales. Which version of their oral narratives saw print: the early ones, which may have been close to truth, or the later ones, which inevitably became ideologically burdened?

The critical zeal for establishing a generic framework also ignores the important difference between the two divisions under which the accounts can be grouped: the accounts that appeared in the Elizabethan and Jacobean periods and those that appeared after 1640. The accounts in the first group were short because the captives knew very little, if anything, about Islam or about Muslim history and culture. After all, captives such as Fox and Hasle-ton had been planning to go not to North Africa but to Spain or other Chris-tian ports in the Mediterranean. Limited in their knowledge, Fox, Hasleton, and Rawlins (whose accounts are included below) focused on themselves, their personal ordeals, their faith, and their commitment to their religious and national identity. Fox's account, however, appeared in a third-person voice (Hakluyt's?) with a pro-Elizabeth conclusion; Hasleton's account included additions that were made by his anti-Catholic editor; and Rawlins's followed the structure of the Anglican sermon. All three accounts included a political message either supporting or opposing the monarch. The narratives written during the Elizabethan period praised the queen and her government for arranging the release of captives or assisting them upon their return to England, while texts written under James obliquely criticized an indifferent monarch and an inefficient admiralty.[184]

Wadsworth's was the only account published during the years leading up to the Civil War, a period during which the printing press was under strict censorship. There, however, the narrative of captivity was overshadowed by the author's anti-Catholicism, which was the chief thrust of the book (as the title– *The English Spanish Pilgrime; or, A new discoverie of Spanish popery and jesuitical strategems*–clearly shows). As soon as censorship was lifted in 1640, an account of captivity and escape was immediately printed (and reprinted the same year). This text, by Francis Knight, changed the whole character of the captivity narrative and was the first of the second group of accounts: it was longer than anything that had preceded it and focused as much on the world of the captors as on the strictly personal aspects of captivity. Knight saw himself as a writer whose aim was to present to his readers a detailed description of territories, peoples, dominions, and experiences that no other compatriot could provide. None of the ten accounts that had been published between 1589 and 1625 achieved any of the breadth, the historical and ethnographical detail, or the geographical variety that the post-1640 accounts provide. Knight, Smith, Elliot, Okeley, Phelps, Brooks, Whitehead, and Pitts, however, combined in their captivity accounts the personal and religious with the descriptive and informative. These later writers knew that their readers wanted to learn about the captives' Christian affirmation as well as about the lands, customs, government, and religion of the Muslims. It is not surprising that some of these captivity accounts have been translated into European languages– and recently into Arabic–given that they provide a rare description of North African history and political society in the early modern period.

Captives-turned-writers in this second group express an anxiety that may have reflected their compatriots' concern. Beginning with the Great Migration to the Americas in the 1630s, some Englishmen had turned into colonialists and plantation owners, dominating and oppressing natives, conquering adversaries, and designating themselves as God's own standard bearers. A national identity was being forged based on Protestant election, capitalist enterprise, and naval superiority. But while this identity of power and expansion was being celebrated in verse and in prose, in masques and in sermons, Britons in North Africa were facing enslavement, humiliation, and Islamic assertiveness. In 1634, when thousands of captives were being held in North Africa, the Secretary of the Privy Council, John Coke, wrote to King Charles I the following warning about the situation in the Mediterranean and in

Europe: "It is also notorious that all nations desire to bee served by their valor. . . . Yet I know not how the world is posesed that our ancient reputation is not only cried down, but wee submit our selves to wrongs & indignities in al places wch are not to bee indurd."[185] Captivity was destabilizing the emergent national identity: whatever "ancient reputation" had existed among Britons and whatever new ideals of valor were being proclaimed, both were being undermined by the indignities that Muslim privateers, among others, were inflicting.

Some of the indignities British captives repeatedly described pertained to the change in food and clothing to which they were subjected in North Africa. Not only did they have to get used to new foods, they also had to wear new clothes that covered their bodies in a totally different way. At a time when people did not have any variety in their diet, when they ate what they or their villages produced, there was fear that a change in diet would induce a change in the identity. After all, food was a national product, and in eating and drinking one confirmed one's sense of community.[186]

Similarly, at a time when sailors and soldiers did not own more than one garment, and when clothes were made and worn in a style that defined them nationally, losing that garment and wearing another invariably changed the way an individual looked and walked and moved, implying a loss of personal nationhood and character. There was such anxiety in English thought associated with the Islamic turban that when a Briton (or any other European) converted to Islam, he was described as having "donned the turban."[187] Nothing revealed conversion and transculturation more than the change in dress. Captives such as Phelps, Brooks, and others, along with "an English slave named Charles Desborough who was carryed from hence [Algiers] in Disguise," escaped after putting on robes and disguising themselves as Moors, showing how well integrated they had become into the society in which they had been held captive.[188] Forced to wear the clothes of the Moors, captives were separated from their national heritage, which in the early modern period was frequently based less on ideals or symbols than on tangible markers. Repeatedly, captives' accounts of the "Mahometan" garments and foods they had to adopt, the even greater humiliation of conversion to Islam and subsequent circumcision, and the "sodomiticall" abuse some captives reportedly suffered reminded Britons of the imperfect dominion of their national authority.[189]

Having experienced the humiliation of being Christian slaves under Muslim masters, the captives-turned-writers used their accounts to establish a Christian teleology and authorize their reintegration into their national community. The former captive—sometimes aided by a narrator or editor—encouraged the reader to recognize that in the encounter between the powerful Muslims and the enslaved English, what was at stake was the certainty that the Christian God was the true God and that a faithful Englishman would always emerge victorious. As John Fox declared in the first captivity account: "Howsoever their [Muslim] God behaved himself, our God showed himself a God indeed, and that he was the only living God."[190] John Rawlins viewed his experience of captivity as divine "purgation," while Thomas Smith deliberately did not include his full name because he wanted to present himself as an archetype of the English Christian who falls into the hands of the "Mahometans" but ultimately prevails; he had been like "Joseph in Egypt . . . promoted to Pharaoh's Elbow," but he had resisted the allure of the Muslims and returned to his native country.[191] A few years later, Edward Coxere (who was captured by the Tunisians) described the "merciless" Moors and the "tormentors" with whom he and other Christians had to contend. The captors had treated them like "dogs" and had beaten them after they had attempted an escape.[192] Later, he presented the Tunisian episode in his autobiography as part of the trials and tribulations that prepared him for salvation as a Quaker. The spiritual progress of the pilgrim passed through the geographical pit of the Barbary Coast.[193] Two decades later, Joshua Gee described his captivity as a "pilgrimage."[194]

Captivity accounts were written to assert English identity and authorize national commitment. They reveal a deep-seated sense of Anglo-Christian self-righteousness, with authors declaiming against the "piracy" and "barbarousness" of the Moors and the Turks without taking into account the more devastating piracy and destruction committed by their own coreligionists against the inhabitants of North Africa. While railing against the "Barbary pirates," some captives seized the opportunity to denounce Islamic religious practices and customs and turn their captivity narratives into polemics. With the authority of experience behind them, the captives-turned-writers presented opinions readers must have viewed as accurate and objective. Even a man such as Pitts, who gave a firsthand account of Muslim life and worship in Algeria, remained indebted to Humphrey Prideaux's venemous 1697 account of Muhammad, as he himself admitted.[195] While the captivity accounts provided the first original information about North Africa, they also embodied a highly charged polemic against the Muslims of North Africa and served to ground the demonization of the Moors not on fancy or fiction but on the authenticity of personal experience.

In these respects, the English captivity accounts fulfilled the same nationalist and religious function performed in Spain by Cervantes's and Lope de Vega's plays, where Spanish captives are presented as victims of Muslim cruelty and torture who resist conversion to the "false religion" of Islam, overpower their captors, and convert them to Christianity.[196] Dramatists in England did not write plays about their captured compatriots, and neither did they address the complex implications and conditions of captivity. A surprising contrast between them and their Spanish counterparts during their respective golden ages is the repeated description by Spaniards of captivity, with all its violence and humiliation and sometimes martyrdom. But not a single English dramatist addressed the theme of English captivity (although they wrote about continental captives), even at a time when thousands of Britons were held in North Africa and when petitions, protests, and parliamentary debates focused attention on their cause. It was left to the captives to describe their experiences and their heroic escapes.[197]

Muslim culture was powerful and dangerous, and nowhere else in the world were there more captive Britons than in the Barbary States. Although Britons were also captured by Native Americans in the period under study, not a single detailed account of such New World captivity appeared in print before 1682 (with the exception of an uncertain account by John Smith), around a century after the first account of captivity among Muslims. Clearly, the encounter with Islam and Muslims was the more threatening, alluring, and problematic: nowhere else in the non-Christian world did Britons face the danger of converting to another religion and emigrating to another society. In America, some Britons (and more Spaniards) went "native," but the accounts written by Englishmen who had been captives in North Africa were ideologically different from those that came out of the North American experience. The attitude of early modern Britons to the two continents and their peoples were poles apart: from the Great Migration on, Britons viewed America as a place of conquest and domination. It was a continent where, promoters of the colonies insisted, wealth, land, and power could be gained. The promoters exercised censorship and control over all publications pertaining to the colonies and produced propaganda that projected images of success and achievement.[198] No accounts were published depicting the captivity of Englishmen (or, worse, Englishwomen) and their humiliation at the hands of the Indians. Only in the last quarter of the seventeenth century, after the colonists were assured of the upper hand, did accounts of captivity among the Indians begin to appear.

Nothing like the colonialist venture was ever entertained in regard to North Africa: from the Elizabethan period on, Englishmen were captives in a territory and among peoples they did not and could not possess. At no point in their exposure to the Muslims of North Africa, even during their twenty-two-year occupation of Tangier, did they feel the sense of establishment and entitlement they felt in America. In 1683 British forces fled Tangier just a few years after they had defeated the Indians in King Philip's war. The accounts produced in the context of North Africa were part of a unique national and mercantile operation whose financial and human impact was felt from London to Edinburgh and fron Whitehall to Westminster and played a significant role in heightening the tension between King Charles and Parliament that precipitated the Civil War.[199] They belong to the distinct historical and political environment that produced the rest of the *corpus captivitis*; they also belong to a religious context in which Britons and other Europeans were repeatedly overpowered and converted to Islam.[200] While Indians captured the body, the Muslims aimed at the soul, too. Indeed, they had—unlike the Indians—a religious ideology that sought to convert Christians and integrate them into the *umma* (community) of Islam.

The penultimate English captivity account in the early modern period (before Pellow's) presents a story of exactly such conversion to Islam but concludes with the triumph of Anglo-Christianity and victory over the cruelty, allure, and exoticism of North Africa. It was written by Joseph Pitts, an Exeter youth who converted to Islam and spent over a decade among the Algerians. After over a century of hearing about thousands of their compatriots who had shamefully converted to Islam, treacherously deserting their monarch and God, kith and kin, English society finally had access to a printed first-person account of such a desertion, along with the first English report of pilgrimage to Mecca and description of the Muslim holy places. Pitts presented a totally unprecedented geographical and psychological range of detail to the English reader: he had traveled in the lands of the Moors as well as into their religion and identity; he had crossed cultural and national demarcations and exposed himself to dislocation, alienation, and exile. Pitts told about a journey to the alien and a return to the familiar, a separation from England and a reassumption of Englishness, a conversion to Islam on the "outside," as he repeatedly affirmed, and an adherence to Christianity on the "inside." Pitts showed how unconquerable the English identity was: despite the power of his captors, despite his (forced) conversion at a tender age, despite the temptations of Algiers and Cairo and Istanbul, Englishness and Christianity could not be defeated. Pitts outsmarted the Muslims and escaped from under their very noses in the city of their power. He had returned home after the ultimate journey into the "Heart of Islam."

Along with the rest of the *corpus captivitis* of petitions, lists, memoranda, appeals, and letters and the vast national apparatus employed in prevention, war, exchange, negotiation, collections, ransom, and escape, the captivity accounts demonstrate that captivity was the central experience in Anglo-Islamic relations in the early modern period. Captivity mingled populations at the most intimate level, bringing men and women into the kitchens and homes, the gardens and shops of their captors. British captives in North Africa, like their North African counterparts in Christendom, became widely familiar with the culture and society of their captors. Despite the mixture of convention with reality, image with truth, and despite the ethnocentrism and sensationalism that inform the accounts, the captives could lay claim to having presented their readers with the first fact-based accounts of the world of Islam, descriptions that were far more substantiated than those provided by any ambassador or traveler, playwright or trader ever could be. The large number of British captives and renegadoes in North Africa brought more new knowledge about Islam and Muslims into British social and religious life than did any other group of British subjects during the early modern period. From North Africa, *semper aliquid novum.*

NOTES

Unless otherwise noted, translations are mine.

1. For European and English knowledge of Islam and Muslims in the Medieval period, see Norman Daniel, *Islam and the West: The Making of an Image* (Edinburgh: Edinburgh University Press, 1960), and Dorothee Metlitzki, *The Matter of Araby in Medieval England* (New Haven: Yale University Press, 1977). For accounts of the European representation of Islamic culture, see Robert Schwoebel, *The Shadow of the Crescent: The Renaissance Image of the Turk (1453–1517)* (New York: St. Martin's, 1967); Kenneth M. Setton, *Western Attitudes to Islam and Prophecies of Turkish Doom* (Philadelphia: American Philosophical Society, 1992); and Samuel Chew, *The Crescent and the Rose: Islam and England During the Renaissance* (1937; reprint, New York: Octagon, 1974). For the representation of Islam in English thought, see Jack D'Amico, *The Moor in English Renaissance Drama* (Tampa: University of South Florida, 1991), and Jonathan Haynes, *The Humanist as Traveler: George Sandys' Relation of a Journey Begun An. Dom. 1610* (London: Associated University Press, 1986). For Muslims in England, see ch. 1 in my *Turks, Moors, and Englishmen in the Age of Discovery* (New York: Columbia University Press, 1999).

2. Abu Fares Abd al-Aziz al-Fishtali, *Manahil al-Safa fi Maathir Mawalina al-Shurafa,* ed. Abd al-Karim Karim (Rabat, 1972), 254.

3. Abd al-Hadi Ben Mansour, "Les immigrés européens à Alger et le lobby français au XVIIᵉ siècle," *Majallat Et-Tarikh* 21 (1986): 27–47; and chs. 2 and 3 in my *Turks, Moors, and Englishmen*.

4. Henry Kamen, *The Iron Century: Social Change in Europe, 1550–1660* (New York: Prager, 1971), 387.

5. Robert Burton, *The Anatomy of Melancholy*, ed. Holbrook Jackson (London: Dent, 1977), part 3, 349; Samuel Hartlib, *The Hartlib Papers* (CD-ROM 1995), 57/4/3/5A.

6. Cervantes, *El Trato de Argel*, in *Obras Completas*, ed. Angel Valbuena Prat (Madrid: Aguilar, 1970), 136.

7. Emanuel D'Aranda, *The History of Algiers and It's [sic] Slavery*, trans. John Davies (London, 1666), 191.

8. I emphasize publication: John Harrison, the English representative in Morocco, wrote extensively but only published one account about Mulay Abd al-Malik in 1633. Nearly all of State Papers (hereafter SP) 71/12 consists of writings about Morocco by Harrison (the State Papers are unpublished documents located in the Public Records Office in London). For a full account of his writings, see my entry in *New Dictionary of National Biography* (New York: Oxford University Press, forthcoming).

9. Captain John Smith's, which is set in Central Europe, and Captain Henry Middleton's, which is set in Mocha (western coast of Arabia). There was also an account by a Greek visiting England who had been seized by Turks—*Christopher Angell, a Grecian, who tasted of many stripes inflicted by the Turks*, published in Oxford in 1617 and reprinted that same year and in 1620.

10. Another edition appeared in 1764. Since the appearance of the second edition, wrote the publisher, the account "is become so extremely scarce as hardly to be had any Rate; the Editor therefore, from the Solicitation of many pious Friends, has now republished it" (*Eben-Ezer; or, A Small Monument of Great Mercy*, 3d ed., 1764).

11. Joseph Pitts, *A Faithful Account*, 3d ed. (London, 1731), xv.

12. "John Whitehead his relation of Barbary," Ms. Sloane 90, British Library.

13. Pellow's account has been excluded from this survey because *The Adventures of Thomas Pellow, of Penryn, Mariner* (London, 1738) contains dozens of pages from previously published sources on Morocco; the text is thus too much of a pastiche. See M. Morsy Patchett, "A Propos de l'Histoire de la longue Captivité et des Aventures de Thomas Pellow Recit Anglais Publié en 1739," *Hespéres Tamuda* 4 (1963): 289–311.

14. D'Aranda, *History*; *A Narrative of the Adventures of Lewis Marott, Pilot-Royal of the Galleys of France* (London, 1677); and *The Travels of the Sieur Mouette, in the Kingdomes of Fez and Morocco, During his Eleven Years Captivity in those Parts*, in *A New Collection of Voyages and Travels* (London, 1708). This last account had appeared in French in 1683.

15. Richard Hakluyt, *The Principal Navigations, Voyages, Traffiques & Discoveries of the English Nation* (Glasgow: James MacLehose and Sons, 1904), 5:298.

16. *Adventures by Sea of Edward Coxere*, ed. E. H. W. Meyerstein (Oxford: Oxford University Press, Clarendon, 1945), 96.

17. G. C. Spivak, "Can the Subaltern Speak?" in *Marxism and the Interpretation of Culture*, ed. C. Nelson and L. Grossberg (Basingstoke, 1988), 271–313.

18. *A true Account of George Pattison's being taken by the Turks; and how redeemed, by God's direction and assistance, without bloodshed, putting the Turks on shore in their own country, about the 8th Month, 1663*, in *The Fighting Sailor Turned Peaceable Christian* (London, 1801).

19. William Okeley, *Eben-Ezer; or, a Small Monument of Great Mercy*, 2d ed. (London, 1684), 85.

20. See Roslyn L. Knuston, "Elizabethan Documents, Captivity Narratives, and the Market for Foreign History Plays," *English Literary Renaissance* 26 (1996): 75–110.

21. See my "Wives, Captive Husbands, and Turks: The First Women Petitioners in Caroline England," *Explorations in Renaissance Culture* 23 (1997): 111–29.

22. *Calendar of State Papers, Domestic, 1652–53*, 118 (hereafter, *Calendar of State Papers, Domestic* will be abbreviated *C.S.P.D.*).

23. SP 71/3/303 ff.

24. *Trinity House of Deptford Transactions, 1609–35*, ed. G. G. Harris (London: London Record Society, 1983), 70.

25. Abu al-Qasim al-Zayyani, *Al-Bustan al-zarif fi dawlat awlad Mulay al-Sharif*, ed. Rashid al-Zawiyya (Risani, 1992), 1:189.

26. SP 71/14/305.

27. The information about the regencies derives from the following studies: R. L. Playfair, *The Scourge of Christendom* (London, 1884); Stanley Lane-Poole, *The Barbary Corsairs* (London, 1890); Sir Godfrey Fisher, *Barbary Legend: War, Trade, and Piracy in North Africa 1415–1830* (Oxford: University Press, 1957); Peter Earle, *Corsairs of Malta and Barbary* (London: Sidgwick and Jackson, 1970); Jamil M. Abun-Nasr, *A History of the Maghrib* (Cambridge: Cambridge University Press, 1971); William Spencer, *Algiers in the Age of the Corsairs* (Norman: University of Oklahoma Press, 1976); John B. Wolf, *The Barbary Coast: Algiers Under the Turks, 1500 to 1830* (New York: Norton, 1979); and C. R. Pennell, ed., *Piracy and Diplomacy in Seventeenth-Century North Africa* (London: Associated University Presses, 1989). For a good Arabic source, see Mahmood Ihsan al-Hindi, *Al-Hawleyyat al-Jaza'iriyya: Tarikh al-Mu'assassat fi-l Jaza'ir* (Damascus, 1979), ch. 2, and the other references I cite below.

28. Muhammad bin Maymun al-Jazairi, *Al-Tuhfah al-Mardiyah fi al-dawlah al-Bakdashiyah*, ed. Muhammad ibn Abd al-Karim (Al-Jazair, 1972), 34–42. See also Taoufik Bachrouch, *Jumhuriyat al-dayat fi Tunis, 1591–1675* (Tunis, 1992).

29. Abun-Nasr, *A History*, 193.

30. Consider the following, written on September 13, 1675: "His Majesty hath by the advice of the lords declared his approval of his selling the negroes, 'and determined that the Greeks (notwithstanding their pretence of being Christians) shall be sent to Tangier, and there employed as slaves on board the galley' " (*A Descriptive Catalogue*

of the Naval Manuscripts in the Pepsyian Library at Magdalene College, Cambridge, ed. J. R. Tanner [London: Navy Records Office, 1909], 3:114).

31. "Una republic Andaluza en el Norte de Africa," in *Etudes sur Les Morisques-Andalous*, ed. Slimane-Mostafa Zbiss (Tunis, 1983), 257–62. For the range of Moroccan seafaring, see the map on page 177 and the detailed description starting on page 149 in Jerome Bruce Weiner, "Fitna, Corsairs, and Diplomacy: Morocco and the Maritime States of Western Europe, 1603–1672" (unpublished Ph.D. diss., Columbia University, 1976). See also Andres Sanchez Perez, "Los Moriscos de Hornachos, Corsarios de Salé," *Revista de Estudios Extremenos (Badajoz)* 2 (1964): 92–149.

32. Richard Blome, *A Description of the Island of Jamaica . . . Together with the Present State of Algiers* (London, 1678), 10. Blome took this sentence from "A Journal kept after my return ye 6th of February," British Library, Sloane 2755, 55r. On one occasion, it was none other than the son of the Algerian "king" who commanded the Algerian fleet; see *C.S.P.D., Charles II, March 1st, 1676, to February 28th, 1677*, 471.

33. Hulaymi Abd al-Qadir Ali, *Madinat al-Jazair* (Al-Jazair, 1972), 288.

34. SP 71/2/437.

35. SP 71/3/212. About the passes, see below.

36. See my *Turks, Moors, and Englishmen*, 165–66.

37. Mahmud Maqdish, *Nuzhat al-Anzar fi Ajaib al-Tawarikh wa-al-Akhbar*, ed. Ali al-Zuwari and Muhammad Mahfuz (Beirut, 1988), 2:92.

38. *Muhammad al-Qadiri's Nashr al-Mathani: The Chronicles*, ed. and trans. Norman Cigar (London: Oxford University Press, 1981), 92.

39. Ibn Abi Dinar, *Kitab al-Munis fi akhbar Ifriqiyah wa Tunis* (Tunis, 1967), 197.

40. *Al-Qadiri's Nashr al-Mathani*, 28. For Algerian gains from privateering, see Norman Robert Bennett, "Christian and Negro Slavery in Eighteenth-Century North Africa," *Journal of African History* 1 (1960): 79.

41. See M. H. Chérif, "Introduction de la piastre espagnole (riyâl) dans la Régence de Tunis au début du XVIIᵉ siècle," *Les Cahiers de Tunisie* 16 (1968): 45–55.

42. For the economic benefits that accrued from privateering, see the assessment of the various incomes generated for the North African regencies by the ransom of Britons: David Delison Hebb, *Piracy and the English Government, 1616–1642* (Aldershot: Scolar, 1994), ch. 7 especially. From 1679 until 1685, for instance, Tripoli gained $247,100 from the ransom of European captives; see Pennell, *Piracy*, 46.

43. The list of "minor operations" provided by R. C. Anderson in chapter 2 of his *Naval Wars in the Levant, 1559–1853* (Princeton: Princeton University Press, 1952) shows a continuous series of attacks from 1573 until 1644 by the Spaniards, the Portuguese, the Maltese, the Tuscans, the English, and other Christian powers on North African cities and harbors, along with uninterrupted raids on Muslim Mediterranean trade and the pilgrimage routes to Mecca. See also Palmira Brummett, *Ottoman Seapower and Levantine Diplomacy in the Age of Discovery* (Albany: State University of New York Press, 1994), chs. 5 and 6 especially.

44. William Byron, *Cervantes: A Biography* (New York: Paragon, 1988), 193.

45. Hakluyt, *Principal Navigations*, 2:190.

46. Ahmad ibn Qasim al-Hajari, *Nasir al-din ala al-qawm al-kafirin*, ed. Muhammad Razzuq (Addar al-Baida', 1987), 30.

47. Jean Pignon, "Un document inédit sur la Tunisie au début du XVIIe siècle," *Les Cahiers de Tunisie* 33 (1961): 129–30.

48. SP 71/1/41v–42r.

49. See my "First Turks and Moors in England," paper presented at the conference "From Strangers to Citizens," London, April 5–8, 2000.

50. Henry De Castries, *Les Sources Inédites de L'Histoire de Maroc: Archives et bibliothèques D'Angleterre* (Paris: Paul Geuthner, 1918–36), 3:75–77; 3:91–93.

51. Francis Knight, *A Relation of Seven Yeares Slaverie Under the Turkes of Argeire, suffered by an English Captive Merchant* (London, 1640), 34.

52 *C.S.P.D., Charles II, October 1668 to December 1669*, 9:385.

53. *C.S.P.D., Charles II, January to November 1671*, 11:235.

54. SP 71/2/1138.

55. Ibn Abi Dinar, *Kitab al-Munis*, 175.

56. Ahmad bin Abi Diyaf, *Ithaf ahl al-zaman*, ed. Muhammad Shammam (Tunis, 1989–90), 2:52.

57. Abderrahmane El Moudden, " 'The Sharif and the Padishah': Three Letters from Murad III to 'Abd al-Malik," *Hesperis Tamuda* 29 (1991): 120 and 125; Muhammad Ibn Ali Ibn Askar, *Dawhat al-nashir*, ed. Muhammad Hajji (Rabat, 1976–77), 31; Husayn Khujah, *Dhayl bashair ahl al-iman bi-futuhat Aal Uthman*, ed. al-Tahir al-Mamuri (Tunis, 1975), 128.

58. Quoted in Mohammad ibn al-Tayyib al-Qadiri, *Nashr al-Mathani*, ed. Muhammad Hajji and Ahmad al-Tawfiq (Rabat, 1986), 1:145.

59. Mohammad Hatamleh, "At-tahjeer al-qusriy lil-moriskiyyeen," *Dirasat* 10 (1983): 123 n. 3.

60. *Tarikh al-dawla al-Saadiya*, ed. Georges S. Colin (Rabat: Editions Felix Moncho, 1934), 53.

61. De Castries, *Sources*, 2:563.

62. Ibid., 3:170 and 214.

63. *Al-Qadiri's Nashr al-Mathani*, 139.

64. Joshua Gee, *Narrative of Joshua Gee of Boston, Mass.*, ed. Albert C. Bates (Hartford, 1943), 4.

65. *Lady Alimony; or, The Alimony Lady* (London, 1659), act 3, scene 2, n.p. For studies on English piracy, see Neville Williams, *Captains Outrageous: Seven Centuries of Piracy* (New York: Macmillan, 1962); Kenneth R. Andrews, *Elizabethan Privateering: English Privateering During the Spanish War, 1585–1603* (Cambridge: Cambridge University Press, 1964); Christopher Lloyd, *English Corsairs on the Barbary Coast* (London: Collins, 1981); and Alberto Tenenti, *Piracy and the Decline of Venice, 1580–1615*, trans. Janet Pullan and Brian Pullan (Berkeley: University of California Press, 1967), ch. 2.

66. SP 71/12/113–15.

67. Henry Barnby, "The Sack of Baltimore," *Journal of the Cork Historical and Archaeological Society* 74 (1969): 127.

68. SP 71/1/pt. 4, fols. 450–53.

69. *The Arrivall and Intertainements of the Embassador, Alkaid Jaurar Ben Abdella* (London, 1637), 28; *C.S.P.D., Charles II, 1668*, 8:576.

70. *C.S.P.D., Charles II, 1670*, 12:294.

71. British Library, Sloane 2755, fol. 48r.

72. SP 71/3/303.

73. SP 71/16/304–5.

74. Hakluyt, *Navigations*, 5:280–282.

75. John Dunton, *A True Journal of the Sally Fleet with the Proceedings of the Voyage* (London, 1637). Another version of the list gives slightly different numbers and identifies the captives from Scotland, Wales, and Ireland, along with twenty-four French, eight Dutch, and five Spanish captives (SP 71/13/31). See also SP 71/13/29 for another copy of the list.

76. Edmond Cason, *A Relation of the Whole Proceedings Concerning the Redemption of the Captives in Argier and Tunis* (London, 1647), 17 ff.

77. Ibid., 11.

78. SP 14/121/139.

79. *Trinity House of Deptford*, 60.

80. James Wadsworth, *The English Spanish Pilgrime; or, A new discoverie of Spanish popery and jesuitical strategems*, 2d ed. (London, 1630), 38.

81. Reported in *Debates of the House of Commons in 1625*, ed. Samuel Rawson Gardner (London: Camden Society, 1873), 116. See also the references to tongue cutting in *Report on Manuscripts in Various Collections* (London, 1914), 7:95, 96; and Abd el Hadi Ben Mansour, *Alger XVIe–XVIIe siècle: Journal de Jean-Baptiste Gramaye, "évêque d'Afrique"* (Paris: Cerf, 1998), 459–61. Cervantes described a captive who had lost his ear after attempting to escape (*Los Baños*, in *Obras Completas*, 280). There is also a scene of martyrological execution in de Vega's *Los Captivos de Argel*.

82. As Ellen Friedman has stated: "Although many captives were forced to do hard labor which caused some to become ill and some even to die, as a rule they do not seem to have been exposed to deliberate, purposeless physical brutality" (*Spanish Captives in North Africa in the Early Modern Age* [Madison: University of Wisconsin Press, 1983], 72, see also 74).

83. T[homas] S[mith], *The Adventures of (Mr. T. S.) An English Merchant* (London, 1670), 21–22. Although the evidence is not yet conclusive that T. S. is Thomas Smith, I have used the full name for the sake of convenience. I am grateful to Professor Gerald MacLean for drawing my attention to this matter.

84. *C.S.P.D., Charles II, March 1st, 1675 to February 29th, 1676*, 12.

85. For the history of the word *bagnios*, see Paul Sebag, *La Régence de Tunis à la Fin du XVIIᵉ Siècle* (Paris: L'Harmattan, 1993), 72 nn. 4 and 9.

86. Richard Hasleton, *Strange and Wonderfull Things Happened to Richard Hasleton* (London, 1595), reprinted in *An English Garner: Voyages and Travels*, ed. E. R. Beazley (New York: Cooper Square Publishers, 1964), 2:173. See also my "English Renaissance Soldiers in the Armies of Islam," *Explorations in Renaissance Culture* 21 (1995): 81–95.

87. John Harrison, *The Tragicall Life and Death of Muley Abdala Melek, the late King of Barbarie* (Delph, 1633), 13. See also "The Renegado-Engineer," in D'Aranda, *History*, 238–42.

88. Edward Webbe, *The Rare and most wonderful thinges which Edward Webbe an Englishman borne, hathe seene and passed in his troublesome travailes*, ed. Edward Arber, English Reprints (London: Alex Murray and Son, 1868), 27.

89. P. Grandchamp, *La France en Tunisie au début du XVIIe Siècle (1611–1620)* (Tunis, 1925), 3:59, see also 66–67, 71.

90. Okeley, *Eben-Ezer*, 59–60.

91. *C.S.P.D., Charles II, March 1st, 1675 to February 29th, 1676*, 424.

92. SP 71/2/65. See also British Library, Sloane 2755, fol. 54v, for the same account in "A Journal kept after my return ye 6th of February out of Holland from ye year 1675 untill 1676."

93. *Fifth Report of the Royal Commission on Historical Manuscripts, Part I* (London: HMSO, 1876), 372.

94. SP 71/14/221.

95. SP 71/15/49.

96. Chantal de la Véronne, *Vie de Moulay Isma'il . . . d'après Joseph de Leon (1708–1728)* (Paris: Librairie Orientalist Paul Geuthner, 1974), 157–58.

97. Okeley, *Eben-Ezer*, 24.

98. For a description of the activities of Franciscan fathers among the captives in Morocco, see Henry Koehler, *L'Eglise chrétienne du Maroc et la Mission Franciscaine, 1221–1790* (Paris, 1934), ch. 2. For chapels in Algeria, see J. Mesnage, *Le Christianisme en Afrique* (Algiers: Adolphe Jourdan, 1915), 203–4.

99. *Los Baños*, 308; D'Aranda is quoted in Guy Turbet-Delof, *L'Afrique Barbaresque dans la Littérature Française aux XVIe et XVIIe Siècles* (Geneva: Droz, 1973), 118; Laurent d'Arvieux, *Mémoires du chevalier d'Arvieux* (Paris, 1735), 4:38–39.

100. Captain Braithwaite, *The History of the Revolutions in the Empire of Morocco* (London, 1729), 67.

101. Moulay Belhamissi, "Captifs chrétiens en Algérie à l'époque ottomane: Histoire ou hystérie?" *Le Maghreb à L'Epoque Ottomane*, ed. Abderrahmane el Moudden (Casablanca, 1995), 75–84. In his account of captivity, for example, Richard Hasleton recalled the torture he had endured under his Catholic captors (on the rack and in solitary confinement) and the kindness shown to him by an old Algerian who protected and fed him; meanwhile, his wife was going around London describing his "most vyle slaverie and miserable bondage" not under the Catholics but under the Algerians (Guildhall Library, London, MS 9234/2, quoted in Knuston, "Elizabethan Documents," 103).

102. See my "Arab Captives Among Europeans During the Renaissance," paper presented at the American Historical Association meeting in Boston, January 4–7, 2001.

103. Knight, *Relation*, 28; *Rome for the Great Turke; or Else, The Great Turke for little Rome* (London, 1664), 3.

104. French Protestants, too, attested to the cruelty of their Catholic compatriots, as Elias Neau reported in *An Account of the Sufferings of the French Protestants, Slaves on Board the French King's Galleys* (London, 1699), and John Bion in *An Account of the Torments the French Protestants Endure Aboard the Galleys* (London, 1708).

105. Blome, *Description*, 10; Edwin Chappell, *The Tangier Papers of Samuel Pepys* (London: Navy Records Society, 1935), 238.

106. *C.S.P.D., Charles I, 1634–35*, 7:325.

107. For the Ostenders, see *C.S.P.D., Charles II, March 1st, 1675, to February 29th, 1676*, 154; for the Portuguese, see *C.S.P.D., Charles II, March 1st, 1676, to February 28th, 1677*, 408.

108. *This is a short Relation of some of the Cruel sufferings (For the Truths sake) of Katharine Evans & Sarah Cheevers, in the Inquisition in the Isle of Malta* (London, 1662). I am grateful to Dr. Vitkus for this reference. For Quakers among Muslims, see my *Islam in Britain, 1658–1685* (Cambridge: Cambridge University Press, 1998), 132–37.

109. "Transactions 1609 to 1625," Trinity House, London, fol. 72.

110. SP 71/1/455.

111. SP 71/16/503.

112. SP 71/16/499.

113. SP 71/16/505–6; SP 71/12/210.

114. SP 71/16/465.

115. Al-Fishtali, *Manahil al-Safa*, 236.

116. For a history of the Jews in North Africa, see the survey of sources in M. Eisenbeth, "Les Juifs en Algérie et en Tunisie a l'époque turque (1516–1830)," *Revue Africaine* 96 (1952): 114–87.

117. See my "Representation of Muslim Women in the English Renaissance," *The Muslim World* 86 (1996): 50–61. For interesting allusions to women's exposure to men, see Abd al-Kareem al-Fakkoon, *Manshur al-hidayah*, ed. Abu al-Qasim Sad Allah (Beirut, 1987), 172–79. The author was Algerian (ca. 1580–1662) and wrote biographies.

118. D'Aranda, *History*, 37.

119. *The Travels of the Sieur Mouette*, 10.

120. *C.S.P.D., Charles II, March 1st, 1675, to February 29th, 1676*, 425.

121. John Whitehead, "John Whitehead his relation," Ms. Sloane 90, British Library, 16r.

122. For the date of Pitts's pilgrimage, see C. F. Beckingham, "The Date of Pitts's Pilgrimage to Mecca," in *Between Islam and Christendom* (London: Variorum Reprints, 1983), item 24.

123. *Calendar of State Papers, Scottish Series, 1509–1589* (London: Longman: 1858), 1:431.

124. *Calendar of the Manuscripts of the Most Honourable the Marquess of Salisbury, Part XXI (1609–1612)*, ed. G. Dyfnallt Owen (London: HMSO, 1970), 250. For a survey of the letters of marque in English history, see R. G. Marsden, ed., *Documents Relating to Law and the Custom of the Sea*, 2 vols. (London: Navy Records Office, 1915).

125. *C.S.P.D., James I, 1623–1625*, 11:430.

126. SP 71/1/152.

127. SP 16/379/162.

128. *Historical Manuscripts Commission: Report on Manuscripts in Various Collections* (London: HMSO, 1901), 1:68.

129. *The Register of the Privy Council of Scotland, 1578–1585*, ed. David Masson (Edinburgh: H. M. General Register House, 1877), 3:177.

130. Ibid., 3:604.

131. For a study and record of Trinity House, see F. W. Brooks, ed., *A Calendar of the Early Judgements of Trinity House* (London, 1951).

132. *Eighth Report on the Royal Commission on Historical Manuscripts, Part I* (London: HMSO, 1881), 237, 239.

133. "Transactions 1609 to 1625," fols. 20v and 87v.

134. Grandchamp, *La France en Tunisie*, 3:61

135. De Castries, *Sources*, 2:526. See also the account of the exchange of captives in *Voyage in a Iournal or Briefe Reportary of all occurrents hapning in the fleet of ships sent out by the King* (London, 1621).

136. De Castries, *Sources*, 2:536.

137. Ibid., 3:152.

138. Grandchamp, *La France en Tunisie*, 5:74; "One Moor for two Captives," SP 71/2/7 (January 4, 1706).

139. SP 71/16/271.

140. SP 71/15/55.

141. SP 71/15/103.

142. SP 71/2/376, 378, 389.

143. Listed in Miguel de Epalza, "Moriscos y Andalusís en Túnês durante el siglo XVII," *Al-Andalus* 34 (1969): 263.

144. *C.S.P.D., 1657–58*, 308.

145. *Acts of the Privy Council of England, 1617–1619*, 146.

146. De Castries, *Sources*, 3:217.

147. SP 71/2/1101, 1035–36.

148. Quoted in Turbet-Delof, *L'Afrique Barbaresque*, 119.

149. SP 71/16/505.

150. Hakluyt, *Navigations*, 5:156.

151. Wadsworth, *The English Spanish Pilgrime*, 38–39.

152. *C.S.P.D., Charles I, 1633–34*, 6:357.

153. SP 71/1/199; for the petitions, see SP 71/1/496–98.

154. *C.S.P.D., Charles II, March 1st, 1676, to February 28th, 1677*, 163.

155. SP 71/2/fol. 983.

156. SP 71/2/fol. 1102.

157. See *C.S.P.D., William III, 1 January–31 December 1697*, 387–388 for an example of ecclesiastical intervention.

158. *Acts of the Privy Council of England, 1623–1625* (London, 1933), 335–36.

159. *C.S.P.D., 1653–54*, 59

160. Francis Brooks, *Barbarian Cruelty* (London, 1693; reprint, Boston, 1700), ix and 58. In *History of the Revolutions*, Braithwaite confirmed that in the last quarter of the seventeenth century, one captive told him that "there were no Hopes of being redeemed" (150).

161. SP 71/16/fols. 503 and 461.

162. John Windus, *A Journey to Mequines; The Residence of the Present Emperor of Fez and Morocco* (London, 1725), 195. The captives were still in Morocco in 1727, when Braithwaite wrote his account; see *History of the Revolutions*, 167.

163. Grandchamp, *La France en Tunisie*, 5:2; see also the reference to "procession habituelle," 5:75. For the processions in France, see Chantal de la Véronne, "Quelques processions de captifs en France à leur retour du Maroc, d'Algérie ou de Tunisie (XVIIe et XVIIIe siècles)," *Revue de l'Occident Musulman et de la Méditerranée*, spec. ed. (1970): 131–42. The only description of such a procession in England appears in *The Arrival and Intertainments of the Embassador*; see my study of this event in *Turks, Moors, and Englishmen*, 35–37.

164. Claude Larquie, "Le Rachat des Chrétiens en terre d'Islam au XVIIe siècle," *Revue d'histoire diplomatique* 94 (1980): 297–351.

165. *A Remonstrance of Many Thousand Citizens* (1646), quoted in Brian Manning, *The English People and the English Revolution, 1640–1649* (London: Heinemann, 1976), 290.

166. Samuel Tuke, *Account of the Slavery of Friends in the Barbary States Towards the Close of the Seventeenth Century* (London, 1848), 7–11.

167. British Library, Add 5489; see also Sloane 5105, fol. 8, "Accompte of Moneys paid towards the Ransom, of the Seamen which were taken Captiues in the Ruth of Dartmouth, of which George Miller Sen: was Masster and Redeemed out of their Slauery att Sally by Harbert Aylwin."

168. SP 71/3/188.

169. Grandchamp, *La France en Tunisie*, 8:238.

170. SP 71/16/503. See the reference to "one of them has been twice captiuated and has not to this day paid his first Ransome; being not of abillity" (SP 71/2/fol. 1101).

171. British Library, Sloane 3511, fol. 162. See also fols. 137, 140–41, 154, 156, 163, 165, 166, 167.

172. SP 18/39/92–93.

173. See SP 71/4/119, which describes an occasion when the Algerians seized a ship for being "more Spanish than English"; British Library Additional MSS 46412, fol. 17. Numerous copies of the 1680 pass survive, attesting to wide circulation and use: British Library Add. 46412, fols. 19 and 20, 25–30, and SP 71/2/fols. 1047–53.

174. SP 71/2/437.

175. *C.S.P.D., Charles II, January to November, 1671*, 455. See the summary of English, Spanish, and French fictional accounts of escape in André Vovard, "Les évasions par mer dans la littérature et dans l'histoire," *Bulletin de la Section de Géographie* 63 (1949–50): 89–104.

176. "Transactions 1609 to 1625," fol. 93v.

177. SP 71/2/437; *Eben-Ezer*, 85.

178. See SP 71/4/161 for a May 1719 account of sailors who deserted their ship in order not to fall into captivity. In *A Brave Memorable and Dangerovs Sea-Fight, foughten neere the road of Titwan in Barbary* (1636), the Water Poet, John Taylor, described the tension between merchants and sailors:

> Therefore, as Merchants make account of men,
> Let men so serve them honestly agen;
> If they pay us, we hold it right and just
> To serve, and to be worthy of their trust.
> With freight and wages, fitting mens desert,
> Shall men turne ill 'cause they are ill inclin'd?
> Or shall their being darke make others blinde?
> If any such there be, we hope they'le mend;
> Or if they mend not, they will one day end.

179. Adam Elliot, *A Modest Vindication of Titus Oates the Salamanca-Doctor from Perjury* (London, 1682), 19.

180. For the Catholic captives, see Mansour, *Alger*, 291 and 397; and Mesnage, *Christianisme*, 216. It is likely that Catholics sometimes ransomed young English Protestant captives in the hope of converting them to Catholicism; the case of "Iacobum Anglum 14. Annorum" may be an instance of this; see Mansour, *Alger*, 400. For the Huguenot captives, see the French captives who promised on March 8, 1706, to pay back their ransoms, described in SP 71/15/103. See also SP 71/15/10, which discusses how Dutch and French Protestant captives were sent to England.

181. British Library, Sloane 3317, fol. 8.

182. G. A. Starr, "Escape from Barbary: A Seventeenth-Century Genre," *H.L.Q.* 29 (1965): 35–52; Joe Snader, "The Oriental Captivity Narrative and Early English Fiction," *Eighteenth-Century Fiction* 9 (1997): 267–98. Snader repeats the "orientalist" thesis in his full-length study of this topic, *Caught Between Worlds: British Captivity Narratives in Fact and Fiction* (Lexington: University Press of Kentucky, 2000), 3, 39, and passim.

183. The lines quoted from "The Church Militant" had nearly prevented *The Temple* from being published; see *The Works of George Herbert*, ed. F. E. Hutchinson (Oxford: Oxford University Press, Clarendon, 1941), 546–47.

184. See my discussion of the political context of early captivity accounts in "English Captivity Accounts in North Africa and the Middle East, 1577–1625," forthcoming in *Renaissance Quarterly*.

185. SP 16/269/51.

186. See, for instance, my discussion of the English reaction to the introduction of coffee in the second half of the seventeenth century in chapter 3 of *Islam in Britain*.

187. See my "Renaissance England and the Turban," in *Images of the Other: Europe and the Muslim World before 1700*, ed. David Blanks, Cairo Papers in Social Science, 19 (Cairo: American University in Cairo Press, 1996), 39–55.

188. SP 71/31/142.

189. After being taken captive, Wadsworth reported that two "Moores . . . secretly select[ed] two of the youngest and fairest among vs, abused their bodies with insatiable lust" (*The English Spanish Pilgrime*, 35). For the use of sodomy in the anti-Muslim polemic, see my discussion of "Sodomy and Conquest" in chapter 4 of *Turks, Moors, and Englishmen*.

190. Hakluyt, *Navigations*, 5:162.

191. John Rawlins, *The Famous and Wonderfull Recoverie of a Ship of Bristoll* (London, 1622), Bv; T.S., *The Adventures*, 2.

192. *Adventures by Sea*, 82–100.

193. Although Puritan autobiography may have played a role in framing some of the accounts, the overall Augustinian/Christian model was also operative, as evidenced by many of the French accounts, in which captivity is seen as providing a lesson in humility and compassion; see, for example, Turbet-Delof, *L'Afrique Barbaresque*, 121–22.

194. Gee, *Narrative*, 27.

195. *The True Nature of Imposture fully display'd in the Life of Mahomet* (1697), cited in Joseph Pitts, *A True and Faithful Account of the Religion and Manners of the Mohammetans* (Exeter, 1704), 13.

196. In Lope de Vega's *El Esclavo de Venecia y Amante de Su Hermana*, Celidero, the Turkish general, gets to the point where he confesses that he does not know whether he is a "cristiano, turco o moro" (*Obras de Lope De Vega* [Madrid, 1918], 5:349). Later, he and Zara, the sultan's kinswoman, convert to Christianity.

197. All but one of the published accounts in the second group present Englishmen who manage to escape, demonstrating thereby that the captives were smarter and more daring than the Muslims; the accounts by Spratt, Coxere, Browne, and Gee, which were not published, presented ransomed captives.

198. Howard Mumford Jones, "The Colonial Impulse: An Analysis of the 'Promotion' Literature of Colonization," *Proceedings of the American Philosophical Society* 90 (1946): 131–61. There had been quite a lot of negative propaganda against

colonization; see David Cressy, *Coming Over: Migration and Communication Between England and New England in the Seventeenth Century* (Cambridge: Cambridge University Press, 1987).

199. See my article "The Barbary Corsairs, King Charles I, and the Civil War," forthcoming in *The Seventeenth Century*.

200. It is unfortunate that in *Caught Between Worlds*, Snader ignored the numerous European captivity accounts that were published on the continent.

Within the illustration, the panel captions read:

Turks taking the English.

Selling slaves in Algers

Execution with A batoone.

Turks burning of A Frier er.

Mayork

FIGURE I. Frontispiece to William Okeley, *Eben-Ezer, or a Small Monument of Great Mercy, Appearing in the Miraculous Deliverance of William Okeley* (London, 1675). Courtesy of the Folger Shakespeare Library.

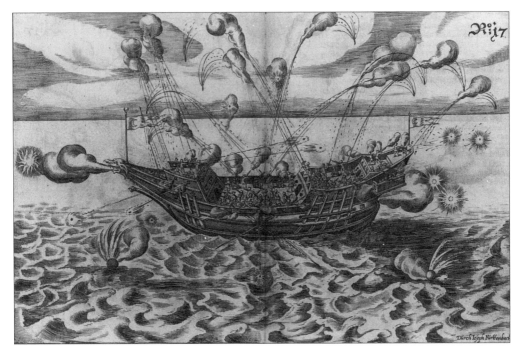

FIGURE 2. From Joseph Furttenbach, *Architectura Navalis* (Ulm, 1629). A Turkish "cara-muzzal" with guns firing. This was the sort of vessel used by the corsairs of North Africa. Courtesy of the Folger Shakespeare Library.

FIGURE 3. From Joseph Furttenbach, *Architectura Navalis* (Ulm, 1629). A seventeenth-century Mediterranean galley. Courtesy of the Folger Shakespeare Library.

Sold by H. Overton
without Newgate.

Mauron delin:

Remember the Poor Prisoners

Ayez Souvenance des Pauvres Prisonniers

Ricordatevi di far carita a Poveri Carcerati

P.Tempest exc:
Cum Privilegio

49

FIGURE 4. From Marcellus Laroon, *The Cryes of the City of London*, 2nd edition (London, 1711). The first edition, published in 1688, includes the same image, showing an Englishman collecting alms to ransom "prisoners" from captivity in Barbary. Courtesy of the Folger Shakespeare Library.

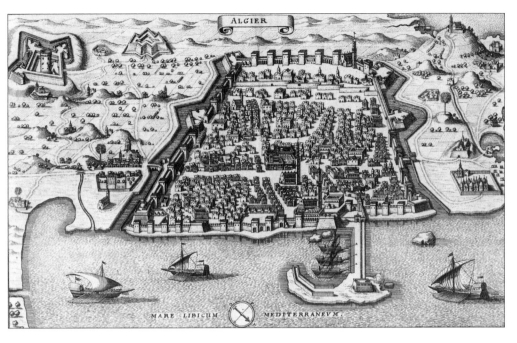

FIGURE 5. Pierre de Montmartin, Sieur d'Avity, *Neuwe Archontologia Cosmica* (Frankfurt, 1646), plate 82. View of the city of Algiers. Courtesy of the Library of Congress.

London

ATLANTIC

OCEAN

*Cape
Finisterre*

BERLENGAS
ISLANDS

S P A I N

Leghorn

Rome

Seville

San Lucar

Cadiz
*Straits of
Gibraltar*

Malaga

Tarifa

Tangier

Fez

Meknes

Mamora

Salé

MAJORCA

IBIZA   •Palma

FORMENTERA

Cape de Gata

Oran

Mostaganem

Tlemcen

Algiers

Blida

Miliana

Bougia

Djidjeli

Bona

Tunis

SICILY

MOROCCO

Tripoli

0   *Miles*   500

FIGURE 6. Map of the Mediterranean region, showing places mentioned in the captivity narratives.

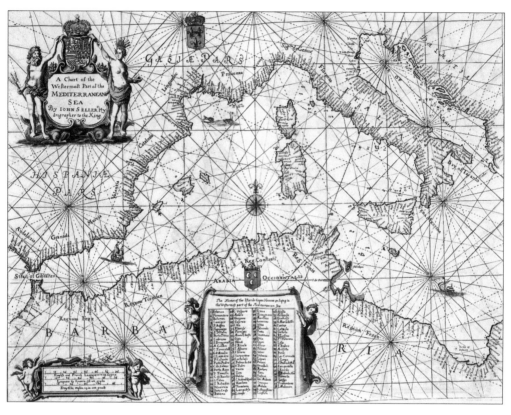

FIGURE 7. John Seller, *Atlas Maritimus; or A Book of Charts* (London, 1672), plate 36. "A Chart of the Westernmost Part of the Mediterranean Sea." Courtesy of the Library of Congress.

Narratives

John Fox, "The Worthy Enterprise of John Fox, in Delivering 266 Christians Out of the Captivity of the Turks," in Richard Hakluyt, Principal Navigations (1589)

(Alexandria, 1563–77)

"The Worthy Enterprise of John Fox" describes a context of enslavement that differs from those presented in the later accounts included in this volume. Egypt, where most of the Fox narrative occurs, had been conquered by the Ottoman Turks in 1517 and was under tighter control by Istanbul than were the regencies in Tunis or Algiers. The international group of slaves that escaped from Alexandria along with Fox in 1577 were galley slaves kept in harbor during the winter season, when weather tended to limit the activity of Turkish galleys. The "keepers" and slave masters in Alexandria are Turks, not the Moors who were native to the Maghreb. By contrast, in Algiers, Tunis, and Morocco, the trade in captives in the century to come was more fully developed, with the local corsair economies targeting Christian vessels and establishing the collection of ransom as their primary profit motive. In Algiers, for example, Christian slaves were frequently employed as laborers (in the galleys or elsewhere), but redemption was always possible for those who could successfully negotiate and pay the price of their ransom. When Fox's ship was captured, however, only the well-connected master and owner were ransomed, while the other captives, including Fox, were held in Egypt or Turkey to "serve in the galleys" as slaves. Fox, as a gunner, had technical knowledge that further encouraged his captors to keep him in their service.

The difference in the conditions of slavery in Salé, Tunis, or Algiers to the west and galley slavery in the Ottoman Empire to the east was still apparent a hundred years later. In his narrative, published in 1704, Joseph Pitts describes an incident that occurred in the 1690s: an Italian corsair facing certain capture at the hands of a combined Algerian-Ottoman fleet intentionally sailed toward the Algerians rather than the Turks, so that the captain and crew would have a chance to regain their freedom by means of ransom. Such redemption was unlikely for Fox and his band of galley slaves, and so they were willing to attempt escape by violent means against overwhelming odds.

Describing events in the 1560s and 1570s, Fox's captivity narrative takes place in a context of friendly relations and active commerce carried out between England and Spain, with English ships like the *Three Half Moons* commonly seen in Spanish harbors, including Seville. During the early Elizabethan period, English maritime activity inside the Mediterranean Sea was minimal, but trade ties to Spain and Portugal were strong. The Spanish Company was formed in 1577, and one of its founding members, William Harborne, was to be the first representative of the English Crown to negotiate a trade agreement with the Ottoman sultan. After formal capitulations were established in 1579 between Queen Elizabeth and the Turkish sultan, Murad III, and the Levant Company was founded in the following year, English maritime traffic moved into the Mediterranean and increased in volume throughout the seventeenth century. This growth in trade embroiled the English in pan-Mediterranean affairs and made their ships and seamen increasingly susceptible to seizure by the Barbary pirates. The seventeenth century would be a period when English merchants sailing in the Mediterranean and the European seaboard region faced the possibility of corsair attack, and this threat would not diminish until the end of the century, when superior technology and naval firepower began to give the English an overwhelming advantage.

The narrative of Fox's captivity and escape is nearly free of anti-Catholic attitudes and celebrates the common cause of Christians who were victimized by their Islamic masters. The documents appended to the narrative were produced by Roman Catholic friars and by officials at the Vatican and at the court of Philip of Spain; these official testimonials accompany the narrative and function as legitimate evidence of the truth of the account and the virtue of the story's Protestant hero, Fox. This alliance between Protestants and Catholics stands in striking contrast to the case of Hasleton, who had the misfortune of falling into Spanish Catholic hands during the peak period of conflict between a militant Spain and its Protestant foes, especially England.

The text reproduced here is taken from Hakluyt's 1589 edition of *The Principal Navigations*, and as such it functions as an inspirational parable promoting the idea of divine favor for the "Elect Nation" and its maritime enterprises. In this regard, the text is typical of the captivity narrative as an early modern genre in which an English Protestant ideology that combines religious and national sectarianism serves as a primary source of the text's social meaning.

"The Worthy Enterprise of John Fox" is told in the third person by a narrator whose identity is unknown. Another account of the same events appeared in 1608 as *The Admirable Deliverance of 266 Christians by John Reynard Englishman from the Captivitie of the Turkes*. Anthony Munday (1553–1633), the purported author of this later account, was a prolific writer of plays, civic pageants, poems, pamphlets, and translations; it is likely he based his text on the account in Hakluyt. The Hakluyt version of the story, which nonetheless differs significantly from Munday's, was probably taken from a previously printed version that was entered in the Stationers' Register on July 23, 1579. Where the Hakluyt version stresses the providentialist framework and draws repeated analogies between the events of the narrative and the Bible, the Munday version mentions God only once and does not include any references to Scripture. The 1608 text opens with an exhortation to pursue "Commerce and Negotiation," not war, in order to strengthen the navy and the nation. The tone is nationalistic and romantic rather than emphatically Christian. Munday's text also features frequent rhetorical and metaphorical flourishes, along with allusions to classical and literary sources. For example, Neptune and the "Gods of the Sea," not the Christian deity, are invoked as controlling powers at the beginning of the account. The later version also refers to Fox as "Reynard" and adds a list enumerating the various nationalities of those who escaped with him.

Only three were English, the rest numbered twenty-six Spaniards, thirty-five Portuguese, twenty-three "Polanders," and thirty-nine Greeks. The list includes many more Christian slaves from the eastern parts of Europe than would have been captive in Algiers or Morocco. A few passages in the Munday text echo verbatim the words of the Hakluyt version, and it is quite possible that both drew on the same earlier source. Hakluyt's version was reprinted in the second edition of the *Principal Navigations*, which appeared in three volumes between 1598 and 1600.

John Fox in Richard Hakluyt, *The Principal Navigations, Voyages and Discoveries of the English Nation, Made by Sea or over Land to the Most Remote and Farthest Distant Quarters of the Earth at Any Time within the Compass of these 1600 Years.*

IMPRINTED AT LONDON BY GEORGE BISHOP AND RALPH NEWBERRY, DEPUTIES TO CHRISTOPHER BARKER, PRINTER TO THE QUEEN'S MOST EXCELLENT MAJESTY, 1589.

The worthy enterprise of John Fox, an Englishman, in delivering 266 Christians out of the captivity of the Turks at Alexandria, the third of January 1577.

Among our merchants here in England, it is a common voyage to traffic into Spain, whereunto a ship, being called *The Three Half Moons*, manned with eight and thirty men and well fenced[1] with munitions, the better to encounter their enemies withal, and having wind and tide, set from Portsmouth, 1563, and bended her journey toward Seville, a city in Spain, intending there to traffic with them. And falling near the Straits,[2] they perceived themselves to be beset round about with eight galleys of the Turks, in such wise that there was no way for them to fly or escape away but that either they must yield or else be sunk. Which the owner perceiving, manfully encouraged his company, exhorting them valiantly to show their manhood, showing them that God was their God and not their enemy's, requesting them also not to faint

---

[1] *fenced*: protected.
[2] *Straits*: Straits of Gibraltar.

in seeing such a heap of their enemies ready to devour them; putting them in mind also that if it were God's pleasure to give them into their enemies' hands, it was not they that ought to show one unpleasant look or countenance there against but to take it patiently and not to prescribe a day and a time for their deliverance, as the citizens of Bethulia did,[3] but to put themselves under His mercy. And again, if it were His mind and good will to show His mighty power by them, if their enemies were ten times so many, they were not able to stand in their hands; putting them likewise in mind of the old and ancient worthiness of their countrymen, who in the hardest extremities have always most prevailed and gone away conquerors, yea, and where it hath been almost impossible. Such (quoth he) hath been the valiantness of our countrymen, and such hath been the mighty power of our God.

With such other like encouragements, exhorting them to behave themselves manfully, they fell all on their knees, making their prayers briefly unto God; who being all risen up again, perceived their enemies by their signs and defiances bent to the spoil, whose mercy was nothing else but cruelty; whereupon every man took him to his weapon.

Then stood up one Grove, the master,[4] being a comely man, with his sword and target, holding them up in defiance against his enemies. So likewise stood up the owner, the master's mate, boatswain, purser, and every man well appointed. Now likewise sounded up the drums, trumpets, and flutes, which would have encouraged any man, had he never so little heart or courage in him.

Then taketh him to his charge John Fox, the gunner, in the disposing of his pieces[5] in order to the best effect and sending his bullets toward the Turks, who likewise bestowed their pieces thrice as fast toward the Christians. But shortly they drew near, so that the bowmen fell to their charge in sending forth their arrows so thick amongst the galleys, and also in doubling their shot so sore upon the galleys, that there were twice so many of the Turks slain as the number of the Christians were in all. But the Turks discharged twice as fast against the Christians, and so long, that the ship was very sore stricken and bruised under water. Which the Turks perceiving, made the more haste to come aboard the ship, which ere they could do, many a Turk bought it dearly with the loss of their lives. Yet was all in vain and boarded

---

[3] *as the citizens of Bethulia did*: The people of Bethulia were ready to surrender to an Assyrian army if God did not send help within five days' time. See the Book of Judith, 8:9–17, in the Apocrypha.

[4] *master*: commanding officer or captain of a merchant ship (usually, as here, distinguished from the ship's owner).

[5] *pieces*: cannons.

they were, where they found so hot a skirmish that it had been better they had not meddled with the feast. For the Englishmen showed themselves men indeed, in working manfully with their brown bills and halberds, where the owner, master, boatswain, and their company stood to it so lustily that the Turks were half dismayed. But chiefly the boatswain showed himself valiant above the rest, for he fared amongst the Turks like a wood[6] lion. For there was none of them that either could or durst stand in his face, till at the last there came a shot from the Turks which brake his whistle[7] asunder and smote him on the breast, so that he fell down, bidding them farewell and to be of good comfort, encouraging them likewise to win praise by death rather than to live captives in misery and shame, which they hearing, indeed intended to have done, as it appeared by their skirmish. But the press and store of the Turks was so great that they were not able long to endure but were so overpressed that they could not wield their weapons, by reason whereof, they must needs be taken, which none of them intended to have been but rather to have died, except only the master's mate, who shrunk from the skirmish like a notable coward, esteeming neither the valor of his name nor accounting of the present example of his fellows. But, in fine, so it was that the Turks were victors. The Christians must needs to the galleys to serve in new offices, and they were no sooner in them but their garments were pulled over their ears and torn from their backs, and they set to the oars.

I will make no mention of their miseries, being now under their enemies' raging stripes.[8] I think there is no man will judge their fare good or their bodies unladen of stripes, and not pestered with too much heat, and also with too much cold, but I will go to my purpose, which is to show the end of those, being in mere misery, which continually do call on God with a steadfast hope that He will deliver them and with a sure faith that He can do it.

Nigh to the city of Alexandria, being a haven town and under the dominion of the Turks, there is a road[9] being made very fencible[10] with strong walls, whereinto the Turks do customably[11] bring their galleys onshore every year in the winter season and there do trim them and lay them up

---

[6] *wood*: enraged.
[7] *his whistle*: the ship's officers, including the chief gunner, wore whistles about the neck, using them to signal the crew to fire a cannon or perform other actions onboard the ship; here, however, "whistle" might mean "throat" or "windpipe."
[8] *stripes*: blows delivered with a whip.
[9] *road*: sheltered harbor area or anchorage.
[10] *fencible*: easy to defend.
[11] *customably*: customarily.

against the springtime. In which road there is a prison wherein the captives and such prisoners as serve in the galleys are put for all that time until the seas be calm and passable for the galleys, every prisoner being most grievously laden with irons on their legs, to their great pain and sore disabling of them to any labor taking. Into which prison were these Christians put and fast warded all the winter season. But ere it was long, the master and the owner, by means of friends, were redeemed, the rest abiding still by the misery, while that they were all, through reason of their ill usage and worse fare, miserably starved, saving one John Fox, who (as some men can abide harder and more misery than other some can, so can some likewise make more shift and work more devices to help their state and living than other some can) being somewhat skillful in the craft of a barber, by reason thereof made great shift in helping his fare now and then with a good meal. Insomuch, till at the last God sent him favor in the sight of the keeper of the prison, so that he had leave to go in and out to the road at his pleasure, paying a certain stipend unto the keeper and wearing a lock about his leg, which liberty likewise six more had upon like sufferance, who by reason of their long imprisonment, not being feared or suspected to start aside, or that they would work the Turks any mischief, had liberty to go in and out at the said road in such manner as this John Fox did, with irons on their legs, and to return again at night.

In the year of our Lord 1577 in the winter season, the galleys happily coming to their accustomed harbor and being discharged of all their masts, sails, and other such furnitures as unto galleys do appertain and all the masters and mariners of them being then nested in their own homes, there remained in the prison of the said road two hundred, threescore, and eight Christian prisoners who had been taken by the Turks' force and were of sixteen sundry nations. Among which there were three Englishmen, whereof one was named John Fox of Woodbridge in Suffolk; the other, William Wickney of Portsmouth, in the county of Southampton; and the third, Robert Moore of Harwich, in the county of Essex. Which John Fox, having been thirteen or fourteen years under their gentle entreatance[12] and being too, too weary thereof, minding his escape, weighed with himself by what means it might be brought to pass and, continually pondering with himself thereof, took a good heart unto him, in hope that God would not be always scourging His children and never ceasing to pray Him to further his pretended enterprise, if that it should redound to His glory.

[12] *gentle entreatance*: kind treatment (ironic).

Not far from the road and somewhat from thence at one side of the city, there was a certain victualing house which one Peter Unticaro had hired, paying also a certain fee unto the keeper of the road. This Peter Unticaro was a Spaniard born, and a Christian, and had been prisoner about thirty years and never practiced any means to escape but kept himself quiet, without touch or suspect of any conspiracy, until that now this John Fox using much thither, they brake to one another their minds concerning the restraint of their liberty and imprisonment. So that this John Fox, at length opening unto this Unticaro the device which he would fain put in practice, made privy one more to this their intent, which three debated of this matter at such times as they could compass to meet together, insomuch that at seven weeks' end they had sufficiently concluded how the matter should be, if it pleased God to farther them thereto; who making five more privy to this their device, whom they thought they might safely trust, determined in three nights after to accomplish their deliberate purpose. Whereupon the same John Fox, and Peter Unticaro, and the other six appointed to meet all together in the prison the next day, being the last day of December, where this John Fox certified the rest of the prisoners what their intent and device was and how and when they minded to bring their purpose to pass, who thereunto persuaded them without much ado to further their device. Which the same John Fox seeing, delivered unto them a sort of files which he had gathered together for this purpose, by the means of Peter Unticaro, charging them that every man should be ready discharged of his irons by eight of the clock on the next day at night.

In the next day at night, this said John Fox and his six other companions, being all come to the house of Peter Unticaro, passing the time away in mirth for fear of suspect till the night came on, so that it was time for them to put in practice their device, sent Peter Unticaro to the master of the road, in the name of one of the masters of the city, with whom this keeper was acquainted and at whose request he would also come at the first, who desired him to take the pains to meet him there, promising him that he would bring him back again. The keeper agreed to go with him, willing the warders not to bar the gate, saying that he would not stay long but would come again with all speed.

In the mean season, the other seven had provided them of such weapons as they could get in that house, and John Fox took him to an old rusty sword blade without either hilt or pommel, which he made to serve his turn in bending the hand end of the sword, instead of a pommel, and the others had got such spits and glaives[13] as they found in the house.

---

[13] *glaives*: broad-bladed weapons or tools.

The keeper now being come unto the house and perceiving no light, nor hearing any noise, straightway suspected the matter and returning backward, John Fox standing behind the corner of the house, stepped forth unto him, who perceiving it to be John Fox, said, "O Fox, what have I deserved of thee, that thou shouldest seek my death?" "Thou villain," quoth Fox, "hast been a bloodsucker of many a Christian's blood, and now thou shalt know what thou hast deserved at my hands." Wherewith he lift up his bright, shining sword of ten years' rust and struck him so main a blow as therewithal his head clave asunder, so that he fell stark dead to the ground. Whereupon Peter Unticaro went in and certified the rest how the case stood with the keeper; who came presently forth, and some with their spits ran him through, and others with their glaives hewed him in sunder, cut off his head, and mangled him so that no man should discern what he was.

Then marched they toward the road, whereinto they entered softly, where were six warders, whom one of them asked, saying, "Who was there?" Quoth Fox and his company, "All friends," which when they were all within proved contrary. For quoth Fox, "My masters, here is not to every man a man, wherefore look you play your parts"; who so behaved themselves in deed that they had dispatched these six quickly. Then John Fox, intending not to be barred of his enterprise, and minding to work surely in that which he went about, barred the gate surely and planted a cannon against it.

Then entered they into the jailer's lodge, where they found the keys of the fortress and prison by his bedside, and there had they all better weapons. In this chamber was a chest wherein was a rich treasure, and all in ducats,[14] which this Peter Unticaro and two more opening, stuffed themselves so full as they could, between their shirts and their skin; which John Fox would not once touch and said that it was his and their liberty which he sought for, to the honor of his God, and not to make a mart[15] of the wicked treasure of the infidels. Yet did these words sink nothing into their stomachs, they did it for a good intent: so did Saul save the fattest oxen[16] to offer unto the Lord, and they to serve their own turn. But neither did Saul scape the wrath of God therefore; neither had these that thing which they desired so and did thirst after. Such is God's justice. He that they put their trust in, to deliver them

---

[14] *ducats*: valuable gold or silver coins.

[15] *make a mart of*: profit from.

[16] *so did Saul save the fattest oxen*: Although Saul was instructed to kill all the Amalekites and destroy all their cattle, he kept the most valuable livestock and therefore failed to carry out God's command. He was subsequently defeated and killed by the Philistines. See Samuel 1:15.

from the tyrannous hands of their enemies (He, I say) could supply their
want of necessaries.

Now these eight, being armed with such weapons as they thought well of,
thinking themselves sufficient champions to encounter a stronger enemy and
coming unto the prison, Fox opened the gates and doors thereof and called
forth all the prisoners, whom he set, some to ramming up the gate,[17] some to
the dressing up of a certain galley, which was the best in all the road and was
called the *Captain of Alexandria*, whereinto some carried masts, sails, oars,
and other such furniture as doth belong unto a galley.

At the prison were certain warders, whom John Fox and his company
slew; in the killing of whom, there were eight more of the Turks which perceived them and got them[18] to the top of the prison, unto whom John Fox
and his company were fain to come to by ladders, where they found a hot
skirmish. For some of them were there slain, some wounded, and some but
scarred and not hurt. As John Fox was thrice shot through his apparel and
not hurt, Peter Unticaro and the other two that had armed them with the
ducats were slain, as not able to wield themselves, being so pestered with
the weight and uneasy carrying of the wicked and profane treasure, and
also divers Christians were as well hurt about that skirmish as Turks slain.

Amongst the Turks was one thrust through, who (let us not say that it
was ill fortune) fell off from the top of the prison wall and made such a lowing that the inhabitants thereabout (as here and there scattering stood a
house or two) came and dawed him,[19] so that they understood the case,
how that the prisoners were paying their ransoms; wherewith they raised
both Alexandria, which lay on the west side of the road, and a castle which
was at the city's end, next to the road, and also another fortress which lay
on the north side of the road, so that now they had no way to escape but
one, which by man's reason (the two holds lying so upon the mouth of the
road) might seem impossible to be a way for them. So was the Red Sea
impossible for the Israelites to pass through, the hills and rocks lay so on
the one side and their enemies compassed them on the other. So was it
impossible that the walls of Jericho should fall down, being neither undermined, nor yet rammed at with engines, nor yet any man's wisdom, policy,
or help set or put thereunto. Such impossibilities can our God make possible. He that held the lion's jaws from rending Daniel asunder, yea, or yet

---

[17] *ramming up the gate*: strengthening the gate against forced entry by barricading
it with earth or other materials to prevent it from being opened.

[18] *them*: themselves (the Turks).

[19] *dawed him*: roused him from unconsciousness.

from once touching him to his hurt, cannot He hold the roaring cannons of this hellish force? He that kept the fire's rage in the hot-burning oven from the three children[20] that praised His name, cannot He keep the fire's flaming blasts from among His elect?

Now is the road fraught with lusty soldiers, laborers, and mariners, who are fain to stand to their tackling,[21] in setting to every man his hand, some to the carrying in of victuals, some munitions, some oars, and some one thing, some another, but most are keeping their enemy from the wall of the road. But to be short, there was no time misspent, no man idle, nor any man's labor ill bestowed or in vain. So that in short time this galley was ready trimmed up. Whereinto every man leaped in all haste, hoisting up the sails lustily, yielding themselves to His mercy and grace, in whose hands is both wind and weather.

Now is this galley on float and out of the safety of the road. Now have the two castles full power upon the galley. Now is there no remedy but sink: how can it be avoided? The cannons let fly from both sides, and the galley is even in the midst and between them both. What man can devise to save it? There is no man but would think it must needs be sunk.

There was not one of them that feared the shot which went thundering round about their ears nor yet were once scarred or touched with five and forty shot which came from the castles. Here did God hold forth His buckler. He shieldeth now this galley and hath tried their faith to the uttermost. Now cometh His special help: yea, even when man thinks them past all help, then cometh He himself down from heaven with His mighty power; then is His present remedy most ready pressed. For they sail away, being not once touched with the glance of a shot, and are quickly out of the Turkish cannons' reach. Then might they see them coming down by heaps to the water side, in companies like unto swarms of bees, making show to come after them with galleys, in bustling themselves to dress up the galleys, which would be a swift piece of work for them to do, for that they had neither oars, masts, sails, gables,[22] nor anything else ready in any galley. But yet they are carrying them into them, some into one galley, and some into another, so that, being such a confusion amongst them, without any certain guide, it were a thing impossible to overtake them; beside that, there was no man that would take charge of a galley, the weather was so rough, and there was such an amazedness

---

[20] *the three children*: three Jewish men who refused to worship other gods and were thrown into a fiery furnace by Nebuchadnezzar but miraculously emerged unscathed. See chapter 3 of the Book of Daniel.

[21] *stand to their tackling*: set to work with their gear.

[22] *gables*: cables.

amongst them. And verily I think their god was amazed thereat. It could not be but he must blush for shame; he can speak never a word for dullness, much less can he help them in such an extremity. Well, howsoever it is, he is very much to blame, to suffer them to receive such a gibe. But howsoever their god behaved himself, our God showed himself a God indeed and that He was the only living God: for the seas were swift under His faithful, which made the enemies aghast to behold them. A skillfuller pilot leads them, and their mariners bestir themselves lustily; but the Turks had neither mariners, pilot, nor any skillful master that was in a readiness at this pinch.

When the Christians were safe out of the enemy's coast, John Fox called to them all, willing them to be thankful unto Almighty God for their delivery and most humbly to fall down upon their knees, beseeching Him to aid them unto their friend's land and not to bring them into another danger, sith He had most mightily delivered them from so great a thralldom and bondage.

Thus when every man had made his petition, they fell straightway to their labor with the oars, in helping one another when they were wearied and with great labor striving to come to some Christian land, as near as they could guess by the stars. But the winds were so diverse, one while driving them this way, another while that way, that they were now in a new maze, thinking that God had forsaken them and left them to a greater danger. And forasmuch as there were no victuals now left in the galley, it might have been a cause to them (if they had been the Israelites) to have murmured against their God, but they knew how that their God, who had delivered them out of Egypt, was such a loving and merciful God, as that He would not suffer them to be confounded, in whom He had wrought so great a wonder, but what calamity soever they sustained, they knew it was but for their farther trial and also (in putting them in mind of their farther misery) to cause them not to triumph and glory in themselves therefore. Having (I say) no victuals in the galley, it might seem one misery continually to fall upon another's neck, but to be brief, the famine grew to be so great that in twenty-eight days wherein they were on the sea, there died eight persons, to the astonishment of all the rest.

So it fell out that upon the twenty-ninth day after they set from Alexandria, they fell on the Isle of Candy[23] and landed at Gallipoli,[24] where they were made much of by the abbot and monks there, who caused them to stay there while they were well refreshed and eased. They kept there the sword

[23] *Isle of Candy*: Crete.

[24] *Gallipoli*: probably Agia Galini, a small port on the south coast of Crete, not the peninsula near the Dardanelles.

wherewith John Fox had killed the keeper, esteeming it as a most precious jewel, and hung it up for a monument.

When they thought good, having leave to depart from thence, they sailed along the coast till they arrived at Taranto,[25] where they sold their galley and divided it, every man having a part thereof. The Turks receiving so shameful a foil at their hand, pursued the Christians and scoured the seas, where they could imagine that they had bent their course. And the Christians had departed from thence one day in the morning, and seven galleys of the Turks came thither that night, as it was certified by those who followed Fox and his company, fearing lest they should have been met with. And then they came afoot to Naples, where they departed asunder, every man taking him to his next way home. From whence John Fox took his journey unto Rome, where he was well entertained of an Englishman who presented his worthy deed unto the pope, who rewarded him liberally and gave him his letters unto the king of Spain, where he was very well entertained of him there, who for this his most worthy enterprise gave him in fee twenty pence a day. From whence, being desirous to come into his own country, he came thither at such time as he conveniently could, which was in the year of our Lord God 1579. Who being come into England, went unto the court and showed all his travel unto the council, who considering of the state of this man, in that he had spent and lost a great part of his youth in thralldom and bondage, extended to him their liberality to help to maintain him now in age, to their right honor and to the encouragement of all true-hearted Christians.

The Copy of the Certificate for John Fox and His Company Made by the Prior and the Brethren of Gallipoli, Where They First Landed

We, the prior and fathers of the Convent[1] of the Amerciates, of the city of Gallipoli, of the Order of Preachers,[2] do testify that upon the 29th of January last past, 1577, there came in to the said city a certain galley from Alexandria, taken from the Turks, with two hundreth fifty and eight Christians whereof was principal Master John Fox, an Englishman, a gunner, and one of the

---

[25] *Taranto*: seaport in southeast Italy.

[1] *Convent*: religious community.

[2] *Order of Preachers*: the Dominicans, an order of preaching friars.

chiefest that did accomplish that great work whereby so many Christians have recovered their liberties. In token and remembrance whereof, upon our earnest request to the same John Fox, he hath left here an old sword wherewith he slew the keeper of the prison, which sword we do, as a monument and memorial of so worthy a deed, hang up in the chief place of our convent house. And for because all things aforesaid are such as we will testify to be true, as they are orderly passed and have therefore good credit, that so much as is above expressed is true and for the more faith thereof, we, the prior and fathers aforesaid, have ratified and subscribed these presents.[3] Even[4] in Gallipoli, the third of Feb., 1577.

I, Friar Vincent Barba, prior of the same place, confirm the premises, as they are above written.

I, Friar Albert Damaro of Gallipoli, subprior, confirm as much.

I, Friar Anthony Celleler of Galls, confirm as aforesaid.

I, Friar Bartlemew of Gallipoli, confirm as aforesaid.

I, Friar Frauncis of Gallipoli, confirm as much.

The Bishop of Rome,[5] His Letters, in the Behalf of John Fox

Be it known unto all men to whom this writing shall come, that the bringer here of John Fox, Englishman, a gunner, after he had served captive in the Turks' galleys, by the space of fourteen years, at length, through God His help, taking good opportunity, the third of January last past, slew the keeper of the prison (whom he first struck on the face) together with four and twenty other Turks, by the assistance of his fellow prisoners, and with 266 Christians (of whose liberty he was the author) launched from Alexandria and from thence arrived first at Gallipoli in Candy[6] and afterwards at Taranto in Apulia, the written testimony and credit of which things, as also of others, the same John Fox hath in public tables[7] from Naples.

Upon Easter eve, he came to Rome and is now determined to take his journey to the Spanish court,[8] hoping there to obtain some relief toward his

---

[3] *presents*: statements contained in this document.

[4] *Even*: here (in this specific place).

[5] *bishop of Rome*: Gregory XIII, pope from 1572 to 1585.

[6] *Candy*: Crete.

[7] *public tables*: official documents.

[8] *Spanish court*: the court of Philip II (reigned 1556–98), who also ruled over the kingdoms of Naples and Sicily.

living: wherefore the poor distressed man humbly beseecheth, and we in his behalf, do in the bowels[9] of Christ desire you that, taking compassion of his former captivity and present penury, you do not only suffer him freely to pass throughout all your cities and towns but also succor him with your charitable alms, the reward whereof you shall hereafter most assuredly receive, which we hope you will afford to him, whom with tender affection of pity we commend unto you. At Rome, the 20th of April, 1577.

Thomas Grolos, Englishman, Bishop of Astraphen.

Richard Silleun, Prior Anglia.

Andreas Ludonicus, Register[10] to our sovereign lord the pope, which for the greater credit of the premises have set my seal to these presents. At Rome, the day and year above written.

Mauricius Clement, the governor and keeper of the English hospital in the city.

The King of Spain, His Letters to the Lieutenant, for the Placing of John Fox in the Office of a Gunner, etc.

To the illustrious prince, Vespasian Gonsaga Colonna, our lieutenant and captain general of our realm of Valentia,[11] having consideration that John Fox, Englishman, hath served us and was one of the most principal which took away from the Turks a certain galley, which they have brought to Taranto, wherein were two hundred fifty and eight Christian captives. We license him to practice and give him the office of a gunner and have ordained that he go to our said realm, there to serve in the said office in the galleys, which by our commandment are lately made. And we do command that you cause to be paid to him eight ducats' pay a month for the time that he shall serve in the said galleys as gunner or till we can otherwise provide for him; the said eight ducats monthly of the money which is already of our provision, present and to come, and to have regard of those which come with him. From Escarole[12] the tenth of August, 1577.

I, the King

Juan del Gado

And under that a confirmation of the council

[9] *bowels*: merciful capacity.

[10] *Register*: administrator in charge of record keeping.

[11] *Valentia*: the province of Valencia, on the east coast of Spain, the site of a recent uprising (1568–71) by the Morisco population.

[12] *Escarole*: the Escorial palace near Madrid.

Verses Written by A.M. to the Courteous Readers,
Who Was Present at Rome when John Fox
Received his Letters of the Pope

Leaving at large all fables vainly used,
All trifling toys that do no truth import;
Lo, hear how th'end (at length) though long diffused[13]
Unfoldeth plain a true and rare report
To glad those minds who seek their countries' wealth
By proffered pains t'enlarge his happy health.
At Rome I was, when Fox did there arrive:
Therefore I may sufficiently express
What gallant joy his deeds did there revive
In the hearts of those which heard his valiantness.
And how the pope did recompense his pains,
And letters gave to move his greater gains.
But yet I know that many do misdoubt[14]
That those his pains are fables and untrue.
Not only I in this will bear him out,
But diverse more than did his patents[15] view.
And unto those so boldly I dare say
That naught but truth John Fox doth here bewray.[16]
Besides here's one was slave with him in thrall,
Lately returned into our native land.
This witness can this matter perfect all.
What needeth more? For witness he may stand.
And thus I end, unfolding what I know:
The other man more larger proof can show.
Honos alit artes.[17]
A.M.

---

[13] *diffused*: obscured or scattered.

[14] *misdoubt*: mistakenly believe.

[15] *patents*: official documents (referring to the testimonials above).

[16] *bewray*: divulge.

[17] *Honos alit artes*: literally, "Honor sustains skill" (Cicero, *Tusculanae Disputationes*: 1.2.4).

Richard Hasleton, *Strange and Wonderful Things Happened to Richard Hasleton . . . in His Ten Years' Travails in Many Foreign Countries (1595)*

(Algiers and Palma, Majorca, 1582–93)

Hasleton served for five years as a slave in the Algerian galleys before his galley was shipwrecked on the island of Formentera. The year was 1587, only eight years after John Fox had been received as a hero at the Vatican in Rome, but relations between England and Spain had taken a turn for the worse. Thus Hasleton arrived in Spanish Majorca as a prisoner of the Inquisition, during a period of open conflict between Spain and England. The authorities apparently wished to make an example of Hasleton, and his captors taunted him with news of the Spanish Armada's preparation and the Spaniards' plan to invade and rule England.

The compulsion to "turn," enforced by the tortures of the Inquisition, is the central trial of Hasleton's long ordeal, and his years as a galley slave (both before and after his escape to Christendom) are glossed over quickly as he develops a detailed account of his treatment at the hands of his Spanish captors. The theological debate between Hasleton and the inquisitor is placed at the center of the narrative. It is clearly meant to serve an ideological function: clarifying the difference, from a Protestant perspective, between true and false faith. Furthermore, it provides the propagandistic picture of a faithful Protestant who is able, all alone with his God, to withstand the cruelty and unjust power of the Spanish other.

Hasleton's absence from England coincided with a period of war between Spain and England. By the time Hasleton finally returned to London in 1593, the Spanish Armada had been launched, dispersed, and defeated. That and subsequent events seemed to have given English Protestants ample evidence that a providential God was on their side. The determined endurance and tenacity of Hasleton as an individual soul, tested by Spanish power, can be read as analogous to the larger spirit of resistance exhibited by the English Protestant nation as a whole.

Ironically, Hasleton must escape from Christendom to Islam, returning to bondage in order to regain his freedom. Near Djidjelli, in Algeria, he fell into the hands of the Kabyles (a Berber group who often asserted their autonomy against the government in Algiers). There, he was offered a rich reward if he would "turn Moor." Thus he experienced a second attempt to convert him from his faith, this time by the offer of financial gain and a Muslim wife, not by torture. Unfortunately, he was unable to recover his freedom either by serving the Berber leaders along the eastern coast of Algeria or by returning to Algiers itself.

Hasleton's account says very little about the circumstances of his ransom but dwells instead on his trials and temptations in Majorca and Cocou. His refusal to succumb, either to the compulsion of the Inquisition or to the tempting rewards offered by the Moors, is emphasized (and perhaps exaggerated) because Hasleton needed his identity as a returned captive to be free and clear of either Roman Catholic or Islamic contamination. His testimony of faith served the purpose of clearing his name, and at the same time it provided a dramatic example of resistance to other faiths and other powers. The Spanish, though Christian, are represented as a more profoundly evil and irrational community, while the Moors of Algeria are motivated not so much by an irrational superstition as by greed.

William Barley, the author of the dedicatory epistle that opens Strange and Wonderful Things, attributes the authorship of this "pamphlet" to Richard Hasleton himself. The 1595 printed text is the only extant version of Hasleton's first-person narrative.

Richard Hasleton. *Strange and Wonderful Things Happened to Richard Hasleton, Born at Braintree in Essex, in His Ten Years' Travails*[1] *in Many Foreign Countries. Penned as He Delivered It from His Own Mouth.*

LONDON: PRINTED BY A.I. FOR WILLIAM BRADLEY AND ARE TO BE SOLD AT HIS SHOP IN GRATIOUS STREET NEAR LEADENHALL. 1595.

To the worshipful Master Richard Staper,[2] one of the worshipful company of merchants adventurers of this honorable city of London, trading to Turkey and the eastern kingdoms. Your worship's faithful well-willer W. Barley wisheth all fortunate and happy success in all your enterprises, with increase of worldly worship, and after death, the joys unspeakable.

Worshipful Sir,

The many reports of your rare virtues generally spoken of all honest travelers who hath tasted the benefit of your bounty, not only in our homeborn country where you have your residence but in those far countries where your honest factors trade. By whose worshipful and express command given them, and the good they daily do for all men which seek them, your worship is accounted and called the pattern of bounty, especially of such as are in their travail distressed with want, which with money are relieved, as well as other great cost their[3] favor or friendship can procure. So that not only the poor and needy are pleasured thereby but those that swim in most abundance. All proceeding of your most kind and courteous disposition.

The remembrance of which moved a longing desire in me, in some sort, to explain your worthiness and fame by your bounty gained. It had never such opportunity until this time when, perusing my store of papers and writings of sundry men's labors, I chanced on this pamphlet, which importeth the troublesome travails of our near neighbor,

---

[1] *travails*: The original spelling is "travailes," which implies both "travels" and "travails."

[2] *Richard Staper*: a leading London merchant and alderman who was heavily involved in the Levant trade and a founder of the Levant Company.

[3] *their*: the factors.'

born at Braintree in Essex, named Richard Hasleton, whose miseries as they were many (being in the hands both of Christian and heathen enemies, for God and our country's cause) and his escapes from death so often and so wonderful, with the constant enduring of the same, his preservation and safe return to England, where his longing desire so often wished him.

All which considered, with your worship's love to all travelers, emboldened me the rather under your worship's patronage to publish the same, especial zeal procuring me thereunto. And partly in regard of your many favors to the said Hasleton in his miseries extended, that your worship's good ensample[4] may lighten others to such good actions.

Hoping your worship will accept of it no less friendly than I offer it willingly; which if you do, then is my desire satisfied and myself rest bounden to your worship's worthiness. Ever beseeching the giver of all good to increase the number of such worthy-minded subjects by whom our prince[5] and country are in foreign parts so much honored.

> Your worship's to command in what I may,
> William Barley.

The Miserable Captivity of Richard Hasleton, Born at Braintree in Essex.

In the year 1582, departing the English coast toward the end of May in a ship of London called the *Mary Marten* (one of the owners was a citizen of London named Master Eastwoode; the other of them named Master Estridge, dwelling at Limehouse), being laden and bound for Petrach,[6] a town of mart being within the dominion of the Turk,[7] where we safely arrived and made our mart and within eight and twenty days were laden homeward; and presently we weighed anchor and set sail, and coming out of the Gulf of Lepanto grounded upon a rock, lying on the larboard side; being in a very great danger, in doubt to lose both ship and goods, yet it pleased God that we recovered. Then, about the midst of the month of July, we came right before Cape de Gatte,[8] when, having a very small wind, we descried two galleys,

---

[4] *ensample*: example.

[5] *our prince*: at that time, Queen Elizabeth I.

[6] *Petrach*: Patras, in Greece.

[7] *within the dominion of the Turk*: under Ottoman rule, "the Turk" being the Ottoman sultan (at this time Murad III).

[8] *Cape de Gatte*: Cabo de Gata, near Almeria, in Spain.

whereupon the master commanded the gunner to put forth the ordinance and to heave the skiff overboard. Then did the gunner demand of the master to make a shot, which he granted. Then did he bestow eight and twenty shot, but to no purpose, for the enemy lay very far out.

Now when we saw our shot and powder spent so much in waste, some of our company cried to our master to show the Turk's letters;[9] but he would not but commanded the gunner still to shoot. For now the galleys were within shot and did shoot at us, both with great shot and muskets. And presently both our gunners were slain (both with one shot), and some others maimed, whereby we were in great doubt, for the galleys lying on both sides of us, one of them had shot us under water, whereby our ship was foundered before we perceived. Then we, perceiving the ship to sink from us, such as were wariest leapt into the skiff, as many as it was able to bear. The rest leaping overboard, such as could swim saved themselves, going aboard the galleys; the others were drowned. Now I being the last man upon the hatches, because I was at the stern, and being sore hurt with a musket shot; the Turks made haste to board our ship, hoping to save some of our goods: two of them came aboard. The first came to me and took me by the bosom. I drew out my knife very speedily and thrust him into the body and so slew him. The other was gone down into the ship, where I left him, for even then was the ship sinking from me. Wherefore I betook myself to swimming, and turning me about to see the ship, I could see nothing thereof but only the flag. Then did I swim to the galleys and, laying hold upon an oar, got into the galley. When I was aboard, I was stripped of my clothes. Then presently was I commanded to the poop to talk with the captain, who inquired of me whether I was a merchant.[10] Which because I would not confess, he gave me fifteen strokes with a cudgel and then put me in the galley's hold, where I was six days, taking very little sustenance, lying in extreme pains by reason of my hurts which I had received in the fight, and with anguish for my hard hap.[11]

About three months after, the galleys returned to Argier,[12] where immediately after my landing I was sold for sixty-six doubles.[13] Then did I fall into

---

[9] *the Turk's letters*: letters of safe conduct granted by the Turkish sultan to English merchant vessels trading in the Mediterranean.

[10] *merchant*: the supercargo of the ship, who was in charge of business dealings on the voyage and might know where money was kept.

[11] *hard hap*: misfortune.

[12] *Argier*: Algiers.

[13] *doubles*: the double pistoles, or doubloons, a Spanish gold coin.

extreme sickness for ten days' space; notwithstanding, I was sent to sea by my master to whom I was sold, to labor in the galleys at an oar's end, where I remained three months, being very feeble and weak, by reason my sickness continued the most part of that time; yet was I constrained either to labor or else to lose my head. I had no other choice. Then, the galleys returning home to Argier, after my coming on shore I was in a marvelous weakness, what with continual labor, with beating, and with sickness, which endured three months, being in a most miserable estate without all succor, seeing no man to pity my misery, having no nourishment but only bread and water and that but small quantity, no apparel on me but a thin shirt and a pair of linen breeches, and lodged in a stable on the cold ground. Thus I, being almost in despair ever to recover, yielded myself to the will of Almighty God, whom it pleased, in the end, to give me a little strength. And after, for the space of two years or more, I was divers times at my labor at the oar's end after my accustomed manner till (such time our fleet of galleys meeting with the galleys of Genoa near the Christian shore, and they following us in chase) it chanced, by reason of tempest, that our galley was cast away near the west side of the island Fermonterra.[14] There were in it, of Christians and Turks, to the number of two hundred and fifty, which were all drowned except fifteen, of which myself, with two others, with great difficulty brake our chains and taking hold of an oar, we escaped to the shore, not without great danger of drowning. We being now gotten to land and accompanied both with Turks and Christians, we took our rest under bushes and thickets. The Turks were very unwilling to depart with[15] us, thinking to find some other galley of the company to take us aboard and carry us back to Argier. But we, hoping now to get our liberties, conveyed ourselves as secretly as we could into the woods and went unto a rock, and with sharp stones we did beat off our irons and fled immediately to the Christians and yielded ourselves. But one of them which escaped with me, who was born in Sclavony,[16] told them that I was an English Lutheran.

Then was I presently carried aboard a galley of Genoa and put in chains. And, upon the morrow, was I sent over into the Isle of Ivisey,[17] being within the jurisdiction of Maiorque,[18] which are all in the dominion of Spain. There

[14] *Fermonterra*: Formentera, a small island in the Balearic group, just south of Ibiza.
[15] *depart with*: separate from.
[16] *Sclavony*: Slavonia.
[17] *Ivisey*: Ibiza.
[18] *Maiorque*: Majorca.

was I imprisoned in the high tower of the town castle, with a pair of bolts upon my heels and a clasp of iron about my neck, there hanging a chain at the clasp; where I remained nine days, fed with a little bread and water. Now, because I had in no respect offended them, I demanded wherefore they molested me, saying it was contrary to law and the profession of Christians. Then did they ask me if I had spoken anything against the king and against the Church of Rome. I answered nothing. Then they told me I should be sent to Maiorque, to answer before the Inquisition. Then the justice, or chief officer, of Ivisey brought me back to Genoa, requesting to have me chained in a galley, which the captain did, asking the justice who should be my surety for running away. He demanded if there were not a spare chain. He said, "Yes." Then he commanded a chain to be brought forth and chained me at the sixth oar before, where I rowed until we came to the Port of Spine[19] in Maiorque, guarding me with fourteen galleys.

Then were the officers of the Inquisition sent for by the captain, which came the second day after our coming there, and at their coming they offered me the Pax,[20] which I refused to touch, whereupon they reviled me and called me "Lutheran," taking me presently out of the galley, carried me on shore in Maiorque, and, finding the inquisitor walking in the market place, presented me to him, saying, "Here is the prisoner." He immediately commanded me to prison, whither they carried me and put a pair of shackles on my heels, where I remained two days. Then was I brought forth into a church, where the inquisitor sat usually in judgment, who being ready set, commanded me to kneel down and to do homage to certain images which were before me.

I told him I would not do that which I knew to be contrary to the commandments of almighty God; neither had I been brought up in the Roman law, neither would I submit myself to it. He asked me why I would not. I answered that whereas in England, where I was born and brought up, the Gospel was truly preached and maintained by a most gracious princess; therefore I would not now commit idolatry, which is utterly condemned by the word of God. Then he charged me to utter the truth, otherwise I should abide the smart. Then was a stool set, and he commanded me to sit down before him and offered me the cross, bidding me reverently to lay my hand upon it and urged me instantly to do it, which moved me so much that I did

---

[19] *Port of Spine*: later called Portpin, now the Bay of Palma.

[20] *the Pax*: a tablet, usually bearing the image of the crucifixion, which was offered to the congregation to be kissed during the Mass.

spit in the inquisitor's face, for which the scribe gave me a good buffet on the face. So for that time we had no more reasoning. For the inquisitor did ring a little bell to call up the keeper and carried me to ward again. And the third day, I was brought forth again to the place aforesaid.

Then the inquisitor asked me what I had seen in the churches of England. I answered that I had seen nothing in the Church of England but the word of God truly preached.

Then he demanded how I had received the sacraments. I replied that I had received them according to the institution of Christ: that is, I received the bread in remembrance that Christ in the flesh died upon the cross for the redemption of man. "How," said he, "hast thou received the wine?" Whereto I replied and said that I received the wine in remembrance that Christ shed his blood to wash away our sins. He said it was in their manner. I said, "No." Then he charged me to speak the truth or I should die for it. I told him I did speak the truth and would speak the truth. "For," said I, "it is better for me to die guiltless than guilty." Then did he with great vehemency charge me again to speak the truth and sware by the Catholic Church of Rome that if I did not, I should die in fire. Then I said, "If I died in the faith which I had confessed, I should die guiltless," and told him he had made a vain oath. And so I willed him to use no circumstance to dissuade me from the truth: "For you cannot prevail. Though I be now in your hands, where you have power over my body, yet have you no power over my soul." I told him he made a long matter far from the truth, for which he said I should die. Then he bade me say what I could to save myself, where I replied as followeth touching the manner of the receiving of sacraments, where he said it was like to theirs: "You," said I, "when you receive the bread, say it is the very body of Christ, and likewise you affirm the wine to be his very blood," which I denied, saying that it was unpossible for a mortal man to eat the material body of Christ or to drink his blood. Then he said I had blasphemed the Catholic Church. I answered that I had said nothing against the true Catholic Church but altogether against the false church. He asked how I could prove it, saying if I could not prove it, I should die a most cruel death.

Note, by the way, that when any man is in durance for religion, he is called to answer before no open assembly but only in the presence of the inquisitor, the secretary, and the solicitor (whom they term the broker). The cause is, as I take it, because they doubt that very many of their own people would confess the gospel if they did but see and understand their absurd dealing. Again, to the matter. Because it was so secret, they urged me to speak the more.

Then he inquired whether I had ever been confessed.

I said, "Yes."

He demanded, "To whom?"

I said, "To God."

He asked me if I had ever confessed to any friar.

I said, "No, for I do utterly defy them. For how can he forgive me my sins, which is himself a sinner, as all other men are?"

"Yes," said he, "he which confesseth himself to a friar, who is a father, may have remission of his sins by his mediation," which I said I would never believe.

Wherefore, seeing they could seduce me by no means to yield to their abominable idolatry, the secretary cried, "Away with him!" The inquisitor and he frowned very angrily on me for the answers which I had given and said they would make me tell another tale. So, at the ringing of a little bell, the keeper came and carried me to ward again. At my first examination, when the keeper should lead me away, the inquisitor did bless me with the cross, but never after.

Two days after, was I brought and set again upon a stool before the inquisitor. He bade me ask *misericordium*.[21] I told him I would crave mercy of Jesus Christ who died for my sins; other *misericordium* would I crave none. Then he commanded me to kneel before the altar. I said I would, but not to pray to any image: "For your altar is adorned with many painted images (which were fashioned by the hands of sinful men) which have mouths and speak not, ears and hear not, noses and smell not, hands and handle not, feet have they and walk not, etc.—which God doth not allow at his altar, for he hath utterly condemned them by his Word." Then he said I had been wrong taught. "For," said he, "whosoever shall see these figures in earth may the better remember him in heaven whose likeness it doth represent, who would be a mediator to God for us." But I replied that all images were an abomination to the Lord, for he hath condemned them in express words by his own mouth, saying, "Thou shalt not make thyself any graven image, etc."[22] "Yea," said he, "but we have need of a mediator to make intercession for us, for we are unworthy to pray to God ourselves, because we are vile sinners." I said there was no mediator but Jesus Christ, where, after many absurd reasons and vain persuasions, he took a pause.

Then I asked him why he kept me so long in prison, which never committed offense to them (knowing very well that I had been captive in Argier

---

[21] *misericordium*: mercy.

[22] *Thou shalt not make thyself any graven image*: the second commandment given to Moses and the Israelites (Exodus 20:4).

near five years' space), saying that when God, by his merciful providence, had through many great dangers set me in a Christian country and delivered me from the cruelty of the Turks, when I thought to find such favor as one Christian oweth to another, I found them now more cruel than the Turks, not knowing any cause why. "The cause," said he, "is because the king hath wars with the queen of England" (for at that instant[23] there was their army[24] prepared ready to go for England). Whereupon they would, divers times, give me reproachful words, saying that I should hear shortly of their arrival in England, with innumerable vain brags which I omit for brevity.

Then did I demand if there were not peace between the king and the queen's majesty, whether they would keep me still. "Yea," said he, "unless thou wilt submit thyself to the faith of the Romish Church." So he commanded me away.

I asked wherefore he sent for me and to send me away, not alleging any matter against me. He said I should have no other matter alleged but that which I had spoken with mine own mouth. Then I demanded why they would have the Romish Church to have the supremacy, whereto he would make no answer. Then I asked if they took me to be a Christian.

"Yes," said he, "in some respect, but you are out of the faith of the true church." Then the keeper took me to prison again. And after, for the space of three weeks, I was brought forth to answer three several times every week. At which times they did sometimes threaten me with death, some while with punishment, and many times they attempted to seduce me with fair words and promises of great preferment, but when they saw nothing would draw me from the truth, they called me "shameless Lutheran," saying many times, "See, he is of the very blood of Luther; he hath his very countenance," with many other frivolous speeches.

After all this, he commanded to put me in the dungeon within the castle, five fathoms[25] underground, giving me once a day a little bread and water, which they let down in a basket with a rope. There remained I one whole year, lying on the bare ground, seeing neither sun nor moon; no, not hearing man, woman, or child speak, but only the keeper which brought my small victual. It happened about the year's end, upon the Feast of Philip and Jacob, being the first day of May,[26] that a pretty boy, being the keeper's son, came to

[23] *at that instant*: in April 1587.
[24] *their army*: the Spanish Armada.
[25] *five fathoms*: thirty feet.
[26] *May*: in 1588.

give me my ordinary food, which he used sometimes to do. Now, when he opened the door[27] and had let down the basket, I asked who was there. He answered by his name, saying, "Here is Matthew!" I asked him where his father was. "He is gone to Mass," said he. So he let down the trapdoor and went his way, leaving the rope with the basket hanging still. And forasmuch as I lay without all comfort, reposing myself only unto God's providence yet unwilling to lose any opportunity that lay in me (if God were pleased) whereby I might be delivered.

So soon as I heard the boy was gone, I jumped up and took hold of the rope and wound myself up to the door. Setting my foot against the wall, with my shoulders did I lift the trapdoor. Now when I was aloft and saw no man (for they were gone to see some ceremonies of their idolatrous exercises in the city), I knew no way to escape away, being now in the midst of the way, wherefore it was unpossible to convey myself so secretly but I should be espied.

Wherefore, for the present shift, I went secretly into a void room of the castle where lay great store of lime and earth, where I tied an old cloth which I had about my head and face to keep the dust out of my eyes and ears, and so did I creep into the lime and covered myself so well as I could, lying there till towards midnight. And then hearing no man stirring, I got up and sought some way to get forth but could find none. Then, being greatly perplexed, I bent myself to the good pleasure of Almighty God, making my humble prayers that he would, of his mercy, vouchsafe to deliver me out of this miserable thralldom. And searching to and fro, in the end I came where three great horses stood, tied by the head and feet. Then did I unloose the halters from their heads and the ropes from their legs and went to the castle wall. When I had tied them end to end, I made it fast to the body of a vine which grew upon the wall, and by it did I strike myself over the wall into the town ditch, where I was constrained to swim about forty paces before I could get forth of the ditch. Then walked I to and fro in the city two hours, seeing no man. Neither could I devise any way forth. Wherefore I returned back again to the town ditch, to see if I could find any way to bring me without the town walls, and following the ditch, at the last I perceived by the noise of the water that there was a watergate through the wall, where I searched and found that the issue of the water was under the wall. Then did I very venturously enter the water and diving under water got into the watergate, and suddenly the force of the water did drive me through with such violence that it cast me

---

[27] *the door*: here, a trapdoor.

headlong against another wall on the outside, which with the blow did much amaze me. Yet, by the help of God, I recovered, swimming down the ditch till I came where was a trough or pipe, which I took to be laid over the ditch to convey some freshwater spring into the city. There did I climb up a post which bare the same and got upon the top of the pipe, where some of the watch, being near the wall, perceived me but could not any way come near to me.

Then cried they, in their tongue, "Who is there?" three or four times, but I made no answer but crept as fast as I could to get off the pipe to land, where, before I could get down, they shot some of their muskets after me, but, thanked be God, none of the shot did hit me.

Thus, with great difficulty, I escaped out of the city and went about six miles from thence before the day brake. Then I went into a thick wood. For I perceived there were very many sent forth, with hue and cry, both footmen and horsemen, to apprehend me. Therefore I lay still the day and night following.

And after, for seven days' space, I wandered through desert ways, among woods and bushes. Many times, as I came near the port ways,[28] I heard the pursuers inquiring after me, demanding of divers[29] whether they had seen me pass. Some were very earnest to take me; others wishing that I might escape. For very many times I was so near them that I heard every word they spake. Thus I imagined, by all possible means, to avoid the hands of these unmerciful tyrants, being in great extremity with hunger and cold. For since the time I came out of the prison, which was at the least eight days, I had none other sustenance but berries, which I gathered from the bushes, and the roots of palm and other like roots, which I digged out of the earth, and no other apparel but an old linen cloth about my body and a red cap on my head, without either hose, shoes, or other furniture. So that, by reason the way was very hard, I was forced to cut my cap in two and lap it about my feet to defend them from the sharp stones and gravel.

Thus traveling for the most part by night, I chanced to come where there was a house standing alone, and near the house there stood a cart wherein lay certain horse collars. Where searching among them, I found the collars lined with sheepskins, which skins I rent from the collars and appareled myself with them in this manner: I put one piece before me like a breastplate and another on my shoulders and back, with the woolly side towards my

[28] *port ways*: the roads to the seaport of Palma.
[29] *divers*: many different people.

body, tying them together over my shoulders and under my arms with palmite,[30] which is a weed like to that whereof our handbaskets are made, which is well known to such as have traveled those parts. And with another piece I made me a cap. And in these seemly ornaments I passed forth, till about three days after, very early in a morning, most unhappily I crossed an highway, where a countryman, traveling with a mule laden with rundlets[31] of wine, espied me and demanded of me whither I was bound. I said I was going to Coothea,[32] which is a town lying on the shore side. But he, suspecting me to be the man which was pursued, bade me stay. But I went onward. He ran after me and threw stones at me, but I (not being able to overrun him, being very feeble) turned back and, with a pole which I carried, began to defend myself, striking at him three or four times. At the last I thrust at him, and hit him on the breast, and overthrew him, whereupon he made a horrible cry. And immediately there came to the number of fifteen more, some having swords, some harquebuses, and others crossbows. When I was thus beset, knowing no way to escape, I yielded myself. Then they bound me hands and feet, laid me on a mule, and carried me back again to the city of Maiorque, delivering me to the inquisitor, who, when he had sent me to prison, commanded a pair of bolts to be put on my legs and an iron clasp about my neck, with a chain of five fathoms a long hanging thereat, which was done accordingly. And on the morrow I was brought forth to the accustomed place and in the same manner, where the Inquisitor, sitting, asked first why I had broken prison and run away. I said, "To save my life." "Yea," said he, "but now thou hast offended the law more than before, and therefore shall the law be now executed upon thee." Then I was carried away again. And immediately there was called an assembly of citizens and such as were seen in the law to counsel and to take advice what punishment they might inflict upon me. Which being deliberated, I was brought forth again and carried to the place of torment, which was in a cell or vault underground.

There were present but four persons, that is to say, the inquisitor; the solicitor (or broker), who is to see the law executed; a Dutch woman that dwelt in the city, who was commanded thither to tell them what I spake because I spake many times in the Dutch tongue; and lastly the tormentor.

The rack now standing ready before them, with seven flaxen ropes lying thereon, new bought from the market, then the inquisitor charged me, as at

[30] *palmite*: probably fiber taken from a variety of palm tree.
[31] *rundlets*: casks.
[32] *Coothea*: Alcudia, located thirty-one miles from Palma.

all other times he used to do, that I should speak what I had to say and to speak the truth; otherwise I should be even now tormented to death. I, seeing myself in the hands of such cruel tyrants as always thirst after the blood of the innocent, even as Cain (who being wroth with his brother, Abel, and carrying a heavy countenance) could be no way eased but with his brother's blood, so I, past hope of life, turned my back towards them, and seeing my torments present before me, I fell down on my knees and besought the Lord to forgive my sins, and to strengthen my faith, and to grant me patience to endure to the end. Then they took me into a void room and stripped me out of my ornaments of sheepskins (which I repeated[33] before) and put a pair of strong canvas breeches upon me. Then bringing me to the rack again, he commanded me to lie down. The bars of the rack under me were as sharp as the back of a knife. Now I, willingly yielding myself, lay down. Then the tormentor bound my hands over my breast crosswise, and my legs clasped up together were fast tied the one foot to the other knee. Then he fastened to either arm a cord, about the brawn of the arm, and likewise to either thigh another, which were all made fast again under the rack to the bars, and with another cord he bound down my head and put a hollow cane into my mouth. Then he put four cudgels into the ropes which were fastened to my arms and thighs. Now the woman which was present, being interpreter, began to persuade me to yield and confess the faith of the Church of Rome. I answered, "If it were the will of God that I should end my life under their cruel hands, I must be content, but, if it please Him, He is able to deliver me, if there were ten thousands against me." Then the tormentor, as he was commanded, began to wrest the ropes, which he did by little and little, to augment my pains and to have them endure the longer. But in the end, he drew them with such violence as though he would have plucked my four quarters in sunder and there stayed a good space. Yet to declare their tyrannical malice, thinking my torment not sufficient, he added more, pouring water through a cane which was in my mouth, by little and little, which I was constrained either to let down or to have my breath stopped until they had tunned in[34] such quantity as was not tolerable to endure, which pained me extremely. Yet not satisfied, they took and wet a linen cloth and laid it over my mouth till I was almost strangled; when my body, being thus overcharged with such abundance of water, after they had thus stopped my breath with the wet cloth, suddenly with the force of my breath and that my stomach was so much

[33] *repeated*: spoke of.
[34] *tunned in*: poured in.

overcharged, the water gushed out and bare away the cloth as if had been the force of a conduit spout.

When the inquisitor saw that all this would not make me yield, he commanded the tormentor for to wind the cord on my left arm more strait, which put me to horrible pains. And immediately the rope burst in sunder. Then said the inquisitor, "Yea, is he so strong? I will make him yield!" and commanded the tormentor to put a new rope. Then the woman again bade me yield, saying it were better to yield than to die so miserable a death. But I, beseeching Almighty God to ease me of my pains and to forgive my sins, answered her that though they had power over my body, yet there was no torment should compel me to yield to their idolatry, whereby I might bring my soul in danger of hellfire. Then the inquisitor asked her what I said. She answered that I had said I would never submit myself to the Church of Rome.

Then did he most vehemently charge me to yield and submit myself to the Romish Church, otherwise he would pluck off one of my arms. Whereupon I denying still, the tormentor, in most cruel manner, wrested the ropes as if he would have rent my body in sunder. I (being now in intolerable pains and looking for nothing but present death) cried out, in the extremity of my anguish, "Now, farewell, wife and children! and farewell, England!" And so, not able to utter one word more, lay even senseless. The inquisitor asked the woman again what I said. She laid her hand upon my head and, perceiving that I was speechless, told him I was dead.

Wherefore the tormentor loosed the ropes, unbound my hands and feet, and carried me into a chamber which they termed St. Walter's Chamber where I came to myself and received some sense and reason but could have no feeling of any limb or joint. Thus I lay in a most lamentable and pitiful manner for five days, having a continual issue of blood and water forth of my mouth all that space and being so feeble and weak, by reason of my torments, that I could take no sustenance.

Till the sixth day, a little recovering my strength, they gave me a little quantity of bread and wine sod[35] together, and presently, the very same day, they carried me forth into the city, and set me upon an ass's back, and whipped me throughout every street of the city of Maiorque, giving me to the number of five hundred lashes, which made the blood to run down my miserable carcass in such abundance that it dropped at the belly of the ass to the ground. Now there were carried with me about the city very many harlots and whores and other malefactors which had offended the law, but none

---

[35] *sod*: sodden.

punished like me. After this, they carried me to the chamber from whence I came, where I lay without all worldly comfort.

Can any man, which understandeth the absurd blindness and willful ignorance of these Spanish tyrants or Romish monsters, think them to be of the true church? Which defend their faith with fire, sword, and hellish torments, without remorse or pity, as you may perceive by a manifest trial here set down to the open view of the world? For when these hellhounds had tormented this miserable creature, as you have heard, with a monstrous and most un-Christian kind of torment, which he endured for the space of three hours, till [he] was at the very point of death and ready to yield up the ghost, they (not yet satisfied with these torments, which he had suffered already) reserved his life, minding to increase his pains, which they were nothing slack to perform so long as he remained in their power.

Now, the second night after they had whipped me about the city as aforesaid, about midnight, I recounting to myself in what misery I both did and had remained, I thought to put in practice once again to get my liberty, craving of the Lord, with hearty prayer, to assist me with His mighty hand. And immediately searching about, I found an old iron stub, with the which I brake a hole through the chamber wall and crept through into another chamber where I felt in the dark many pieces of plate, which I little regarded. After, I found many towels and table napkins. Then, seeking further, I found a long cane whereon there hung many puddings and sausages. I plucked down the cane but had little mind on the victual. Then I found certain knives. Then I espied some light at a great window in a garret or loft over me. Wherefore I tied a crooked knife to the cane and thrust up a long towel, and with the knife at the end of the cane, I drew the towel about a bar of the window and drew it to me, and with that towel I did climb up into the window. But then I could not get forth between the bars, wherefore I digged forth one of the bars, and tied my towels and napkins together end to end, and fastened one end to a bar of the window, and then did slide down by them till I came within three or four fathoms[36] of the ground, when the towels brake in sunder, and I fell down into a well which was direct under me, where I was almost drowned. Yet it pleased God to deliver me. And being then in the city, without the castle walls, I (knowing no other way to get out) went again to the town ditch, where I got through the watergate with less peril than before, by reason there was less water than was the other time. Then went I with all speed into the woods, lying all days in woods as close as I could, and trav-

---

[36] *three or four fathoms*: eighteen or twenty-four feet.

eled by nights through woods and mountains. And upon the third night, about midnight, I happened into an olive garden, not above half a bow shot from the seaside, in which garden I found a little skiff or boat lying under a pomegranate tree, and there lay in the boat a hatchet. All which served happily for my delivery.

Now I, being unable to carry the boat to the waterside, did cut small truncheons of wood, and upon them did slide it down to the waterside. Then I cut an arm of an olive tree, to make my boat a mast, and having no other shift, made a sailcloth with my breeches and a piece of mantle which I had about me. And for[37] my oars were very mean, yet durst I stay to look for no better but presently set sail and, yielding myself to the good pleasure of Almighty God, betook myself to the sea, willing rather to abide what the Lord would lay on me than to die among these most cruel tyrants.

And by the providence of God, upon the second day, in the forenoon, I descried the coast of Barbary, for the wind stood northeast, which served me most happily. Understand that this cut[38] is, from shore to shore, one hundred and fifty leagues, which is four hundred and fifty English miles, and at that time a very rough sea, insomuch if it had not been by the great and wonderful power of God, my vessel and I had both been overwhelmed.

But I fell in with the country of Kabyles,[39] commonly called the King of Cookooe's land,[40] near a town called Gigeley,[41] where I went onshore, leaving my boat to swim which way the wind and weather would conduct it, thinking it had done me sufficient service.

But see now, when I had escaped through the surges of the sea from the cruelty of the Spaniard, I was no sooner landed and entered the mountains but I was espied by the Moors which inhabit the country, who pursued very earnestly to take me, supposing me to be come from the Christian shore to rob in their coast. For many times the Spaniards will pass over in some small vessel and go onshore, and if they can catch any men of the country, they will carry them away to make galley slaves, wherefore the Moors are very diligent

---

[37] *for*: because.

[38] *cut*: course.

[39] *the country of Kabyles*: The Kabyles are a group of Berber tribes in Algeria and Tunisia. Their "country" may refer to the area known as the Little Kabylia, in the present province of Constantine, Algeria.

[40] *the King of Cookooe's land*: "Cookooe" is spelt, in maps later than this narrative, Couco or Cocou. It was not far from the left bank of the river Sahel that falls into the Bay of Bejaia, the present Akbou.

[41] *Gigeley*: Djidjelli, in Algeria.

to pursue them at their landing, and if it chance they take any Christian, they use him in like sort. Wherefore I, being very unwilling to fall into their hands, was constrained to go into a river, which ran between two mountains, and there to stand in water up to the chin, where the bushes and trees did grow most thick over me, where I stood certain hours, until they had left searching for me.

Now, when I perceived they were departed, I went out of the water, being very feeble, for I ate nothing all that time but the bark of the trees, which I cut with my hatchet. I went forth as secretly as I could, minding to pass to Argier.

I had not gone above three miles when I espied a Moor, a very well favored old man, who was weeding a field of wheat.

I spake to him in the tongue of Franke[42] and called him to me. I, having my hatchet in my hand, cast it from me. He came unto me and, taking me by the hand, demanded very gently what I would have. I, perceiving that he did, even at the first sight, pity my poor and miserable estate, told him all things that had happened unto me: how I was an Englishman; how I had been captive in Argier; how I chanced to come to Genoa; their sending me to Maiorque; and all the torment which I had suffered there; and finally my escape from thence, with all the rest that followed.

This good aged father, when he had heard my lamentable discourse, showing himself rather a Christian than a man brought up among the Turkish Mahometists,[43] greatly pitied my misery and forthwith led me home to his house and caused such victuals as the country yieldeth to be set before me, which was dried wheat and honey, and baked a cake upon the fire hearth and then fried it with butter, which I thought very good meat, for I had not been at the like banquet in six years before, the good father showing me what comfort he could.

There I remained four and twenty hours. In the meantime the Moors which dwelt in the villages by, understanding of my being there, came and, calling me forth, inquired of me what I was, from whence I came, and whither I would, and with great vehemency charged their weapons against my breast, insomuch that I thought they would verily have slain me. But mine host, that good old man, came forth and answered for me and so dissuaded them from doing me any harm and took me back again into his house.

[42] *the tongue of Franke*: the lingua franca, a hybrid language spoken in the ports of the Mediterranean.

[43] *Mahometists*: followers of Mahomet (Muhammad), i.e., Muslims.

This being past, I requested him to help me to a guide to conduct me to Argier, and he presently provided two, whereof the one was his son, to whom I promised to give four crowns for their pains. So, taking my leave of my good host, we took our way towards Argier. When we had not passed above twenty-four miles on the way, we chanced to meet a gentleman of that country who was, as it were, purveyor to the king and went about the country to take up corn and grain for the king's provision. He, meeting us upon the way, asked whither we were traveling. My guides answered that we were going to Argier. He asked what had we to do there. They said to deliver me there. Then he demanded what I was. They told him I was an Englishman that came from the Christian shore and was bound towards Argier. Then did the gentleman take me from them, sending them back from whence they came, but compelled me to go with him to a village by and very earnestly persuaded me to turn Moor, promising, if I would, he would be a mean to prefer me greatly, which I still denied. Then, upon the next day, he carried me further, to a town called Tamgote,[44] and delivered me to a nobleman of great authority with the king, which was lieutenant-general for the wars (for this king of Cookooe holdeth continual war with the king of Argier, although they be both subject to the Great Turk). I was no sooner brought before this nobleman, but he demanded whether I would turn Moor. I answered that I would not. Wherefore immediately he commanded a pair of shackles to be put on my heels and a clasp of iron about my neck, with a chain threat. Then was I set on a mule and conveyed to Cookooe, where the king lay.

When I was come thither, I was presently brought before the king, who inquired what I was, and from whence I came, and what my pretense was. I answered that I was an Englishman and that I came from the Christian shore, intending to pass to Argier. Then he asked me what I could do. I told him I could do nothing. Then he demanded whether I were a gunner. I said, "No." Then he persuaded[45] me very instantly to yield to their religion, offering to prefer me, wherefore I desired him to give me liberty to depart, "for my desire is to be in England, with my wife and children." "Yea," said he, "but how wilt thou come there?" For they minded to keep me still, and evermore the king assayed to seduce me with promises of great preferment, saying, if I would serve him and turn Moor, I should want nothing. But on the contrary, I besought him to give me liberty to go to Argier, where I was in hope to be delivered and sent home to mine own country.

[44] *Tamgote*: Tamgout.
[45] *persuaded*: tried to convince.

Now he, seeing he could win me by no gentle means, commanded me to prison, saying that he would either make me yield and turn Moor or else I should die in captivity.

In this while that I remained in prison, divers of the king's house came to me, persuading me to yield to the king's demand, alleging how hardly the king might use me, being now in his power, unable to escape, and again how bountifully the king would deal with me if I would submit myself.

Within a little time after, it happened there was great preparation to receive the king of Abbesse,[46] whose country adjoineth to the king of Cookooe's land, and [they] are in league together and join their armies in one against the king of Argier. Now at his coming, I was fetched forth of prison and commanded to charge certain pieces of ordinance, which were three sacres[47] and two minions[48] of brass, which I refused not to do, trusting thereby to get some liberty. Wherefore, at the coming of the king of Abbesse into the town, I discharged the ordinance as liked them very well, for they are not very expert in that exercise. For which I had some more liberty than before.

This king of Abbesse, tarrying some certain time there in consulting with the king of Cookooe for matters touching the wars with Argier and understanding of me, sent for me, being very desirous to talk with me, where, after certain questions he desired of the other king that he might buy me, which he would not grant. Then the king of the Kabyles or Cookooe persuaded me very seriously to serve him wil[ling]ly and to turn Moor and offered to give me seven hundred doubles by the year, which amounteth to the sum of fifty pounds of English money, and moreover to give me by the day thirty aspers (which are worth twelve pence English) to find me meat, and likewise to give me a house and land sufficient to sow an hundreth bushels of grain yearly and two plow of oxen furnished to till the same, also to furnish me with horse, musket, sword, and other necessaries, such as they of that country use. And lastly he offered to give me a wife freely, which they esteemed the greatest matter, for all buy their wives at a great price. Yea, if there were any in his court could content me, I should make my choice, but if there were not, he would provide one to my contentment, whatsoever it should cost him. But when he perceived all he said was in vain, he sent the queen and her gentle-

---

[46] *king of Abbesse*: probably a leader of the tribe of the Beni-Abbas, or Beni-Abbés.

[47] *sacres*: small cannons used in sieges and on ships.

[48] *minions*: small cannons weighing eleven hundred pounds, with a mouth measuring about three and a quarter inches in diameter.

women to talk with me. When she came, she very courteously entreated me to turn and serve the king and to consider well what a large offer the king had made, saying that I was much unlike to come to any like preferment in my country. And many times she would show me her gentlewomen and ask me if none of them could please me, but I told her I had a wife in mine own country, to whom I had vowed my faith before God and the world, which vow, I said, I would never break while we both lived. Then she said she could but marvel what she should be whom I esteemed so much as to refuse such offers of preferment for her sake, being now where I must remain in captivity and slavery all the days of my life. But when she could prevail no way with me, when she had uttered these foresaid speeches, and many others which were frivolous to rehearse, she left me. Yet by her means I had more liberty than before.

After this, I was set to saw boards and planks and was commanded to make a carriage for a piece of ordinance. Thus they compelled me to labor daily, which I did the more willingly because I hoped still to get my liberty thereby in the end. Then they willed me to show the fashion of our edge tools, after the English, which when they saw the fashion, their smiths wrought them very artificially[49] and gave them very good temper. For these things I was had in more estimation, insomuch that they took off my irons and let me walk abroad with a keeper. Then was I commanded by the king to teach the carpenters to frame a house after the manner of English building, and for that purpose there were sent forth carpenters and workmen with me to the woods to fall timber, all which were to do what I appointed upon the king's commandment. Now I, being chief master of the work, appointed out the trees which were very special good timber. In small time, we had finished our frame, which liked the king very well. By this means I had more liberty than before and was very well entreated. Yet I was greatly grieved in mind that I could not procure any means for my liberty, although at that time I wanted few necessaries. Yet was I daily devising how I might escape away, for three special causes: one was for the special care I had of my salvation because (as you have heard) there were many temptations laid before me to draw me from a Christian to be an abominable idolater. The second cause was for the love and dutiful allegiance which I owe to my prince and natural country. The third was the regard of the vow which I vowed in matrimony and the care of my poor wife and children. Which causes moved me so much that whereas, by reason of my diligence in these foresaid matters, I walking

---

[49] *artificially*: skillfully.

abroad with my keeper who, not suspecting me, was not so attentive as before he had been. So soon as our frame was finished, I took opportunity and, showing them a clean pair of heels, took my way over the mountains intending to go for Argier. But presently there was a great store of men, both on horseback and on foot, who, being more perfect in the way[50] than I was, quickly overtook me and carried me back again to Cookooe.

I was presently brought before the king, who asked me why I ran away. I told him, "To have liberty." Then he called certain of his servants to him and commanded them to lay me down at his feet, which four of them did, and laying me flat upon the belly, one of them gave me seventy-five stripes with a great cudgel, till I was not able to remove out of the place. Then the king commanded to carry me to prison again, whither two of them carried me and put me in irons and there left me, where I remained for the space of two months.

Then was I brought forth of prison and sent daily to a fountain or well, about half a league from the town, to fetch water with a couple of asses, for the use of the king's house. Now in this time, many artificers (as smiths, joiners, and carpenters, and many others) came to me to understand the fashion of many English tools (as plane irons, gouges, chisels, and such like), for which they showed me some favor and gave me some money. And when I had gotten a little money, I bestowed it upon apparel and caused it to be made like to theirs, which I carried secretly when I went to fetch water and did hide it in a dry cave under the side of a rock. I bought me likewise a sword and a lance, such as they use to travel with. I also provided a file. All which I laid up with my apparel.

It happened that the king of Abbesse came again to visit the king and to take counsel about warlike affairs, as usually they did. Wherefore when they heard of his coming, making great preparation for him, it fell out so that there wanted water in the offices,[51] where, in an evening, there was exceeding thunder and rain and lightning, so that there was no man would go for water, but everyone calling for the Englishman. Then I, which durst say no "nay," took the vessels and hung them upon the asses and so went, through rain and wind and thunder and all, till I came to the well, where I left my asses to wander whither they would, and went to my apparel, and with my file cut off my irons, and made me ready in my suit of Moors' clothing, and, with my sword

---

[50] *more perfect in the way*: faster and more able to maneuver.

[51] *offices*: those parts of the building where household work takes place, including the kitchen and rooms connected with it.

by my side and my lance on my shoulder, took my way once again towards Argier. And that night I went about twenty miles over rocks and mountains, keeping myself out of beaten ways, casting[52] my way by the moon and stars. When the day began to be light, I lay me down in a brake of thick bushes, and there I slept the most part of the day, and in the evening I began to travel forth on my way.

Now on the third night I was to pass a bridge where was continual watch and ward, both day and night, where I must of necessity pass, by reason the river[53] ran betwixt two mountains which were so steep that no man can neither go down to enter water nor yet, being in, can by any possible means get up on the other side, which river is a great defense to the country. Where I used no delay but entered the bridge in the beginning of the night, about nine of the clock, being in great doubt[54] of the watch. But at the first end of the bridge, I saw no man, until I was happily passed over. Then there came one after me and asked, "Who goes there?" It being somewhat dark, and I, in apparel and with my weapons like a Moor, answered boldly that I was a friend and told him I was coming to the governor to deliver letters from the king. For near the river's side there is a village where dwelleth he who hath charge of the keeping of this passage. Whereby I went onward through the village, but before I was far passed, I heard horsemen upon the bridge which asked whether any man had passed that night. The watermen told them there was one gone even now which said he went to deliver the king's letters to the officer. But I thought no time now to hear any more of their talk but betook me to my heels, and so soon as I was without the town, I went out of the port way[55] into woods and kept desert ways that night and day following. And the next night I came within the liberties of the king of Argier, where I knew the Kabyles could not fetch me back again.

In this order I escaped their hands, by the mighty power of God. For understand, in these desert mountains there are all manner of wild beasts, in great number, as lions, bears, wolves of marvelous bigness, apes, wild swine, and also wild horses and asses, with many other hurtful beasts, yet was I never in danger of any of these.

In this country of Kabyles, there is divers kinds of very pure metals, as gold, silver, and lead, and good iron and steel, but they, for want of knowledge

---

[52] *casting*: directing.

[53] *the river*: the river Isser.

[54] *doubt*: fear.

[55] *the port way*: the road to the port of Algiers.

and skill, make no use of any metal except iron and steel. Although at such times I have been present, while the smiths have tried their iron, I have seen among the dross of the iron, very perfect gold. Which they, perceiving me to behold, were very inquisitive to understand whether it were gold or any other metal of substance. But I told them it was but a kind of dross whereof we made colors for painting in England.

They carried me out to the mountains and showed me the rocks where they gathered their iron, which rocks had veins of very pure gold, which I would not reveal to them but answered as before, because I doubted[56] if the king once knew me to have experience in such mysteries, he would keep me the more strait, whereby I might have remained in bondage during my life.

Now when I was within the country of Argier, I was out of dangers from the pursuers, and then did I walk by day and kept the common ways. Where, coming within the view of Argier, upon the way I met a Turk who knew me at the first sight and demanded if I had not been captive with such a man.

I said, "Yes." He then inquired whether I went to the city.

I said, "Yes." Then returned he back and did accompany me to the city.

When I came there, I would have gone to the English house, but he led me violently to my old master, where I rested me a day and night, my master not being very earnest, for because in this time[57] that I was absent, all the English captives were redeemed and sent home. Wherefore I went to the English consul, hoping to be presently delivered, who gave me very good words but did not show me that favor which he professed.

I could make some discourse of his unkind dealing with me and others of our countrymen, which I will leave till more fit occasion. For understand that while I was with him there came a messenger from my old master, with whom I was before I went to Genoa, who would have carried me away by force but I would not go, requesting the consul to take order for my delivery. But he persuaded me to go with him, saying that he would, in time, provide for my liberty.

But by means I would not yield to go to my master, nor yet the consul would not take order for me. I was taken by the king's officers and put in chains in the king's prison, among other captives. And at the next setting out of the galleys, I was put to my old occupation, where I remained a galley slave for three years and above after, in which time I was eight voyages at sea, and at such times as the galleys lay in harbor, I was imprisoned with the rest

---

[56] *doubted*: feared.
[57] *in this time*: 1587–88.

of the captives, where our ordinary food was bread and water and, at some times, as once or twice in a week, a small quantity of sodden wheat.

To conclude, I passed my time in sickness and extreme slavery until, by the help of an honest merchant[58] of this city of London and having a very fit opportunity by means of certain our English ships which were ready to set sail, bound homeward, upon Christmas Even, being the twenty-third of December, 1592, I came aboard[59] the *Cherubim* of London, which, weighing anchor and having a happy gale, arrived in England towards the end of February following.

Thus have you heard how it hath pleased the Almighty God (after many and great miseries) to bring me to the port which I longed greatly to see, beseeching God of his mercy to prolong the days of our most gracious and renowned queen, whose fame reacheth far and whose most happy government is in admiration with foreign princes. So wishing all to the glory of God and furtherance of the gospel, I end.

[58] *an honest merchant*: Richard Staper, to whom Barley's dedicatory epistle is addressed.

[59] *I came aboard*: in Algiers.

John Rawlins, *The Famous and Wonderful Recovery of a Ship of Bristol, Called the* Exchange, *from the Turkish Pirates of Argier (1622)*

(Algiers, 1621–22)

This brief book, the "unpolished work of a poor sailor," is dedicated to George Villiers, marquis of Buckingham, who was King James's greatest favorite and who held the post of lord high admiral. The dedicatory epistle alludes to the royal government's neglect of common seamen, an issue that was often raised against James I by those who wished to see more support for the development of an English navy and greater efforts to ransom poor sailors from captivity in the Barbary ports. The text provides an interesting picture of the place of renegade corsairs in the Algerian maritime economy, with an English renegade, Henry Chandler, purchasing an English ship taken by Algerian corsairs and then buying English and Dutch slaves who had the skills necessary to sail it.

The opening and closing sections of the text stress the truth value of the text and assert the didactic importance of this "relation" as proof of the "power and providence" of the Christian deity. The narrative depicts the struggle for freedom as a clearly delineated opposition of good to evil, of Christian "power and goodness" fearlessly and violently opposed to "the cruelty and inhumanity of Turks and Moors . . . who from a native barbarousness do hate all Christians and Christianity." As such, it focuses on the suspenseful events of that struggle and only pauses slightly to offer the more nuanced ethnographic observations of Muslim culture that appear in some of the other narratives. When the text describes Islamic culture, it stresses either superstitious customs and misbeliefs or cruel practices such as the methods supposedly used in Algiers to force Christians, under duress and pain of torture, to turn Turk.

The 1622 text is the only extant version of this narrative; no subsequent editions are known. Most of the tale is told from the third-person point of view, but occasionally the narrator slips into the first person, and the opening and closing paragraphs frame the text with passages of moralizing, first-person commentary on the events. These framing passages and the statement near the end that "Rawlins himself dare justify the matter" may be the signs of a ghost writer or second author at work, and it is possible that the author was one of the other English seamen captured in Rawlins's group of merchant ships and also present during the uprising at sea, therefore an eyewitness to all the events involving Rawlins. At the outset, there is an attempt to gain narrative authority by using the rhetoric of a plain-speaking, truth-telling sailor, but then the text shifts into a more formal third-person narration. The parenthetical comment on p. 101 implies that Rawlins is the author but that he employs the third-person narrative voice to "make the discourse equal," that is, to render the account more accurately, from an objective distance. The text then reverts to first person for two paragraphs before returning to the third person. The first-person voice resumes, however, in the final section, which offers Rawlins's successful revolt against his Turkish masters as an inspirational model for heroism in the service of an English God, king, and commonwealth.

John Rawlins, *The Famous and Wonderful Recovery of a Ship of Bristol, called the Exchange, from the Turkish Pirates of Argier, with the Unmatchable Attempts and Good Success of John Rawlins, Pilot in Her, and Other Slaves; Who, in the End, with the Slaughter of About Forty of the Turks and Moors, Brought the Ship into Plymouth, the 13th of February Last, with the Captain a Renegado, and Five Turks More; Besides the Redemption of Twenty-Four Men and One Boy from Turkish Slavery.*

LONDON: PRINTED FOR NATHANIEL BUTTER, DWELLING
AT THE PIED BULL, AT SAINT AUSTIN'S GATE. 1622.

To the Right Honorable George, Marquis of Buckingham, Viscount Villiers, Baron of Whaddon, Lord High Admiral of England; justice in eyre[1] of all His Majesty's forests, parks, and chases beyond Trent; Master of the Horse to His Majesty, and one of the Gentlemen of His Majesty's Bedchamber; Knight of the most noble Order of the Garter, and one of His Majesty's most honorable Privy Council of England and Scotland.

Right Honorable,

Seeing it hath pleased God by so weak means as my poor self to have His power and goodness made manifest to the world, as by this following relation may appear, I thought it my duty to present the same unto you, whom the Majesty of England hath presented unto us as our patron and chief commander of our sea affairs. Accept it then, I humbly beseech you, as an unpolished work of a poor sailor and the rather for that it exemplifies the glory of God. For by such men as myself, your Honor must be served, and England made the happiest of all nations. For though you have greater persons and more braving spirits to lie over our heads and hold inferiors in subjection, yet are we the men that must pull the ropes, weigh up the anchors, toil in the night, endure the storms, sweat at the helm,

---

[1] *justice in eyre*: justice presiding over a circuit court.

watch the biticle,[2] attend the compass, guard the ordnance, keep the night hours, and be ready for all impositions. If, then, you vouchsafe to entertain it, I have my desire. For, according to the oath of jurors, it is "the truth, and the very truth." If otherwise you suppose it trivial, it is only the prostitution[3] of my service, and wisdom is not bought in the market.

> Your Honor's humbly to be commanded,
> John Rawlins

The Psalmist saith that "He that goeth to sea shall see the wonders of God,"[4] and I may well say that he that converseth with mariners and sailors shall hear of the wonders of men, as by this following discourse shall appear. Not that I am willing to be the author of novelty or amaze you with incredible reports, but because I would not let slip so remarkable an accident and so profitable a relation. Remarkable, as extending to manifest the power and glory of God, who hath variety of supportation[5] in store to sweeten affliction and make all endurances[6] subject to fortitude and patience; profitable, as being thus far exemplary, to teach all men of action and employment not to despair in distress and to know thus much: that brave attempts are compassed by resolution and industrious employment, and whether they thrive or not, yet shall the enterprise be charactered with a worthy exploit. And if it end with success, oh how shall the actors be remembered to posterity! And make their fame immortal that either purchased their liberty, even out of fire, or delivered themselves (though by death itself) from slavish captivity or the thralldom of barbarous infidels who glory in nothing more than the perdition of our souls and the derision of our Christ. Hearken then, I pray you, to this following relation, and learn thereby, as I said, both to give God the praise of all deliverances and to instruct one another in the absolute duties of Christianity. By the one, the power and providence, with all the attributes belonging to so immense a deity, shall be made manifest; by the other, the weak brother shall be comforted, the strong confirmed, the wavering reduced, the faint-hearted erected, and the presumptuous moderated. By both, religion

---

[2] *biticle*: binnacle.

[3] *prostitution*: devoted, submissive offering.

[4] *"He that . . . of God"*: from Psalm 107.

[5] *supportation*: assistance.

[6] *endurances*: hardships.

shall have a sweet passage in the consciences of men, and men made the
happy instruments of God's glory and their own increases of good example
and imitation. And thus much for preamble or introduction; now to the matter itself.

In the year 1621, the first of November, there was one John Rawlins (born
in Rochester and dwelling twenty-three year in Plymouth) employed to the
Straits of Gibraltar by Master Richard and Steven Treviles, merchants of Plymouth, and freighted in a bark[7] called the *Nicholas* of Plymouth, of the burthen[8] of forty tons, which had also in her company another ship of Plymouth
called the *George Bonaventure*, of seventy tons burthen or thereabouts,
which, by reason of her greatness beyond the other, I will name the admiral[9]
and John Rawlins' bark shall, if you please, be the vice-admiral. These two,
according to the time of the year, had a fair passage and by the eighteenth of
the same month came to a place at the entering of the straits, named Trafal-
gar, but the next morning, being in sight of Gibraltar, at the very mouth of the
straits, the watch descried five sail of ships, who, as it seemed, used all the
means they could to come near us, and we, as we had cause, used the same
means to go as far from them. Yet did their admiral take in both his topsails,
that either we might not suspect them or that his own company might come
up the closer together. At last, perceiving us Christians, they fell from devices
to apparent discovery of hostility and making out against us. We again suspecting them pirates took our course to escape from them and made all the
sails we possibly could for Terriff[10] or Gibraltar, but all we could do could not
prevent their approach. For suddenly one of them came right over against us
to windward and so fell on our quarter. Another came up on our luff and so
threatened us there. And, at last, all five chased us, making great speed to surprise us.

Their admiral was called *Callfater*, having upon her main topsail two top-
gallant sails, one above another. But whereas we thought them all five to be
Turkish ships of war, we afterwards understood that two of them were their
prizes, the one a small ship of London, the other of the West Country, that
came out of the Quactath[11] laden with figs and other merchandise but now
subject to the fortune of the sea and the captivity of pirates. But to our busi-

---

[7] *bark*: sailing vessel.
[8] *burthen*: carrying capacity.
[9] *the admiral*: the flagship.
[10] *Terriff*: Tarifa, a port on the Spanish side of the straits, to the west of Gibraltar.
[11] *the Quactath*: I have been unable to identify this location.

ness. Three of these ships got much upon us, and so much that, ere half the day was spent, the admiral, which was the best sailer, fetched up[12] the *George Bonaventure* and made booty of it. The vice-admiral again, being nearest unto the lesser bark whereof John Rawlins was master, showed him the force of a stronger arm and by his Turkish name, called Villa Rise,[13] commanded him, in like sort, to strike his sails and submit to his mercy, which, not to be gainsaid nor prevented, was quickly done. And so Rawlins, with his bark, was as quickly taken, although the rear-admiral, being the worst sailer of the three, called *Riggiprise*, came not in till all was done.

The same day, before night, the admiral (either loath to pester himself with too much company, or ignorant of the commodity [that] was to be made by the sale of English prisoners, or daring not to trust them in his company for fear of mutinies and exciting others to rebellion) set twelve persons who were in the *George Bonaventure* on the land, and divers other English whom he had taken before, to try their fortunes in an unknown country. But Villa Rise, the vice-admiral that had taken John Rawlins, would not so dispense with his men but commanded him and five more of his company to be brought aboard his ship, leaving in his bark three men and his boy, with thirteen Turks and Moors, who were, questionless, sufficient to overmaster the others and direct the bark to harbor. Thus they sailed directly for Argier, but the night following followed them with great tempest and foul weather, which ended not without some effect of a storm, for they lost the sight of Rawlins' bark, called the *Nicholas* and, in a manner, lost themselves (though they seemed safe ashipboard) by fearful conjecturing, "What should become of us?"

At last, by the twenty-second of the same month, they, or we (choose you whether, for I would not be mistaken in altering the persons, by either naming the first for the third or the third for the first, but only make the discourse equal, by setting down the business honestly and truly, as it chanced) arrived in Argier and came in safety within the mole[14] but found not our other bark there; nay, though we earnestly inquired after the same, yet heard we nothing to our satisfaction, but much matter was ministered to our discomfort and amazement. For although the captain and our overseers were loath we should have any conference with our countrymen, yet did we adventure to inform ourselves of the present affairs, both of the town and of the shipping.

---

[12] *fetched up*: overtook and came alongside.

[13] *Rise*: Arabic *rais* meaning "captain" or "leader" (literally, "head").

[14] *mole*: fortified harbor located at the foot of the city.

So that finding many English at work in other ships, they spared not to tell us the danger we were in and the mischiefs we must needs incur, as being sure if we were not used like slaves, to be sold as slaves, for there had been five hundred brought into the market for the same purpose and above a hundred handsome youths compelled to turn Turks or made subject to more vilder prostitution[15]–and all English! Yet, like good Christians, they bade us be of good cheer and comfort ourselves in this: that God's trials were gentle purgations, and these crosses were but to cleanse the dross from the gold and bring us out of the fire again, more clear and lovely. Yet I must needs confess that they afforded us reason for this cruelty, as if they determined to be revenged of our last attempt to fire their ships in the mole[16] and therefore protested to spare none whom they could surprise and take alone but either to sell them for money or to torment them to serve their own ends. Now their customs and usages, in both these, were in this manner.

First, concerning the first. The bashaw[17] had the overseeing of all prisoners, who were presented unto him at their first coming into the harbor, and so chose one out of every eight for a present or fee to himself. The rest were rated by the captains and so sent to the market to be sold, whereat, if either there were repining or any drawing back, then certain Moors and officers attended, either to beat you forward or thrust you in the sides with goads. And this was the manner of the selling of slaves.

Secondly, concerning their enforcing them either to turn Turk or to attend their filthiness and impieties: although it would make a Christian's heart bleed to hear of the same, yet must the truth not be hid, nor the terror left untold. They commonly lay them on their naked backs or bellies, beating them so long till they bleed at the nose and mouth, and if yet they continue constant, then they strike the teeth out of their heads, pinch them by their tongues, and use many other sorts of tortures to convert them. Nay, many times, they lay them their whole length in the ground like a grave and so cover them with boards, threatening to starve them if they will not turn. And so many, even for fear of torment and death, make their tongues betray their hearts to a most fearful wickedness and so are circumcised with new names

[15] *more vilder prostitution*: implying the use of English boys as sexual slaves.

[16] *attempt to . . . the mole*: In May 1621 an English fleet under the command of Sir Robert Mansell (1573–1656) attempted to burn the Algerian corsair fleet by sending fireboats into the harbor.

[17] *the bashaw*: the ruling official of the Ottoman regency in Algiers, appointed by the Ottoman sultan.

and brought to confess a new religion. Others again, I must confess, who never knew any god but their own sensual lusts and pleasures, thought that any religion would serve their turns and so for preferment or wealth very voluntarily renounced their faith and became renegadoes,[18] in despite of any counsel which seemed to intercept them. And this was the first news we encountered with at our coming first to Argier.

The twenty-sixth of the same month, John Rawlins his[19] bark, with his other three men and a boy, came safe into the mole and so were put all together to be carried before the bashaw, but that they took the owner's servant[20] and Rawlins' boy and by force and torture compelled them to turn Turks. Then were they, in all, seven English besides John Rawlins, of whom the bashaw took one and sent the rest to their captains, who set a valuation upon them. And so the soldiers hurried us, like dogs, into the market, where, as men sell hackneys[21] in England, we were tossed up and down to see who would give most for us. And although we had heavy hearts and looked with sad countenances, yet many came to behold us, sometimes taking us by the hand, sometimes turning us round about, sometimes feeling our brawns and naked arms, and so beholding our prices written in our breasts, they bargained for us accordingly, and at last we were all sold, and the soldiers returned with their money to their captains.

John Rawlins was the last who was sold, by reason of his lame hand. He was bought by the captain that took him, even that dog Villa Rise, who (better informing himself of his skill fit to be a pilot and his experience to be an overseer) bought him and his carpenter at very easy rates. For as we afterwards understood by divers English renegadoes, he paid for Rawlins but 150 doublets,[22] which make (of English money) seven pound, ten shilling. Thus was he and his carpenter, with diverse other slaves, sent into his ship to work and employed about such affairs as belonged to the well rigging and preparing the same. But the villainous Turks perceiving his lame hand, and that he could not perform so much as other slaves, quickly complained to their patron, who as quickly apprehended the inconvenience. Whereupon he sent for him the next day and told him he was unserviceable for his present

---

[18] *renegadoes*: former Christians who have converted to Islam and have joined the Muslim community.

[19] *Rawlins his*: a possessive form; Rawlins's.

[20] *the owner's servant*: probably the supercargo.

[21] *hackneys*: horses.

[22] *doublets*: doubloons; Spanish gold coins.

purpose, and therefore unless he could procure fifteen pound of the English there, for his ransom, he would send him up into the country, where he should never see Christendom again and endure the extremity of a miserable banishment.

But see how God worketh all for the best for His servants and confoundeth the presumption of tyrants, frustrating their purposes, to make His wonders known to the sons of men, and relieves His people when they least think of succor and releasement. Whilst John Rawlins was thus terrified with the dogged answer of Villa Rise, the *Exchange* of Bristol, a ship formerly surprised by the pirates, lay all unrigged in the harbor, till at last one John Goodale, an English Turk,[23] with his confederates (understanding she was a good sailer and might be made a proper man-of-war) bought her from the Turks that took her and prepared her for their own purposes. Now the captain that set them on work was also an English renegado, by the name of Rammetham[24] Rise, but by his Christian name Henry Chandler, who resolved to make Goodale master over her. And because they were both English Turks (having the command, notwithstanding, of many Turks and Moors), they concluded to have all English slaves to go in her and, for their gunners, English and Dutch renegadoes, and so they agreed with the patrons[25] of nine English slaves and one French slave for their ransoms, who were presently employed to rig and furnish the ship for a man-of-war. And while they were thus busied, two of John Rawlins' men (who were taken with him) were also taken up to serve in this man-of-war; their names, James Roe and John Davies, the one dwelling in Plymouth and the other in Fowey, where the commander of this ship was also born, by which occasion they became acquainted. So that both the captain and the master[26] promised them good usage, upon the good service they should perform in the voyage and withal demanded of him if he knew of any Englishman to be bought that could serve them as a pilot, both to direct them out of harbor and conduct them in their voyage. For, in truth, neither was the captain a mariner, nor any Turk in her of sufficiency to dispose of[27] her through the Straits in security nor oppose any enemy that should hold it out bravely against them. Davies quick replied that, as far as he understood, Villa Rise would sell John Rawl-

---

[23] *English Turk*: an English renegade who has converted to Islam.

[24] *Rammetham*: Ramadan.

[25] *patrons*: owners.

[26] *master*: here, the second-ranking officer on the ship.

[27] *dispose of*: maneuver, navigate.

ins, his master and commander of the bark which was taken, a man every way sufficient for sea affairs, being of great resolution and good experience, and for all he had a lame hand, yet had he a sound heart and noble courage for any attempt or adventure.

When the captain understood thus much, he employed Davies to search for Rawlins, who, at last lighting upon him, asked him if the Turk would sell him. Rawlins suddenly answered that by reason of his lame hand he[28] was willing to part with him, but because he had disbursed money for him, he would gain something by him and so priced him at 300 doublets, which amounteth to fifteen pound English, which I must procure or incur sorer endurances. When Davies had certified thus much, the Turks ashipboard conferred about the matter, and the master, whose Christian name was John Goodale, joined with two Turks who were consorted with him and disbursed 100 doublets apiece and so bought him of Villa Rise, sending him into the said ship called the *Exchange* of Bristow,[29] as well to supervise what had been done as to order what was left undone but especially to fit the sails and to accommodate[30] the ship, all which Rawlins was very careful and indulgent in, not yet thinking of any particular plot of deliverance more than a general desire to be freed from this Turkish slavery and inhuman abuses.

By the seventh of January, the ship was prepared, with twelve good cast pieces and all manner of munition and provision which belonged to such a purpose, and the same day hauled out of the mole of Argier, with this company and in this manner.

There were in her sixty-three Turks and Moors, nine English slaves and one French, four Hollanders that were free men to whom the Turks promised one prize or other and so to return to Holland or, if they were disposed to go back again for Argier, they should have great reward and no enforcement offered but continue as they would, both their religion and their customs. And for their gunners, they had two of our soldiers, one English and one Dutch renegado. And thus much for the company. For the manner of setting out, it was as usual, as in other ships, but that the Turks delighted in the ostentous bravery[31] of their streamers, banners, and topsails, the ship being a handsome ship and well built for any purpose. The slaves and English were employed under hatches about the ordnance and other works of order and

---

[28] *he*: Villa Rise.

[29] *Bristow*: Bristol.

[30] *accommodate*: fit out.

[31] *ostentous bravery*: showy, elaborate decoration.

accommodating themselves, all which John Rawlins marked, as supposing it an intolerable slavery to take such pains and be subject to such dangers and still to enrich other men and maintain their voluptuous lives, returning themselves as slaves and living worse than dogs amongst them.

Whereupon, after he had conceited[32] upon the indignity and reproach of their baseness and the glory of an exploit that could deliver himself and the rest from this slavish captivity, being very busy among the English in pulling of ropes and placing of ordnance, he burst into these, or such like, abrupt speeches: "Oh hellish slavery, to be thus subject to dogs! To labor thus to enrich infidels and maintain their pleasures! To be ourselves slaves and worse than the outcast of the world! Is there no way of releasement? No device to free us from this bondage? No exploit, no action of worth to be put in execution, to make us renowned in the world and famous to posterity? Oh God strengthen my heart and hand, and something shall be done to ease us of these mischiefs and deliver us from these cruel Mahometan[33] dogs!"

The other slaves pitying his distraction (as they thought) bade him speak softly lest they should all fare the worse for his distemperature.[34]

"The worse!" quoth Rawlins, "What can be worse? Death is the determiner of all misery, and torture can last but a while! But to be continually a-dying, and suffer all indignity and reproach, and in the end to have no welcome but into the house of slaughter or bondage, is insufferable and more than flesh and blood can endure! And therefore, by that salvation which Christ hath brought, I will either attempt my deliverance at one time or another or perish in the enterprise. But if you would be contented to hearken after a release and join with me in the action, I would not doubt of facilitating the same and show you a way to make your credits thrive by some work of amazement and augment your glory in purchasing your liberty."

"I prithee, be quiet!" said they again, "and think not of impossibilities: yet if you can but open such a door of reason and probability that we be not condemned for desperate and distracted persons, in pulling the sun (as it were) out of the firmament, we can but sacrifice our lives, and you may be sure of secrecy and taciturnity."

"Now, blessed be my genius," said Rawlins, "that ever this motive was so opportunely preferred, and therefore we will be quiet a while, till the iron be hotter, that we may not strike in vain."

[32] *conceited*: meditated.
[33] *Mahometan*: Muslim.
[34] *distemperature*: disordered state of mind.

The fifteenth of January, the morning water[35] brought us near Cape de Gatt,[36] hard by the shore, we having in our company a small Turkish ship of war that followed us out of Argier the next day and now joining with us, gave us notice of seven small vessels, six of them being settees[37] and one a pollack,[38] who very quickly appeared in sight, and so we made toward them. But having more advantage of the pollack than the rest and loath to lose all, we both fetched her up and brought her past hope of recovery, which when she perceived, rather than she would voluntarily come into the slavery of these Mahometans, she ran herself ashore, and so all the men forsook her. We still followed as near as we durst and for fear of splitting let fall our anchors, making out[39] both our boats, wherein were many musketeers and some English and Dutch renegadoes who came aboard home at their congé[40] and found three pieces of ordnance and four murtherers,[41] but they straightway threw them all overboard to lighten the ship. And so they got her off, being laden with hides and logwood for dyeing, and presently sent her to Argier, taking nine Turks and one English slave out of one ship and six out of the lesser, which we thought sufficient to man her.

But see the chance—or, if you will, how Fortune smiled on us: in the rifling of this Cataleynia,[42] our Turks fell at variance, one with another and in such a manner that we divided ourselves: the lesser ship returned to Argier, and our *Exchange* took the opportunity of the wind and plied out of the Straits, which rejoiced John Rawlins very much, as resolving on some stratagem when opportunity should serve. In the meanwhile, the Turks began to murmur and would not willingly go into the Marr Granda,[43] as the phrase is amongst them; notwithstanding, the Moors (being very superstitious) were contented to be directed by their Hoshea,[44] who with us signifieth a witch

[35] *water*: tide.

[36] *Cape de Gatt*: Cabo de Gata, near Almeria, in Spain.

[37] *settees*: "decked vessel[s], with a long sharp prow, carrying two or three masts with a kind of lateen sails, in use in the Mediterranean" (*O.E.D.*).

[38] *pollack*: polacca or polacre, a three-masted sailing vessel, usually combining a square sail on the mainmast with lateen sails on the other masts.

[39] *making out*: sending out.

[40] *came aboard home at their congé*: entered the vessel at their leisure, without opposition.

[41] *murtherers*: small cannons.

[42] *Cataleynia*: Catalonian.

[43] *Marr Granda*: the Atlantic Ocean, beyond the Straits of Gibraltar.

[44] *Hoshea*: soothsayer (Hoshea being an ancient Hebrew prophet).

and is of great account and reputation amongst them, as not going in any
great vessel to sea without one, and observing whatsoever he concludeth out
of his divination. The ceremonies he useth are many, and when they come
into the ocean, every second or third night he maketh his conjuration. He
beginneth and endeth with prayer, using many characters[45] and calling upon
God by divers names. Yet, at this time, all that he did consisteth in these par-
ticulars.

Upon the sight of two great ships, and as we were afraid the chasing, being
supposed to be Spanish men-of-war, a great silence is commanded in the
ship, and when all is done, the company giveth as great a screech, the captain still coming to John Rawlins and sometimes making him to take in all
his sails and sometimes causing him to hoist them all out, as the witch find-
eth by his book and presages. Then have they two arrows and a curtal axe
lying on a pillow, naked. The arrows are one for the Turks, and the other for
the Christians. Then the witch readeth, and the captain or some other taketh
the arrows in their hand by the heads, and if the arrow for the Christians
cometh over the head of the arrow for the Turks, then do they advance their
sails and will not endure the fight, whatsoever they see, but if the arrow of
the Turks is found, in the opening of the hand, upon the arrow of the Christians, then will they stay and encounter with any ship whatsoever. The curtal axe is taken up by some child that is innocent, or, rather, ignorant of the
ceremony, and so laid down again. Then they do observe whether the same
side is uppermost which lay before and so proceed accordingly. They also
observe lunatics and changelings,[46] and the conjurer writeth down their say-
ings in a book, groveling on the ground, as if he whispered to the Devil to tell
him the truth, and so expoundeth the letter, as it were, by inspiration. Many
other foolish rites they have, whereon they do dote as foolishly, and whereof
I could entreat more at large, but this shall suffice at this time.

Whilst he was thus busied and made demonstration that all was finished,
the people in the ship gave a great shout and cried out, "A sail, a sail!" which
at last was discovered to be another man-of-war of Turks. For he made
toward us and sent his boat aboard us, to whom our captain complained that
being becalmed by the southern cape[47] and having made no voyage, the
Turks denied to go any further northward, but the captain resolved not to
return to Argier, except he could obtain some prize worth his endurances,

---

[45] *characters*: magical symbols or symbolic emblems.
[46] *changelings*: feeble-minded persons.
[47] *the southern cape*: of Portugal, i.e., Cape St. Vincent.

but rather to go to Salee[48] and sell his Christians to victual his ship. Which the other captain apprehended for his honor and so persuaded the Turks to be obedient unto him, whereupon followed a pacification amongst us, and so that Turk took his course for the Straits and we put up northward, expecting the good hour of some beneficial booty.

All this while our slavery continued, and the Turks, with insulting tyranny, set us still on work in all base and servile actions, adding stripes[49] and inhuman revilings, even in our greatest labor. Whereupon John Rawlins resolved to obtain his liberty and surprise the ship, providing ropes with broad specks[50] of iron and all the iron crows,[51] with which he knew a way, upon the consent of the rest, to ram up or tie fast their scuttles, gratings, and cabins, yea, to shut up the captain himself with all his consorts, and so to handle the matter that upon the watchword given, the English being masters of the gunner room, ordnance, and powder, they would either blow them into the air or kill them as they adventured to come down, one by one, if they should by any chance open their cabins. But because he would proceed the better in his enterprise, as he had somewhat abruptly discovered himself to the nine English slaves, so he kept the same distance with the four Hollanders that were free men, till finding them coming somewhat towards them, he acquainted them with them the whole conspiracy, and they, affecting the plot, offered the adventure of[52] their lives in the business. Then, very warily, he undermined[53] the English renegado which was the gunner and three more, his associates, who at first seemed to retract. Last of all, were brought in the Dutch renegadoes, who were also in the gunner room, for always there lay twelve there, five Christians and seven English and Dutch Turks. So that when another motion had settled their resolutions, and John Rawlins his constancy had put new life, as it were, in the matter, the four Hollanders very honestly, according to their promise, sounded the Dutch renegadoes, who with easy persuasion gave their consent to so brave an enterprise. Whereupon John Rawlins, not caring whether the English gunners would yield or no, resolved, in the captain's morning watch, to make the attempt. But you must understand that where the English slaves lay, there hung up always four

---

[48] *Salee*: Salé, a center for piracy and slave trading on the Moroccan coast, near modern-day Rabat.

[49] *stripes*: blows of the whip, and the marks they leave on the body.

[50] *specks*: spikes.

[51] *iron crows*: crowbars.

[52] *offered the adventure of*: offered to risk.

[53] *undermined*: won over by means of subtle persuasion.

or five crows of iron, being still under the carriages of the pieces,[54] and when the time approached, being very dark, because John Rawlins would have his crow of iron ready, as other things were, and other men prepared in their several places, in taking it out of the carriage, by chance, it hit on the side of the piece, making such a noise that the soldiers hearing it, awaked the Turks and bade them come down. Whereupon the boatswain of the Turks descended with a candle and presently searched all the slaves' places, making much ado of the matter, but finding neither hatchet, nor hammer, nor anything else to move suspicion of the enterprise more than the crow of iron, which lay slipped down under the carriages of the pieces, they went quietly up again and certified the captain what had chanced, who satisfied himself that it was a common thing to have a crow of iron slip from his place.

But by this occasion, we made stay of our attempt yet were resolved to take another or a better opportunity. Only I must tell you what John Rawlins would have done if this accident had not happened. He was fully minded, with some others, with their naked knives in their hands, to press upon the gunner's breast and the other English renegadoes and either force them to consent to their designs or to cut their throats, first telling them plainly that they had vowed to surprise the ship and, by God's assistance, to obtain their liberty; and therefore either die or consent that when you hear the watchword given, "For God and King James and St. George for England," you presently keep your places and advise to execute what you are commanded.

But as you have heard, God was the best physician to our wounded hearts and used a kind of preventing physic rather than to cure us so suddenly. So that, out of His providence, perceiving some danger in this enterprise, He both caused us to desist and, at last, brought our business to a better period and fortunate end. For we sailed still more northward, and Rawlins had more time to tamper with his gunners, and the rest of the English renegadoes, who very willingly, when they considered the matter and perpended[55] the reasons, gave way unto the project and with a kind of joy seemed to entertain the motives. Only they made a stop at the first onset,[56] who should begin the enterprise, which was no way fit for them to do because they were no slaves, but renegadoes, and so had always beneficial entertainment amongst them. But when it was once put in practice, they would be sure not to fail them but venture their lives for God and their country. When Rawlins had heard them

[54] *carriages of the pieces*: frames for holding the heavy guns.
[55] *perpended*: pondered.
[56] *made a stop at the first onset*: would not go so far as to begin the revolt.

out, he much liked their contradiction[57] and told them plainly he did require no such thing at their hands but the slaves and himself would first sound the channel and then adventure the water. And so, after reciprocal oaths taken and hands given, Rawlins once again lay in wait for the fittest opportunity. But once again he is disappointed, and a suspicious accident brought him to recollect his spirits anew and study on the danger of the enterprise, and thus it was:

After the renegado gunner had protested secrecy, by all that might induce a man to bestow some belief upon him, he presently went up the scuttle but stayed not aloft a quarter of an hour. Nay, he came sooner down and in the gunner room sat by Rawlins, who tarried for him where he left him. He was no sooner placed and entered into some conference, but there entered into the place a furious Turk with his knife drawn and presented it to Rawlins his body, who verily supposed he intended to kill him, as suspicious that the gunner had discovered something. Whereat Rawlins was much moved and so hastily asked what the matter meant, or whether he would kill him or no, observing his countenance and (according to the nature of jealousy) conceiting[58] that his color had a passage of change, whereby his suspicious heart condemned him for a traitor but that, at more leisure, he sware the contrary and afterwards proved faithful and industrious in the enterprise. And for the present, he answered Rawlins in this manner: "No, master, be not afraid. I think he doth but jest." With that, John Rawlins gave back a little and drew out his knife, stepping also to the gunner's sheath and taking out his (whereby he had two knives to one), which when the Turk perceived, he threw down his knife, saying he did but jest with him. But as I said, when the gunner perceived Rawlins took it so ill, he whispered something in his ear that at last satisfied him, calling heaven to witness that he never spake word of the enterprise, nor ever would, either to the prejudice of the business or danger of his person.

Notwithstanding, Rawlins kept the knives in his sleeve all night and was somewhat troubled for that he had made so many acquainted with an action of such importance, but the next day when he perceived the coast clear and that there was no cause of further fear, he somewhat comforted himself and grew bolder and bolder in disposing the affairs of the ship. Only it grieved him that his enterprises were thus procrastinated, whereby the Mahometan tyranny increased and the poor slaves even groaned again under the

[57] *contradiction*: reservation.
[58] *conceiting*: imagining.

burthen[59] of their bondage and thought every day a year till something was put in execution for their deliverance. For it was now full five weeks since Rawlins first projected the matter.

All this while, Rawlins drew the captain to lie for[60] the northern cape,[61] assuring him that thereby he should not miss purchase, which accordingly fell out, as a wish would have it, but his drift was, in truth, to draw him from any supply or second[62] of Turks, if God should give way to their enterprise or success to the victory. Yet for the present, the sixth of February, being twelve leagues from the cape, we descried a sail and presently took the advantage of the wind in chasing her and at last fetched her up, making her strike all her sails, whereby we knew her to be a bark belonging to Torbay,[63] near Dartmouth, that came from Averare,[64] laden with salt. Ere we had fully dispatched, it chanced to be foul weather, so that we could not, or at least would not, make out[65] our boat but caused the master of the bark to let down his and come aboard with his company, being in the bark but nine men and one boy. And so the master, leaving his mate with two men in the same, came himself (with five men and the boy) unto us, whereupon our Turkish captain sent ten Turks to man her, amongst whom were two Dutch and one English renegado who were of our confederacy and acquainted with us.

But when Rawlins saw this partition of his friends, before they could hoist out their boat for the bark, he made means to speak with them and told them plainly that he would prosecute the matter either that night or the next, and therefore, whatsoever came of it, they should acquaint the English with his resolution and make towards England, bearing up the helm whiles the Turks slept and suspected no such matter. For, by God's grace, in his first watch, about midnight, he would show them a light by which they might understand that the enterprise was begun or at least in a good forwardness for the exe-cution. And so the boat was let down, and they came to the bark of Torbay, where the master's mate being left (as before you have heard) apprehended quickly the matter and heard the discourse with amazement. But time was precious and not to be spent in disputing or casting of doubts whether the Turks that were with them were able to master them or not, being seven to

---

[59] *burthen*: burden.
[60] *to lie for*: set a course for.
[61] *the northern cape*: probably Cape Finisterre.
[62] *second*: reinforcement.
[63] *Torbay*: Torquay, a port on the coast of Devonshire, south of Exeter.
[64] *Averare*: probably Aveiro, on the west coast of Portugal.
[65] *make out*: let down.

six, considering they had the helm of the ship, and the Turks (being soldiers and ignorant of sea affairs) could not discover whether they went to Argier or not, or if they did, they resolved, by Rawlins' example, to cut their throats or cast them overboard. And so I leave them to make use of the renegadoes' instructions and return to Rawlins again.

The master of the bark of Torbay and his company were quickly searched and as quickly pillaged and dismissed to the liberty of the ship, whereby Rawlins had leisure to entertain him with the lamentable news of their extremities and the adventure of their voyages, whereby he understood of his first setting out from the West Country; of his taking and surprising at sea by Villa Rise; of his twice being sold as a slave and so continuing to his heart-burning and excruciation; of the making the *Exchange* of Bristol a man-of-war, which they were now in; of the captain and master, who were both English renegadoes; of the cruelty of the Turks in general and his own fortunes in particular; of his admission into the ship as a pilot; of the friendship which passed between him and the Hollanders; of the imparting the secret of surprising the ship, both to the slaves and Christian renegadoes; of their consent and courageous apprehension of the matter; of the first attempt and their twice disappointing; of his still resolution presently to put it in practice; of his last acquainting the Dutch renegadoes who went aboard his bark; and, in a word, of every particular which was befitting to the purpose. Yea, he told him that that night he should lose the sight of them, for they would make the helm for England, and he would, that night and evermore, pray for their good success and safe deliverance.

When the master of the bark of Torbay had heard him out and that his company were partakers of his story, they all became silent, not either diffident of his discourse or afraid of the attempt but as wondering at the goodness of God and His mercy in choosing out such weak instruments to set forth His glory.

"True," quoth Rawlins, when he found them coming toward him, "it is so. For mark but the circumstance of the matter, and you shall see the very finger of God to point us out our deliverance. When we came into the main ocean[66] to hunt after prizes, according to the nature of pirates, and that I resolved on the enterprise, there were sixty-five Turks in our ship and only seventeen of our confederacy. Then it pleased God to abate us ten of the Turks, who were sent with the polacre before recited. And when we were disappointed again of our purposes, you see now what hath chanced. We are

---

[66] *main ocean*: Atlantic Ocean.

rid of more Turks and welcome you as a new supply. So that, if you please, we shall be twenty-four strong, and they, in all, are but forty-five. Be therefore courageous, and let us join heart, hand, and foot together that we may execute this brave attempt for God's glory, our country's honor, the good example of other,[67] our own deliverance, and (if we may not be counted vainglorious) our everlasting memory."

By that time he had finished this discourse also, the master of the bark and his company resolved to assist him, as projecting[68] the misery and wretchedness they should endure by being slaves to the Turks and the happiness of their liberty besides the reputation of the enterprise. As for death, it was in community[69] to all men and so in the hands of God to dispose, at His pleasure, and either could not happen before the hour of limitation or could not be prevented, for human policy must submit to divine providence. Yet to show himself an understanding man, he demanded of Rawlins what weapons he had and in what manner he would execute the business, to which he answered that he had ropes and iron hooks to make fast the scuttles, gratings, and cabins. He had also in the gunner room two curtal axes, and the slaves had five crows of iron before them. Besides, in the scuffling, they made no question of some of the soldiers' weapons. Then for the manner, he told them they were sure of the ordnance, the gunner room, and the powder and so, blocking them up, would either kill them, as they came down, or turn the ordnance against their cabins, or blow them into the air by one stratagem or other. And thus were they contented on all sides and resolved to the enterprise.

The next morning, being the seventh of February, the prize of Torbay was not to be seen or found, whereat the captain began to storm and swear, commanding Rawlins to search the seas up and down for her, who bestowed all that day in that business, but to little purpose, whereupon, when the humor was spent,[70] the captain pacified himself, as conceiting he should be sure to find her at Argier. But, by the permission of the ruler of all actions, that Argier was England and all his wickedness frustrated. For Rawlins being now startled, lest he should return in this humor for the Straits, the eighth of February went down into the hold and finding a great deal of water below, told the captain of the same, adding that it did not come to the pump, which he did

---

[67] *of other*: to others.
[68] *projecting*: foreseeing.
[69] *in community*: common.
[70] *when the humor was spent*: when his angry mood had passed.

very politicly, that he might remove the ordnance. For when the captain asked him the reason, he told him the ship was too far after the head.[71] Then he commanded to use the best means he could to bring her in order.

"Sure then," quoth Rawlins, "we must quit our cables[72] and bring four pieces of ordnance after,[73] and that would bring the water to the pump." Which was presently put in practice. So the pieces being usually made fast thwart the ship, we brought two of them, with their mouths right before the biticle. And because the renegado Flemings would not begin, it was thus concluded: that the ship having three decks, we that did belong to the gunner room should be all there and break up the lower deck. The English slaves who always lay in the middle deck should do the like and watch the scuttles. Rawlins himself prevailed with the gunner, for so much powder as should prime the pieces, and so told them all, there was no better watchword, nor means to begin, than upon the report of the piece to make a cry and screech, "For God and King James and Saint George for England!"

When all things were prepared and every man resolved, as knowing what he had to do and the hour when it should happen to be two in the afternoon, Rawlins advised the master gunner to speak to the captain, that the soldiers might attend on the poop, which would bring the ship after.[74] To which the captain was very willing, and upon the gunner's information, the soldiers gat themselves to the poop to the number of twenty, and five or six went into the captain's cabin, where always lay divers curtal axes and some targets.[75] And so we fell to work to pump the water and carried the matter fairly till the next day, which was spent as the former, being the ninth of February and (as God must have the praise) the triumph of our victory.

For by that time, all things were prepared, and the soldiers got upon the poop as the day before. To avoid suspicion, all that did belong to the gunner room went down, and the slaves in the middle deck, attended their business, so that we may cast up our account in this manner: first, nine English slaves, besides John Rawlins; five of the Torbay men and one boy; four English renegadoes and two Dutch; four Hollanders—in all, four and twenty and a boy. So that lifting up our hearts and hands to God for the success of the business, we were wonderfully encouraged and settled ourselves till the report of the

[71] *too far after the head*: with the bow riding lower in the water than the stern.

[72] *quit our cables*: leave off tending the ropes that control the ship's sails.

[73] *after*: toward the rear of the ship.

[74] *bring the ship after*: cause the rear of the ship to go down.

[75] *targets*: shields.

piece gave us warning of the enterprise. Now, you must consider that in this
company were two of Rawlins' men, James Roe and John Davies, whom he
brought out of England and whom the fortune of the sea brought into the
same predicament with their master. These were employed about noon
(being, as I said, the ninth of February) to prepare their matches, while all the
Turks, or at least most of them, stood on the poop, to weigh down the ship,
as it were, to bring the water forward to the pump; the one brought his match
lighted between two spoons, the other brought his in a little piece of a can.
And so, in the name of God, the Turks and Moors being placed as you have
heard, and forty-five in number, and Rawlins having proined[76] the touch-
holes, James Roe gave fire to one of the pieces, about two of the clock in the
afternoon, and the confederates, upon the warning, shouted most cheerfully.
The report of the piece did tear and break down all the biticle and compasses,
and the noise of the slaves made all the soldiers amazed at the matter, till seeing the quarter of the ship rent and feeling the whole body to shake under
them, till understanding the ship was surprised and the attempt tended[77] to
their utter destruction, never bear robbed of her whelps was so fell and mad!
For they not only called us dogs and cried out, "*Usance de la mer*,"[78] which
is as much as to say "the fortune of the wars," but attempted to tear up the
planks, setting a-work hammers, hatchets, knives, the oars of the boat, the
boathook, their curtal axes, and what else came to hand, besides stones and
bricks in the cook room, all which they threw amongst us, attempting still
and still to break and rip up the hatches and boards of the steering,[79] not
desisting from their former execrations and horrible blasphemies and revilings.

When John Rawlins perceived them so violent and understood how the
slaves had cleared the decks of all the Turks and Moors beneath, he set a
guard upon the powder and charged their own muskets against them, killing
them from divers scout holes, both before and behind, and so lessened their
number, to the joy of all our hearts. Whereupon they cried out and called for
the pilot, and so Rawlins, with some to guard him, went to them and understood them, by their kneeling, that they cried for mercy and to have their lives
saved, and they would come down, which he bade them do. And so they
were taken one by one and bound, yea, killed with their own curtal axes,

[76] *proined*: primed.
[77] *tended*: intended.
[78] usance de la mer: the custom of the sea (French).
[79] *steering*: the area in the stern, near the helm.

which, when the rest perceived, they called us English dogs and reviled us with many opprobrious terms, some leaping overboard, crying, "It was the chance of war!" Some were manacled and so thrown overboard, and some were slain and mangled with the curtal axes, till the ship was well cleared, and ourselves assured of the victory.

At the first report of our piece and hurly-burly in the decks, the captain was a-writing in his cabin and, hearing the noise, thought it some strange accident and so came out with his curtal axe in his hand, presuming by his authority to pacify the mischief. But when he cast his eyes upon us and saw that we were like to surprise the ship, he threw down his curtal axe and begged to save his life, intimating to Rawlins how he had redeemed him from Villa Rise and ever since admitted him to place of command in the ship, beside honest usage in the whole course of the voyage. All which Rawlins confessed but withal added the fearfulness of his apostasy from Christianity, the unjustifiable course of piracy, the extreme cruelty of the Turks in general, the fearful proceedings of Argier against us in particular, the horrible abuses of the Moors to Christians, and the execrable blasphemies they use both against God and men. I will not dwell on his reply, nor on the circumstances of atonement, only I am sure Rawlins at last condescended to mercy[80] and brought the captain and five more into England. The captain was called Ramtham Rise, but his Christian name, Henry Chandler and, as they say, a chandler's son in Southwark. John Goodale was also an English Turk. Richard Clarke, in Turkish, Jafar; George Cooke, Ramedam; John Browne, Mamme; William Winter, Mustapha; besides all the slaves and Hollanders, with other renegadoes, who were willing to be reconciled to their true Savior, as being formerly seduced with the hopes of riches, honor, preferment, and suchlike devilish baits to catch the souls of mortal men and entangle frailty in the terriers[81] of horrible abuses and imposturing deceit.

When all was done and the ship cleared of the dead bodies, John Rawlins assembled his men together and with one consent gave the praise unto God, using the accustomed service on shipboard,[82] and, for want of books, lifted up their voices to God, as He put into their hearts or renewed their memories. Then did they sing a psalm and, last of all, embraced one another for playing the men[83] in such a deliverance, whereby our fear was turned into joy

[80] *condescended to mercy*: agreed to show mercy.
[81] *terriers*: literally, small dogs known for their ability to pursue and then fasten onto their quarry with fierce tenacity.
[82] *accustomed service on shipboard*: traditional prayer of thanksgiving.
[83] *playing the men*: exhibiting courage and boldness.

and trembling hearts exhilarated that we had escaped such inevitable dangers, and especially the slavery and terror of bondage, worse than death itself. The same night, we washed our ship, put everything in as good order as we could, repaired the broken quarter, set up the biticle, and bore up the helm for England, where, by God's grace and good guiding, we arrived at Plymouth the thirteenth of February and were welcomed like the recovery of the lost sheep or as you read of a loving mother that runneth with embraces to entertain her son from a long voyage and escape of many dangers.

Not long after, we understood of our confederates that returned home in the bark of Torbay that they arrived in Penzance in Cornwall the eleventh of February, and if any ask after their deliverance, considering there were ten Turks sent to man her, I will tell you that, too. The next day after they lost us, as you have heard, the three renegadoes had acquainted the master's mate and the two English in her with Rawlins' determination and that they themselves would be true to them and assist them in any enterprise; then, if the worst came, there were but seven to six. But as it fell out, they had a more easy passage than turmoil and manslaughter. For they made the Turks believe the wind was come fair and that they were sailing to Argier, till they came within sight of England, which one of them amongst the rest discovered, saying plainly that that land was not like Cape Vincent.

"Yes!" saith he that was at the helm, "and you will be contented and go down into the hold and trim the salt[84] over to windward, whereby the ship may bear full sail; you shall know and see more tomorrow."

Whereupon five of them went down very orderly, the renegadoes feigning themselves asleep, who presently start up and, with the help of the two English, nailed down the hatches. Whereat the principal amongst them much repined and began to grow into choler and rage, had it not quickly been overpassed. For one of them stepped to him and dashed out his brains and threw him overboard. The rest were brought to Exeter and either to be arraigned according to the punishment of delinquents in such a kind or disposed of as the king and council shall think meet. And this is the story of this deliverance and end of John Rawlins' voyage.

Now, gentle reader, I hope you will not call in question the power and goodness of God, who from time to time extendeth His mercy to the miraculous preservation of His servants; nor make any doubt that He hath still the same arm and vigor as He had in times past, when Gideon's three hundred

---

[84] *trim the salt*: shift the cargo of salt.

men overcame the Midianites;[85] and many ancient stratagems are recorded to have had a passage of success, even within our memories, to execute as great a wonder as this. Nor do I think you will be startled at anything in the discourse touching the cruelty and inhumanity of Turks and Moors themselves, who from a native barbarousness do hate all Christians and Christianity, especially if they grow into the violent rages of piracy or fall into that exorbitant course of selling of slaves or enforcing of men to be Mahometans. Nor can I imagine you will call in question our natural desire of liberty and saving of our lives, when you see, from instinct of nature, all the creatures of the world come to the law of preservation, and our Savior Himself alloweth the flying out of one city into another in the time of persecution,[86] and Paul, by saying he was a Roman, procured his delivery.[87] Well then, it is only the truth of the story that you are amazed at, making doubt whether your belief of the same may be bestowed to your own credit. I can say no more. The actors in this comic tragedy are most of them alive. The Turks are in prison; the ship is to be seen; and Rawlins himself dare justify the matter. For he hath presented it to the marquis,[88] a man not to be dallied withal in these things nor any way to be made partaker of deceit. Nay, I protest I think he durst not, for his ears[89] (concerning the substance[90]), publish such a discourse to open overlooking, if it were not true. As for illustration, or cementing the broken pieces with well-tempered mortar, blame him not in that, for precious stones are worn enameled and wrought in gold which otherwise would be still of value and estimation but polished and receiving the addition of art and cunning, who doth not account the better and esteemeth himself the richer for their possession? So then, entertain it for a true and certain discourse: apply it, make use of it, and put it to thy heart for thy comfort. It teacheth the acknowledgment of a powerful, provident, and merciful God, who will be known in His wonders and make weak things the instruments of His glory.

---

[85] *Gideon's . . . the Midianites*: See Judges 7, which describes the miraculous defeat of a vast army by only three hundred men of Israel.

[86] *our Savior . . . of persecution*: See Matthew 10:23.

[87] *Paul, by . . . his delivery*: See Acts 22:25–29.

[88] *the marquis*: George Villiers, the marquis of Buckingham and lord high admiral, to whom this book was dedicated.

[89] *for his ears*: for fear of punishment (thieves, vagabonds, and other criminals were sometimes punished by having a hole bored in an ear with a hot iron or by having their ears cut off).

[90] *concerning the substance*: because the subject matter deals with the serious crime of piracy.

It instructeth us in the practice of thanksgiving when a benefit is bestowed, a mercy shown, and a deliverance perfected. It maketh us strong and courageous in adversity, like cordial restoratives to a sick heart, and our patience shall stand as a rock against the impetuous assaults of affliction. It is a glorious sun to dissipate the clouds of desperation and cheer us thus far that God can restore us when we are under pressure of discomfort and tribulation: for preferment comes neither from the East, nor the West, but from Him that holdeth the winds in His hands and puts a hook in the nostrils of Leviathan.[91] So that if He do not give way to our contentment, it is because He will supply us with better graces or keep us from the adder's hole of temptation, whereat if we tarry, we shall be sure to be stung unto death. In a word, it is a mirror to look virtue in the face and teach men the way to industry and noble performances, that a brave spirit and honest man shall say, with Nehemiah, "Shall such a man as I fly?"[92] Shall I fear death or some petty trial when God is to be honored, my country to be served, my king to be obeyed, religion to be defended, the commonwealth supported, honor and renown obtained, and in the end, the crown of immortality purchased?

---

[91] *puts a hook in the nostrils of Leviathan*: refers to the Book of Job, chapter 41.

[92] *with Nehemiah . . . I fly?*: See Nehemiah 6:11. Nehemiah led the Jews out of captivity in Babylon to rebuild the temple in Jerusalem.

News from Sally of a Strange Delivery of Four English Captives from the Slavery of the Turks (1642)

(Salé, 1642)

A plain pamphlet merely six pages in length, *News from Sally* is one of many brief printed texts from the seventeenth century that offered "news" from the sea about the exploits, successes, and misfortunes experienced by English vessels in the Mediterranean, Africa, Asia, and the New World. The text was written so simply and its length is so brief that its existence testifies to the interest in such matters that must have existed among English readers at the time. Such small pamphlets would have functioned as sensational and entertaining news flashes that provided short-lived pleasure to some or as records of events in the maritime sphere that would have been of interest to English citizens involved in maritime enterprise.

The fate of the captured crew, which was taken to Salé but then sold to a merchant in Algiers, demonstrates that the trade in bodies in North Africa involved a cooperative economy that linked the various entrepôts of the slave trade.

No other edition of this narrative is known.

News from Sally of a Strange Delivery of Four English Captives from the Slavery of the Turks

PRINTED IN THE YEAR 1642.

About the beginning of October last, four English ships (the one from Rye, the other from Barnstable, the third from Apsum, and the fourth from Dartmouth), being bound homeward from Rochelle[1] after a day and a night's sail, it was their fortune to meet with a Turkish man-of-war of Sally,[2] who, being well provided, with small resistance took them (they being merchant's men and not for service)[3] [and] carried them to Sally, where after some few days arrival, one of each ship was sold to a merchant of Argier[4] for slaves, who having not opportunity of passage, remained some days in Sally with his slaves, in which time he gave order that shackles should be made for each slave weighing fifty pound weight; but the Lord most graciously delivered them after this manner: viz.,[5] for being chained every night (as the custom is) to an iron bar until their shackles were made and in the daytime employed about the town, they found means to speak with a Portugal slave concerning their escape, who assured them that if they could conveniently get out of the town, they might take their course along the seashore, and in three or four hours they may recover a town of the Spaniards,[6] not distant from that place above eighteen miles; which having learnt, they employ their best endeavors for their escape, so that having gotten a piece of clay and finding opportunity to make the impression of the key of their prison in the aforesaid clay, by

---

[1] *Rochelle*: a port on the west coast of France, in the Bay of Biscay.
[2] *Sally*: Salé.
[3] *merchant's men and not for service*: commercial vessels, not equipped to fight.
[4] *Argier*: Algiers.
[5] *viz.*: an abbreviation for the Latin *videlicet*, meaning "that is."
[6] *town of the Spaniards*: Mamora.

which they made a wooden key and making trial found that it would stand them in stead. The night before they should have departed for Argier and that their shackles should have been put on, having got a strong nail, they begun about twelve o'clock to tamper with the lock which held the chain to the iron bar, to which they were fastened. But having spent two hours and not being able to pick the lock, despairing of their purpose, laid themselves down to sleep, but God putting into the heart of James Cadman (master of that ship from Rye) once more to assay the lock, rose up, and being next unto the lock, at the very first trial opened it, which having done, opened the door with the wooden key. Then coming to another door, they easily lifted it off from the hooks with an iron bar which they there found; so likewise a third door, which led them into the street. But mark the wonderful works of the Lord: for all the time that this was a-doing, a dog continued barking in the house, which their patron[7] and another Turk never heard, although they lay the very next wall unto them. So being come into the street, the one having the iron bar, the other an axe, the third a staff, and the fourth an iron ladle (such as they melt lead in), they ran presently to the town wall and leaped down without any harm, it being eighteen foot high, and so took their way towards the shore, not meeting with any scouts or watch in all the way. After which, as the Portugal directed them, they run along the seashore, in far more danger of the wild beasts (which use to haunt those places) than formerly they were of the Turk their master; but God which delivered them out of the hands of the one saved them also from the jaws of the other, for they met but with one wild boar, who so soon as he had set eye on them, fled from them. They did hear in divers places the barking of a small beast, which usually follows the lions, by which they guessed divers lions were thereabout, but met with none. So with running, by break of day they obtained the Spanish town, where the governor gave them noble entertainment and within the space of an hour, took them into a turret, where he showed them twenty-four Turkish horsemen, which had pursued them; but God be praised, they were out of their reach. The iron bar, the axe, and the ladle, the governor hanged up in the chief church of the town, in memorial of their strange delivery. So having occasion of passage for Calais, they came away from thence and finding a Dover ship at Calais, came for England, where they now are to give God praise for their safe delivery.

FINIS

---

[7] *patron*: owner.

William Okeley, *Ebenezer; or, A Small Monument of Great Mercy, Appearing in the Miraculous Deliverance of William Okeley (1675)*

(Algiers, 1639–44)

When he was captured by pirates in 1639, William Okeley was a crew member on a ship sailing to help found a new colony in the West Indies, "in pursuance of a commission from . . . the earl of Warwick, the Lord Saye, and the Lord Brooke." These three men were leading members of the Puritan faction in Parliament, which had been dissolved in 1629 by Charles I. During the period of Charles's personal rule (1629–37), there were elements among the "godly people" who saw the New World as an alternative space for worship free from Laudian practices and restraints. The "Governors and Company of Adventurers for the Plantation of the Islands of Providence, Henrietta and the adjacent Islands" were granted a royal charter in 1630 under the leadership of Robert Rich, earl of Warwick; William Fiennes, Viscount Saye; and Robert Greville, Lord Brooke. John Pym, who would be a leader of the parliamentary cause, was also an early investor. The settlements they sponsored were located on two islands off the coast of Nicaragua (known today as Santa Catalina and Santa Andreas). Okeley's citation of a verse from Herbert's "The Church Militant," with its personification of true "Religion . . . ready to pass to the American strand," is an allusion to the emigration of religious dissenters to the New World.

There are many signs of a Calvinistic, providentialist agenda in Okeley's text, and the revival of antiroyalist Protestantism in England may account for the printing of the text after so many years, in 1675. This was the era immediately preceding the Popish Plot ("revealed" by Titus Oates in September 1678), and popular suspicion of "popery" was strong. Okeley's narrative is accompanied with a theological apparatus that is much more substantial than any included in the other texts in this collection, with frequent digressions proclaiming a militant Protestantism and a virulent anti-Catholicism. The prefatory verses declare that "this book is Protestant, and hates a lie." Claiming to be reporting a story "of God's own working, not of man's inventing," the text makes strong claims for the theology of militant Protestantism and for the truth-bearing authority of the narrative itself. Like the religious beliefs professed by the author, the narrative is said to be "all plain and true."

The minister Okeley meets in Algiers, Devereux Spratt, was a low church divine, whom the Muslim authorities in Algiers allowed to preach to the Christian slaves resident there. But Okeley accounts for this religious tolerance by attributing venal motives to the Muslim slavemasters: "For whilst we intermeddled not with their superstitions but paid our patrons their demands, we might without any disturbance from them worship our God according to our consciences."

Okeley's narrative includes frequent diatribes against Islam and the Turks of Algiers, much of which derives from a long tradition of anti-Islamic polemic. The text provides ethnographic material, including detailed descriptions of life in Algiers, but much of this is filtered through a demonizing mechanism that deploys old stereotypes and anti-Islamic tales. For example, Okeley describes the Prophet Muhammad as a "religious thief" whose religion is based on the offering of "booty" to "his idol," and he echoes one of the conventional Christian accounts of the origins of Islam: "Mahomet, by the help of Sergius, a Nestorian monk, and Abdalla the Jew, had patched up a cento of Jewish and monkish fopperies, which was now their religion." According to Okeley, "their prophet was but a cobbler," and his theology merely a plagiarized hybrid taken from earlier monotheistic traditions. For an English Protestant, the combination of Nestorian Christianity, monasticism, and Judaism demonstrated both heresy and an irrational inconsistency. This account of the origins of Islam seeks to define it as a religion by and for renegades and apostates. Stories about Sergius the Monk and the "impostures" of Mahomet were widely disseminated in the late Middle Ages and the early modern period, and the legend of Sergius was well known to English readers. George Whetstone's *The English Mirror* (1586), for example, features a moralizing tale about "the envy of Sergius, a monk of Constantinople, who being banished for heresy, fled into Arabia, unto Mahomet; by devilish policies, ambitious Mahomet forced the people to hold him for a Prophet, which damnable sect, until this day hath been nourished with the blood of many thousands" (1.7.55 ff.). A hundred years later, this legend was still prevalent, and Okeley perpetuates it.

It may not have been Okeley himself, however, who provided all of the Protestant, anti-Islamic theology in *Ebenezer; or, A Small Monument of Great Mercy*. In the "Preface," in fact, Okeley tells the reader that someone else has taken his manuscript and prepared it for publication: "It has been drawn out many years with my own hand, and many have had the perusal of it, . . . yet till I could prevail with a friend to teach it to speak a little better English, I could not be persuaded to let it walk abroad: the stuff and matter is my own, the trimming and form is another's." He may have composed the original manuscript not long after his homecoming, but it was printed much later, in 1675, thirty-two years after he returned to England from captivity. The theological apparatus that frames and accompanies Okeley's text may be a part of the "trimming and form" produced by Okeley's nameless "friend."

The Okeley narrative was reprinted in 1676, and a second edition appeared in 1684 with "A Further Narrative of James Deane and Others" appended. Deane's "Narrative" is a brief account of events that occurred after his ship, which was bound for Barbados, was taken by Algerian pirates on June 25, 1679. Deane himself lived as a slave in Algiers for two and a half years before being ransomed. A third edition of Okeley's text was printed much later, in 1764.

William Okeley, *Ebenezer;*[1] *or, A Small Monument of Great Mercy, Appearing in the Miraculous Deliverance of William Okeley, John Anthony, William Adams, John Jephs, John --,*[2] *Carpenter, from the Miserable Slavery of Algiers with the Wonderful Means of Their Escape in a Boat of Canvas; the Great Distress and Utmost Extremities Which They Endured at Sea for Six Days and Nights; [and] Their Safe Arrival at Mayork,*[3] *with Several Matters of Remark During Their Long Captivity and the Following Providences of God Which Brought Them Safe to England.*

Bless the Lord, O my soul, and forget not all His benefits, who redeemeth thy life from destruction, who crowneth thee with loving kindness and tender mercies.   *—Psalms 103:2–4*

LONDON: PRINTED FOR N. V. PONDER, AT THE SIGN OF THE PEACOCK, IN THE POULTRY NEAR CORN HILL AND IN CHANCERY LANE NEAR FLEET STREET, 1676.

Upon This Book and Its Author
This author never was in print before
And (let this please or not) will never more.
If all the press-oppressors of the age
Would so resolve, 'twould happiness presage.
He should as soon another voyage take,
As be obliged another book to make.
His canvas boat escaped seas and wind;
He fears this paper vessel will not find
Such gentle gales, when every reader hath
Power with a puff to sink the writer's faith.
For whoso prints a book goes off from shore

---

[1] *Ebenezer*: in Hebrew, literally, "stone of help." After a victory over the Philistines, Samuel erected a stone as a monument declaring, "Thus far the Lord has helped us" (I Samuel 7:12).

[2] *John --*: For some reason the last name of this member of Okeley's escape party has been omitted throughout the text. He is apparently a carpenter by trade and thus is given "Carpenter" as a pseudonym, but it is not his surname.

[3] *Mayork*: Majorca.

To hazard that which was his own before:
As one poor pinnace overmatched that fights
With an armado, so doth he who writes.
If books (like goodly merchant ships) set forth,
Laden with riches of the greatest worth;
With councils, fathers, text men, school men manned;
With sacred cannon[4] mounted at each hand;
Are hard beset and forced to make defense
Against armed atheism, pride, and impudence,
How can this little cockboat[5] hope escape,
When scripture suffers piracy and rape?
Noah's ark (wherein the world epitomized
And mankind in octavo was comprised),
Though in the deluge 'twas preserved found,
By infidelity itself lies drowned.
That Moses with a rod the sea should cane
And beat the coward streams into a plain,
With the same cane should broach a flint and bring
Out of its fiery womb a flowing spring;[6]
That a dry stick assigned for Levi's share
Should bud and blossom and ripe almonds bear;[7]
That Sampson with the jawbone of an ass
(And atheists think him one that lets it pass
Without a scomme[8]) should slay a thousand men
And being weary with the slaughter, then
The kind jawbone, that was his falchion[9] first,
Should turn a flagon and allay his thirst.[10]
These miracles, and all the sacred store
Which faith should grasp and piety adore,

---

[4] *cannon*: a pun on "cannon" as artillery and "canon" as religious law.

[5] *cockboat*: a small boat propelled by oars, especially a ship's tender.

[6] *Moses with . . . flowing spring*: Moses parted the Red Sea, and later, during the forty years of wandering in the Sinai Desert, he struck a rock with his staff and water came out (see Exodus 14:21 and 17:1–6).

[7] *dry stick . . . almonds bear*: In Numbers 17:8 God makes Aaron's staff miraculously bear almonds.

[8] *scomme*: scoff.

[9] *falchion*: sword.

[10] *Sampson with . . . his thirst*: See Judges 15:14–19.

Meet with arrests, arraignments, and a doom
More harsh than tales of heathen Greece or Rome.
Yet o the folly of confounded man!
Who cannot truth believe but fables can.
When truth that cannot lie shall be belied,
Its power defied, and weakness deified;
When our diseased appetite shall lust
For Egypt's leek[11] or Gibeon's moldy crust;[12]
Ephraim[13] will feed on ashes and disdain,
The manna comfits, and the candied rain.[14]
An heaven-born truth (like poor men's infants) may
For lack of godfathers, unchristened stay
And find no priest; when every stander-by
Will be a gossip to a great man's lie.
O miracle of love! God-Man was fain,
Each miracle he wrought, to make it twain,
The fact, and faith, too, else the fact in vain.
There is a generation alive
That live on lying miracles and thrive.
There is a guild of priests will undertake
To make that God who doth all wonders make:
Can make him, bake him, break him, eat him, too,
And with a thought can all again undo.[15]
Had but some monk this history to dress,
He would have made the iron teeth of th' press
Turn edge and grin,[16] to chew the stuff and style;

[11] *Egypt's leek*: The Israelites in the wilderness of Sinai complained that they had only manna to eat and wished for what they had eaten in Egypt (Numbers 11:4).

[12] *Gibeon's moldy crust*: The Gibeonites deceived the Israelites by offering dry and moldy provisions as evidence that they had come from a far country (Joshua 9:3).

[13] *Ephraim*: In the Book of Hosea, Ephraim is the object of divine judgment and is chastised for neglecting God's laws. See also Psalm 78.

[14] *manna comfits . . . candied rain*: God rained manna, or bread from heaven, to provide food to the Israelites in the wilderness of Sinai (Exodus 16:13–16).

[15] *guild of priests . . . again undo*: "Guild of priests" refers to the Roman Catholic clergy, and the allusion is specifically to the Catholic doctrine of transubstantiation (which claims that the communion rite produces a miraculous change in substance whereby the bread and wine become Christ's flesh and blood).

[16] *grin*: draw back the lips and gnash the teeth.

Compared with which all's pap in Mandeville.[17]
Had these five comrades been good sons of Rome,[18]
Nothing but miracles had brought them home.
Okeley had been inspired; Jephs had seen
An apron dropped down from heaven's Virgin Queen
To make a sail; Carpenter should have prayed
Saint Joseph to assist him at his trade;
And the next morn did in the cellar find
The keel, ribs, pins, all modeled to his mind.
An holy sea-calf in St. Peter's coat
Had then appeared and danced before the boat.
Saint Christopher[19] with a sweet babe on's back
Had stalked along to save from rock and wrack.
Saint Nicholas[20] (or in his shape, Old Nick)
Had with a straw steered the Boat Catholic.
The tortoise taken napping in the flood
Had first said grace and then become their food.
Yea, and his sacred shell had been preferred
To make fine combs for Wilgefortis' beard.[21]
And who can tell (for now 'tis thirty years
Since this strange expedition from Algiers)
What use the friars of Mayork have made
Of the poor skiff to raise their legend trade?[22]
But be it as it will, buy or not buy,
This book is Protestant and hates a lie.
The reader shall find in this breviary
All paternosters, not one "Ave Mary."
If gentleman and Christian may avail,

[17] *Mandeville*: Sir John Mandeville, putative author of a fourteenth-century book of fantastic travels.

[18] *good sons of Rome*: pious Roman Catholics.

[19] *Saint Christopher*: patron saint of travelers.

[20] *Saint Nicholas*: patron saint of sailors.

[21] *Wilgefortis' beard*: The Christian daughter of a pagan king of Portugal, St. Wilgefortis asked God to give her a beard so that she might evade the command of her father to marry a pagan prince. After a beard grew on her chin, her father had her crucified.

[22] *raise their legend trade*: increase the amount of money made from the sale of relics or from charitable contributions encouraged by the telling of legends, miracles, and the like.

If honor and religion can be bail
For this poor pilgrim's truth and faithfulness,
It may with leave and safety pass the press.
Let him who scorns to read, or reads to scorn,
And thinks this story might have been forborne,
First, buy the book, then give security
To do the like; the bookseller and I
Will give him bond, when he returns to land,
To pay a thousand pounds into his hand.
Meanwhile, this narrative (all plain and true)
Is worth a sixpence to a Turk or Jew,
But to a Christian (were the story gone)
The preface is a pennyworth alone.
The whole hath no erratas or mistakes,
Save what the printer and the poet makes.

A PREFACE TO THE FOLLOWING NARRATIVE

Courteous reader,

I do readily agree with thee that there is no sort of writings more liable to abuse than this of the narrative: lying much at the mercy of the composer to be corrupted and as much in danger to be misimproved by the reader. The reader therefore I am sure will demand good security that he is not imposed upon in the ensuing relation, and the writer craves leave, too, to maintain a modest jealousy, lest the reader should miss the benefit that is designed to him in it. The author will engage and pawn his credit not to wrong the narrative, and he would take some care also that the reader may not wrong himself.

It is very true that every narrator is under a strong temptation to season his discourse to the gusto[23] of the time, not imposing a severe law upon himself to report what was true but accommodating his story to the liquorish[24] appetite of others. I have observed that some men are ashamed to recount mean and humble matters: if they bring us anything below prodigy and miracle, if they stuff not their farces with gorgons, harpies, centaurs, and enchanted islands, they neither please

---

[23] *gusto*: taste.
[24] *liquorish*: greedy.

themselves nor hope to take their readers by the heartstrings. Hence it
is that we have so many lean, barren stories, larded with the additaments[25] of fruitful invention, as if they had been penned by the pattern
of Xenophon's *Cyrus*.[26] *Non ad historiae fidem, sed ad justi imperii
exemplar:*[27] not for counterpanes[28] of truth but counterfeits of fancy.
They tell us not what was really done but what they would have had
done if they might have had the contrivance of the scene and tragedy.
They first form ideas of ingenious romances in their own heads and
then obtrude them upon the world for historical verities.

Just as our hydrographers,[29] in the delineating of countries, with one
wanton, extravagant frolic of their graver can raise mountains where
nature left us valleys and sink deep valleys where God has stretched
out a champaign; can create bays and creeks where the Creator made
firm land; and jut out promontories and capes where there's nothing in
nature to answer them; and to fill up vacuities (out of pure good husbandry, that not an inch of ground may be lost) present us with flying
fishes, tritons, and mermaids which spend their hours *inter pectinem et
speculum;*[30] and lest *Mare del Zur*[31] should still be a desolate wilderness, have courteously stocked it with the Painter's Wife's Island and
terra incognita:[32] at this rate are we dealt with by this kind of men who
love to blow up lank stories into huge bladders and then put something
in them to make them rattle to please children, and yet they are but
bladders still, though swelled with the tympany[33] and wind colic.[34]

[25] *additaments*: added ingredients.

[26] *Xenophon's* Cyrus: the *Cyropaedia*:, by the Greek historian Xenophon. It is a
romanticized account of the education of Cyrus the Great of Persia.

[27] Non ad . . . imperii exemplar: Latin: "Not for the sake of historical truth but for
the example of just authority."

[28] *counterpanes*: copies.

[29] *hydrographers*: makers of maps and seacharts.

[30] inter pectinem et speculum: Latin: "between the comb and the mirror."

[31] Mare del Zur: Spanish: *Mar del Sur*, i.e., the South Seas.

[32] *stocked it* . . . terra incognita: To avoid leaving a blank space on the map, the area
representing the unexplored South Seas has been filled with imaginary islands and
continents: "the Painter's Wife's Island" would probably be drawn with naked nymphs
or female natives (for whom the original model was a "painter's wife"), and *terra incognita* (Latin: "unknown land") would be the Australian land mass, which remained
unexplored until the eighteenth century.

[33] *tympany*: a swelling in the belly.

[34] *wind colic*: griping pains in the lower intestine caused by or accompanied by flat-
ulence.

There are also a sort of stories, which by the way of courtesy we miscall histories, that scorn to give us an account of anything but dreadful and terrible battles and how one great man above all the rest chopped off heads and arms, and cut off some sheer by the waist, and with his trenchant blade mowed down whole files of armed enemies, the fields all this while running with streams of blood and purple gore, and all this with as much confidence and exactness in every minute circumstance as if, like the familiar daemon of Paracelsus,[35] they had been enclosed in the pommel of the general's sword or had hovered like victory with her doubtful wings over both the armies, where they might securely take notes of all that was said or done, in Shelton's brachygraphy.[36] But from what principles or interests these warriors were acted, by what rules they proceeded, with what councils and intrigues designs were managed, and to what point all these policies steered, is as much below their spirits as above their abilities to inform us.

To secure the reader against the fear of such entertainment in this narrative, let him know that he shall meet with nothing in fact but what is precisely true. What of wonderment he may encounter was of God's own working, not of man's inventing. Let others make tragedies to gratify the bookseller and cheat the simple buyer; we need not Peter Lillicrap's *Essex Serpent*,[37] not Livewell Chapman's *Greater Monsters*,[38] to aggrandize our title page. God's works need no foil to set them off: the greatest beauty of truth is its nakedness and symmetry.

There is a vast difference between the most elaborate products of art and the most homely[39] pieces of nature, for though the former will needs ape the latter, yet how pitifully does she bungle in the imitation!

[35] *familiar daemon of Paracelsus*: A "familiar" or "daemon" is a spirit raised and controlled by magical means. Phillipus Aureolus Paracelsus (1493?–1541) was a physician and natural philosopher who claimed that such spirits could be raised and commanded by a mage (as Ariel is by Prospero in *The Tempest*).

[36] *Shelton's brachygraphy*: a system of shorthand outlined in S. Shelton's *Brachygraphy; or, The Art of Short-Writing* (London, 1672).

[37] *Lillicrap's* Essex Serpent: Peter Lillicrap (active 1647–72) was a London printer and pamphleteer. A pamphlet titled *A True Relation of a Monstrous Serpent Seen at Henham [in Essex] on the Mount of Saffron Walden* appeared in 1669.

[38] *Chapman's* Greater Monsters: Livewell Chapman (fl. 1651–65) was a London bookseller who in 1655 was accused of printing seditious pamphlets. Perhaps Okeley refers to the pamphlet that Chapman published in 1657 titled *A Monstrous Birth*.

[39] *homely*: simple.

Look upon the subtle point of the finest needle through a microscope, and you will soon be satisfied that art is but a dunce, for the needle will appear as blunt and dull as a drumstick, but come and view one of God's handiworks in the same glass, [e].g., the sting of a bee, and you shall see it perpetually acuminated[40] till it ends in something which the eye must either confess to be a point or nothing. The same difference we may observe between those romances which are the issues of fine wits and the serious, grave contrivances of divine providence. What clumsed[41] things are the Cassandras[42] to one of those pieces of proportion to be seen in God's government of this lower world! So that it were unpardonable to strive to recommend the wonderful providences of God to the genius of this age by a lie or to talk deceitfully for Him. Whatever therefore this narrative is, yet it's a naked account of His own workings, and gold needs no gilding.

But now the reader's great danger lies in running over some of God's works and yet not seeing God in His works. Little children, we see, do hugely please themselves with the gilded covers and marbled leaves of books but concern not themselves [with] what is within, and if they chance to look a little overly upon the forms and shapes of the letters yet understand not the sublime matter that may be couched in them; now, to divide the words from the meaning is morally to annihilate them, and so whilst they see letters and word only, they see just nothing. There are a great many such *paido-gerontes*,[43] such old children in the world that gaze upon the surface of God's works but never are led by them to admire the wisdom, power, goodness, and holiness of God. They deal with the works of providence just as they do with the works of creation. God has engraven his own name in legible characters upon the heavenly bodies. The stars in their single beauties, their combined asterisms,[44] their mutual aspects, their intricate yet regular motions, speak their author. Nay, upon the lowest recreations, the leisure sports of nature,

---

[40] *acuminated*: brought to a point.

[41] *clumsed*: dull, stupid.

[42] *Cassandras*: those who try to predict the future (Cassandra, the daughter of Priam, was given the power of prophecy by Apollo, but no one believed her predictions).

[43] paido-gerontes: Greek: "children who are old."

[44] *asterisms*: constellations.

there is written *Deus fecit*.[45] But now the common observer, whose thoughts are terminated by his eye and his eye with the visible heavens, as 'tis bespangled with glittering things called planets and stars, loseth quite their main design, which is to conduct and argue our thoughts up to a first cause; for they were not so much out[46] who cried up the music of the spheres to be so ravishing, and we should confess it, could we but hear them sing this anthem: "Glory be to God on high."[47] Can we be so brutish as once to imagine that the wise God who creates nothing little, nor for a little end, should create such great and glorious bodies only to be the objects of ignorant and blind amazement? Surely, no, but that by the contemplation of them we might be led into the admiration of Him whose being, wisdom, power must needs be infinitely glorious when His very works are excellently so. Here then will be the reader's danger lest all his spirits should evaporate in a confused admiration that a boat, a little, a canvas boat, should like the ark convey so many persons so many leagues safe to shore, whilst he misses the true intent and meaning of it: to behold a watchful providence (as well as the being of a deity) over all affairs. Now, that he may not split upon this dangerous rock but improve the narrative to his best advantage, I shall submissively lay before him a few directions.

1. Sect. Learn from this narrative to trust and in all thy ways to acknowledge God, who by the most contemptible means can effect the most considerable things. Created beings, as they cannot act beyond the sphere of their activity, so neither can they operate further than the suitableness of their instruments will enable them. It were ridiculous to attempt to cut down a forest with a penknife or lave the ocean with a spoon, but if the great God can make the dullest tool to cut, can serve himself of the most unfit instruments and accomplish the most noble works with the most wooden engines, he will sure deserve our greatest trust and confidence. As great princes are attended with a numerous train of servants, more for state[48] than absolute necessity, so God uses second causes, not because he cannot work without them but to teach us to admire his strength in their weakness, his all-sufficiency in their insufficiency.

---

[45] Deus fecit: Latin: "God made [it]."

[46] *so much out*: so wrong.

[47] *"Glory be . . . on high"*: song of the angels praising God (Luke 2:14).

[48] *state*: display of power.

The Grand Seignior had heard of the famous achievement of Castriot's scimitar[49] and was very desirous to make an experiment whether its excellency answered the report. He sends for it, proves it, it does no execution; he sends it back with scorn and indignation, that lying fame should magnify a sorry ammunition sword so far above its merits, but Scanderbeg, before the messenger's face, hews in pieces helmets, corselets. "Go now," says he, "and tell your master, though I sent him my sword, I did not send him my arm. None can work with God's means that has not God's arm: hast thou an arm like God?" (Job 40:9). Here then the reader may see (and if he sees not, he forfeits his eyes) the same God who in an ark of bulrushes[50] preserved Moses and in another ark saved Noah, in a small canvas sculler[51] (which was our ark, though in a lesser volume) waft us over the ocean and bring us all safe to land. As God is seen in the smallest works of creation, so in the smallest instruments of His providence. The little fly or ant expresses creative power and omnipotency in miniature, as well as the great, castle-bearing elephant. I have read somewhere of a goldsmith that made a lock and key and chain so small and subtle that a fly would draw them all about a table and never be stalled. Surely the spectator would not predicate[52] the strength of the poor fly but the skill of the artist.

> *Est in tenuibus, et pusillis reculis*
> *Laus optimiq; maximiq; maxima.*
> Gaz. Pia Hilar.[53]

> The glory of the great wise king
> Shines greatly in the smallest thing.

---

[49] *Castriot's scimitar*: George Castriota (ca. 1404–68), or "Scanderbeg," was an Albanian hero and prince who was raised as a Muslim at the Ottoman court but renounced Islam, returned to Albania, and led the Albanians in successful resistance to the Turks. Legends about his exploits circulated throughout Christian Europe.

[50] *ark of bulrushes*: actually, a papyrus basket (Exodus 2:3).

[51] *sculler*: rowboat.

[52] *predicate*: commend.

[53] Gaz. Pia Hilar.: an abbreviated citation of the source for the Latin (from St. Jerome, who refers to the monk St. Hilarion, founder of a monastery in Gaza). *Pia* means "pious."

Indeed, our whole passage was wonder. Suppose we had met with one night of hazy weather; we might have plied back into the jaws of that destruction which we had so far escaped. Had we met with one storm (and an ordinary puff of wind had been a storm to us), it had presently overset us, but the same God that commands a calm for the halcyon commanded halcyon days and nights for us, till under the wings of his gracious care he had hatched his own purposes of mercy into perfect deliverance. It was a wonder, too, that in our six days' voyage in the Mediterranean, the very high road of navigation, both for honest men and knaves, merchants and pirates, we should not meet with one vessel, friend or foe. Had we met with a friendly vessel, they had pitied us, taken us up, and then the power of God had not been so signalized in our preservation. Had we fallen in with an enemy, we had immediately become a prey to their teeth: they had swallowed us up quick, we had made but one poor morsel to their greedy stomachs and thereby defeated a work of God gloriously begun and robbed Him of the revenue of his praise.

If then "they that go down to the sea in ships see the works of the Lord and his wonders in the deep" (Psal. 107:23–24), what wonders, what miracles of providence have we seen, and may others see in us, who went down to the sea, not in a ship but in a canoe, which for want of a better name we call a boat! Let the reader therefore admire God with me, and both of us with the Psalmist (Psal. 86:8): "Amongst the gods there is none like unto thee, O Lord, neither are there any works like thy works."

He deals unrighteously with God who measures Him by the smallness of the means that He uses and not by the greatness of those effects He produces by those means. And therefore,

> *Disce a cymbula, quisquis es; et Deo*
> *Da pro tenuibus, et pusillis reculis,*
> *Laudem optimoq; maximoq; maximam.*
> *Gaz. Pia Hilar.*

Let this our little skiff thy spirits raise,
To give to this great God thy greatest praise.

2. Sect. Let the reader improve this relation to fortify his faith against the little cavils of atheistical spirits who lay out their ill-placed wit in forging objections against Him that gave it. There is a creature famous in Proverbs 6: *Qui lacte materno impletus calcibus petit lactantem* (that being filled with the liberal dug ungratefully kicks his dam). Thus this sort of men are ambitious to be accounted witty in creating knots and difficulties in the historical passages of God's great providences recorded in Scripture and particularly in His preservation of Noah and his family in the ark, but he that had seen with us the watchful eye of God superintended and the steady hand of God to hold a poor canvas boat built without regular proportion, ill victualled, without anchor, helm, compass, or tackle, and thereby preserve the lives of five inconsiderable persons of no great use in the world and after six days' great extremity and distress land them all safe may easily credit the report how the same God should preserve eight persons, upon whose lives the repeopling of the whole world did depend, in a vessel of most exact proportions, strong built, and well laid in with all manner of provisions. He that can see a creator in the works of creation, and a governor in the works of providence, may reasonably believe all divine revelations.

3. *Sect*. Let all that would not abuse this narrative beware, lest whilst they are admiring providence in this instance of our preservation, they do not overlook those eminent appearances of God towards themselves every moment, which, though perhaps they carry not so much of rarity in them, yet may have in them as much of real power, wisdom, and goodness. We are apt to deal with our mercies, just as we do with our sins, where the commonness and frequency of either abates and takes off from the observation and notice which we owe them. We gaze and wonder at comets and their flaming beards but seldom admire the sun, a far more glorious body, because he rises and sets every morning and evening upon the just and the unjust. Dost thou admire God in our preservation? Learn to admire Him in thy own. Art thou surprised with wonder that we were kept a few days when there was not half an inch between us and death? Consider, God has kept thee many days and many years, and every minute of those many days and years, when there was but a hair's breadth between thee and death: dost thou then admire God preserved us alive in a vessel of cloth? Admire that God that holdeth thy soul in life, and that in a more frail vessel, a vessel of clay: dost thou still wonder we were not blown over with every breath of wind? Admire also that the lamp of thy life which thou carriest in a paper lantern is not blown out by every blast of sickness. But if thou

wilt still wonder how such a boat should carry us, then wonder also how thy food nourishes thee, how thy clothes keep thee warm, how thy sleep refreshes thee: there's not a moment in our lives but is filled with real miracle and wonder. "I will praise thee," says the Psalmist (Psal. 139:14), "for I am fearfully and wonderfully made." Let us all praise God, for we are fearfully and wonderfully preserved. If preservation be but a continued creation, how should we adore that power that created us once but preserves us always! God expects that we should equally magnify His skill in making us out of nothing and securing us that we drop not into nothing and as much admire His goodness that we crumble not, molder not, into our dust, as that we were at first formed out of dust.

4. Sect. Let the reader learn from our slavery to prize and improve his own liberty. If we serve not our God sincerely and cheerfully in plenty, He can send us where we shall serve our enemies in want. If we glorify Him not with our liberty but turn it into licentiousness, He can clap us up close where we shall learn to prize it higher and wish we had improved it better. It argues great disingenuity and baseness in our spirits that we provoke our God to teach us the worth of mercies by the want of them: "The Lord does not willingly afflict nor grieve the children of men" (Lam. 3:33), but we provoke Him to take his rod into His hand and lay it smartly upon our backs because that folly which is bound up in our hearts will not otherwise b[e] lashed out of us. Thus God threatened His people of old (Deut. 28:48): "Because thou servedst not the Lord thy God with joyfulness and gladness of heart, for the abundance of all things, therefore shalt thou serve thine enemies, in hunger, thirst, and nakedness and in the want of all things." Thus He taught Judah, by the captivity of Babylon, to prize the freedom of Canaan.[54] We might learn our duty much cheaper from God's word, but we, like truants, will not learn it there till God sends us to school with a rod at our backs.

5. Sect. Let all learn from hence, in what state soever the providence of God shall place them, therewith to be content. Perhaps thou art a servant to a Christian: dost thou murmur? It shows thou little knowest

---

[54] *He taught . . . of Canaan*: God taught the ancient Israelites (Judah) to value their freedom when He allowed Nebuchadnezzar, king of Babylonia, to conquer Jerusalem. After the conquest of the Jewish kingdoms in Canaan, thousands of Israelites were sent to live in bondage in Babylon.

what it is to be a slave to an imperious Turk. Thou servest him that
prays with thee and for thee: dost thou repine? God might have made
thee serve one who would curse and torture thee and make little provision for thy body and none at all for thy soul. The Christian religion
is surely the most excellent religion in the world because it holds the
balance so even between superiors and inferiors: it enjoins the one to
give the most full obedience and yet prohibits the other to exercise
rigor. It is peremptory for duty and yet abhors tyranny. Whoever has
known Turkish slavery is obliged to become a more loyal subject, a
more dutiful child, a more faithful servant; and whoever has not
known it is yet obliged to become all these lest God make him know it
and whip out of him that restive spirit of grumbling and disobedience
with the briars and thorns of the wilderness.

God commanded all masters amongst the Jews to allow their servants a day of rest (Deut. 5.14), and He gives this reason for it: "Remember that thou wast a servant in the land of Egypt." The equity of which
reason holds stronger for the Christian. Remember thou wast a servant
to the worst of masters, a drudge in the basest of works, and liable to
receive the worst of wages: has Christ set thee free? And art thou
become a servant to the best of masters? Employed in the most reasonable and honorable services? And in expectation of the most glorious rewards? Let it teach thee, if thou beest a master, to command gently; and if a servant, to obey cheerfully.

6. Sect. Let all learn to walk worthy of the Gospel. It is that which
sweetens all our mercies and mitigates the bitterness of all afflictions,
and if we sin away that, we either sin away all the rest or whatever is
useful and desirable in all the rest. If we enjoy the light and yet walk in
darkness, it's righteous with God to overspread our habitations with
Egyptian or Babylonish, Turkish or popish darkness. God can carry us
to Rome or Algiers or else send Rome and Algiers home to us: for what
should a people do with light that only intend to play or fight by it? The
once-famous churches of Asia are now swallowed up by the Ottoman
sword and the Mahumedan unbelief, and those sometimes famous
cities, Carthage and Hippo, which knew those burning and shining
lights, Cyprian and Augustine,[55] are now possessed with Moors and

---

[55] *Cyprian and Augustine*: saints and fathers of the early church in North Africa,
Cyprian as bishop of Carthage (248–58) and Augustine as bishop of Hippo (395–430).

defiled with the abominations of the greatest impostor that ever seduced the nations, but one.[56] And thinkest thou, O man, O Christian, that do'st these things so alien from the Gospel of Christ, that art drunk in the day and cursest that God whom thou worshipest, that thou shalt escape the judgment of God? I tell thee, nay, and I tell all those that read these lines and are guilty, and I tell myself, so far as I am guilty, that except we repent, we shall all likewise perish.

The Lord Jesus Christ, in his epistle to the church of Ephesus, gives her this memorial (Rev. 2:5): "Remember therefore from whence thou art fallen, and repent, and do thy first works, or else I will come unto thee quickly and remove thy candlestick out of its place, except thou repent." But Ephesus would none of his counsel, none of his caution, and Christ was as good as his word: he put out her candle and removed her candlestick.[57] I have often wondered what should be the grounds of their confidence, who speak as if the Gospel were entailed upon England by virtue of some ancient charter, as if God would make us exceptions from his general rule, which is to take away abused, despised means and mercies, and we must own much of prerogative in our case; but yet let us rejoice with trembling, lest when profaneness and debauchery dog religion so close at the heels, she fly not thither where she may find better quarter. It has made great impression upon me when I read the divine Herbert[58] in his "Church Militant":[59]

> Religion stands on tiptoe in our land,
> Ready to pass to the American strand.
> When height of malice and prodigious lusts,
> Impudent sinning, witchcrafts, and distrusts
> (The marks of future bane) shall fill our cup
> Unto the brim and make our measure up, etc.

---

[56] *the greatest imposter . . . but one*: presumably the Prophet Muhammad (second only to Satan?).

[57] *Christ was . . . her candlestick*: refers to the fact that Ephesus, in Asia Minor, was under Muslim rule.

[58] *the divine Herbert*: George Herbert (1593–1633), a Protestant divine and author of religious poetry.

[59] *"Church Militant"*: When the lines that follow were first submitted for publication in 1633 in Herbert's collection of verse, *The Temple*, the Cambridge licenser objected to the implication that true religion was preparing to leave England with the religious dissenters who were emigrating to the colonies.

7. *Sect*. Let it be every man's care to be found in God's way. The promise of protection is annexed to God's way (Psal. 91:11): "He shall give His angels charge over thee to keep thee in all thy ways." And the blessing of God is annexed to His own way, too (Psal. 128:1): "Blessed is every one that feareth God and walketh in His ways." When we are overtaken with the evil of affliction, let the first question we propound to ourselves be this: am I not in the way of transgression? Did this danger find me in my duty? Was I in God's highway or in some by-path of my own? Was I doing His work? Serving His glory? If we observe not the way of His precepts, I know no reason we should plead the promise of his protection. There are two things upon which I look upon it as my great duty to reflect: first, whether we were in the way of God's precepts when we fell into our enemies' hands; secondly, whether we were in the way of God's promise when we escaped out of their hands. For the former, I am abundantly satisfied that we were in the way of our duty, for we were sent out by commission from the right honorable Robert, earl of Warwick, the Lord Saye, and the Lord Brooke, who by patent from His Majesty, King Charles the First, were governors of the Isle of Providence,[60] whither we were bound. For the latter, if the more severe reader shall make it a question whether we could in faith expect protection in an adventure visibly so rash and precipitous and shall determine it against us that we tempted God by casting ourselves upon extraordinary protection, expecting deliverance without warrant, in a way little on this side miracle, I shall first say, let him shun that rock in his own conversation upon which he supposes us to have dashed. Let our shipwrack be a buoy to warn him of the like presumption, and let him learn more wisdom at our cost and charges. I shall further say, let him not discover greater rashness in censuring our adventure than he charges upon our adventure but modestly consider himself lest he also be tempted; and if we were guilty of folly, he may thus gain wisdom by our folly. But I shall add, extremity of misery is none of the

---

[60] *Robert, earl of . . . Isle of Providence*: The "Governors and Company of Adventurers for the Plantation of the Islands of Providence, Henrietta and the adjacent Islands" were granted a royal charter in 1630 under the leadership of Robert Rich, earl of Warwick; William Fiennes, Viscount Saye; and Robert Greville, Lord Brooke. These men were leaders of the Puritan opposition and after the dissolution of Parliament in 1629 they contemplated emigration to the New World colonies.

best counselors: let him put himself under our circumstances, and if cowardice did not hinder him from making our attempt, I am confident conscience would not. Our lives were bitter to us by reason of cruel bondage and (though mine was at that time much mitigated) yet there is a secret magnetism in a native soil, with which our hearts being once strongly touched, could never admit of the least variation but still pointed directly homewards; and such a land, too, as was like Goshen,[61] all light, when the land of our captivity was like Egypt, both for slavery and darkness, that might both be felt; and we thought it below men, for the love of life, to lose the reasons of our lives, for "All may have / (If they dare try) a glorious life, or grave" (Herbert, "The Church Porch").

In a word, though success will not warrant an evil action, yet there's much of justification in it, on the behalf of those which are not so; nor did we tempt God to work miracles but trusted Him to afford us special protection. But if this will not satisfy, let none imitate us wherein we failed but rather admire divine condescension that engaged in our deliverance, notwithstanding our failing.

8. Sect. Let all that read this narrative be instructed never to promise themselves great matters from men: I have observed it in the whole course of our captivity and constant tenor of those gracious providences which brought us thence, and the series of mercy, wisdom, and power that was our convoy home, that we ever found most of favor from God when we expected least from men and the least of kindness from those where we might, or thought we might in reason, have promised ourselves most. When we met with unexpected friendship, God would teach us to own Himself. When we met with disappointment, God would teach us the folly of idolizing the creature. I have seriously admired the compassion and relief we found at Mayork, and yet we knew them to be Romanists,[62] and they knew us to be Protestants; and how little respect we found from some of our own country at Alicante, Cadiz, and St. Lucar's,[63] and yet we were tied together in the strictest triple bonds of *Un Dieu, Un Roy, Un Ley*—One God, One King, One Law—but God was seen in both. I could relate a passage during our captivity in Algiers that had more of bitterness in it than in all our

[61] *Goshen*: fertile region of Egypt occupied by the Israelites (see Genesis 45:10).
[62] *Romanists*: Roman Catholics.
[63] *St. Lucar's*: Sanlucar, a Spanish port at the mouth of the Guadalquivir River.

slavery, and yet they were Christians, not Algerines; Protestants, not Papists; Englishmen, not strangers, that were the cause of it. But I have put a force upon myself and am resolved not to publish it. In our return homewards, we met with some who would talk to the grief of those whom God had wounded and was now in a way to heal again. Some would interpretatively say, with the churlish Nabal[64] (I Sam. 25:10), "Who are these? And whence come they? There are many servants nowadays that break away, every one from his master." But then was the season when we had most experience of God's faithfulness. And I shall never cease to own before the world the great respect we found from some English merchants to whom we were perfect strangers; and the civilities of Captain Goodson, Captain Smith, his mate, and his son are not to be forgotten.

Perhaps, after all this, the reader will be earnest to be satisfied why this narrative has lain so long dormant and appeared no sooner in the world? And I shall herein also endeavor to give him all reasonable satisfaction.

1. When we returned into England, we found our native country embroiled in a most dreadful civil war, and most men had enough to do to bear their own personal calamities and had little need to be troubled with the miseries of others. They were other kind of declarations that flew abroad then, and that was enough to supersede a narrative of this nature for some years.

2. The great mercies of God have not always their due weight upon our hearts at first, and I have received signal deliverances from eminent dangers since that great one, and it's well if all the mercies of our lives, all our deliverances put together, will amount to an argument strong enough to overcome our backwardness to make public acknowledgments.

3. I thought a long while that it was not worth the while to trouble the world with my particular concerns, till the importunity of several ministers and others (both in city and country) overcame my reluctancy, in whose reasons I did acquiesce.

4. I was conscious to myself of great unfitness to recommend it to public view in such a garb as might vindicate it from contempt; for

---

[64] *churlish Nabal*: churlish because he greeted the sons of David with insults, declaring them to be runaway servants and outlaws.

though it has been drawn out many years with my own hand, and many have had the perusal of it, have approved it and desired it, yet till I could prevail with a friend to teach it to speak a little better English, I could not be persuaded to let it walk abroad: the stuff and matter is my own, the trimming and form is another's, for whom I must vouch that he has done the truth, myself, and the reader, justice.

Having overcome all these difficulties, I do here erect my Ebenezer as a small monument of great mercy and as an obligation upon my soul to great duty and do pray that it may stand as an abiding witness for God in my conscience, that whenever I am tempted to sin, I may have an answer ready to stop the mouth of the tempter with indignation: how can I do this great evil and sin against my good God? When I am tempted to distrust, I may encourage my faith from my own narrative, saying, "Remember that God who delivered thee at the sea." When I am tempted to murmur, I may suppress those mutinous thoughts from my own narrative, saying, "Remember what thou enduredst in Algiers." When my heart grows cold and unthankful, I may chide and shame it, from my own narrative, into gratitude to God, that God who remembered us in our low estate, for His mercy endureth forever! Who preserved us at the sea, the great sea, for His mercy endureth forever! And secured us in a boat, a contemptible boat, for His mercy endureth forever! Who gave us favor in the eyes of strangers, for His mercy endureth forever! And opened to us the hearts of enemies, for His mercy endureth forever! And taught us to look up to His never-failing mercy when friends failed, for His mercy endureth forever! Who returned us safe to England, for His mercy endureth forever! We called upon Him in the day of our trouble: He delivered us, and we will glorify Him.

Reader, this narrative is true: peruse it seriously, and let not vanity tempt thee to say, "Things might have been better contrived, wiselier managed." It was God that did what was good in all: call not His wisdom in question because He did not create more wonders to gratify thy itching humor. Perhaps thou wouldst have had us been brought over upon a floating island or in a whale's belly, but I do not understand that the great God is bound to work miracles to save men's longings: God has done His work well, and none can mend it, for "what can the man do that comes after the King?" (Eccl. 2:12). For the matter of fact recorded herein, I might safely call God to record upon my soul that I lie not. The thing is known to many and has been sifted and scanned by such eyes and ears as are not guilty of easy credulity. I have evidence that may storm the most obstinate unbelief: Mr. Thomas Saunders, my wife's brother, being in Mayork not long after we came from thence, saw our boat hanging up for a monument upon the side of the great church there. Mr. Robert Hales, who was there 1671, assures me he saw the naked ribs and skeleton of it then hanging in the same place. Now I assure thee, reader, I should be much ashamed of myself if strangers unconcerned in my personal deliverances should be so far concerned as to preserve a memorial of them and yet unthankful I should erect no standard or pillar as an evidence of God's wonderful appearing for me.

It's true, I am informed by one that some affirm, there are more boats hanging up in Mayork, in memory of some suchlike escape. Now if others have really escaped the same danger, by the same means, it greatly confirms our narrative, and I do heartily rejoice that providence has appeared in the same method for others as for ourselves. We never intended to monopolize God's providences to our sole use and behoof, and we rejoice if our attempt and success may have encouraged others to make the like attempt and have found the like success, but I do assert it with great confidence that when we were in Mayork, there was no such boat hanging up, but the inhabitants there entertained our deliverance as such whereof they had no parallel. But if on the other side, these, or some of these succeeding boats, were but imposture, then the goodness of God appears more remarkable towards us, that we really were the subjects of such wonder, which others durst only pretend to, and it sets a luster upon this great salvation, which others have thought so considerable that they judged it worth the while to tell a lie to entitle themselves to the credit of it, for it's gold and silver, not copper or baser metals, that they who drive the coining trade strive to counterfeit.

Let then everyone that reads, understand and seriously sit down and consider with himself whether he has not had many eminent personal deliverances in one kind or other, which this marvelous providence of God towards us may not refresh his memory withal, and if he shall hence be taught to blush at his forgetfulness of lapsed mercies, if this narrative shall recover any lost providences and fix them on and rivet into his soul, if he shall find himself awakened to due thankfulness to God for all His benefits towards him, let him join with me in ascribing all the power, and therefore all the glory, to the Almighty, and let him kindly accept the assistance of him who shall reckon it amongst his other mercies to have been serviceable to anyone in reviving a better frame of heart. I am,

reader,

thy friend and servant,

W. Okeley

SECT. I. A BRIEF ACCOUNT OF THOSE PROVIDENCES WHICH LED TOWARDS OUR CAPTIVITY IN ALGIERS

This narrative would be too happy if it should not meet with some hasty and impatient spirits that grudge the time that's spent in preface and introductions, and such as these are wild to come at the story of the boat. All the rest is but one great tedious impertinency; they'll not give a fig for all the other. I shall make never the more haste for unreasonable importunity, but the remedy is in their own hands: they may turn over a few leaves and meet with it in its proper place, if they sit upon thorns. But to the more judicious and considerate, it will be acceptable to know how our foot was taken in the snare, as well as how the snare was broken and we delivered.

In the month of June, in the year of Our Lord, one thousand six hundred thirty and nine, in pursuance of a commission from the right honorable, the earl of Warwick, the Lord Saye, and the Lord Brooke, we took ship at Gravesend in the *Mary* of London, carrying six guns, Mr. Boarder being master and James Walker the master's mate. The ship was chiefly laden with linen and woolen cloth, having in her, seamen and passengers above sixty, bound for the Isle of Providence in the West Indies. Five weeks we lay in the Downs,[65] wishing and waiting for a wind, and then we set sail and came to an anchor near the Isle of Wight, but by this time all our beer in the ship stunk, and we were forced to throw it overboard and to take in vinegar to mix with water for our voyage. The next Lord's day[66] we set sail again, and coming between the island and the mainland, we stuck fast in the sands, but the tide coming in hove us off. These circumstances seem very inconsiderable to

[65] *the Downs*: a roadstead in the English Channel, along the east coast of Kent between North and South Foreland. It is protected by the Goodwin Sands, which act as a natural breakwater.

[66] *Lord's day*: Sunday.

those that were not concerned in the products of them, but God has given us the advantage and leisure to see what great things were in the womb of these little things. Had the wind stood longer against us, it had been more for us, and the danger had been past; had it stood less while against us, it had been for us, too, and we had been gone past the danger. But God appoints it the moment when it should come about to blow us into the mouths of our enemies. We see the truth of that, "Ye know not what to pray for." We prayed for a wind, and we had a whirlwind. If we always knew what mischief the answer of our prayers would do us, we should be glad to eat our words and pray against our prayers. Denial is often the best answer, and we had need leave all petitions to the wisdom of God to be interpreted according to His good pleasure and returned as they may be good for us and make most for His own glory. We were also taught that the sea may sometimes be our best friend and the earth our worst enemy and that nothing can do us good or hurt but by the direction and commission of the Almighty.

We were now three ships in company, and one of the other I remember carried nine guns; Mr. Church, master. The sixth day after our setting sail from the Isle of Wight, by break of day in the morning, we discovered three ships about three or four leagues to leeward. The masters of our ships presently consulted what was most advisable: whether to stay and speak with them or to make the best of our way. At last (upon what reasons I know not) it was determined that we should stay. It was not long before we discovered those other three ships to be Turk's men-of-war, who espying their prey, endeavored to come up with us, which about night they effected. Whilst they were coming up, the masters of our ships seemed resolved to fight them and accordingly made preparation to receive them, but in the night the master and company of the ship wherein I was altered their counsels, let their resolutions die, and agreed to run for it. Uncertain counsels never produce better success: when we might have gone, then we would stay; and when there was no way to escape, then we must needs attempt it. Had we either at first resolved not to fight them or, resolving to fight, had prosecuted our resolutions like men of courage, we might, perhaps, either have avoided the danger or bravely mastered it. The Turks, perceiving us begin to run, sent one of their number to chase us, whilst their other two attended the remaining two of our company till the morning. At break of day they began to fight us and after a short dispute boarded us and took us all three. In the *Mary*, six were slain and many wounded; so small was the difference between flight and fight, but that the death and wounds of those that fly are dishonorable but of them that fight, beautiful and glorious.

Many weeks they kept us close prisoners at sea. We found many English-men in their ships, slaves like ourselves, from whom we had no other comfort but the condoling of each other's miseries and that from them we learnt a smattering of the common language,[67] which would be of some use to us when we should come to Algiers, whither, after five or six weeks, we were brought.

SECT. II. THE DESCRIPTION OF ALGIERS, WITH
THEIR MANNER OF BUYING AND SELLING SLAVES

Algier is a city very pleasantly situated on the side of the hills overlooking the Mediterranean, which lies north of it, and it lifts up its proud head so impe-riously, as if it challenged a sovereignty over those seas and expected tribute from all that shall look within the straits. It lies in the thirtieth degree of lon-gitude and hath somewhat less than thirty-five degrees of north latitude. The city is considerably large, the walls being above three miles in compass, beau-tified and strengthened with five gates: *Port Marine* towards the north and *Port Piscadore* not far from thence; and *Porta Nova* towards the south, built, as they report, by the Spaniard whilst it was in their possession; the West Gate, which they call *Bubawite*; and the Eastern Gate, which in their tongue is called *Bubazoon*. They have also several strong castles besides that upon the point of the mole, so that the town is judged impregnable. The city is built very stately and yet more strong than stately, and more famous than strong, but not more famous for anything than for infamy, being the retreat, the nest, of those Turkish corsairs which have long tyrannized in and been a terror to the neighboring seas. It is supposed by some to contain four thousand fami-lies, by others, four score thousand persons, but they must needs be very short in their reckoning, it having been judged, that of all nations, there could be no less than twenty-five thousand slaves. The private buildings are very beautiful, flat-roofed, adorned with galleries towards their courts, supported by pillars. And they may afford to build sumptuously because they build at cost and with other men's hands. Their temples are also very magnificent and much too good for their religion, whose practice and conversation speaks them to say, "There is no God."[68] And yet we read of a religious thief who

[67] *the common language*: the lingua franca, a hybrid dialect used by merchants throughout the Mediterranean.
[68] *There is no God*: a mocking allusion to the first "pillar" of Islam, the *shahadah*, or profession of faith: "There is no god but Allah, and Muhammad is the Messenger of God."

never went about the works of his calling (for so he called stealing) but he would solemnly implore the assistance of his idol: a strange god, sure, that would be accessory to his devoto's[69] robberies; and a strange worshiper, that either hoped to flatter his god to become his accomplice in villainy with the vow of a good round share of the booty or would be such a fool to think that god worth the worshiping that should be thus flattered. They have also many stately baths, to which the men resort in the morning and the women in the afternoon. But they want one, worth them all, wherein they might by faith and repentance wash away their filthiness.[70]

To this fair city we were brought, yet in our eyes it was most ugly and deformed, for the French proverb is universally true: *"Il n'y a point de belle prison"* (there is no such thing as a fair prison). I confess, for a jail, it's one of the best built that I have seen. There's nothing that the soul of man bears with more regret than restraint: the body itself is judged by some to be but the soul's little-ease,[71] or cage, where though it seems to dwell, yet 'tis but in honorable durance;[72] and though it dares not break the prison, yet it listens and longs for a jail delivery. There can be nothing large enough for a soul but God, from whom since it once at first came, it must needs be restless till it return to him again; and surely it has much forgot its self and extract,[73] if it can take up with satisfaction in anything on this side its Creator.

As soon as we were put ashore for the first night, we were locked down in a deep, nasty cellar. Some inconveniences we felt, but they were nothing to what we feared. The next day we were carried or led, or rather driven, to the viceroy's (or bashaw's) palace,[74] who according to the custom and his own right, is to have the tenth man for his dividend of the slaves.

When the next market day came, we were driven like beasts thither and exposed to sale; and there is a great deal of God's goodness in that one word, that it was not to the slaughterhouse to be butchered, as well as to the market to be sold. Their cruelty is great, but their covetousness exceeds their cruelty; could they make as much of us dead as they make alive, that so both the interests of cruelty and of covetousness might be secured and reconciled, we

---

[69] *devoto's*: zealous worshiper's.

[70] *one, worth . . . their filthiness*: the baptismal font (implying a conversion to Christianity).

[71] *little-ease*: a prison, specifically the name of a dungeon in the Tower of London.

[72] *honorable durance*: imprisonment without dishonor (playing against the prevalent usage, "durance vile").

[73] *extract*: essence.

[74] *bashaw's palace*: palace of the Ottoman-appointed viceroy of Algiers.

are well assured which way it should have gone with us. But it must be a great deal of tallow and fat that will answer two or three dollars a month.

Their manner of selling slaves is this: they lead them up and down the fair, or market, and when a chapman[75] bids any money, they presently cry, "a-rache! a-rache!" That is, "Here's so much money bidden, who bids more?" They that cheapen[76] the exposed slaves are very circumspect persons: they carry their eyes in their heads, as well as their money in their purses, and use the one in laying out the other, for they are loath to buy a pig in a poke. Their first policy is to look in their mouths, and a good, strong entire set of grinders will advance the price considerably; and they have good reason for this practice: for first, they are rational creatures and know that they who have not teeth, cannot eat; and they that cannot eat, cannot work; and they that cannot work, are not for their turn; and they that are not for their turn, are not for their money. And secondly, they intend to keep them at hard meat[77] all the year, and it must not be gums but solid teeth (nay, if it were possible, case-hardened teeth) that must chew it, and when all is done, they had need of the ostrich's stomach[78] to digest it. Their next process is to feel their limbs, as whether there be any fracture or dislocation in the bones, anything analogical to spavin or ringbone,[79] for these will bring down the market wonderfully, and to be clean-limbed, close-coupled,[80] well jointed, will advance it as much. The age is very considerable, but they that sell them did not breed them, and therefore they know nothing, more or less, of that. Two ways they have to find out the age: the one is to stand to the courtesy of the slaves,[81] but they are not bound to make any such discovery, and therefore they go by general conjectures from the beard, face, or hair; but a good set of teeth will make anyone ten years younger and a broken one ten years older than the truth; for if they were five hundred years old, all is a case,[82] if they could but eat and work, or if they could not eat, yet if they could but work, or if neither

[75] *chapman*: trader or dealer.

[76] *cheapen*: haggle over.

[77] *hard meat*: "corn and hay used as fodder, as opposed to grass" (*O.E.D.*) and also "under close confinement" (*O.E.D.*).

[78] *the ostrich's stomach*: the ostrich was proverbial for its ability to eat the indigestible.

[79] *spavin or ringbone*: bone diseases affecting horses and causing lameness.

[80] *close-coupled*: used to describe horses that have strong joints in the back and hindquarters.

[81] *stand to . . . the slaves*: rely upon the slaves themselves to state their true ages.

[82] *all is a case*: it is all the same.

eat nor work, if their skins would but fetch in the money again. You shall have the seller commend his goods to the sky and the buyer, on the other hand, as much undervalue them, and the true market price commonly lies just between them, but so it is all the world over.

"O," says the seller, "mark what a back he has, what a breadth he bears between the shoulders! What a chest! How strong set! How fitted on the nonce[83] for burdens! He'll do but e'en too much work."

"Pish," says the buyer, "He looks like a pillard,[84] like a very meacock[85] at his provender, and on that seems to be surfeited."

But they are very curious in examining the hands, for if they be callous and brawny, they will shrewdly guess they have been inured to labor; if delicate and tender, they will suspect some gentleman or merchant, and then the hopes of a good price of redemption[86] makes him salable.

When any are sold, they must be trotted once more to the viceroy's that he may have the review of them, and if he likes any of them at the prices they went off at, there's no more dispute, they are his own.

As for myself, I was sold the first market day to a Tagarene,[87] and that the reader may not stumble at that hard word, he may understand that when the Moors were driven out of Spain[88] by Ferdinand the Great, they, upon their return into Africa, assumed names that might argue gentility and be an evidence of their ancient extract from such places where they had been great dons, and accordingly there are many families thus denominated as Tagarenes, Jarbeens, etc.

SECT. III. AN ACCOUNT OF SOME DIFFICULTIES THAT
I MET WITH DURING MY CAPTIVITY IN ALGIERS

Those miseries which it is dreadful to endure are yet delightful to be remembered, and there's a secret pleasure to chew the cud and ruminate upon escaped dangers; however, the reader may afford to run over with his eye in an hour that which I ran through in five years and, supposing him-

[83] *fitted on the nonce*: well suited for the particular purpose.
[84] *pillard*: robber.
[85] *meacock*: weak, timid creature.
[86] *redemption*: ransom.
[87] *Tagarene*: a Morisco from Andalusia.
[88] *the Moors . . . of Spain*: Ferdinand II expelled the Moors from Granada in 1502. Later, in 1609, Philip III expelled the Moriscos, those Moors who remained in Spain and were forced to convert to Christianity.

self safe upon the amphitheater, may behold poor slaves combating with beasts below.

The first adventure I met with after I was brought to my patron's[89] house (for so I must now style him) had well nigh cost me my life. My patron's father, being desirous to see his son's pennyworth, commanded me up into a gallery which looked into the court. He began to insult over me with insupportable scorn, reflecting upon me because I was a Christian, and cast out some expressions which did really reflect upon the person of my Redeemer (though I have heard worse since). My neck was not yet bowed nor my heart broken to the yoke of bondage; I could not well brook because I had not been used then to such language, and because I could not express myself in the Moresco, or *lingua frank*,[90] I supplied it with signs; and imitating the cobbler's yark,[91] I signified both ways as well as I could that their prophet was but a cobbler. I confess my meaning was no more but that Mahomet, by the help of Sergius, a Nestorian monk, and Abdalla the Jew, had patched up a cento[92] of Jewish and monkish fopperies, which was now their religion. But he, without the preamble of many railing words, fell upon me with severe blows. Whatever rage and fury his hands or feet could execute, that I felt, and my entreaties did but enrage his choler, so that I saw I might sooner blow out the fire with a pair of bellows than lenify[93] his passion with prayers. I had no other way but this, to make an offer of leaping down out of the gallery into the court, and therefore clapping my hands upon the rails, as if I would throw myself headlong down over them and rather choose to receive my death from the pavement than his hands, he presently assuages, if not his rage, yet the execution of it. The old gentleman knew very well that if I lost my life, his son must lose his present money and future profit; for there's little made out of a dead man's skin, and therefore he respites my further punishment till my patron's return, and then indeed this reputed blasphemy of mine with full cry was carried to his ears, and it lost nothing in the telling but was aggravated to purpose. My patron, being naturally a very passionate man, said nothing but without examination drew out his long knife (which they constantly wear by their sides) and made at me, and had there doubtless put an end to my life and captivity at once, had not his wife, who was there seasonably present,

---

[89] *patron's*: master's.
[90] *Moresco, or* lingua frank: lingua franca.
[91] *yark*: the action of drawing stitches tight when making shoes.
[92] *cento*: patchwork text, plagiarized from various sources.
[93] *lenify*: soothe and moderate.

taken him in her arms and sweetened him into more moderate counsels. Some will be ready enough to say that I was but a martyr to my own folly: this was not a place for dispute, but obedience. Well, I learnt from hence two lessons: one, that when the body is a slave, the reason must not expect to be free; and where the whole outward man is in bondage, the tongue must not plead exemption. A second, that it's fair for slaves to enjoy the freedom of their own consciences without reviling another's religion, though erroneous, and this wit I bought, as it fell out, a pretty good pennyworth.

When the storm was over, my employment was assigned me (for they had rather see a slave dead than idle), and for about half a year it lay in trudging on errands, bearing burdens, and discharging other domestic services at command, wherein the only consideration was that it was commanded, and not what was commanded.

At this time my patron had a part in a man-of-war which carried twelve guns. She being at sea (with some others of the same place) met with an English merchant laden with plate and other rich commodities from Spain and bound for London (one Isaac being master), and after a very sharp though short dispute, the Algerines carried her and brought her safe home. The adventurers divide their booty and being high-flown with this success, they resolve to fit her out again to carry more guns, and from hence grew my new employment. Upon the carpenters I attended, waited on the smiths to get the ironwork fitted and finished, and truly he allowed me more for portage than to the ordinary *hammels*, or common porters.

When this ship was now fitted for another adventure, my patron tells me I must go in her. It was a nipping word. I pleaded that I was no seaman, understood nothing of the mariner's art, and therefore as he could expect little service from me in that kind, so I must expect most rigorous treatment because I could not acquit myself in the service as well as others. He removed my pleas and promised I should not be wronged, but there was more at the bottom than all this: for here a case of conscience offered itself, whether I might without sin in any case fight against Christians on the p[a]rt of the common enemy of all Christianity? The best resolution I could give myself was this: that first, my employment would only lie in managing the tackle, which will kill nobody, but it was replied that without the due management of the tackle, all the guns in the ship would kill nobody. Secondly, therefore I answered that it was not evident that they would engage against Christians more than all the rest of mankind, for all the world are their enemies who are rich enough to invite them and too weak to resist them. But my patron had a solution worth all these: he told me peremptorily, I must and should go. I found myself under force. I was a pressed man who could not examine the justice of the cause. In a word, his commands were backed with compulsion, and whatever his authority was, he had more power than I had courage to deny or strength to resist, and go I did. Yet this I will say for him: he spoke to the captain and officers of the ship to treat me civilly, that is, less cruelly than other slaves were treated. He gave me some money also in my pocket, bought me clothes, and laid me in provision above the ship's allowance.

Nine weeks we were at sea, within and without the straits, cruising and picarooning[94] up and down. At last we met with one poor Hungarian-French man-of-war whom we took, and so returned.

My patron having been at great charges in fitting and manning out this ship, and the reprisals[95] so slenderly answering his great cost and greater hopes, told me I must allow him two dollars[96] per month and live ashore where I would and get it where I could. This was a hard chapter that he that could not maintain himself should be compelled to contribute to the maintenance of another. It was difficult to raise increase out of no stock and to pay interest out of no principal, but there was no contending. It cost me much debate with myself, and I turned my thoughts into all forms and shapes, but all projects that presented themselves were encumbered with so many difficulties that they amounted very near to impossibilities. The more I consulted, the further I found myself from a conclusion, and I could see no way but one (but that was worth a thousand, could I have made the best of it), and that was to commit myself to God, who had brought me into this strait, beseeching Him that He would bring me out of it.

But that my trusting to God might not be a cloak for laziness or a pillow for sloth to rest upon, I addressed myself to an Englishman whose condition was that of a slave, whose calling was that of a tailor. He at first word counseled me to come and stay with him, and he would teach me to work of his trade. I accounted nothing base that was honest, and necessity would ennoble a far meaner employment, and very readily closed in my thoughts with his motion and was suddenly elevated into huge hopes that I should now be in a capacity to answer my patron's demands and escape his lash. But my straits were not (it seems) great enough to glorify God, nor my condition mean enough to magnify his power in raising me. I was not reduced to that extremity which would make an opportunity to exalt his appearing mercy, for

---

[94] *picarooning*: keeping watch for a prize, as a pirate might do.
[95] *reprisals*: property taken by force.
[96] *two dollars*: two Spanish pieces of eight, each worth eight Spanish reals.

when I came to him the next day, I perceived by his silence that his mind was changed, and I was loath, either out of modesty or pride, to give him further trouble, and therefore interpreting his silence to be a more civil way of denial, I left him and once more launched out into the wide world.

In this forlorn posture I wandered, but neither knew nor much cared whither, though the wise God both knew and cared, and His providence directed me to another Englishman who was sitting in a little shop. He asked me, "What news?" And (as that which is uppermost always comes out first) I presently began the story of my desperate condition: how the rigid law of my patron had imposed two dollars per month upon me, and I knew not where to levy the least mite of it. He heard, considered, pitied my condition, and invited me to come and sit in the shop with him, but seeing nothing but bare walls, I asked him, "To what end? What trade should we drive there? There's not much difference between starving in the streets and in the shop."

"Countryman," said he, "I drive here an unknown trade. Here I sell lead, iron, shot, strong waters, tobacco, and many other things." This motion was a great deal too good to be refused, and I think at that time no tolerable condition would have stuck with me.

I acquainted my patron with my design, pleaded I wanted stock to set up with. He lent me a small modicum, and with another pittance that I had privately reserved of my own, I began to trade. That very night I went and bought a parcel of tobacco. The next morning we dressed it, cut it, and fitted it for sale, and the world seemed to smile on us wonderfully. In this way of partnership we continued for some while, and what we got clear, we divided every week according to the proportion of our respective stocks. In a while, finding the world to come in upon us, we ventured upon no less than a whole butt of wine. Some money we had, and some credit. This wine we drew out and got considerably by it. But it's very difficult to maintain moderation in an exalted state, for even our state was capable of better and worse, for my partner, being elevated with our good success, grew a good fellow and a bad husband, neglected his business, went tippling and fuddling[97] up and down, and the concerns of the shop and trade lay wholly upon my shoulders.

It fell out that one John Randal who with his wife and child were taken in the same ship with myself, being put to the same shifts with myself and, as 'tis very common, having a monthly tax imposed upon him by his patron, which he must scrape up where he could and besides maintain himself, his wife, and child, went up and down seeking for relief. At last the poor man

[97] *fuddling*: boozing.

straggled to our shop. His case made great impression upon me. I could not but consider the goodness of God to me, that should now be in a condition to advise and help another, who so lately wanted both myself, and it had this operation upon me, that I would not suffer a poor, distressed countryman, a fellow captive, a fellow Christian, to stand begging at that door where I had so lately stood myself. Shall I shut the door, or my heart, upon him when God had opened a door of hope to me in the day of my trouble? Shall I so ill requite the Lord's kindness to me? Surely that God who comforts us in our tribulations expects that we should comfort others in theirs (2 Cor. 1:4)? I had him therefore come in and, knowing him to be a glover by trade, advised him to learn to make canvas clothes for seamen that are slaves, and, for my own part, he should sit rent-free, but if my partner would insist upon his moiety, he must be willing to satisfy him, for I had no power to determine of another's right.

It were tedious to trouble the reader how I wore out three or four irksome years in this way of trading. All this while there was no dawning of deliverance from our bondage. As one year left us, another found us and delivered us over captives to the next. Our condition was bad and in danger every day of being worse, as the mutable humors of our patrons determined upon us, for our shop and trade was no freehold. The truth is, in time we were so habituated to bondage that we almost forgot liberty and grew stupid and senseless of our slavery. Like Issachar,[98] "we couched down between our burdens; we bowed our shoulders to bear and became servants to tribute" (Gen. 49:14–15) and were in danger to be like those Israelites in Babylon, who being once settled, "forgot Canaan and dwelt with the king for his work" (I Chron. 4:23). We seemed as if our ears had been bored,[99] and we had vowed to serve our patrons forever. Long bondage breaks the spirits; it scatters hope off and discourages all attempts for freedom. And there were more evils attended our condition than the bodily torture which we were always liable to and sometimes endured.

1. We were under a perpetual temptation to deny the Lord that bought us, to make our souls slaves that our bodies might recover liberty. As Satan

---

[98] *Issachar*: one of the tribes of Israel, described here as contented with its lot and willing to surrender its independence in subservience to the Canaanites.

[99] *ears had been bored*: a mark of a slave who loves his master and renounces his right to freedom after six years' labor: "His master shall pierce his ear with an awl; and he shall serve him for life" (Exodus 21:6).

once tempted Job to curse God and die,[100] so he knew how to change his note to us and accommodate his snare to our condition, to curse God that we might live. How many have made shipwreck of faith that they might not be chained to the galleys? I can never enough admire the grace of that promise (Psal. 125:3), "The rod of the wicked shall not always rest upon the lot of the righteous, lest the righteous put forth their hands to iniquity," nor ever enough adore the faithfulness of him, who "will not suffer us to be tempted above that we are able" (I Cor. 10:13).

And 2. Evil is the unmanning and dispiriting of the soul to worthy actions, for we are apt to put on the temper and spirit of slaves with the habit, and the Christians of the Greek communion are a very sad instance of this truth.[101]

And 3. We were very much at a loss for the preaching of the Word, and yet herein the gracious God stepped in for our relief.

SECT. IV. HOW GOD PROVIDED FOR OUR SOULS BY SENDING US AN ABLE MINISTER TO PREACH THE GOSPEL TO US IN OUR BONDAGE

The gracious God, looking upon the affliction of His poor servants and remembering us in our low estate, was pleased many ways to mitigate the load of our captivity. We have reason to say, with the church (Ezra 9:9), "We were bondsmen, yet our God hath not forsaken us in our bondage, but hath extended mercy to us, to give us a reviving and a [wall] in His holy place." And thus he brought about His design of grace and mercy. There was an English ship taken by some of our Algerine pirates, and in her one Mr. Devereux Sprat,[102] a minister of the Gospel. It deserves our consideration and greatest admiration that the wise God should supply our necessities at the cost and charges of others of His dear servants, but thus providence sent Joseph into Egypt, where he endured a thirteen years' slavery that he might preserve the lives of his father's family, within whose narrow walls the most

[100] *Satan once . . . and die*: See Job 3.

[101] *the Christians . . . this truth*: This refers to the alleged complacency of Greek Orthodox communities who were tolerated as *dhimmi* subjects under Ottoman rule. Greeks made up a large portion of the population of Istanbul and other major cities in the Ottoman empire.

[102] *Devereux Sprat*: There is a manuscript narrative extant in which Spratt recorded his own experience as a captive in Algiers (see bibliography).

visible church of God in those days was enclosed (Gen. 45:5). Now, some of us observing this Mr. Sprat to be a person of very sober, grave, and religious deportment, we addressed ourselves to him and humbly entreated him that we might enjoy the benefit of his ministry; in order whereto, we desired him that he would compound with his patron at so much a month as he could, and because we were abundantly convinced of our duty to administer to him of our carnal things, who should administer to us of his spirituals, we engaged to allow him a competency[103] to maintain himself and satisfy the expectations of his patron. The good man hearkened to us with much readiness, and now indeed we found our burdens much lighter and our conditions not press so hard upon our spirits. Thrice a week this godly, painful[104] servant of Jesus Christ prayed with us and preached to us the Word of God. Our meeting place was a cellar, which I had hired at some distance from our shop, where I stowed some goods that were peculiarly my own when we fell into a greater stroke of trade.[105] To our meetings resorted many, sometimes three or fourscore, and though we met next [to] the street, yet we never had the least disturbance from the Turks or Moors, for whilst we intermeddled not with their superstitions but paid our patrons their demands, we might without any disturbance from them worship our God according to our consciences. It's true that such were the circumstances of the slavery of many poor Christians that they could not attend, and such the wretched carelessness of others that they would not attend, and such the provisions that God had made for others, by other means, that they needed not, perhaps, attend upon God's worship with us; but thus was our God pleased to give us the means of strengthening our faith and comforting our drooping spirits.

At length came one Captain Wildy of Ratcliff to trade there, who with the assistance of the Leghorn merchants freed our minister from his patron. After his freedom from his patron, yet there remained a duty of sixty dollars, which was a particular charge payable to the public treasury, before he could be fully enlarged from the city. We petitioned therefore the captain that he might, and Mr. Sprat himself that he would, still continue to be serviceable to our poor souls in the work of the Gospel, and we easily prevailed and had the benefit of his ministry whilst I stayed there.

---

[103] *competency*: sufficient income.

[104] *painful*: painstaking.

[105] *fell into . . . stroke of trade*: began to do a larger volume of business.

SECT. V. SOME REMARKABLE OBSERVATIONS THAT I
GLEANED UP WHILST I REMAINED IN ALGIERS

They that are pressed with their own personal grievances have little leisure
to look abroad and observe the motions of others, and indeed our own afflictions, however sweetened, lay still gnawing and grating upon our spirits that
we must needs be very ill qualified to treasure up materials to make a history.
Such a design required leisure, liberty, privacy, retiredness, intelligence, and
strict correspondence, to all which we were perfect strangers. Yet sometimes
I could make a truce with my troubles and obtain so long a cessation from
my vexatious pressures as to make observation.

And 1., the hypocrisy of their profession was so notorious that he must put
out his eyes that did not see it. One month in the year they observe their
Ramadan, which is their Lent, and indeed they observe it by day with more
than monkish austerity, imposing upon themselves a total abstinence. An
observation which they may be presumed to owe to that Nestorian monk[106]
who clubbed with Mahomet in the cursed invention of the Alkoran. But for
all their demure quadragesimal[107] looks by day, they give or sell themselves
to commit with greediness all manner of the most execrable villainies by
night, and they cheat themselves with this evasion: that forsooth Mahomet
commanded them to fast so many days but not so many nights. For now they
beat up their drums[108] and call their friends first out of bed, then out of doors.
They provoke, challenge, dare one another to eat, drink, and run into all
excess of riot. They will neither spare man in their rage nor woman in their
lust. The two hungry meals of the day makes the third of the night an
errand[109] glutton. By day they create themselves a purgatory, and by night the
poor slaves find a hell. Now, when they have crammed their guts all night
and are maw-sick[110] in the morning, they put on their Lenten face again and
call that a fast which is but physic[111] and pretend religion for that which they

[106] *that Nestorian monk*: Sergius, who according to the tradition of Christian, anti-
Islamic polemic conspired with Muhammad to invent a new religion.
[107] *quadragesimal*: forty-day, i.e., Lenten.
[108] *they beat up their drums*: Drums were beaten by the *musahhariti*, who came
each morning during Ramadan to rouse Muslims so that they could wake up and eat
a meal before the sun rose and the day's fast began.
[109] *errand*: thorough.
[110] *maw-sick*: nauseous or vomiting.
[111] *physic*: a necessary remedy.

are compelled to by nature. That is, they fast when they can eat and drink no longer. But indeed their fast by day is nothing but a dry drunkenness, for when they have drunk and whored themselves into sin, they fancy they merit a pardon by abstinence, a piece of hypocrisy so gross that whether it be to be sampled anywhere in the world, unless perhaps by the popish carnivals, I cannot tell.

2. I could not but observe that though they allow that every man may be saved in that religion he professes, provided he walks by its rules, and therefore that at last, the Jews, under the banner of Moses, the Christians, under the banner of Christ, and the Turks, under the banner of Mahomet, shall all march over a fair bridge into I know not what paradise, a place far beyond the Elysian fields, yet they afford no mercy to one who having once professed, afterwards revolts from Mahumetanism, an instance whereof I shall now present the reader with.

The Spaniards every year return a considerable sum of money to Algiers, to be employed in the redemption of such of their own country as are there in slavery. Some say there is a particular treasury set apart for that service, but this I know: that they use the charitable benevolence of well-disposed persons to advance it. Now there was a Spanish friar that was a slave, who being passed by in the redemption that year, took it very heinously[112] to be neglected, thought himself much wronged, hereupon he grows discontented, and the Devil (who never works with greater success than upon that humor) takes the advantage to push him on, and he, in a pet, renounces the Christian religion, declares himself a Mussulman, and accordingly appears in his Turkish habit. I knew him very well by sight: he was a fat, corpulent person, but after he had turned renegado, I observed him to become strangely lean and dejected in his countenance. But I little suspected that the root of his distemper lay in his conscience, but it seems he had severely reflected upon his apostasy, for he had not renounced only his popery but his Christianity. His own conscience, which was a thousand witnesses against him, was a thousand tormentors to him. Long he bore its secret and stinging lashes, but when he could no longer stand under them, he goes to the viceroy's palace and there openly declares himself a Christian and protests against the superstition and idolatry of Mahomet, as a most execrable and damnable imposture. Immediately he is convened before the council, and there strictly examined. He persists resolutely in his profession, whereupon he is clapped in irons and for some time there secured. Now, they pretended this reason for their

[112] *heinously*: angrily.

procedure: that there had been some practicing and tampering with him, either morally by argument or naturally by some dose of intoxicating drugs, that had thus distempered him, for loath they were it should be thought that any man of sound mind, or master of his reason, would ever revolt from their religion. But when they saw him fixed in his resolution and that neither what he felt or might fear, what they had inflicted or could threaten, did unhinge him from his profession, they proceeded to the last remedy and inexorably condemned him to the fire, a way of punishment which they learnt from the Spaniards themselves, who first set up the Inquisition against the Moors and have now turned the edge of it against the Protestants. And now they proceed to the execution of the sentence, which was performed with some pomp and state. And first they formed a crown with a cross upon the top of it, within the plates and bars whereof they put flax. Thus crowned, they guard him through the city, out of the West Gate about half a mile, which was the appointed place of execution. And first one puts fire to the flax in his mock crown, to take possession of his head in the name of the rest of his body. At first he shook it off, but another put fire again to it with a cane, and then the poor man stood patiently, and presently they put fire to the whole pile and there burnt him. I saw some of his bones and scorched flesh after he was dead, and the same evening came a zealous Spaniard and carried away some of his scorched flesh and bones as the holy relics of a martyr, saying, "I have now done enough to make satisfaction for all the sins that I have committed."

3. It's worth admiration to see in what great awe they stand of the meanest officer, who is known to be such by his turbant[113] and habit. If any affray be made, or a murder committed in the streets, the chiaux,[114] or officer, presently comes without any weapon or person to assist him, and if he seizes the offenders, none is so hardy as to resist even unarmed authority.

4. The great reverence which the Moors pay to the Turks, though both Mahometans, is remarkable. If a Moor shall dare to strike a Turk, he is punished with great severity. I saw two Moors whilst I was there whose right hands were chopped off for this one crime and hung about their necks in strings. The one was set upon an ass, the other walked by on foot, the common crier proclaiming before them their offense through the chief streets of the city. I saw another also with his heels tied to a horse's tail. He was wholly naked, only he had on a pair of linen drawers, and thus was he dragged through the streets. It was a most lamentable spectacle to see his body all

---

[113] *turbant*: turban.

[114] chiaux: or *chiaus*, a Turkish term meaning "sergeant" or "messenger."

torn with the rugged way and stone, the skin torn off his back and elbows, his head broken, and all covered with blood and dirt, and thus was he dragged through the city out at *Bubazoon*, or the East Gate, where he ended his miserable life.

Two others of their own countrymen I saw executed in a most terrible and dreadful manner (but either I did not know or do not remember their crimes). The one was thrown off from a high wall, and in his fall he was caught by the way by one of the great sharp hooks which were fastened in the wall. It caught him just under the ribs, and there he hung roaring in unspeakable pain till he died. The other was fastened to a ladder, his wrists and ankles being nailed through with iron spikes, in such a posture as somewhat resembles the celebrated cross of St. Andrew,[115] and lest his flesh and sinews should fail and the nails not hold, his wrists and ankles were bound fast with small cords to the ladder. Two days I saw him alive under this torture. How much longer he lived under it I cannot tell.

5. They are generally great enemies to debauchery in public. It's a great scandal to them when they see any Christians (who brought that bestiality out of their own countries with them) to be guilty of it. I have heard them say of a drunken slave, "A Christian? No, he's a swine." And though they will indulge themselves by night (especially in their Ramadan month), yet woe be to him that shall offend by day in that kind. There was an Englishman who had brought over with him his drunken humor, and his captivity had not made him sober, and when religion has not firm hold of the heart, a little matter will make such a one let go his hold of religion. This Englishman turned a renegado, and of a drunken Christian became a drunken Turk, and was not able to keep the pot from his head[116] during their holy time of Ramadan. Being one day found thus like a sot, he was brought into the *cassabal*, or chief court of judicature, where he was adjudged to receive many hundreds of violent blows, some upon his naked back and reins,[117] others upon his naked belly. He could not creep from the place of punishment but was carried away by the *hammels*. His belly and back were so excoriated that Sampson Baker, an Englishman who was his chirurgeon,[118] assured me he was forced to cut off abundance of his flesh before he could be cured.

---

[115] *cross of St. Andrew*: St. Andrew is said to have died on an X-shaped cross.
[116] *keep the pot . . . his head*: restrain himself from drinking to excess.
[117] *reins*: kidneys.
[118] *chirurgeon*: surgeon.

6. What cruelties they exercise upon poor slaves need not be mentioned, and there will be an occasion to speak of the most ordinary way of punishment ere long. Let it suffice that all is arbitrary and unlimited. If a patron shall kill his slave, for aught I could perceive, he suffers no more for it than if he should kill his horse. There was a Dutch youth, a slave to a Turk, who upon some provocation drew his knife at his patron. For this offer, he was sentenced to be dragged out at one of the gates and there to have his arms and legs broken in pieces with the great sledgehammer, which sentence was accordingly executed, for though I could not see his face for the crowd, yet I heard the blows and the miserable cries of the poor dying young man.

SECT. VI. THE GRIEVOUS PUNISHMENT INFLICTED UPON
JOHN RANDAL, THE AUTHOR'S DANGER AND DELIVERANCE
FROM THE SAME, UPON PRETENCE THAT THEY HAD
ATTEMPTED TO MAKE AN ESCAPE

It is time to reassume my own concerns and look a little into my own condition, which, through the good providence of God, was much better than that of many of my poor brethren and fellow captives, and yet I met with great ebbings and flowings in my tranquillity. Whilst I was managing my trade very stoutly and successfully (John Randal working with me in my shop), my partner having now knocked off[119] and left all to me, one day I changed a twenty-shilling piece of gold for silver with a friend, and having the money chinking in my hand, John Randal asked me what I did with so much money. I desired him to keep it for me till our return, and he should know; for he being not very well, we agreed to walk out of the town to take the fresh air, a liberty which for somewhat above a mile is indulged to the slaves. When we had walked almost to the end of our tedder,[120] I was desirous to walk a littler further to view the coasts, if perhaps any advantage might offer itself afterwards for an escape, though we actually designed no such thing. As we were prying about the seaside, one of the spies appointed constantly to watch, lest any of the slaves should run away, came to us and charged us with an attempt to make an escape. We flatly denied it, but he laid hold on us. There was no resisting: obey we must and accordingly attended his mastership towards the city. As we drew near, I espied some English men at quoits (for with such recreations and diversions they are willing now and then to beguile the

---

[119] *knocked off*: discontinued his work.
[120] *tedder*: tether.

tedious minutes of lingering thralldom). I beckoned to one of them whom I knew, and pretending only to whisper with him, I secretly conveyed to him my purse, wherein were seven pieces of eight. We were presently met by another spy, and those two led us to a little blind[121] house where they searched us. They took away the twenty shillings which I had put into my friend's hand and, finding nothing upon me, took away my doublet and then brought us before the viceroy and his council. We were straitly examined and strongly charged with an attempt to escape. We peremptorily denied all and stood upon our innocency, affirming that our only design of walking abroad was to take the fresh air, occasioned by my fellow's sickness. This purgation would not be accepted, and the batoon[122] was commanded to be brought forth. We answered we durst not falsely accuse ourselves nor make ourselves criminal when we were not so, and therefore if such was their will and pleasure, we must abide by it, and so we sat down by the sticks.

The way of punishment by the batoon, or cudgel, is this: they have a strong staff, about six foot long, in the middle whereof are bored two holes. Into these holes a cord is put, and the ends of the cord fastened on the one side the staff with knots so that it makes a loop on the other side. Into this loop of the cord both the feet of the person condemned to this punishment are put. Then two lusty fellows, one at each end of the staff, lifts it up in their arms, and twisting the staff about till his feet are fast pinched with the cord by the ankles, they raise up his feet with the soles upwards, well nigh as high as their shoulders, and in this posture they hold them, the poor man the mean while resting only with his neck and shoulders on the ground. Then comes another lusty, sturdy knave behind him and with a tough short truncheon gives him as many violent blows on the soles of his feet as the council shall order.

But the viceroy, with his council, gathering from circumstances and induced to believe us by our constant and resolute denial of the fact, omitted at present any further punishment and only commanded us to be laid in chains in the viceroy's prison till our patrons should demand our liberty and fetch us out. And the next day we were both delivered, though with differing fates, as Pharaoh's chief butler and chief baker were both taken from prison, the one to be advanced, the other to be hanged,[123] for John Randal's

---

[121] *blind*: out of the way, or perhaps dark and windowless.

[122] *batoon*: stick or club used to administer a beating, usually on the soles of the feet.

[123] *Pharaoh's chief . . . hanged*: See Genesis 40.

patron being a very Termagant,[124] used that absolute and unlimited sovereignty which they pretend to over their slaves and commanded him to receive three hundred blows upon the soles of his feet with the batoon, in manner before described. As for myself, when I was brought home, the spy that seized us came and demanded money of my patron for his good service (not reckoning that he had anything of me) which put him into a most desperate fit of passion and, calling me dog and Jew, and all to naught, commanded me to go work in the looms with two other Englishmen that were slaves and linen cloth weavers. But alas, I was a very bungler and understood nothing of the craft and mystery[125] of weaving, more or less, but there I wrought till I had spoiled all that I laid my hands on. Now, when he saw that my labor this way would not turn to account, he rated me for a loggerhead[126] and bade me fill quills[127] for the other two. Being now degraded from a bungling weaver to an excellent filler of quills, I continued about a month. My shop all this while lay at sixes and sevens. What was become of it I knew not and durst not for my life discover any desire to return to that employment. At last, my patron asked me for the money that he had lent me when I first began to trade. I answered submissively that I had not a farthing; all my small estate lay in a few goods, and till they were sold I could not possibly repay him. He calls one of his slaves, a Dutchman, and commands him to go with me and turn all into ready money and bring it him. When I came to my old shop, there was the nest indeed, but all the birds were flown, for in my absence (poor John Randal being lame and not able to work, my partner sometime before having left me, and I confined to another employment) some of these rascals had broken open my shop and thence carried the best of my goods, though my cellar was still safe and some of my goods I heard of and recovered. What money I had was hid in the ground, as it was my constant way. That night the Dutchman and myself returned to our patron and told him we could sell nothing, whereupon he remanded me to my shop, there to trade, paying him the two dollars a month as I had done before.

[124] *Termagant*: a violent, overbearing bully; also, an imaginary deity referred to in romance tales and mystery drama and said to be the object of Muslim worship.
[125] *mystery*: trade.
[126] *loggerhead*: thick-headed, stupid person.
[127] *fill quills*: wrap yarn around a bobbin or spool.

SECT. VII. THE AUTHOR'S PATRON GROWING POOR, HE IS SOLD
OR MORTGAGED TO ANOTHER; THE WONDERFUL KINDNESS
THAT HE FOUND FROM HIS SECOND PATRON

Here was nothing yet working towards a deliverance, nor could I yet see the least glimmering of possibility which might so much as flatter my willing mind with a hope of escaping, but it's observed that the night is always darkest towards daybreak, and God is often drawing nearer to us in mercy when we conceive He is departing further off in displeasure.

My patron had been sinking in his estate a pretty while; the last ship he had put to sea broke his back. At last he was grown (insensibly) so low that it could no longer be daubed up[128] with his repute, but he must be forced to sell all his slaves to pay his debts. It was not much to me whither I was chopped and changed. I might change my jailer and my jail, but still I was like to be a prisoner. I might be bought and sold, and sold again, but still my condition was slavery; yet one thing methought was comfortable, that the last instrument of my bondage was come into misery as well as myself.

In the partage[129] of his slaves, it fell to my lot and another's to be mortgaged for a certain sum of money jointly to two persons, the one a capmaker, the other a grave old gentleman who amongst his own people had the repute of a good-natured and moderate person (as good nature and moderation go at Algier). The day of payment came; the money was not paid; the capmaker and the old gentleman seize on us and hold us in common, but in a while they resolved to divide us, that each of them might know his proper goods and chattels, and each of us might know whom to call master and whose whistle we were bound to obey. We are both summoned to appear in a certain place at midday, and much ado there was about our dividing. At last they agreed to cast lots for us, only, because I was in a handsome way of trade, it was accorded that he to whose share I should fall should pay the other fifty doubles,[130] which, if I compute aright, is something more than fifty shillings sterling. I was exceeding fearful I should fall to this capmaker, for he had the character of a brutish, ill-humored creature, and therefore I was concerned to lift my petition to God, that seeing when the lot should be cast into the lap, yet the whole disposition thereof is of God, He would give me forth a gracious lot. Whatever there is of contingency as to us, there's nothing accidental to

---

[128] *daubed up*: literally, covered up with whitewash.
[129] *partage*: division.
[130] *doubles*: copper coins worth about a shilling each.

God. Well, God delivered me from that tyrant, and I was adjudged by the decision of the lot to the old gentleman. And if I should be silent here, I should be the most ungrateful wretch living. I found not only pity and compassion but love and friendship from my new patron. Had I been his son, I could not have met with more respect nor been treated with more tenderness. I could not wish a friend a better condition than I was then in, except my bonds. If anything could be mingled with bondage to make it sweet, if anything could reconcile slavery to nature, if anything could beget an acquiescence in such a state, I did not, I could not, want it.

And indeed the freedom that I found in servitude, the liberty I enjoyed in my bonds was so great, that it took off much of the edge of my desire to obtain and almost blunted it from any vigorous attempt after liberty that carried hazard in its face, till at last I was awakened upon this occasion.

My patron had a fair farm in the country, about twelve miles from the city, whither he took me along with him. He had me to their markets, showed me the manner of them, and at my return he loaded me home with all manner of good provisions, that I might make merry with my fellow Christians. And I had some reason to conclude from his great kindness to me that he intended to send me thither to manage the farm for him. I saw now evidently that if I once quitted my shop, I should lose with it all means, all helps, and therefore all hopes to rid myself out of this slavery. And though I might have been there a petty lord and bashawed it[131] over the rest of my fellow servants, yet slavery had in it something of I know not what harshness that I could not brook. Fetters of gold do not lose their nature; they are fetters still. Had Bajazet's cage been of gold, as 'twas of iron, yet it was a cage, and that was provocation enough to a haughty spirit to beat out his own brains against its bars.[132] This therefore quickened my dull temper, and I began to resolve to make an attempt once for all. Now therefore mustering those few wits captivity had left me, I set them on work and ran through all things possible and impossible. He that will find what he has lost must look where 'tis not, as well as where 'tis, and forming stratagems in my head, some idle and vain, some desperate, others impossible, at last I pitched upon one that seemed to me feasible and practicable.

---

[131] *bashawed it*: played the basha, lorded it.

[132] *Bajazet's cage . . . its bars*: Bajazet, or Bayezit I, was Ottoman sultan from 1389 to 1403. Bajazet and his army were routed by Tamerlane at the battle of Ankara, and while held captive he is said to have committed suicide by hurling himself against the bars of his cage. See Christopher Marlowe, *Tamburlaine, Part I*, act 5, scene 1.

SECT. VIII. THE CONTRIVANCE FOR OUR ESCAPE, THE PERSONS
ACQUAINTED WITH IT, AND ALSO THOSE THAT WERE ENGAGED
IN IT; SOME DEBATES ABOUT LEAVING MY PATRON

Having formed the design, or at least the rude draft and general model of it, my first care was to open it to some skillful and faithful counselors who might more impartially discover to me its inconveniences, where it was like to prove leaky or take wind. And first I acquainted Mr. Sprat, our minister, with it and laid before him the whole of the contrivance, and he so far approved it that he judged it possible. Next, I acquainted one Robert Lake, a very wise and religious person, who bestowed his blessing on it and wished it all good success. And lastly, I acquainted my friend John Randal, who approved, yet none of these could, or would, run the risk of its miscarriage. Mr. Sprat was already delivered from his patron and in a fair way to be absolutely enlarged in a more safe and regular way, for not long after our escape came Captain Park of London and paid the sixty dollars and took him along with him for England. John Randal had a wife and child, and these were too dear pledges to be left behind and yet too tender things to undergo our difficulties. Robert Lake was an ancient person and neither able passively to be carried in nor actively to carry on a design that required much hardiness of body and mind to endure and much strength to go through with it. We had nothing more from them than prayers and counsels, which yet was the main,[133] and then my next care was to take in partners and accomplices in the design.

And herein I had a threefold respect: first, to such as were necessarily required to form the instrument of our escape and deliverance. Secondly, to such whose tried and approved fidelity I might presume would be obstinately and religiously secret in concealing it. Thirdly, to such whose courage of mind and strength of body would render them capable to pursue the ends of it, to put it in execution, and go through with it.

But before I would reveal the project to any of them in particular, I required an oath of secrecy: that whereas I should now reveal to him, or them, a matter of great concernment to their happiness and welfare, they should solemnly promise and swear that in case they did not approve it, or would not join in it, yet they should, neither directly nor indirectly, for fear or flattery, discover it or the persons engaged in it to any person whatsoever. When a project was once mentioned which promised in general their

---

[133] *the main*: the principal part.

happiness and welfare, I needed not tell them in particular what it drove at: they could smell out that with ease, for what could be good or happy to slaves without liberty? This oath therefore they willingly took. I judged seven persons would be enough to manage, carry on, and execute it, and therefore, except the three forementioned, I communicated it to no one person but these following, who engaged in it, though all of them did not go through with it. John Anthony, a carpenter, who had been a slave fifteen years. His trade sufficiently shows how useful he would prove in the design. William Adams, who since his captivity had learnt and used the trade of a bricklayer. His serviceableness in it will be evident in the sequel. He had been a slave eleven years. John Jephs, who was a seaman and must therefore be presumed one of the quorum in a project of this nature. He had endured slavery about five years. John --, a carpenter, who was a skillful man in his trade, lusty of body, and therefore must be a good wheel in this engine, and he had been a slave five years. And two others, whose employment it was to wash small cloths at the seaside, and those had also their parts in carrying on the work, though they went not along with us. And William Okeley, who presents the reader with this narrative, who was taken August 11, 1639, and escaped June 30, 1644. These made up the number of seven. There arose a scruple; nay, it amounted to a question: whether to attempt an escape from my patron, one that so dearly loved me, so courteously treated me, had so fairly bought me, were justifiable before God and men.

And, 1. It might be a question in point of prudence; for where could I hope to mend myself? Or better my condition? I might possibly find worse quarter in England where the civil wars were now broke out, and to that height of exasperation that those of the same nation, and perhaps blood, would hardly give quarter of life to one another. If the name of native country bewitched me, if that dazzled my eyes, surely wherever we are well is our country, and all the world is home to him that thrives all over the world. And why should the name of bondage, why should a word grate so harshly upon my delicate spirit when the sting of it was taken away? Liberty is a good word, but a man cannot buy a meal's meat with a word. And slavery is a hard word, but it breaks no man's back. Thousands are more slaves than I who are yet their own masters, and less at liberty than myself, who have the free rake[134] and range of the whole world. But yet my patron's favor was no freehold: I held not my happy time in fee simple;[135] all was *ad voluntatem*

---

[134] *rake*: course.
[135] *fee simple*: belonging to the owner and his heirs forever.

domini.[136] Besides, he might die and leave me to another or live to sell me to another who might be of another character, and then my condition would be therefore worse because I had known a better.

2. I might be questioned in point of ingenuity:[137] how I could be so unworthy to leave him who had loved me? Would not all that should hear of it condemn me of ill nature, to leave without taking leave one that had been a father to me, who might have used the right of a lord and used me as a child, who might have treated me as a slave? But really I thought there was more of manners and courtship in the objection than of weight and cogency. Still I dwelt with Meshech and had my habitation amongst the tents of Kedar,[138] and one thought of England, and of its liberty and Gospel, confuted a thousand such objections and routed whole legions of these little scruples. It was no time to stand upon the punctilios of honor and ingenuity, no time to complement and strain courtesy; here was no "Farewell, patron," in the case, and therefore I soon overcame that.

But, 3. It might be questioned in the court of conscience whether it were not downright theft to withdraw myself from his service, who had bought me, paid for me, entered upon me, possessed and enjoyed me as his own proper goods, and now I was not my own, had no right to myself. Whether might not a man be felo-de-se[139] in stealing himself as well as killing himself? And whether he is not the greater self-robber that steals away himself than he that steals away from himself? But I much questioned their propriety to me. My patron's title was rotten at the foundation. Man is too noble a creature to be made subject to a deed of bargain and sale, and my consent was never asked to all their bargains, which is essential to create a right of dominion over a rational creature where he was not born a subject. If I had forfeited my life or liberty, the law might take it; but I was not conscious to myself of any such forfeiture, but that I was at my own disposal.

Thus all was clear and quiet, and we went on with our design, which I now first opened to them: that I had contrived the model of a boat, which being formed in parcels[140] and afterwards put together, might by the superintendency of divine providence prove an ark to deliver us out of the hands of our

---

[136] ad voluntatem domini: Latin: "the Lord's will be done."

[137] *ingenuity*: honorable or fair dealing.

[138] *I dwelt . . . tents of Kedar*: a reference to Psalm 120, which is an exile's prayer for deliverance from enemies.

[139] *felo-de-se*: corrupt Latin for "a traitor to oneself."

[140] *parcels*: separate pieces.

enemies. This was soon said and greedily entertained. To escape was a pleasant word, the name of liberty made music in our ears, and our wishing hearts
danced to the tune of it, and a boat was as promising a means as anything
could be imagined. But when once their thoughts cooled and came more
sedately to look into the difficulties of it, they appeared innumerable, and
some of them seemed insuperable, and some things that had passed current[141] in my own thoughts, and I went cle[a]r away with them, without any
rub,[142] yet when they came to be pierced into with more eyes and scanned
upon more fingers, they were attended with considerable impediments.
Where this boat should be built was one staggering question. Where it should
be launched, and where put to sea, was a choking objection. How we should
escape those Argus[143] eyes, which are always observing us by day, was a grav-
eling query, or how to get out of the city by night, whose walls are so high,
whose gates are so close shut and strongly guarded, was another vexatious
query. How we should be rigged and victualed for such a voyage was a considerable inquiry. And whither we should design[144] was not to be slighted.
But how such a little skiff, rather than boat, should be able to weather all the
accidents of the sea was a neck question,[145] enough to strangle faith and sti-
fle us with despair.

To these objections I answered that I had designed[146] my own cellar as the
meetest place wherein to build the boat, that when it was there built, it might
be taken in pieces again and carried out of the city in parcels and bestowed
in private places till things were ripe for execution. That for a place where to
put to sea, it would be time enough to determine upon that when we had finished our vessel. That Mayork was the most commodious place to design to
land in. But in general I told them to this purpose: that if we never attempted
anything till we had answered all objections, we must sit with our fingers in
our mouths all our days and pine and languish out our tedious lives in
bondage. Let us be up and doing, and God would be with us. To begin is one
half of our work. Let us make an essay and answer particular objections as
they offered themselves and as we met with them in our work. That the project had its difficulties was confessed, but what has not that is commendable

---

[141] *passed current*: seemed acceptable.
[142] *rub*: obstacle.
[143] *Argus*: mythical giant with a hundred eyes.
[144] *whither we should design*: where we should try to go.
[145] *neck question*: a test question, with one's life at stake for an incorrect answer.
[146] *designed*: intended to use.

and glorious? Yet whatever difficulties and dangers we could meet with, liberty, kept in our eye, would sweeten the dangers we might encounter in attempting. They were all well satisfied with what was said, and all engaged to venture the utmost they were, and had, to accomplish it.

SECT. IX. THE MODEL OF THE BOAT, CARRYING IT OUT OF THE CITY, AND BESTOWING IT IN CONVENIENT PLACES

In the cellar where we had worshiped God, we began our work, and it was not the holiness but the privacy of the place that invited us and advised us to it. And first we provided a piece of timber about twelve foot long to make the keel, but because it was impossible to convey a piece of timber of that length out of the city but it must be seen, and of that shape but it must be suspected, and that suspicion would bring us into examination, and the rack or batoon might extort a confession out of the most resolved and obstinate breast, we therefore cut it in two pieces and fitted it for jointing, just in the middle. Our next care was the timbers or ribs of the boat, which we contrived thus: every one of the timbers was made of three pieces and jointed in two places because a whole rib at its full length would be liable to the same inconveniences with the keel. Now understand that the joints of the ribs were not made with mortise and tenon, but the flat side of one of the three pieces was laid over the other, and two holes were bored at every joint, into which two nails were to be put when we should join the parcels of our boat together. You must understand further that these two holes at every joint were not made in a straight line, parallel with the sides of the pieces, for then the three pieces, which make one rib, being joined together would have made one straight piece; a form which would by no means comport with the use and design of the timbers, but so that when both the nails were in the holes, each joint would make an obtuse angle and so incline so near towards a semicircular figure as our occasion required. All this while, here is no visible provision made for boards to clothe the naked ribs of our boat, without which the keel and timbers looked but like an useless anatomy,[147] but neither had we, nor was it possible we should have, any boards in our vessel. Necessity is the best artificer when all is done, if we except her sister Contingency, to which two the world has been beholden for the most useful inventions which at this day do ease the labor and toil of wearied mankind. For the jointing of these boards and the nailing of them to make the boat watertight would require

---

[147] *useless anatomy*: lifeless skeleton.

such hammering, and that hammering would make such a clamorous echo in the cellar as must have drawn upon us the jealous eyes of the Algerines, who about their wives and slaves are insupportably suspicious. And therefore, from the first conception of the design, I always resolved upon a canvas. In pursuance of which thought, being all satisfied that it was practicable, we bought as much strong canvas as would cover our boat twice over upon the convex of the careen.[148] We provided also as much pitch, tar, and tallow as would serve to make it a kind of a tarpaulin cerecloth to swaddle the naked body of our infant boat, with earthen pots to melt do[wn] our materials in, and prefixed a night wherein we might execute that part of our labor. The two carpenters and myself were appointed to this service, and the cellar was the place where we met. Matters had hitherto run on very evenly and smoothly, but here we met with some discouraging rubs. For when we had stopped all the chinks and crannies of the cellar, that the steam of the melted materials might not creep out and betray us (there being no chimney), we had not been long at our work before I felt myself exceeding sick with the strong and unusual scent of the melted liquor.[149] I was forced to go out into the streets to gulp for breath, where meeting with the cool air, it overcame me. I swooned, fell down, brake my face, and there lay. My companions, missing me, made out to seek me, found me in this sad plight, and carried me in again, though exceeding sick and unserviceable. They had not proceeded much further before I heard one of them complain he was sick and could proceed no further, and now our work stood still. I plainly saw that our hopeful project, that had hitherto so smoothly proceeded, must needs miscarry and prove abortive, for it would be impossible to finish it this night. And if we once parted and suffered our spirits to cool over the design, they would never cease cooling till they were stone-cold and hard frozen, and therefore I advised to set open the door and commit ourselves and our work to God's protection. For I told them they could not but know that if any discovery were made, the burden would fall heaviest upon my shoulders, and my back or feet must pay for all. At length we resolved to set the cellar door wide open, and as soon as that was done, and the steam pretty well gone out, we came to ourselves again, courageously went on with our business, and pitched one-half that night. The next night we met again, set open the door, and whilst they plied the work, I stood sentinel at the door to give notice of

[148] *convex of the careen*: outer surface of the boat.

[149] *liquor*: liquefied substance used to treat the canvas (here, the "pitch, tar, and tallow").

approaching danger, but we happily finished the whole and while it was yet dark carried it to my shop, which was about a furlong from the cellar, and there at present secured it.

I shall not question the reader's ingenuity so much but that he will suppose there goes a great deal more to a boat than I have described, but what should I trouble him with those things that are common to all other boats? I mention only what was peculiar to our own, and I do not intend to trouble him with the boatwright's lecture.

In our cellar we fitted all things: we made the timbers fit to the keel, and the canvas fit for the timbers, and the seats fit to the whole, and then took all in pieces again, and laying our heads together, plotted how to convey all out of the town and lodge them in secure and trusty places.

And first, for our keel, we all with unanimous consent judged Will Adams the fittest person to execute that part of the design, for he had long exercised the trade of a bricklayer, and his employment lay much without the town, and besides he used such pieces in leveling his work. He therefore, accoutered with his apron before him, his trowel in his hand, and one of the pieces upon his shoulder, undertook it, and without the least observation went cleverly away with it and, as he saw his opportunity, hid it in the bottom of a hedge and not long after conveyed out its fellow and lodged it in the same place. This succeeding so happily, we saw no great difficulty in the timbers, for we put one nail into a hole of every joint, and then you will easily conceive that the two extreme pieces of one rib being folded inwards upon the middlemost will lie in the room of one of the pieces for length, excepting that little that the ends of each piece were beyond the holes. Now, by general consent, the conveying these out of the city was committed to one whose employment was to wash small clothes by the seaside. He puts them into his bag amongst his clothes and so very orderly carried them out and hid them where he could find most commodious[150] stowage, but yet with respect to nearness to that place where the keel was laid.

But how to convey our tarpaulin safe out of town seemed most difficult. By night it was impossible, and by day the difficulties very considerable and the danger proportionable, for the gates are strictly watched, the streets crowded, the spies pickeering[151] in every corner, and the bulk of the canvas thus dressed was very great. To divide it had been to ruin ourselves, for no stitching together again could so cheat the searching water but it would find

---

[150] *commodious*: convenient.
[151] *pickeering*: reconnoitering.

out the needleholes. At last we ventured upon this way: we put it into a large
sack and committed it to him that used to wash clothes, and lest any should
clap a jealous hand upon it, we put a pillow over our canvas within the bag,
that so its softness might delude the inquisitor and make it pass for clothes.
Let none despise or condemn these as low, mean pieces of contrivance, for
we had not politicians' tools[152] to work withal, but the less was our policy,
the more glorious does the wisdom of God shine in succeeding it, and yet
even that little policy we were guilty of, was of His bestowing also. What of
sin was in all of it was entirely our own; what of power, wisdom, and success
was all His. But our agent escaped happily with it and, lodging it in a secret
place, returned.

We had yet many things to provide, and oars are absolutely necessary:
they were of the quorum to[153] an escape by sea. As fins are the fish's oars, so
oars are the boat's fins, by help whereof she makes her way. Now, to supply
this defect, we took two pipe staves,[154] and slitting them across from corner
to corner with a handsaw, we made of each pipe staff two rude things which
necessity was pleased to entitle the blades for a pair of oars, and these were
easily conveyed out without suspicion.

Next we considered that provision must be laid in for our voyage, and
therefore we provided a small, and but a small, quantity of bread, presuming
our stay at sea must be but short, for either we should speedily recover land
or speedily be drowned or speedily be brought back again. Two goat's skins
also, stripped off whole and so tanned (a kind of bottle much used by the
Algerines to carry milk and water in), we had, which we lined[155] with fresh
water, and we know that must needs be a great rarity in the Mediterranean.

We remembered also that a sail might be of right good use to us for expedition, and therefore we bought as much canvas as would answer that end,
and when some dispute was made about carrying it out, I offered to undertake that last part of our work. I had not gone a quarter of a mile but as I cast
my wary eye back, I espied the same spy who once before had seized me and
given me trouble, following me very roundly. My heart began to ache; I was
loath a design of so near and dear concernment to all of us should be brought
to the birth, and there should be no strength to bring forth. It's sad, after a
voyage, to shipwrack in the haven, but methought it was more sad to sink a

[152] *politicians' tools*: statesmen's strategies.
[153] *of the quorum to*: necessary for.
[154] *pipe staves*: strips of wood used for making casks or barrels.
[155] *lined*: filled.

vessel before it could be launched. And here I first found the difference between innocence and guilt, for how boldly could I hold up my head to this spy and his betters (at least, his masters) when I was not conscious of any such design in hand, whereas now the reflection of my conscience was enough to write guilt in my countenance (for some things are sin there which are not so in other places), and this had betrayed me, had I not suddenly plucked up my spirits, and spying an Englishman washing clothes by the sea, I went the ready way to him and desired him to help me wash that canvas. As we were washing it, the leering spy came and stood upon the rock just over our heads to watch our motions. As soon as we had a little formally washed[156] it, to cast a mist before his observing eyes, I took the canvas and spread it before his face upon the top of the rock to dry; he stayed his own time and then marched off. But I was as jealous of him as he could be of me for his heart and therefore, fearing he might lie in ambush for me, took it when 'twas dry and very fairly carried it back into the city and faithfully acquainted my accomplices how the matter squared. This discouraged them not a little, for that they seemed timorous to proceed in the enterprise.

At last we comforted and encouraged one another and entered into close counsel: where we should meet that night? At what time? Where we should put our boat together, and where put to sea? The time was an hour within night; the rendezvous on a hill, about half a mile from the sea; and so we dispersed some one way, some another, and privily lurking in hedges and ditches, lay close till the time appointed.

There is one thing that the reader will be ready to ask, and I shall be more ready to answer him for a special reason: viz., what I did with my shop and goods? When I had once resolved upon this adventure and saw it go on hopefully, I gave my patron my wonted visits, kept fair correspondence, paid him his demands duly, but secretly I made off my goods as fast as I could and turned all into ready money. I had a trunk, for which John Anthony made me a false bottom, into which I put what silver or gold I had and into the body of the trunk whatever it would hold and was worthy holding. This trunk I committed privately to the fidelity of our dear minister, Mr. Sprat. He took the charge of it, and he was now ready to receive his full discharge. This trunk he faithfully secured and carefully brought over and as honestly delivered to me when he heard I was come safe to London, and I was willing to move that question merely for the answer's sake, which witnesses his fidelity.

---

[156] *formally washed*: pretended to wash.

SECT. X. THE PUTTING OF OUR BOAT TOGETHER, THE
DIFFICULTIES WE MET WITH THEREIN, AND OUR
PUTTING OUT TO SEA, JUNE 30, 1644

As soon as we were met all together at the appointed place, we began to think
of executing our long intended design, but we were divided in our counsels [as
to] where to begin our work. It had been a question propounded before, and
we thought we had fully resolved upon the place, but at our meeting we were
strangely discomposed. There were two places which stood in competition,
each pretending good conveniences for that end: the one was a hill about half
a mile from the sea; the other was a valley, encompassed with two hedges,
about a furlong from the hill but of the same distance with it from the sea. It
was urged for the valley that it was a place of more secrecy and privacy, less
obvious to view, but then it was objected that we might there be surprised and
seized by the clutches of our enemies ere we could have notice to shift for ourselves. For the hill, it had been argued that we might there make better discovery of danger and make provision to avoid it, and in short, we all agreed
overnight to put our boat together upon the hill, promising ourselves much
advantage from its situation. But when we were met, we all altered our resolution without any visible reason and carried it for the valley. God is much in
the dark to us, but all our ways are in the open light to Him. It's very difficult
to give an account what God is doing at present, but we shall know, if we can
but patiently wait till future providences comment upon the former, and in a
while we saw the reason why God overruled our purposes.

We had hid several of our materials near the top of the hill, where also
grew a small fig tree which we had marked with our eye, as judging it would
be useful to strengthen the keel of our boat. Two of our company were immediately dispatched to saw down this fig tree and bring it, and the parcels of
our boat there deposited, away with them. They were hardly come to the
place, but we heard dogs bark about the top of the hill, and indeed two men
with dogs came very near them, but our men being aware, lay close and still,
and so they passed by without making any discovery, and then our men
bestirred themselves and brought away the fig tree and the other materials
and returned to us.

And now we had once more brought the scattered limbs of our boat into
one place, which, like those of Absyrius,[157] had been dispersed up and down

---

[157] *Absyrius*: Osiris, Egyptian god of the underworld, slain by his evil brother Set,
who then cut him into pieces and spread the body parts throughout Egypt.

the fields. It was no time to trifle, and therefore we all buckle to our work in good earnest. But we were so nigh some that were at work in the neighboring gardens that we could hear them speak and therefore must needs suppose they might hear us, too, and therefore we acted by signs and pointed and pulled and nodded but were all mutes. It might have been an expedient for the builders of Babel,[158] when their languages were divided, to have carried on their great project by signs, but certainly there was confusion poured out upon their hearts and counsels, as well as division in their tongues and languages.

The two parts of our keel we soon joined. Then opening the timbers, which had already one nail in every joint, we groped out for the other hole and put its nail into it. Then we opened them at their full length and applied them to the top of the keel, fastening them with rope yarn[159] and small cords, and so we served all the joints to keep them firm and stable. Then we bound small canes all along the ribs lengthways, both to keep the ribs from veering and also to bear out the canvas very stiff against the pressing water. Then we made notches upon the ends of the ribs, or timbers, wherein the oars might ply, and having tied down the seats and strengthened our keel with the fig tree, we lastly drew on our double canvas case, already fitted, and really the canvas seemed a winding sheet for our boat, and our boat a coffin for us all.

This done, four of our company took it upon their shoulders and carried it down towards the sea, which was about half a mile off. It was a little representation of a funeral, to see the four bearers marching in deep silence with something very like a hearse and coffin upon their shoulders, and the rest of us decently attending the ceremony, but we wanted torches, and besides it's not usual for any to wait upon their own coffins. But we durst not grudge our boat that small and last office, to carry it half a mile, for we expected it should repay us that service and civility with interest, in carrying us many a league. We carried it at land where it could not swim, that it might carry us at sea where we could not walk. As we went along, they that were in the gardens heard us passing by and called to us, "Who comes there?" But it was dark, and we had no mind to prate, and therefore without any answer we silently held on our way.

When we came to the seaside, we immediately stripped ourselves naked and, putting our clothes into the boat, carried it, and them, as far into the sea

---

[158] *builders of Babel*: Noah's descendants, who tried to build a tower to reach heaven (Genesis 11:1–9).

[159] *rope yarn*: thick twine.

as we could wade, and this we did lest our tender boat should be torn against the stones or rocks, and then all seven of us got into her. But here we soon found how our skill in calculating the lading of our vessel failed us, for we were no sooner embarked, but she was ready to sink under us, the water coming in over the sides, so that once again we must entertain new counsels. At last, one whose heart most failed him was willing to shut out[160] and rather hazard the uncertain torments of the land than certainly be drowned at sea. Then we made a second experiment, but still she was so deep laden that we all concluded there was no venturing out to sea. At length another went ashore, and then she held up her head very stoutly and seemed hearty enough for our voyage.

It was time now to commit and commend ourselves and vessel to the protection and conduct of that God who rules the winds and the waves and whose kingdom is in the deep waters, imploring mercy for the pardon of our sins and resigning up our souls to God, as if we had been presently to suffer death by the hand of the executioner. And taking our solemn farewell of our two companions, whom we left behind, and wishing them as much happiness as could be hoped for in slavery and they to us as long a life as could be expected by men going to their graves, we launched out, upon the thirtieth day of June in the year of our Lord, one thousand six hundred forty and four: a night forever to be remembered by His poor creatures, who are ourselves great monuments of divine providence and do set up this little monument of His goodness and mercy that may survive us and bear up the name of God to aftertimes, that by us men may learn to put their trust in God. And the bill of lading is as followeth: John Anthony, William Adams, John Jephs, John --- (Carpenter), and William Okeley.

SECT. XI. THE GREAT EXTREMITIES WE ENDURED AT SEA FOR
SIX DAYS AND NIGHTS, WITH THE COINCIDENT PROVIDENCES
OF GOD THAT APPEARED FOR US IN OUR EXTREMITIES, AND
OUR MIRACULOUS LANDING AT MAYORK, JULY 6, 1644

We are now out at sea without helm or pilot, without anchor, tackle, or compass, but God was these, all these, and more than all these. Our number was small, our work was great: we could not afford one idle hand, not one idle finger. Four of the company continually wrought at the oars, and indeed we

160 *shut out*: be excluded.

wrought for our lives, and then I shall not need to say how we wrought. But this I shall say, I can truly say it: I never saw strength so strained, nor the utmost of what nature could do for life and liberty exerted so much in all my life. The employment of the fifth man was more easy but no less necessary, which was to free the boat of that water which by degrees leaked through our canvas.

We labored the harder that night because we would gladly be out of the ken[161] of our old masters by day, but when day appeared we were yet within sight of their ships that lay in the haven and road and off the land. But our boat being small, and lying close and snug upon the sea, either was not at all discovered or else seemed something that was not worth the taking up. A little hope in the midst of great fears made us double, and redouble, our diligence. We tugged at the oars like those who are chained to the galleys because we had no mind to be slaves to our old patrons in their galleys.

But upon all occasions we found our want of forecast,[162] for now our bread, which was to be the staff of our decayed strength, had lain soaking in the salt water, like a drunken toast sopped in brine, and was quite spoiled. And our fresh water in the bottles stank of the tanned skins and owze,[163] having lain sobbing[164] in the salt water, which made it nauseous. But yet that hope, that hovered over us and flattered us that we should one day mend our commons,[165] sweetened all again. So long as bread was bread, we complained not. Three days with good husbandry it lasted, but then pale famine (which is the worst shape death can be painted in) stared us in the face, and there was no substitute for bread at sea. At land, the roots of grass, the tops of trees, and the vilest excrements[166] have served to stop the clamor of a ravenous stomach, but that which slaves despised we should have admired and prized. Water indeed we might have, either cold or hot. We had choice, but it was a hard choice: either the cold salt water out of the sea or that warmer which had been strained through our bodies, and that we chose of the two, but we must not have that, after a while, unless we would first accept the other. And the misery was, these did not assuage our thirst but increase it,

---

[161] *ken*: range of vision.
[162] *forecast*: forethought.
[163] *owze*: solution used to tan hides.
[164] *sobbing*: soaking.
[165] *mend our commons*: improve our daily allotment of food and drink.
[166] *excrements*: parts of plants without nutritional value.

nor increase o[u]r strength but diminish it, yet these were the means of life, strange means, that would destroy the end.

Several things added to our misery, for trouble seldom comes solitary. For first, we had the wind for some time full against us, and this was both an evil in itself, an evil in its effect, and an evil in its cause. It was a great evil in itself: it increased our labor and then defeated it. We rowed harder, to less purpose; we moved but did not advance; we spent our strength for nought and in vain. It was an evil in its effect, for it engaged the waters against us and drew them into its party. The sea is a perfect neuter of itself and willing to maintain its neutrality, but the powerful winds drew her into the faction. And that sea which serves the north today, shall comply with the more prevailing south tomorrow, for the waves are the greatest timeservers in the world. But it was far the greatest evil in its cause, for the winds being against us argued that God was against us, for the wind we know was His. He brings the wind out of His magazines.[167] We were now so dispirited that we debated whether we should bear up[168] with the wind or make the best of our way and row against it. That is, whether it were not better to go back to Algiers with ease than painfully make towards freedom. At last, like persons that, though we knew not what to do, yet resolved not to return, we resolved whilst we had life and strength and breath, we would struggle with it. And now the great God interposed: He rebuked His wind; it was not against us. Nay, He reconciled His wind, and it became our friend. He that can turn the rivers in the south could turn the wind out of the north. Here we might have had a notable demonstration of God's sovereignty. He determined the quarter of the wind, the quantity of the wind, and the continuance of the wind: the quarter, whence it should blow; the quantity, how much it should blow; and the continuance, how long it should blow. The quarter was our enemy, the continuance had quite brought us to despair, but had He opened His hand and let out one blast more, the proud waters had gone over our souls; we had perished in the deep. But we see that our times are in God's hand, the ocean in the hollow of the same hand, and the winds in the same hand, and happy it was for us that we, and they, were all there.

A second great inconveniency was that our labor was without intermission. Though we advanced not forwards at many strokes, yet cessation had driven us backwards. The poor sentinel that stands upon the watch yet comforts himself that another will relieve him, but we had none to take the toil off our hands and give us respite: we might shift our places but not our pains.

---

[167] *magazines*: storehouses.
[168] *bear up*: turn and go.

A third great evil that lay sore upon us was the extremity of the heat by day. The season was raging hot, being the beginning of July. The climate was hot, being under or about the fourth climate.[169] We wanted fresh water to cool the heat and were engaged in continual labor to enrage the heat, and all these made it insupportable to our bodies, and our little or no hope (which now, like a candle burnt down to the socket, did rather blink than burn) made it grievous to our souls. One small help we had (if it was a help): that the fifth man, who emptied the boat of the salt water, threw it upon the bodies of the rest to cool them, but this was a miserable remedy, for our bodies were so bleached between the scorching sun and the cooling water that they rose up in blisters all over. Great pain we felt, great danger we were in, great miseries were endured, great wants we were under and had nothing little but hope, food, and strength. By day we were all stark naked; by night we had our shirts or loose coats, and that was all our clothing: the rest we left ashore to ease our boat.

If any shall be so inquisitive as to ask by what directions we steered our course that we did not tack about insensibly in the dark night or day, he may know that for the day, one of the company had a pocket dial[170] which supplied the place of the compass, e'en well enough for such a vessel and such mariners. By night, when the stars appeared, we had our advice from them, and when they disappeared we guessed at our way by the motions of the clouds.

In this sad and woeful plight we continued four days and nights. On the fifth day, we were on the brink of the brink of despair, and all hope that we should be saved utterly perished. And now, as persons despairing of the end, we ceased to pursue the means, laid by our oars, left off our labor. Either we had no strength left or were loath to throw away that little we had to no purpose. Only we kept still emptying the boat: loath to drown, loath to die, yet knew no ways to avoid death. When the end is removed, all means perish with it.

They that act least commonly wish the most. Thus when we had left fruitless labor, we fell upon fruitless wishes that we might meet with some vessel, some ship to take us up. If it was but a ship, we considered no further—English or African, Tros,[171] Tyriusve[172]—all was a case.[173] Or if not, yet the worst

---

[169] *fourth climate*: the fourth of the seven classical climates, this one located between the parallels of Rome (42) and Rhodes (36).

[170] *pocket dial*: small mariner's compass.

[171] *Tros*: from the Troas, scene of Homer's *Iliad*.

[172] *Tyriusve*: Tyre, ancient city of Phoenicia.

[173] *all was a case*: all was one.

was better than our bad case, and therefore [we] resolved, could we have discovered any ship, to have made towards her, though it had been one of
Algiers. How many wished themselves again in Egypt, when they combated
with the unexpected difficulties of the wilderness! How oft have the people
of God been more afraid of the means of their deliverance than of their danger! When Christ came to save his disciples from the storm, yet because he
came in a way uncouth[174] and unexpected, "they cried out for fear" (Mat.
14:26). Whether the reader will pity or condemn us, I know not, but to that
pass were we now brought, that we would have accepted life upon any terms
not base and sinful, and whether we should have stuck at such or no, I have
no such security from my own heart as to resolve him.

   Whilst we were at this dead ebb of hope, the great God whose most glorious opportunity to help is His creatures' greatest extremity, He that
appeared for Abraham in the mount[175] and to the three young men in the
fiery furnace,[176] He that delivered Israel at the sea, at the Red Sea, He who
times all His mercies for their advantage, even He sent us some relief, and a
little relief is great in great exigences. As we lay hulling up and down, we discovered a tortoise not far from us asleep in the sea. Had the great Drake[177]
discovered the Spanish plate fleet,[178] he could not have more rejoiced. Once
again we bethought ourselves of our oars, and now our little boat showed
itself to be of the right breed of Algiers, made of piratic timber, and to its poor
ability would become a corsair. We silently rowed to our prey, took it into the
boat with great triumph. We cut off her head and let her bleed into a pot; we
drank the blood, ate the liver, and sucked the flesh. Warm flesh and hot
liquor[179] (except our own) had been a great rarity with us a long time. It was
a novelty of providence, and really it wonderfully refreshed our spirits,
repaired our decayed strength, and recruited nature. At least, poor, exhausted
Nature was willing to be cheated and fancy herself recruited. But there was
no cheat in't: we were really refreshed and with fresh vigor and courage fell

---

[174] *uncouth*: unfamiliar.
[175] *Abraham in the mount*: at the sacrifice of Isaac (Genesis 22:2).
[176] *three young men . . . fiery furnace*: Nebuchadnezzar punished three Jews who
refused to worship his idols by casting them into a furnace, but they were protected by
the Hebrew god and emerge unharmed (Daniel 3).
[177] *Drake*: Sir Francis Drake (ca. 1540–96), English sea captain, explorer, and buc-
caneer.
[178] *Spanish plate fleet*: Spanish treasure fleet carrying gold and silver from the New
World.
[179] *liquor*: drink.

to our work. We left our fears behind us; we picked up some scattered crumbs of hope; and about noon we discovered, or thought we discovered, land. It's impossible to express the joy and triumph of our raised souls at this apprehension. The poets tell us that as often as Hercules threw the great giant against the earth, his Mother Earth gave him new strength against the next encounter.[180] It was new strength, new life to us, though not to touch, yet to see or, if not to see, to think we saw it. It brought fresh blood into our veins, fresh color into our pale cheeks. We looked not like men awaked from sleep, not like captives broke from the chains of Algiers, but like persons raised from the dead. But hope and fear made a strange medley passion in our souls, like the repartees[181] of two contrary jostling tides or the struggling of the eddy with the mainstream. Hope would persuade us that we saw the land, but chill fear bade us pause upon it, for as we easily believe what we desire to be true, so we are as ready to fear lest it should not prove true; for fear had got long possession of our souls and would hardly admit hope to stir but was ready to suppress it as a disturber of its empire. We had seen nothing but air and sea, sea and air, in five days and nights; that though our reason told us there was such a thing as land, yet the impressions that fear had made upon us made it questionable whether ever we should see it. And we durst not give too much credence to our eyes that had been used to bring sadder stories to our hearts.

Yet still we wrought[182] hard. Hope did us that kindness: it put us upon an earnest desire to see whether we were deceived or no. After some further labor, we grew more confident and, at last, fully satisfied that it was land. I hope I shall never forget what a sense we had of God's goodness upon that assurance. Extremes do equally annoy and sometimes infatuate the mind. They tell us that in Greenland the extremity of cold will make the iron stick to the fingers, as our experience assures extremity of heat will do, for now like distracted persons we all leapt into the sea, quitting our boat, and being all good swimmers, we there bathed and cooled our heated bodies. An adventure, which if well considered, had as much of the desperado in it as our putting to sea, for now we were at the mercy of the sharks, which might have sheared off a leg or arm, and now our overheated bodies were open to receive the impressions of that cold element. But as we never considered our

[180] *Hercules threw . . . next encounter*: A classical myth recounts a struggle between Hercules and Antaeus, a giant who drew his strength from his mother, the earth.

[181] *repartees*: opposed forces.

[182] *wrought*: worked.

danger, the great and good God delivered us from the ordinary effects of such folly. We presently returned to our boat, and being both wearied with labor and cooled a little with the sea, we lay us all down to sleep in as much security as if we had been in our own beds. Nature being almost spent must have a truce. She will not undertake to keep our bodies upon their legs if we will not submit to her great standing ordinance of rest. And here we saw still more of divine goodness, that our leaky vessel did not bury us in the sea and we awaking find ourselves in the other world, but He that gave us sleep measured it, and He measured it exactly, not suffering us to outsleep the season of plying our pump or that which supplied the place of it.

Being thus refreshed with sleep, we found new strength for our work, and God found us new work for our strength. We tugged the harder at the oar because we hoped ere night to sleep upon a more stable and faithful element. But we made our way very slowly and when we cast up the account of our progress, found that we had gone but little way in a long time. Towards evening we discovered another island: the first we saw was Mayork; the second, Fromentere;[183] and some of our company that had sailed in these seas would undertake to assure us of it. We debated not long to which of these we should direct our course, for the latter being much infested with venomous serpents and little if at all inhabited, we resolved all for Mayork. All that night we rowed very hard, and the next, being the sixth of July and from our putting to sea. We kept within sight of it all day, and about ten o'clock at night we came under the island, but the rocks were there so craggy and steep that we could not climb up.

Whilst we were under these rocks there came a vessel very near us. Let the reader put himself in our stead: let him but copy out our thoughts; let him imagine how loath we were to lose all our toil and travel, to forgo our deliverance, to have this rich mercy, which God had put into our hands, wrested out of them again by some Turkish picaroon[184] or corsair that are always skimming those seas. It concerned us therefore to lie close, and when they were passed by, we gently crept along the coast as near the shore as we durst till we found a convenient place where we might thrust in our weatherbeaten boat.

If these papers should fall into the hands of some that are great clerks[185] in the art of navigation and have conned the mariner's terms of art, they will smile at my improper wording of these matters and say I am one of Paul's

---

[183] *Fromentere*: Formentera.
[184] *picaroon*: pirate.
[185] *clerks*: scholars.

mariners.[186] But I can be content to be accounted one of his mariners whilst I have shared in his mercies. How many of those that speak the language of the sea yet have found her billows deaf to their cries and prayers and their stately ships made the scorn of winds and the reproach of waves; when we, who had none of their ships and little of their skill, have had experience of those providences to which they have been strangers.

SECT. XII. THE GREAT KINDNESS WE RECEIVED AT MAYORK FROM THE VICEROY AND THE INHABITANTS OF THAT ISLAND AND CITY

When we were come to land, we were not unsensible of our deliverance, though like men newly awakened out of a dream, we had not the true dimensions of it. We confessed God had done great things for us, but how great things He had done was beyond our comprehension: we had escaped the sea, but yet death might be found at land, and we were ready to say, with Sampson (Judg. 15:18), "Lord, thou hast given this great deliverance into the hands of thy servants, and now shall we die for thirst?" We had had no food since we ate the liver and drank the blood of the tortoise, and therefore leaving three of our company with the boat, the other two, viz., John Anthony and myself, were sent out to scout abroad for fresh water. And the rather were we sent because this John Anthony could speak both the Spanish and Italian tongues very perfectly, and I had as much of the Spanish as might serve to express our wants and desires if perhaps we might meet with any persons thereabouts. We were not far gone before we fell into a wood, and we were in a wilderness in our thoughts which way to take: he will needs go his way, and I mine. Good Lord! What a frail, impotent thing is man! That they whom common dangers by sea, common deliverances from sea, had united should now about our own wills fall out at land. And yet thus we did: he gave me reproachful words, and it's well we came not to blows. But I went my own way, and he seeing me resolute, followed me, and the providence of God, not dealing with us according to our frowardness, followed us both: this way led us to a watchtower of the Spaniards, many of which they keep upon the seacoasts to give the country timely notice of any picaroons that come ashore to rob and spoil.

[186] *Paul's mariners*: According to the Bible, St. Paul was taken on a ship bound for Rome, and after the crew exhibited poor seamanship and then panicked in the face of a terrible storm, he brought the crew and passengers safely to shore at Malta, though the ship was wrecked (Acts 27).

When we came within call, fearing he might discharge at us, we spoke to him upon the watch, told him our condition, what we were, whence we came, how we escaped, and earnestly begged of him to direct us to some fresh water and in the meantime to bestow upon us some bread. He very kindly threw us down an old moldy cake, but so long as it was a cake and not a stone, nor a bullet, hunger did not consider its moldiness. Then he directed us to fresh water, which was hard by. We stood not telling stories. We remembered ourselves; we remembered our brethren left with our boat and observing the sentinel's directions, came to a well where there was a pot with strings to draw with. We drank a little water and ate a bit of our cake, but the passage was so disused that we had much ado to force our throats to relieve our clamorous stomachs. But here we stayed not, but with the four lepers in the tents of the Syrians (2 Kings 7:9) rebuked ourselves: "We do not well: we have glad tidings to carry, and do we hold our peace?" We return to our boat, are welcomed by our companions, acquaint them with the good success of our embassy, and all prepare to make to the well.

And now we must leave our boat, that faithful instrument of God's providence, which had so trustily served His purpose to deliver us. It was not without some recoiling upon our spirits that we should so much as in appearance imitate the ingratitude of those who having served their private ends on their friends and have now no further use of them most ungratefully shake them off. That we should be like the waterdog which uses the water to pursue his game and when he comes to land, shakes it off as troublesome and burdensome. But it was no time to stand upon compliments: hunger, thirst, weariness, desire of refreshment and rest, those importunate duns[187] commanded us away, and tying our boat as fast as we could to the shore, we left her to mercy, which had been so good to us.

As we were going, or rather creeping or crawling, towards the well, another quarrel started amongst us, the memory whereof is so ungrateful that I shall give it a burial in silence, the best tomb for controversies.

And now we are at the well, and the well is provided of water, and we have something to draw; all these helps God has given us, but He must give us one more, even a throat to swallow it, without which, all the rest signify nothing. This was the evil disease Solomon had observed in his days (Eccles. 6:2): "A man to whom God had given riches, wealth, and honor, so that he wanteth nothing for his soul, of all that he desireth; yet God giveth him not power to eat thereof." He that gives us water to drink and meat to eat must give us

---

[187] *duns*: insistent demands.

power to eat and drink also. How totally do we depend upon Him for life and breath and all things! One of our company, William Adams, attempting to drink, after many essays was not able to swallow it, but still the water returned so that he sunk down to the ground, faintly saying, "I am a dead man." We forgot ourselves, to remember him, and after much striving and forcing, he took a little, and when he and we were refreshed with our cake and water, we lay down by the well side till the morning. None of us could watch for the rest, but one God watched over us all. There we lay locked up and buried in sleep. The heavens covered us when we wanted a canopy. Each might say in the morning, with David (Psal. 3:5), "I laid me down and slept; I awaked, for the Lord sustained me."

When it was clear day, we addressed ourselves once more to the man upon the watchtower, entreating him to direct us the ready[188] way to the next house or town where we might find relief. He civilly points us towards a house about two miles off, whither, with wearied steps and joyful hearts, we now began to travel. Our feet had been so parboiled and quodled[189] with the sun's heat in the saltwater pickle that they were very raw and more blistered, and long it was before we could overcome the tediousness of those two miles. When we approached the house, the owner espying us and concluding by our shabby garb that we were some pilfering rascals, presented a fowling piece at us and charged us to stand. The foremost of our company, who could speak that language well, meekly told him he might spare that language; we were not able if we had so wicked a will, nor willing (if we had been able) to offer him the least injury; that we were a company of poor creatures whom the wonderful providence of God had rescued from the slavery of Algiers and hoped he would show mercy to the afflicted. The honest farmer, moved with our relation, sent us out bread, water, and olives, with which when we had refreshed ourselves, we lay down and rested three or four hours in the field and returning thanks for his charity, prepared to crawl away at our lame rate. He seeing us thankful beggars, enlarged his civility to us, called us into his house, and gave us good warm bean pottage, which seemed to me the most pleasant food that ever I eat in my life. Our leave once more taken, we advanced towards the city of Mayork, which from this place is about ten miles. No water could we meet with upon our way, but towards evening we discovered one drawing water at a well. We hasted to him, and he drew for us; that was our supper, and there was our lodging that night.

---

[188] *ready*: most direct or convenient.
[189] *quodled*: boiled.

The next morning we came into the suburbs of the city. The strangeness of our attire, being barefoot, barelegged, having nothing on but loose coats over our shirts, drew a crowd of inquirers about us: who we were? whence we came? whither we went? We gave them a particular account of our deliverance, with its circumstances, and they as willing to pity as to know our estate, and as ready to relieve as pity, accommodated us for the present with food. They gave us wine and strong-waters,[190] and whatever else might recover our exhausted spirits, but told us we must be obliged to tarry in the suburbs till the viceroy had notice that such strangers were arrived. He had soon information of us, and we as soon a command to appear before him. He examined us about many affairs: what men of war the Algerines had at sea? what strength they were of at land? But above all, he was most curious and exact in satisfying himself about our escape, our boat, our hazards at sea; wherein when we had fully obeyed him, he ordered we should be maintained at his own cost till we could have passage to our own country.

In this while the people gathered us money to buy us clothes and shoes, and we wanted nothing that nature called for but thankful hearts to God. And they endeavored to help to that mercy, too. As I was walking in the streets viewing the city, a young man steps to me.

"Friend," said he, "are you one of those that came lately over in the canvas boat?"

I answered, "Yes, I was one of them."

"Well," replied the young man, "it was not the little boat, but the great God that brought you over."

I must needs say, I often think of this young man's words, and as often as I think of them they chide me that I have not hitherto more publicly owned[191] God in his gracious and wonderful deliverance. However others may be concerned to read, I know not yet; I am concerned to write of the great things God has done for me.

SECT. XIII. THE PROVIDENCES OF GOD WHICH ATTENDED US AND CONDUCTED US ALL SAFE TO ENGLAND

It may not prove ungrateful to the reader to see how the great God who begun to work for us perfected His work concerning us; how He that had, and did, deliver, would still deliver us. As single stars have their glories, yet

---

[190] *strong-waters*: alcoholic spirits, such as brandy.
[191] *owned*: acknowledged.

constellations are more glorious: so each providence of God is admirable, but taken together, as one serving another, and this helping forwards that, so indeed they are most admirable. When the Creator viewed His each day's work, it so punctually answered its idea according to which, and obeyed that power by which it was created, that He pronounced it good; but when He reviewed the product of the six days, He pronounced all to be very good. Each letter in a book speaks skill, but when those letters form words, those words sentences, there is a greater excellency and more skill discovered. Separate providences speak out eminently some of God's attributes, but when we put them together, all the attributes of God shine forth in them, and one illustrate another, which reflects a light upon the former.

Mayork is a city where our English ships did seldom trade, and we being full of desire to see our native country, preferred our humble petition to the viceroy that we might have passage in the king of Spain's galleys, which were then in the road, bound for Alicante in Spain, which he graciously granted us. What cold entertainment we met with there from some of our own country, I shall draw a veil over, yet even there we found the mercies of God. One merchant took compassion on us and conducted us to an Englishman's house, where we lodged, and gave us half a dollar to defray our charges. The next day, understanding that there was an Englishman in the road, bound for England, we went aboard to see for passage. We made our condition our best argument to prevail. The master told us he had but little provision, but if we would be content with bread and beverage, we might go. We accounted that royal fare and accordingly waited till he set sail. Whilst we were aboard, two English merchants came thither also and were very earnest that we would give them the short of our adventure. We gratified them, and one of them said, "Countrymen, we have heard your story." After a few days we set sail and when we were at sea were hotly chased by two Turkish men-of-war, but being near Gibletore,[192] we got in there and escaped. We had known slavery too much and long to be ambitious of it again, and therefore three of us, John Anthony, John –– (Carpenter), and myself, went ashore and there stayed; our other companions ventured along with the ship and came into England before us. Whilst we were at Gibletore, the Spaniards understanding our condition, much pitied us, and one told us that if we would accept it, we might have lodging in his vessel, and he had fish enough that we might make use of. There we stayed till our money was gone and then resolved to go with the foot post[193] by land to Cadiz,

---

[192] *Gibletore*: Gibraltar.
[193] *foot post*: letter carrier or messenger who travels on foot.

which is about sixty miles. But whilst my two companions were gone to inquire for the courier, I stayed upon the shore and saw a small Spanish vessel coming from Malaga, bound for Cadiz. I went aboard him to desire passage. He freely granted it, and the next morning early we set sail and in little time came into Cadiz road, but not nigh enough to go ashore, the captain told us. Our passage was paid; we might freely go ashore when we would. Now, because we found no ship here bound for England and hearing that there was one at St. Lucar's, we traveled thither by land, which is about twelve miles. After a short stay there, I met with the master's mate, of whom I earnestly entreated for passage. He told me he had very little provision and that it would be hard to be obtained. Whilst we were talking, the boat came to fetch him aboard, and in her there was a youth, who was the master's son. He asked his father's mate, who was also his uncle, who we were. He told him we were poor men escaped from Algiers, but for want of provision he doubted we could not go for England. "No!" said the youth, "Do you think my father will deny passage to poor Englishmen that come from Algiers?" "Come, countrymen," said he, "come into the boat, you shall have passage." He presently acquaints his father with us and our condition. He treated us with great kindness. He prevailed with the merchants to lay in provision for us. We continued in his ship till we came away. In the time of our stay, I went aboard one Captain Goodson,[194] who lay then in the road. He was extremely civil to me; at my departure he gave me twenty shillings and set me aboard our ship in his own boat. We met with contrary winds and were very near engaging with a Hamburger. It was five weeks before we could reach the Downs, where we arrived in September 1644. The commander of the ship was Captain Smith of Redriff.

TO HIS INGENIOUS FRIEND, MR. WILLIAM OKELEY, UPON
HIS MIRACULOUS DELIVERANCE IN HIS CANVAS BOAT

Thy boat thy coffin call, and greet
The canvas as thy winding sheet:
From coffin, shroud, delivered;
Call't resurrection from the dead!
And since thy life's [thus] great, thy lines present
As God's great mercy's lesser monument.
FINIS

[194] *Captain Goodson*: Captain Goodson's ship.

Thomas Phelps, *A True Account of the Captivity of Thomas Phelps, (1685)*

(Meknes, 1684–85)

In 1685, the year that Phelps's *True Account* appeared with its dedication to Samuel Pepys, James II had just succeeded to the English throne, and Pepys had been reinstated as secretary of the admiralty in time to preside over the operation to demolish and abandon the fortress occupied by the English at Tangier, in Morocco. Unable to negotiate an agreement with the Moroccan sultan, Mulay Ismail, the English decided to pull out of the colony they had maintained since 1661. It was Mulay Ismail, a cruel but highly effective leader, whose troops had besieged Tangier and whose slaves were set to work building the opulent new capital that he founded at Meknes. Thomas Phelps was one of the slaves employed in the construction of this royal city. Phelps's connection to Pepys, and his occupation as master of a transatlantic merchant vessel, position him within the network of commerce, patronage, and government that directed the course of the British maritime economy during the late seventeenth century.

Phelps expresses a patriotic, nationalistic ideology, and his purpose in reporting events is more practical than polemical, offering helpful information and a cautionary tale for other seamen bound for Barbary. The sort of militant, puritanical pronouncements that are found in Okeley's narrative are absent from Phelps's account, and this is not surprising since such an attitude would not have been welcome under the patronage of either Pepys or James II, to whom Phelps says he was granted the privilege of an introduction at court. Phelps's experience did not so much lead him to thank God or invoke divine providence (though occasionally he does) as teach him to value what he terms "the immunities and freedom of my native country and the privileges of a subject of England."

The account the Salé corsairs' capture of Phelps's ship offers a telling example of the complex and subtle negotiations that were necessary in a maritime economy where force and fraud were constantly used to take ships, cargo, and crew as booty. In the late seventeenth century, the system of the "pass" (see appendix 7) was formally established in a series of Anglo-Algerian treaties that allowed English vessels to sail in the Atlantic and Mediterranean unmolested by Algerian corsairs as long as they did not carry passengers from countries hostile to Algiers (such as Portugal). The treaty gave Algerian ships the "right of search": when an Algerian ship encountered an English one, the Algerians were allowed to send two crew members to inspect the English ship's passenger and cargo lists. This is the right the renegado captain invokes when he plays the role of an Algerian corsair. Despite Phelps's suspicion that the other ship is from Salé, the Englishman is taken in by the strategy of the Salé corsairs, who pretend to be Algerians until they have taken control over most of Phelps's crew. Phelps's readers are thus given a warning about the deceptive methods practiced by renegade pirates who might be encountered quite close to England.

Not only does Phelps offer his own example as a warning to others, but in the concluding episode of the tale, in which the English seamen return to destroy the Moroccan corsairs' ships in their home harbor, Phelps offers a positive example of bravery in the service of the British navy and the nation. The opening and concluding episodes of the narrative stand in opposition, balancing Phelps's victimization with his triumphant revenge. With the drama of enslavement and escape taking up the center of the text, closure and symmetry are then neatly effected in the English raid when Phelps helps to burn the "very ship" that had taken him captive a year before. The text ends with Phelps returning to England as a hero, not a dupe.

No other edition of Phelps's narrative is extant.

Thomas Phelps, *A True Account of the Captivity of Thomas Phelps at Machaness in Barbary and of His Strange Escape in Company of Edmund Baxter and Others, as Also of the Burning Two of the Greatest Pirate Ships Belonging to That Kingdom, in the River of Mamora, Upon the Thirteenth Day of June 1685.*

Hac olim meminisse juvabit.[1]

LICENSED, AUGUST THE 21ST. R. L.'S. LONDON: PRINTED BY H. HILLS, JUN[IOR], FOR JOSEPH HINDMARSH, AT THE GOLDEN BALL OVER AGAINST THE ROYAL EXCHANGE IN CORNHILL, 1685.

To the Honorable Samuel Pepys,[2] Esquire;

Sir,

Having by your generous favor had the honor of being introduced into His Majesty's presence, where I delivered the substance of this following narrative, and being pressed by the importunity of friends to publish it to the world, to which mine own inclinations were not adverse, as which might tend to the information of my fellow seamen, as well as satisfying the curiosity of my countrymen, who delight in novel and strange stories, I thought it would be very far wanting to myself, if I should not implore the patronage of your ever honored name, for none ever will dare to dispute the truth of any matter of fact

---

[1] *Hac olim meminisse juvabit*: from Virgil (*Aeneid* 1:203). The complete phrase is "Forsan et haec olim meminisse iuvabit," meaning "One day this may be sweet to remember."

[2] *Samuel Pepys*: Pepys (1633–1703), a celebrated diarist, was a naval official who served as secretary of the admiralty from 1672 to 1679 and again from 1684 to 1688.

here delivered, when they shall understand that it has stood the test of your sagacity. Sir, your eminent and steady loyalty, whereby you asserted His Majesty's just rights and the true privileges of your country in the worst of times,[3] gives me confidence to expect that you will vouchsafe this condescension to a poor yet honest seaman who have devoted my life to the service of his sacred Majesty and my country; who have been a slave but now have attained my freedom, which I prize so much the more in that I can with heart and hand subscribe myself,

Honorable sir,
your most obliged and humble servant.
Tho. Phelps

THE PREFACE TO THE READER

Since my escape from captivity and worse than Egyptian bondage, I have, methinks, enjoyed a happiness with which my former life was never acquainted. Now that, after a storm and terrible tempest, I have by miracle put into a safe and quiet harbor, after a most miserable slavery to the most unreasonable and barbarous of men; now that I enjoy the immunities and freedom of my native country and the privileges of a subject of England; although my circumstances are otherwise but indifferent, yet I am affected with extraordinary emotions and singular transports of joy. Now I know what liberty is and can put a value and make a just estimate of that happiness which before I never well understood; which observation agrees very well with a lesson in morals I remember I have been taught, viz.,[4] that all happiness here below is only relative and has a value only put upon it by comparison: riches and abundance have their measures of good and convenience from the consideration of the miseries and inconveniences that attend poverty and want; health can be but slightly esteemed by him who never was acquainted with pain or sickness; and liberty and freedom are the happiness only valuable by a reflection on captivity and slavery. They who are unacquainted with, and have no notice of, the miseries of the latter will never put a due value and consideration upon the former; of which general rule, the most part of my countrymen, I am sorry to say, are too par-

---

[3] *the worst of times*: Pepys had just been reappointed as secretary of the admiralty after losing that post in 1679, when he was accused of betraying naval secrets to the French. He was briefly imprisoned in the Tower but was vindicated and freed in 1680.

[4] *viz*:. abbreviation for the Latin *videlicet*, meaning "namely" or "that is."

ticular an instance, who of all the nations of the earth are possessors of the greatest liberty but least sensible of the happiness. Here the government secures every man in the possession and enjoyment of what God's blessing and his own industry has allowed. Here even the poor and needy, the impotent, and those who the hand of God has touched have a comfortable subsistence and plentiful provision against all extremities. Here the industrious mechanic or country farmer can sit down at his table better provided than many barons of German, marquises in France, and knights in Spain. In a word, slavery is so strange a condition to England, that to touch its soil is ipso facto manumission, and the generality of the people have but little heard and less understood the miserable state which the most part of the world is now subject to, so that the plenty and great liberty of the English subjects is no great happiness to them because they never weigh their condition with what is the lot of other nations. Upon this consideration, I have adventured to publish this account of the miseries I underwent with many others during our captivity in Barbary and of my escape thence. My design is, Christian reader, to work in thee by this true though plain narrative some pity towards the sharp sufferings of thy poor brethren at the hands of infidels; to instruct thee to prize the blessings of that pleasant place where thy lot is fallen and where having only the benefit of air, thou hast a goodly heritage; and lastly, with me, to magnify the name of God, who in His Word commands us to tell what things He hath done for us and to show forth His works with gladness.

A TRUE ACCOUNT OF MY BEING TAKEN, AND SUFFERINGS DURING MY CAPTIVITY

Upon the twenty-seventh day of August 1684, I, Thomas Phelps, set sail from the Downs[5] in a vessel called the *Success*, of London, about forty tons, laden with salt, bound for a place in Ireland called the Ventrey,[6] where we arrived the tenth day of September. I stayed there some while and killed beef, designing[7] for the Madeiras and Montserrat. Accordingly, on the twentieth

---

[5] *the Downs*: a roadstead in the English Channel, along the east coast of Kent between North and South Foreland. It is protected by the Goodwin Sands, which act as a natural breakwater.

[6] *the Ventrey*: a fishing village on Dingle Bay, located four miles west of Dingle in County Kerry.

[7] *designing*: intending to sail.

of September, I set sail for the Madeiras, but my design was crossed, and my voyage stopped as followeth. Upon the fifth of October (being then a hundred leagues west off the Rock of Lisbon)[8] we saw a sail to windward of us, which immediately we found to give us chase. We made what sail we could from him, and night coming on, we had, for about two hours, lost sight of him, but at the rising of the moon, he got sight of us and quickly came up with us, hailing[9] us whence our ship. We answered "from London," demanding the like of him, who made answer "from Algier" and withal commanded us hoist out our boat, which we refused to do, but we braced our headsails[10] for him. Immediately he sent his boat towards us. When it was got almost by our side, we gave them three shouts, which so surprised them that they thought it convenient to retire aboard their own ship. We were not a little cheered at their departure and made from them with all the sail we could make, for we had not one great gun, and as for powder, I believe one single pound was the outmost[11] of our store. In the meantime he was hoisting in of his boat, I had got above two miles from him, which made me think I was clear of him, and withal that the ship must be an Algerine, she appearing so great that, according to the stories in England, I thought no such ship could belong to Salé; but I found myself, within a little while, mightily mistaken, for as soon as his boat was hoisted in, he presently fetched us up[12] again. We had tried his sailing all ways but found we could not wrong him any way; so seeing him astern, and a thing impossible to lose sight of us, I put out a light for him, notwithstanding I was possessed at that time (God knows) with fear enough, but I thought, in the dark, my seeming confidence and resolution might impose upon him, so as to fancy I was of some force, and truly afterwards he confessed to me that he thought I had six guns aboard and that I did intend to fight him.

He kept astern of me all night, and in the morning he put out Turkish colors, which I answered with our English. Then he came up and saw I had no boat in sight, for my boat was stowed down betwixt decks. He commanded me therefore to brace to my headsails, and then he sent his boat to demand

---

[8] *Rock of Lisbon*: possibly Cape Roca.

[9] *hailing*: "hailing of a ship is calling to her to know whence she is, or whither she is bound, or any other occasion" (H. Manwaring, *Seaman's Dictionary*, 1644).

[10] *braced our headsails*: drew in our main sails to stop the ship from moving forward.

[11] *outmost*: utmost.

[12] *fetched us up*: caught up to us.

my pass.[13] Aboard her was an antient[14] Moor, who formerly had been a slave in England and spoke good English and who was set at liberty by our late gracious king Charles the Second. He, seeing us in readiness with what arms we had, asked me if I had a mind to break the peace. He told me I needed not trouble myself to keep them out of our vessel, for none of them could be persuaded to come aboard me.

I brought him my customhouse cockets,[15] for I had no pass. The Moor aforesaid carried them to the captain but soon after returned and told me that would not satisfy the captain, unless the master[16] himself would come. I made answer that I would not come, that I had done what I was obliged to by the articles[17] 'twixt England and Algiers. The boat a second time put away for their ship, and whilst they were hoisting in their boat, I made what sail I could and was got a mile or more from them again, entertaining better hopes than I was in the night before; but as soon as the boat was in and stowed, the Moors made sail and came up with me again, the captain ordering to tell me that if I refused to come aboard him, he would come aboard me with his ship. With that he ranged up my weather quarter;[18] I immediately put a-stays,[19] which put him into some confusion, so that he was forced to put a-stays also. He had then no gun which I could perceive. I saw his ports,[20] and his waist[21] was man-high. As I came about, I run under his stern, then bore away right before the wind. He soon came up with me, but not one shot passed all this while. He demanded of me why I clapped a-stays for to run athwart his halse.[22] I answered that I doubted[23]

---

[13] *pass*: According to the terms of the peace treaty signed between the English crown and the Algierian regency, the lord high admiral of England issued official passes that allowed English ships to travel freely, without molestation by Algerian ships.

[14] *antient*: old.

[15] *customhouse cockets*: "document[s: sealed by the officers of the custom-house, and delivered to merchants as a certificate that their merchandise has been duly entered and has paid duty" (*O.E.D.*).

[16] *master*: commanding officer aboard the ship.

[17] *articles*: the peace treaty signed by Britain and the Algerian Regency in 1676.

[18] *ranged up my weather quarter*: moved into a position on the windward side of the ship, next to the area between the beam and the stern.

[19] *put a-stays*: turned the head of the ship into the wind.

[20] *ports*: "that place out of which the ordnance are put through the ship's sides" (Manwaring, *Seaman's Dictionary*).

[21] *waist*: a length of board or rail running along the sides of the ship's middle deck.

[22] *run athwart his halse*: cut across in front of his ship (the "halse" or "hawse" being the front portion of the ship where the hawseholes are located).

[23] *doubted*: suspected that.

he was not of Algier. He swore in English to me that he was, else before this he would have discovered himself, and withal he told me that if I did not come aboard he would straightway sink me, and so he hoisted out his boat. In the mean time I bore away, but his boat coming up made me bring to again and brace aback.[24] His boat then came aboard. I asked this Moor who spoke English what ship of Algiers this was. He very readily, without stammering, told me she was called the *Tagerene*; young Canary, commander.[25] I immediately then went into his boat. So soon as I came aboard, the captain asked me why I was so hard of belief. My distrust was such then that I prayed the captain now that he had me aboard in his power, to resolve me whether he were a Salé man or not. He swore to me again that he was of Algiers and that I should not be wronged. He made me sit down and caused them to set dates and figs before me. A little after, the captain told me that he was made acquainted by his men that they saw two Portugueses[26] aboard my ship and that he would have them out, and then I should be gone about my business. I told him I had none such aboard, but he would see them two men, so two men were sent for. After that, he told me there were three more and them he must have. Well to be short, at last he was suspicious that I was a Portuguese also, and to convince me that I was one, I found my entertainment presently withdrawn! Thus did this faithless Barbarian[27] serve me, until he had wheedled all my men aboard him except two, and then the valiant Moors entered my vessel with abundance of courage, heaving the two remaining English over the head of the vessel into the boat.

Thus were we all stripped, the vessel plundered in a moment, which they did resolve to have sunk because they were too far at sea distant from their own coast, but immediately we saw five sail bearing down upon us, which startled the Moors, putting them into a great fright, obliging them to quit my vessel with abundance of beef and three boxes of dry goods aboard, which their fear would not give them leisure to rummage for. In some small time, the five vessels discovered us. When they came within two leagues of us, had

---

[24] *bring to again and brace aback*: turn into the wind while drawing the sails out of the wind, thus bringing the ship to a halt again.

[25] *Tagerene; young Canary, commander*: The name of the ship refers to the Tagerene, or Morisco, inhabitants of Algiers who had come from Andalusia; the captain's name also suggests an Algerian provenance.

[26] *two Portugueses*: According to the agreement between Britain and Algiers, the transportation of other foreign nationals, including Portuguese, was cause for search and seizure by Algerian ships.

[27] *Barbarian*: a native of Barbary; also, an uncivilized person.

they bore down afterwards with that resolution that they threatened before, the pirate would never have stood to look them in the face, but alas, like distracted, fearful game, every of the five ships took a several course, and being now night they all escaped.

After that we cruised about thirty leagues to the west of the northern cape[28] and so to the Burlings,[29] but no nearer than twenty leagues to the shore, and therefore I imagine there is more safety for small vessels bound that way, to keep the shore as near as is possible, for I know certainly they never attempt to come near but endeavor as much as they can to avoid the shore because our men-of-war use[d] to careen[30] at Lisbon.

I am likewise pretty well satisfied for the small time that I was amongst them (although it was too long for my profit) that no Salé man will fight a ship of ten guns, which I found true by observation of a countryman from Bristol whilst I was aboard. We came up with him and hailed him and would have had him put out his boat, but he refused and withal showed himself ready in his own defense, upon which we were glad to leave him.

So that to satisfy all my countrymen who follow my trade, I dare confidently affirm that if I had a ship of ten guns, and it should be my fortune to encounter any of these Salé rogues (who all go under the notion of Algerines, who are now at peace with England), I would encourage him to send his boat, by acquainting him that our master would come aboard and show his pass (which is the thing they aim at). And when the boat was come to my side (any man of reason may judge then whether she were from Salé or Algiers, but however I would commit nothing should be judged a breach of the peace 'twixt England and Algiers), I would heave in a grappling and secure the men, all save two, whom I would permit to return aboard and bring me a Christian or else aver my pass. If they will not do that, I am then satisfied what he is and think myself obliged to defend myself from slavery, but this I am very confident of: that he will never stay to dispute the case afterward.

About a fortnight after I was taken, we met one Samuel Crampton who came from Faro[31] and whom we soon took without any resistance. The week

[28] *the northern cape*: possibly Cape Roca.
[29] *the Burlings*: the Berlengas Islands, just off the coast of Portugal.
[30] *to careen*: "bringing the ship over to lie on one side, she being afloat" (Manwaring, *Seaman's Dictionary*) for the purpose of caulking, scraping, or repairing the portion of the hull below the waterline.
[31] *Faro*: port on the southern coast of Portugal.

following, we took a small ketch come from Calais, laden with sherry and
raisins and bound for Limerick; John Elliot, master.

The number of us Christians taken aboard the three prizes was twenty-
five, besides twelve which were aboard the pirate, in all thirty-seven. We who
were newly taken were kept in irons in the hold.

After the taking of these three vessels, the pirate made all the sail he could
for Salé to save the spring tide,[32] which flows at Salé and Mamora south-
southwest about thirty leagues. To the northward of Salé, we met a Fleming
who came from Salé and told our commander that the English men-of-war
were at Tangier then, attending Captain Nicholason,[33] which caused us to
bear directly for Salé and fell in directly with the Castle, where were no English men-of-war, according to the advice.

On the bar[34] of Salé, there run[s] a great sea,[35] which obliged us to come
to an anchor near the bar, where we rid six hours. Then were we poor Christians all let loose from our iron shackles, wherein we had been confined for
twenty days preceding. The captain sent the boat as near the shore to the
south of the bar as possibly he could, to inquire what news. There they were
acquainted that they might safely come in the next high water. Whilst the
boat was gone ashore, the Moors, we observed, fell all fast asleep, the captain also, with his head over the rail upon the half-deck, seemed deeply
engaged. This opportunity, methought, was very inviting. I made a proposal
of it to my fellow slaves and undertook to do the captain's business myself.
The Christians were forward enough to comply with the motion, and eleven
of the twelve (which were slaves retained in the ship before our being taken),
they also were willing, if the twelfth who was steward in the ship would have
consented, but this sneaking varlet proved recreant, and for fear of him the
other eleven turned also renegadoes to this heroic and Christian resolution.
I had a mind to have dispatched this troubler of our peace out of the way first,
but the fear that his fellow slaves would have severely resented it restrained

---

[32] *save the spring tide*: arrive shortly after a new or full moon, when the high tide
is at its maximum.

[33] *at Tangier . . . Captain Nicolason*: a naval officer named Nicolson served under
the last English governor of Tangier, Colonel Percy Kirke. Tangier was held by the English crown from 1661 until February 5, 1684, when it was demolished and evacuated by
the English, who had failed to reach a treaty agreement with the Moroccan ruler,
Mulay Ismail. The English men-of-war mentioned here were probably there at this
time to supervise the destruction of the city and the withdrawal of its garrison.

[34] *bar*: sandbar.

[35] *great sea*: powerful tide or current.

my resolution. The slave's name was Will Robinson. He professed himself a Christian in words, but indeed we found more civility from the Moors than him.

At four in the afternoon, we weighed anchor and stood in for the bar. We struck twice going over, but without any damage. It was upon the first day of November, after we had helped to moor our ship, at night we were all carried ashore and conveyed to our lodging, which was an old stable but without litter or straw, having nothing save the bare dirty ground for our bed or pillow. The next day we were all carried aboard the ship to unrig her and get out her ballast, which we did. About four in the afternoon, I was sent for ashore to come to the governor, who passed his sentence on us three masters, that we should go to his house and there remain until we were sent for by the king. We remained at his house ten days, where our daily employment was to grind the corn for the use of his family. At length there came an order for us and all the rest of the Christians to be carried to the king, whose ordinary and then residence was at Machaness,[36] a place which this present emperor has set his fancy upon and bestows most of his care and employs all Christian slaves in building there. It is distant from Salé about seventy miles and from Fez thirty.

In our journey thither, I cannot forget our captain's extraordinary civility, in accommodating us sometimes with borricoes[37] to ride on, so that in two days and a half we arrived thither. The first night we were not brought before our great master, but the following our captain presented us before him, and withal some Portuguese plate which was taken in Mr. Crampton's vessel. As the captain gave it into his hand, the surly tyrant with a seeming scorn and disdain heaved it against the wall, which was the first action I observed and did a little discover the temper of my new patron Mulay Ishmael, emperor of Morocco[38] and Fez, etc. He ordered us to be sent amongst the rest of our fellow slaves. As we went, we were entertained with the civilities of the place and welcomed by the joyful acclamations and compliments of the Moors kicking and slapping us all along, which appeared very uncouth to me, who was but a stranger; but that night my fellow captives allayed my wonder by acquainting me that what had past was nothing: it was only a suitable prologue to all the tragical sufferings that Christians must endure there whilst

[36] *Machaness*: Meknes, the newly founded royal capital, a city near Fez in Morocco.

[37] *borricoes*: burros.

[38] *Mulay Ishmael, emperor of Morocco*: reigned 1672–1727.

they are slaves, which were so dreadful that I could willingly, that very night, have ventured my life to endeavor an escape. They painted out to me the tyrannical humor of the emperor, both towards the Christians and natives, in such bloody colors, viz., how they had seen him butcher many thousands with his own hands, how that none can be secure in his presence for that the varying of a look, a small spot in the garment, or any such inconsiderable circumstance will raise such a caprice in the emperor's noddle, without any other provocation, as to endanger all the heads before him, and it is very rare if the company escape with one or two only beheaded or lanced through the body.

The second day after my arrival thither, I saw him lance seven and twenty negroes, one after another, and every day after, until New Year's Day (when he parted to Santa Cruz[39] with his army), I either saw or heard of his inhumane but yet (through custom) to him natural barbarities, killing and dragging, but this latter is a piece of respect observed only to minions and favorites, vice-kings and alcaides.[40] Yea, his women are not able by all their charms to avoid his fury but are more the objects of his implacable rage than any other passion. I have been several times in the West Indies and have seen and heard of divers inhumanities and cruelties practiced there. I have also read in books and have heard learned men discourse of the Sicilian tyrants and Roman emperors, but indeed I forget them all; they are not to be named in comparison with this monster of Africk, a composition of gore and dust, whom nothing can atone but human sacrifices and to be in whose court it is much more eligible[41] to be his horse or his mule than to be his privado[42] or wife of his bosom, from whose greatest kindness my good God ever defend me, for his mercies are cruel. Yea, even Hamed Ben Haddu who was his ambassador here in England three years ago,[43] although he was received and entertained here with extraordinary civilities and caressed everywhere by all the endearments of kindness and respect, and although by his fineness and Moorish subtlety he stole into the inclinations of the well-meaning and good-natured English, so that he obtained the reputation of ingenuity and candor,

---

[39] *Santa Cruz*: Agadir, on the southwestern coast of Morocco.
[40] *alcaides*: governors or commanders.
[41] *eligible*: desirable.
[42] *privado*: confidant or court favorite.
[43] *Hamed Ben Haddu . . . three years ago*: A Moroccan ambassador, Mohammed Ohadu, arrived in London in January 1682, where he met with Charles II at Whitehall to negotiate an Anglo-Moroccan treaty. He remained until July, when he departed for Morocco. Mulay Ismail subsequently refused to ratify the agreement.

yet the dog has returned to his vomit, and by woeful experiment all my countrymen who come under his power find him a harsh and cruel master who managed his affairs here with deep dissimulation and now improves his knowledge of English affairs, to the detriment and ruin of all the king's subjects with whom he has to do; if it be his fortune to meet or pass by any of them, his custom is (as all the English can attest) to salute them with a devilish curse to the best of my remembrance expressed thus: "Alli Haztebuck," i.e., "God roast your father." He is indeed reckoned a great master in the art of dissimulation and flattery, a qualification which seems very requisite in a courtier of such a barbarous, bloody tyrant as his master is.

But to proceed: my fellow Christians in the next place showed me the staff of their life there, i.e., their bread, which was of barley but black, and withal it stunk, the corn being kept seven years underground before used. One day's allowance, if sold, would yield only nine fluces,[44] which amount to three farthings. Flesh is cheap, both mutton and beef, but money is scarce: two pounds and a half of beef are ordinarily sold for four blankil (i.e., two pence half-penny) and two pounds of mutton at the same rate. Good white bread is also plentiful, half as cheap as in England, but what is this to the slaves who have not a farthing? And not a bit is allowed us without money. I am confident there is many a Christian there who hath not tasted a morsel of flesh in five month's time.

The country is a pleasant champion[45] country, very fruitful, well watered, productive of all sorts of fruit in plenty. We Christians who arrived last were excused for two days from labor; only we were instructed in our deportments to our negro taskmasters,[46] who afterwards gave us severe chastisement for our mistakes and lapses. Our work and daily labor was continually building of houses and walls. The materials and method is very foreign and will appear strange to my countrymen here. There are boxes of wood of dimensions according to pleasure;[47] these we fill with earth powdered and lime and gravel, well beat together and tempered with water, and when full we remove the box according to order and withdraw the box planks and leave this matter to dry, which then will acquire an incredible hardness and is very lasting,

[44] *fluces*: small copper coins.

[45] *champion*: level, open.

[46] *negro taskmasters*: The Moroccan sultan was traditionally served by a personal army of black soldiers recruited or taken from the southern oases and the Niger River valley.

[47] *according to pleasure*: as needed.

for we have seen walls of some hundred years standing (as we were informed), and all that time has not been able to do them any prejudice.[48]

The king himself (what the reason of his humor may be, I never had the curiosity to ask him) will sometimes vouchsafe to work in the lime and dirt for an hour together and will bolt out an encouraging word to the slaves then, viz., as I remember, "liferus," that is, "God send you to your own countries," but I judge he either does not speak from his heart or else he hopes God will not answer the prayers of such a wicked wretch. With this sort of labor I made a shift to pass away all the winter and indeed without a quibble: I had no other shift[49] or shirt; only the charity of my fellow slaves (who were better provided) accommodated me with a covering from the cold, which else would have endangered my life.

The reader, I suppose, will not think it strange if I was dissatisfied and very weary of my condition, and therefore I did often rummage all my thoughts for some expedient to ease me of this accursed way, not of living, but starving and dying daily. My mind did often flatter me with the greatest possibility of liberty by running away, and so confident I was that I discovered my intentions to several Christians, especially to those of my near acquaintance, who by no means could be induced to hear the difficulties and dangers that attended such a resolution. In the meantime, my friends in England had taken some care for my ransom and had given order to Mr. Luddington, an English merchant in Barbary, to endeavor my relief if one hundred and fifty pounds would effect it, which sum Mr. Luddington acquainted me he was ready to disburse, if I could cut (that is, agree with my patron for my ransom) for six hundred or seven hundred pieces of eight. I proffered the said sum, but it would not be accepted, upon which I looked upon my condition as desperate, my forlorn and languishing state of life without any hopes of redemption (which only could support our spirits in the midst of such great afflictions and bondage to those upon whom God and Nature seems to have impressed characters of slavery to the rest of mankind) appeared far worse than the terrors of a most cruel death. I set up then my fixed and unalterable resolution to escape whatever fate attended it, leaving the event to providence. I had more than conjecture that present death was to be the reward of my endeavors if I were retaken, for three Spaniards, who some two months before were taken, making their escape, the king caused them to be brought before him and with his own hands proved their butcher and exe-

---

[48] *prejudice*: harm.

[49] *shift*: a pun, meaning both "stratagem" and "loose-fitting linen shirt."

cutioner, which cruel proceedings did wholly dishearten the poor-spirited Christians and banished all such resolutions quite out of their minds. At length I opened my mind to Mr. Baxter (who about a year and a half before had made an unlucky attempt to run away, but being brought back, he had the bastinado[50] in such a sort that he could not work for a twelve month, having irons continually upon his legs), but notwithstanding, such was his love of Christian liberty that he freely told me that he would adventure with any fair opportunity. After I had him thus engaged by his promise, I gave him no rest until we had pitched upon[51] a day. We also took into our cabal and share of our fortunes two Bristol men, who were ready at an hour's warning, when we appointed.

There are at Machaness at present about eight hundred Christians of all nations, two hundred and sixty whereof are English, several of which have tendered money for their ransom: some seven hundred, some five hundred pieces of eight; some more, some less. But the king still put them off with this: that he would clear none particularly but that they should go all together.

January the first, the king set forward towards Santa Cruz with an army of about sixty thousand men, designing to quell his nephew, who had made a formidable insurrection against him in that part of his dominions. We Christians could not inform ourselves of the certain proceedings of these armies, neither did we much care—fight dog, fight bear[52]—but this we learnt: that it will be two or three years before his return, and it is not to be supposed that any particular Christian will be released until he return. Besides, there is no hopes to be laid upon the most solemn word and protestation of this swarthy infidel Mulay Ismael, for as I have been informed, about four or five years ago, by an agreement with Colonel Kirk, all the English slaves were to be set at liberty at the rate of two hundred pieces of eight a head, and the bargain was so far struck that the Christians were got a mile out of town, but the accursed Jews (the stench and pest of the nations of the earth, malicious to all mankind and loathsome and abominable wherever they come, who not only have the blood of the Savior of the world lying upon their heads but are accountable for the blood of many thousands of his members which they daily shed), these wicked enemies of Christianity, brought back these poor Christians into the house of bondage thus: they proffered the emperor as

---

[50] *bastinado*: a beating delivered with a stick, usually on the soles of the feet.

[51] *pitched upon*: resolved upon.

[52] *fight dog, fight bear*: an English proverb alluding to bearbaiting, expressing a desire to see rival forces fight to the death without interference from spectators.

much money as the king of England tendered for the Christians' ransom, if so be he would only lend them for a while to build a city for the Jews, and then they should be restored to the king. The covetous tyrant soon closed with these advantageous terms, and the Christians were turned over to the Jews, who employed them three years in building a city. But when finished, see the just judgment of God! The Jews were turned out and forced to give place to the Moors. Another remarkable story concerning the Jews I cannot but insert upon this occasion. About three years ago, Mr. Bowrey of Bristol was, with twenty sail more, taken by the Salé men. Bowrey had a parcel of soap in his ship, which then did belong to the king. Ben Haddu, ambassador in England, desired to buy this soap of the king, but a Jew outbid him and so had the soap, for which dealing the ambassador kept a grudge in his mind against the Jews and was revenged on them after this manner, whilst I was there. He informed the king that the Jews had imposed upon him and cozened him of fifty thousand pieces of eight in the matter of the soap, upon which the king clapped up ten of the chief Jews in prison, until they should either pay the said sum or else restore the soap, which it is to be supposed hath been sold in Christendom two years ago.

AN ACCOUNT OF MY ESCAPE, MR. EDMUND BAXTER, AND OTHERS FROM BARBARY

After a serious consideration, finding that no proffers for my redemption would be accepted, I committed the conduct of my proceedings to almighty providence, resolving to make an escape in company of three more: Edmund Baxter, Anthony Bayle, and James Ingram.

On the twenty-ninth of May, agreeing with our guardian Moors for a blankil (i.e., 2d., ob.[53]) apiece, we had the liberty to be excused from work that day, we went therefore to the town of Machaness, and having but a small stock of cash about us (viz. nine blankils), we laid it out in bread and two small bullock's bladders, with a little burdock, to carry water in.

About three of the clock in the afternoon we began our journey, designing to go as far as an old house called the king's house, distant about three miles from Machaness, resolving to conceal ourselves about that house until night and promising to ourselves the greater security because we knew some Christians used commonly to work there; but proceeding in our journey, we

---

[53] 2d., ob.: abbreviation for "two pence, obiter" (the Latin obiter means "in passing").

discovered upon a loaded horse the Moor who lived at that house, which obliged us to quicken our pace and keep ahead of him, for if he should come up with us, he would easily discover that we did not belong to the said house. We made haste therefore before him, and coming near the house, we discovered about twenty Moors sitting there, which accident of being hemmed in behind and before by these our enemies put us into a great fright and had in all likelihood spoiled our design in the very entrance, if providence had not presented to our view, on one side of the house, a parcel of limekilns, to which, without the Moors observation, we immediately struck up,[54] where we absconded ourselves by lying flat upon our bellies. About half an hour after, came two Moorish women thither to gather up some loose wood. We, considering it very inconvenient to show ourselves fearful, lest we should be taken for renegadoes, spoke to them, but they returned us no answer, following their business and taking us, as we judged, either for Moors or Christians employed about the said limekilns, so we continued there without any further molestation until night, when we proceeded on our journey, traveling about eighteen miles that night. We passed by a great many tents, whence the dogs came out and barked at us, and the Moors also saw us but said nothing, mistaking us for their countrymen.

That night we crossed the great river[55] which runs down to Mamora, about eighteen miles distance from Machaness, and about a mile from the bank of the river, we found a convenient bush where we took up our lodging all the day following, without any disturbance. At night we found ourselves obliged to return to the said river to furnish us with water, the littleness of our vessel, which contained not above a gallon, being a great hindrance in our journey. We continued our progress twelve miles that night, which proved very tiresome by reason of the weeds and bushes, and the nights were not so long as we wished. Just about daybreak, we found a convenient bush near to a great valley, where we reposed ourselves. As soon as the day broke clear, we saw abundance of cattle grazing in the bottom, with Moors who looked after them, but by God's providence none came near us, so that we lay safe all that day, being the last day of May.

At night we set forwards, keeping the woods, where were no Moorish inhabitants, only wild beasts, the less savage and formidable, which we often saw, but they never attempted to come near us. We traveled about ten miles that night and then crossed a river which supplied us with water, whereof we

[54] *struck up*: made our way.
[55] *the great river*: presumably, the Sebou River.

were in want. On the other side of the river, we observed the footsteps of a great many cattle, which rendered the place, as we thought, unsafe for us. We made therefore a little further progress in the morning, to the top of the hill, where under a large oak we found a bush convenient for our reception that day, but within a little while we were disturb[ed] in our repose, observing the cattle to come grazing up the hill, directly to that bush, with Moors at their heels. With all haste therefore we packed up our luggage and ran a mile further without being discovered, until we came to a pear tree furnished with long grass around him. There we took up our quarters all that day, being the first of June.

The night following, we intended to proceed, but it pleased God to strike me lame with the gout, so that I was not able to stand. I was forced therefore to remain there all that night and the day ensuing, which was a great hindrance to my companions and affliction to myself. The readiest expedient to remedy my distemper which I could think upon was this: we made a fire in a hole in the ground, and I put my foot into the hole to draw away the pain. Having also a lancet with us, I endeavored to breathe a vein[56] in my foot, but I could not effect it, for the lancet would not enter. However, I found some ease by the force of the fire. My company, being sensible of the delay which my distemper occasioned, began to be moved, insomuch that they told me that if I could not march with them that night, they must hold themselves obliged to take leave of me, which added a great affliction to my sorrow, insomuch as I was the author and first mover of the escape. That I might not therefore be forsaken by my companions, and in compliance to their importunity, I resolved to strain my outmost power.

The third of June at night I endeavored to go, but in great pain, so that we could not proceed above three miles, when I was forced to pray my companions to stay but that night, and I did not question, but by God's blessing, to be able to travel with them the next. They consented, and so we took up our lodging for the remainder of that night under another pear tree.

The fourth of June I kept baking my foot all the day in the ground, till about two in the afternoon. In the meanwhile, I procured Mr. Baxter to make me a wooden leg,[57] which accordingly he did. I persuaded them then to travel about three or four miles that afternoon, which would a little ease the labor of the night. They agreed. I traveled about four miles with that leg and then rested till night on the top of a high hill, whence we saw a great plain valley before us.

---

[56] *breathe a vein*: lance a vein so as to let blood.
[57] *wooden leg*: a crutch or splint.

At night we shaped our course clear of the tents and traveled over the edge of the plain, about six miles. We passed by several fields of corn, the Moors in the meantime hallowing to frighten the wild beasts from them. Crossing of a river that night, we saw and heard several lions. Some approached so near that we could almost have touched them, but as soon as we struck fire, which we had prepared for that very purpose, they presently vanished. When the light began to display itself, we took our quarters for the next day, which was June the fifth. At night we continued our course, when I was still lame, which was a great hindrance to my company, but we were loath to part. Our bread also was almost at an end, the consideration whereof obliged me to strain hard to get eight miles that night. By resting the next day I found myself to be something better but then to qualify my joy for this, another companion, Anthony Bayle, began to sink and give over.

June the sixth we set onward and measured ten miles that night, when we came to a great swamp, there my pain renewing. I fain would have persuaded them to stay but by no entreaties could persuade them, so resolving to part, we shared our bread, which came to two half-rusks[58] apiece. I endeavored to allure my weak wearied brother to abide with me, comforting him with the expectation of gardens where we two, more easily than the company of four, might provide for ourselves. He would not stay. Being pressed thus with the consideration of being left alone, I resolved to put forward, when it pleased God that my foot became perfectly whole and clear of the gout. That night we traveled over a high, barren hill, where we fancied we heard the suss[59] and noise of the sea, which encouraged us to mend our pace until we met with a garden where we gathered about a dozen of small pumpkins, a very comfortable assistance to us, now that our bread was all spent, for some we eat raw, and some we roasted in the ground, whereby we found ourselves considerably refreshed. That night we made no more than eight miles, for meeting with a great oak which was blown down, we thought it inconvenient to overslip such an advantageous retirement for the next day, which we were the more desirous of because we heard a great many Moors, though we could not see them.

All the next day we lay still, and with exceeding contentment we heard the noise of the sea. At night we put on and came to the shore, where we found whereabout we then were, viz. to the southward of Mamora. We directed our course then northward for two miles, when we could discern the castle, but

---

[58] *rusks*: pieces of bread toasted to make them hard and crisp.
[59] *suss*: hiss made by the surf.

knowing that we could not go to the northward of the castle because the great river goes directly up into the country, we turned back about a mile, and finding a convenient bush, we rested there all the next day, hearing and seeing a great many cattle, but none came near us.

June the eighth we gathered about half a peck of snails and caught a land tortoise, which we roasted and ate heartily. That day also, we saw a ship in the offing. When night was come, we made down towards the castle, and before we were aware we fell upon a Moor making a fire, which forced us to draw back. The Moor not discerning us, we fetched then a compass and by another way came down to the castle. There we found a strong watch, which did wholly discourage our expectations of relief from that place, so we set up our resolutions for Salé, about eighteen or twenty miles to the southward, to see what good could be done there. But before we parted with Mamora, we made bold with a little barley and guinea corn[60] growing under the castle, of each whereof we gathered about a quarter of a peck to serve our necessities, and then we betook ourselves to our former night's refuge, the bush, and after having consulted how to steer our course for Salé, the result whereof was along the seaside, we rested all the next day without disturbance.

June the ninth we traveled along the seaside, where we saw a great deal of raft timber. We concluded therefore, seeing the ship in the offing, to make a raft, which accordingly we did and put off with it, but it would not swim, boyart with us all.[61] We came therefore ashore and cut all our lashings, leaving it to the mercy of the sea. We traveled five miles towards Salé that night, fearing lest by staying long thereabout we should be discovered, for our footing and trailing of the timber had made such an impression in the sand as if an hundred men had been there. That night we took up our quarters in a fig tree about seven miles short of Salé, where was no inhabitant.

June the tenth at night we made forward to Salé, in the road. We fell upon a parcel of tents, where though the dogs were ready to seize us and the Moors themselves called to us, we made no answer and traveled on, without any farther trouble or danger, until we came to Salé. As soon as we came thither, we made towards the gardens and gathered some pumpkins, and because night was far spent, we retreated about a mile out of town, to find some place which might secure us from discovery. We pitched[62] upon a bush in a great valley, wherein we resolved to enclose ourselves the day following. About

[60] *guinea corn*: durra, a variety of sorghum grain.
[61] *boyart with us all*: while keeping us all afloat.
[62] *pitched*: decided.

eleven of the clock of that day, we espied a boy with a dog keeping of sheep but yet not forgetting his game, which was hunting of partridges. He beat the bush wherein we were lodged and threw in stones, and the dog also did his part, barking and coursing about the bush, but by miracle (as we thought) we were not espied, though we discovered abundance of fear amongst ourselves, for if we had been taken notice of, we could not otherwise consult[63] our own safety than by the death of that poor silly[64] lad.

The eleventh day being past, at night we made a descent to the river of Salé, about a mile above the town, where we found a boat but could not with all our strength launch her. Anthony Bayle and I, who were the only swimmers in our company, made over to the south side of the river, to see what purchase we could make there. We found indeed three boats, but they were all aground, so that we could do no good with them; but in searching about the new ships (which five in number are building there), we found two oars, with which we swam over to our consorts, and all together we went down by the river's side to the harbor's mouth, but we could meet with no boat to put our oars in. We saw two Dutchmen in the river, but they kept a diligent watch, which hindered us from carrying away their boat. We concluded therefore to bury our oars in the sand at some remarkable place,[65] and so we betook ourselves to find out a sanctuary for the day following. We found a fig tree full of leaves, in an unfrequented place, as we thought, on the north side of the river yet within call of the ships, which then were a-building! Under the covert of this little tree, though surrounded with enemies and dangers, we resolved to expect the protection of the next day. The reader may possibly judge this an instance of a romantic[66] courage and an effect rather of rash boldness than prudent consideration. Truly, he is in the right, for we ourselves were of the same mind. About the middle of the next day, upon this occasion, a Moor who had newly washed his clothes directs his course directly to our tree, and there hangs up his *al hage*[67] to dry whilst he himself sat down not far off to louse[68] himself, an't please you. If providence did hinder him from discerning us, I assure you it was not for want of provocation,

[63] *consult*: bring about.
[64] *silly*: simple, innocent.
[65] *remarkable place*: place that they could remember and find again.
[66] *romantic*: impractical and extravagant.
[67] al hage: jocular use of the title of respect given to an older Muslim, referring here to his turban or robe.
[68] *louse*: delouse.

as we all confessed, and indeed I never in my life was in such a trembling fit as that lousy rascal put me into.

The twelfth day of June being past, at night we came down again to the river to look after a boat which we had observed was moored in the river, half a mile higher than where we found the oars. This we who could swim found and brought to our consorts. We paddled her down the river close by the Dutchmen, who saw us but said nothing; then we put ashore and fetched our oars. We continued paddling until we had passed a Frenchman lying at the bar's mouth, who plainly saw us but said nothing. So soon as we had left him behind us, we shipped out our oars, and rowing right into the sea, our course by the North Star was west-northwest. When we had rowed four miles or thereabout, we discerned a ship at anchor, which obliged us to alter our course and row northward until we had passed her, fearing lest she might be a Salé ship, and we had learned at Machaness that two of them were a-cruising at that time and not yet come in. Therefore it was that in distrust of this ship we altered our course. We rowed about two leagues without[69] the ship and lay upon[70] our oars. When day broke up clear, we saw the ship with her sails loose. I then acquainted my consorts that in my judgment, if the ship were of Salé, she would make in for the bar at that time because the tide and the sea breeze were then both favorable, it being high water at seven of the clock, but if she were an English man-of-war, as we incessantly wished, then we thought the sea breeze would make her stand off to sea.[71] Notwithstanding, our opinions were various, and we were doubtful what to do. At length I persuaded my consorts, with much ado, to row in and make her hull.[72] Then the ship stood off and at length saw us. We pulled aboard and found her to be the *Lark*, frigate; Captain Leighton, commander. After some examination and discourse about the methods and means of our escape, I propounded to the captain a design which had newly taken strong possession of my fancy. It was this: that if he would accommodate me with his boat and those belonging to the other two men-of-war which were in company, I would undertake to pilot them in and to burn what ships were then at Mamora. The captain immediately stood[73] to the northward and came up with the other two ships, which were the *Bonaventure* and the *Greyhound*. The admiral was then sick at Calais, so Captain Mac-

---

[69] *without*: away from.
[70] *lay upon*: rested.
[71] *stand off to sea*: go further out toward the open sea.
[72] *make her hull*: catch up to the other ship.
[73] *stood*: directed his course.

donald being eldest captain,[74] we went aboard him, and sending for Mr. Fairborne, who was then captain under Captain Priestman, who was sick as abovesaid, they held a council about those propositions which I had made. At first they seemed unpracticable, by reason of many difficulties, but especially of the bar, which is worse than that of Salé, but then when upon second thoughts they considered the forwardness of men, who but that very day had escaped a heavy slavery and yet were willing that very night to engage in the action, they concluded it both possible and feasible, so they entertained with approbation what I had proposed. After which, I immediately returned with Captain Leighton aboard the *Lark* and communicated the result of the council with my comrade, Mr. Baxter, who was heartily pleased with what was undertaken and willing to go along, so he was ordered to go in the *Bonaventure*'s boat and was very serviceable and who was better acquainted with that bar than I was. Immediately orders were given to shave some deal boards[75] and saw some tar barrels[76] and make ready with all expedition. By seven at night, all things were in readiness. The frigates were riding two leagues from shore. Orders were given that the boat in which I was, the *Greyhound*'s, should go ahead, commanded by Captain Macdonald, who behaved himself indeed with great courage and resolution, and the rest had orders to follow us. There were three barges in all and one yawl. The number of men concerned in the action was forty-two, who all had strict charge upon pain of death not to seek after plunder, which was punctually observed. About eight at night we put off from the ships, and betwixt nine and ten we fell a little to the northward of the bar, but by Mr. Baxter's assistance, we quickly righted ourselves and found the bar. There was a great noise upon the shore: all thereabout had taken the alarm, which did nothing discourage us. We proceeded lustily, without any concernment at their hideous outcries, which when the Moors perceived and that we advanced with undaunted resolutions, they thought it best to fly betimes and secure themselves and their castle. In the meantime we pursued our design towards the ships, aboard which, there being a great many lights, we observed the Moors looking over the sides of the first we came to, which was the bigger of the two. They called to us to keep off. We answered them with about twenty granado-shells,[77] which soon drove them overboard.

---

[74] *eldest captain*: senior and therefore commanding officer.

[75] *shave some deal boards*: make wood shavings from pine boards.

[76] *saw some tar barrels*: cut up tar barrels (another combustible material, one that is difficult to extinguish).

[77] *granado-shells*: mortar shells or grenades.

They had not far indeed to escape, for the castle wall was within a boat's length of the ship, so without any difficulty we presently entered. One Moor we found aboard, who was presently cut in pieces. Another was shot in the head, endeavoring to escape upon the cable.[78] We were not long in taking in our shavings and tar barrels and so set her on fire in several places, she being very apt to receive what we designed, for there were several barrels of tar upon the deck, and she was newly tarred as if on purpose. Whilst we were setting her on fire, we heard a noise of some people in the hold. We opened the scuttles and thereby saved the lives of four Christians, three Dutchmen and one French, who told us that the ship on fire was admiral[79] and belonged to Aly Hackum and the other which we soon after served with the same sauce had the name of *Plummage Cortible*, which was the very ship which in October last took me captive. I cannot deny that I was possessed with an extraordinary satisfaction to see this ship on fire, and I could not but admire the wonderful providence of God, to whom alone vengeance belongeth,[80] in vindicating my cause and making me an unwitting instrument of revenge for the injuries I received from the owners of this vessel.

Such was the fierceness of the flames that we were forced to keep off from the ships' sides, whereby we became obnoxious to[81] the shot of the Moors, who from the walls of the castle made a great firing upon us, both of small and great guns, but with little or no execution, for our men, by the light of the great fire having them in perfect view upon the walls, made smart returns upon them, firing incessantly upon them and with that eagerness that they quite neglected their oars, so that if the tide had not turned to ebb, we should have run a great risk: our men were so full of joy, whooping and hallowing at the sight of so desirable a bonfire, that they never minded the dangers they might be subject to. We were therefore forced to row the *Bonaventure*'s yawl, who had lost all her oars. In all this action we had but one man mortally wounded and two or three more slightly hurt. After we had completed our business and absolutely destroyed these ships, we returned out of the river, over the bar, and pulled aboard the frigates. Captain Macdonald received us kindly and gratified us with the entertainment of his ship very frankly,[82]

---

[78] *cable*: heavy rope tied to the anchor.

[79] *was admiral*: was a flagship.

[80] *to whom alone vengeance belongeth*: "Vengeance is mine, I will repay, saith the Lord" (Romans 12:19).

[81] *obnoxious to*: exposed to harm from.

[82] *frankly*: generously.

aboard which we stayed until we came to Calais. There we went ashore, designing a passage for England with the first opportunity. Captain Macdonald gave us certificates of our service in the late action, and then Mr. Baxter and I took leave of him. We did not stay long at Calais before we met with an opportunity for England aboard Captain Atkins,[83] who came from Leghorn and was bound for London, who very willingly granted us passage with him and gave us civil and welcome entertainment, whom God reward and all other our benefactors, particularly (though to some readers it may seems immaterial, yet when occasion offers, not to remember, to all good men, will appear unthankful, and I had rather be taxed with impertinence than ungratitude) Mr. Hodges, who bestowed upon us four pieces of eight in our necessity (God return his charity into his own bosom with blessing and increase), and honest Captain Gutteridge, who sent a barrel of beef and a hundred weight of bread, lest we should lie too chargeable upon Captain Atkins in our passage home, who the first day of July, 1685, set sail from Cadiz and arrived in the Downs the twenty-sixth of that month.

Thus have I given a short and plain account of my captivity and escape, with the circumstances that attended it, and though possibly my style may appear rough and unpolished, which the courteous reader I hope will a little excuse, expecting no other from a blunt seaman acquainted with nothing so much as dangers and storms, yet I do profess I have penned this narrative with all the sincerity and truth that becomes a plain-dealing Englishman. My design and aim in all (kind countryman and courteous reader) is to excite with me thy praises to our God the only deliverer, who hath delivered me from a cruel and severe captivity; and withal to stir up thy grateful resentments[84] for the happiness, peace, and freedom that thou enjoyest under so excellent and well tempered a government; but most especially to move thy pity for the afflictions of Joseph;[85] to excite thy compassionate regard to those poor countrymen now languishing in misery and irons; to endeavor their releasement according to thy power, at least by importuning heaven, that during their captivity God would support them with His grace to bear patiently their afflictions and to resist all temptations until, in His good, appointed time, He vouchsafe them a happy deliverance. Amen.

FINIS.

[83] *aboard Captain Atkins*: aboard Captain Atkins's ship.
[84] *resentments*: feelings.
[85] *Joseph*: the biblical Joseph, whose brothers sold him into slavery amongst the Ishmaelites (Genesis 37:28).

Joseph Pitts, *A True and Faithful Account of the Religion and Manners of the Mohammetans, with an Account of the Author's Being Taken Captive* (1704)

(Algiers and Mecca, 1678–94)

As its title indicates, Joseph Pitts's *True and Faithful Account of the Religion and Manners of the Mohammetans* is more than just a captivity narrative. Its primary function is to provide firsthand, ethnographic reportage about Islamic culture, religion, and customs. Pitts's thick description of Algiers and of the pilgrimage to Mecca includes a wide range of observations, from public wrestling matches, to the conduct of war, to the details of Islamic religious practice and belief. Like the other narrators whose writings are collected here, Pitts strongly, even anxiously, asserts the truth value of his account, but in his case, there is an emphasis on empirical truth and accuracy of information rather than the "revealed truth" of religion. Pitts is keen to correct the errors and inaccuracies of other writers and to contribute thereby to the store of European, Christian knowledge about the Islamic world.

Pitts offered his text, and undertook the labor of writing it, "to do some good" and "also make some manner (at least) of restitution and reparation for my past defection." He is the only author of the captivity narratives included here who formally converted to Islam during his captivity. By the end of his career in Algiers, he had become a full-fledged "renegado," enjoying the privileges of a free citizen of the "Turkish" community and serving in a corsair fleet that preyed upon Christian shipping in the Mediterranean. As such, his need to purify himself and to clear his name is much greater than any of the other narrators.' Pitts's contemporaries in England would have seen him as contaminated by his intimate and extended contact with the Islamic other. His apostasy was a crime that called for atonement. Pitts's, *True and Faithful Account of the Religion and Manners of the Mohammetans* not only claims to be a revelation of the truth about Islam from an insider's point of view; it also asks the reader to acknowledge the "true and faithful" nature of the narrator, in spite of the fact that he had "turned Turk." Pitts offers an exchange: information and testimony about and against Islam in return for his redemption and reintegration. His narrative is a confessional tract, but it also represents the narrator's attempt to atone for his apostasy by offering something substantial—intelligence about the Muslims—that will be useful to his own society and therefore a valid form of compensation for his crime.

The use value of Pitts's text is apparent in the numerous reprints and excerpts that followed the first edition in 1704. A second edition was printed in 1717 and reprinted in 1719. In 1731 a third edition appeared, corrected and supplemented with maps and plates, including a "map of Mecca" and "a cut of the gestures of the Mahometans in their worship." This was reprinted in 1738, and further appearances of Pitts's narrative occurred in various compilations of ethnographic materials published in the eighteenth and nineteenth centuries.

Joseph Pitts, *A True and Faithful Account of the Religion and Manners of the Mohammetans. In which is a Particular Relation of Their Pilgrimage to Mecca, the Place of Mohammet's Birth, and a Description of Medina and of His Tomb There. As Likewise of Algier and the country adjacent: and of Alexandria, Grand Cairo, etc. With an Account of the Author's Being Taken Captive, the Turks' Cruelty to Him, and of His Escape. In Which Are Many Things Never Published by Any Historian Before.*

BY JOSEPH PITTS OF EXON. EXON: PRINTED BY S. FARLEY, FOR PHILIP BISHOP AND EDWARD SCORE, IN THE HIGH-STREET. 1704.

To the honored William Ray, esquire, late consul of Smyrna.

Sir,

I humbly beg your leave to lay the following sheets at your feet as the best acknowledgment I can at present make for the great kindnesses you showed me at Smyrna.

Sir,

Next to almighty God, I am indebted to you, who so readily ventured your life to procure my liberty. I am sensible what hazards you run to facilitate my escape, and I am at a loss how to express my sense of so great a favor and benefit.

With what sympathizing goodness did you allay those fears and terrors I lay under when I designed to make my escape! Your good book you lent me did much support me, and your noble and generous pity to me upheld me amidst all my discouragements.

'Tis through your means that I once more breathe in English air. 'Tis by your means that I enjoy the Gospel. Through you, I am delivered from Mohammet, a privilege greater than my life itself!

I can never make you suitable returns for the obligations you have laid on me, but God is able to recompense you, and my constant and earnest prayers to Him shall be for your welfare, honor, and prosperity in this world and immortal happiness in the next.

I want words to express my resentments of[1] your past kindnesses and favors and to implore your pardon of this my boldness in offering to you this poor testimony of my gratitude, which if you shall please to forgive and accept of this mean offering, I shall reckon it one of the happiest circumstances of my whole life that I have an opportunity of thus declaring, that

> I am,
> honored sir,
> Your most obliged, most devoted,
> And most obedient servant,
> Joseph Pitts.

THE PREFACE

It may be thought presumption in me to put forth this little book of the religion and manners of the Mohammetans, etc., after so many great and learned men and travelers, capable of making their observations with the greatest exactness, have published on the same subject. And indeed I thought an offer towards a publication of my poor memoirs to be so, but I was importuned by many of my friends to write the following account, and upon a serious consideration of the intent of their requests, I was induced to do it, hoping thereby to do some good to one or other and also make some manner (at least) of restitution and reparation for my past defection.

I may undergo the censures of some, but I hope not of the best and most candid men. I do not pretend to give an exact and methodical account of what I have observed, for I cannot pretend to the abilities that are required for a person that writes such an history. Only I beg leave to say plainly, I have the most valuable qualification of an historian on my side, i.e., truth.

I never thought, till importuned thereto, of exposing my observations to the public view. I had many objections in myself to the contrary and great reluctancy, which the reader may guess at. But I have now launched out and therefore entreat the reader that he would first pass by the inexactness of the method, and secondly, the mean style, and thirdly, the errors that happen to be seen, though I know of none material except what are in the errata.

One thing I will desire of the learned reader, which is that if the Arabic words in any place be not rightly written, he will please to take notice that I

---

[1] *resentments of*: continued feelings about.

aimed at the vulgar sound of the word and writ as near as I could to their way of speaking it. And moreover, I can't pretend to a perfection in the Arabian language. If I happen in any place to be mistaken in point of time, it is not willfully done, and therefore I hope the reader will pass it by.

I might have contrived it so as to have made a much bigger book of it, if I had thought fit, but I was willing that it should be for everybody's reading, and therefore I was unwilling to make the price too great.

I have hinted at some mistakes in authors who are persons of great learning and worth and whose names I acknowledge myself unworthy so much as to mention, were it not for the sake of truth, which ought to be the dearest thing in the world to every man, and upon that account alone I have made bold to mention some things in which I am sure they are misinformed. What I speak I know to be true and have not recited things merely upon hearsay.

I question whether there be a man now in England that has ever been at Mecca, and if I were assured of it, yet I would never take encouragement from thence to tell the world anything but truth. If I should, I am sensible it would be but a bad testimony of my repentance for my apostasy, and I dread the thoughts of so doing, so that the reader may be assured of my sincerity in the following relation.

But after all, 'tis not to be expected but that I shall come under the censures and reproaches of some, yet this is my comfort: who is there that ever published a book of this nature and did not come under censure? You must give him leave (say they, in a way of proverb): travelers must be allowed to tell what stories they please; 'tis better believe what he saith than to go and seek out the truth of it. I have borne much more than this ere now, etc., but censure is no proof. If I have committed any error, it is an involuntary one, and I shall be glad to be informed of it and will correct it, but for such men as are partial in the censure, or critics at random, and find fault for the sake of finding fault, I think those are more unreasonable than the people I came from, and therefore I desire no familiarity with them.

In the sixth chapter, which contains an account of the Mohammetan faith and worship, it behooved me to be as exact as possible I could, and there is nothing material, as far as I can remember, that I have omitted, unless it be in p. 53[2] where the first of the practical duties, as I call them, should be set down *seun et meck*, i.e., to observe circumcision, and so on to the second, third, etc. This omission is among the errata.

The seventh chapter, which treats chiefly of the Mohammetans' pilgrim-

---

[2] *p.53*: See p. 259 in this edition.

age to Mecca where Mohammet was born (though some deny that he was born there, yet it is universally believed among the Turks) and of their visit at his tomb at Medina, I think it to be very exact, as to truth, though the method and the wording may need an apology.

How many stories have been scattered about in the world concerning Mohammet's tomb? As of its hanging up by the virtue of a lodestone, etc., which are all as false as any thing can be.

The story of the pigeon, which was said to be taught by Mohammet to pick corn[3] out of his ear, which the vulgar took to be the whispers of the Holy Ghost, hath no better foundation that ever I could learn than a castle, or his tomb, in the air. And since I came from Algier, I have seen many books, some of which have treated of Algier in particular and others of the Mohammetan religion in general, which are stuffed with very great mistakes. I speak not this to raise a value to myself in what I have here written, for I protest I am ashamed and in pain about publishing it (notwithstanding the encouragement and importunity my friends have used towards me) because I am sensible[4] I want ability to do a thing of this nature as I ought. But whatever the success of this book may be, I declare my principal end in its publication is giving glory to God, by whose gracious providence I am released from slavery and reduced[5] into my own native country where there are no means of salvation wanting and where the blessed doctrine of Jesus is established and the Holy Trinity adored.

It is a shame indeed to Christians to take a view of the zeal of those poor blind Mohammetans, which in the following account will be found to be in many things very strict. If they are so strict in their false worship, it must needs be a reprimand to Christians who are so remiss in the true. And I pray God they may take the hint and learn thereby to bless the goodness of God, that He hath continued His Gospel to them while such a vast part of the globe is devoted to a vile and debauched impostor.[6]

'Twas, as I have read, the many heresies and divisions and blasphemous errors broached in that age that provoked God to deliver the eastern churches over to cursed Mohammet and to remove the candlestick out if its place.[7] God

[3] *corn*: grain.
[4] *sensible*: aware.
[5] *reduced*: brought back.
[6] *vile and debauched imposter*: the prophet Muhammad.
[7] *remove the candlestick . . . its place*: an allusion to Christ's epistle to the Ephesians (Revelation 2:5), which threatens to remove the Ephesian's "candlestick" if they do not repent. This threat is realized, Pitts implies, in the fact that all the churches in Asia Minor, including Ephesus, were under Muslim rule.

grant the same cause may not have the same direful influence on us but that all professing Christianity may both entirely believe the doctrine of our blessed Savior and sincerely conform their practice to their belief. And though the former in some instances may seem difficult to reason and the latter to corrupt nature, yet both, duly and humbly considered, will be found to be our rational service. And according to the best of my capacity, I see not much difference between a man's refusing to embrace and believe the mysterious doctrines of our religion because they exceed his reach and comprehension, so long as they are clearly revealed, and his denying to obey the practical and moral precepts of Christianity because some of them are not suited to his humor and complexion and adapted to his own scheme. We must have a new religion to please all, but the old must and will stand in spite of the gates of hell. For our Lord hath assured us that they shall not prevail against it and that He will be with His church to the end of the world, wheresoever it may be transplanted for the sins of men.

I shall a little further trouble the reader's patience in recommending to all parents an early and religious education of their children and that they take all imaginable care that they do betimes, in their tender years, instruct them well in the principles of Christianity. For I am truly apt to think had I myself had as little knowledge as some have that are taken slaves, I had been forever lost. And I am verily persuaded that many poor ignorant souls which have turned Mohammetans would never have done what they did had they been catechized as they ought: no man knows how far the benefit of a good and pious education extends.

One thing more and I have done, which is this: I think myself obliged to make my apology for calling the Turkish imam[8] or *emaum* "priest" and their mosques "churches," but I hope the reader will pardon it because I knew not well otherwise how to express myself so as to be understood.

CHAPTER I. CONTAINING AN ACCOUNT OF THE AUTHOR'S BEING
TAKEN, OF AN INSURRECTION DESIGNED BY THE SLAVES BUT
DISAPPOINTED, OF THE MANNER OF SELLING SLAVES IN ALGIER

When I was about fourteen or fifteen years of age, my genius led me to be a sailor and to see foreign countries (much contrary to my mother's mind, though my father seemed to yield to my humor), and after having made two

---

[8] *imam*: actually, a prayer leader and sometimes a theological scholar but not the full equivalent of a Christian priest.

or three short voyages, my fancy was to range further abroad, for which I sufficiently suffered, as in the sequel of the story will appear.

Having shipped myself Easter Tuesday, *anno* 1678, with one Mr. George
Taylor, master[9] of the *Speedwell* of Lymson near Exeter (Mr. Alderman
George Tuthill of Exon, owner), bound to the western islands[10] from thence
to Newfoundland, from thence to Bilboa, from thence to the Canaries, and
so home, had God permitted. We got safe to Newfoundland, and our business being ended there, with a fair wind we put out for Bilboa, and after we
had been out about forty days from Newfoundland, coming near the coast of
Spain (which we knew was the place where the Algerines used to haunt for
poor ships that come from the westward) we looked out sharp for ships,
avoiding all we saw, but especially did we look out in the morning at sunris-
ing and in the evening at sunsetting. The day in which we were taken, our
mate, Mr. John Milton, was early at topmast-head[11] and cried out, "A sail!"

The master asked him, "Where?"

"At leeward," replied the mate, "about five or six leagues."

And so, to be brief in my relation, about midday, being almost overtaken
by them (the enemy being but about a mile distance from us), our master
said, "It will be in vain for us to make our flight any longer, seeing it will be
but an hour or two ere we shall be taken and then probably fare the worse if
we continue our flight." I may leave any person to judge what an heartless
condition we were in, but yet still we could not forbear kenning[12] the ship,
that unwelcome object, who devil-like was eager in the pursuit of us. All
hope now failing and there being no place for refuge, we hauled up our sails
and waited for them. As soon as the pirate came up with us, the captain,
being a Dutch renegade and able to speak English, bid us hoist out our boat,
which we could not do without much trouble and time, by reason that a few
days before one of our men in a great storm was washed overboard, and I
myself was scalded and so disabled for working, so that we had but four men
that were able. And therefore before we could make half-ready to hoist out
our boat, they came aboard us in theirs. I being but young, the enemy seemed
to me as monstrous, ravenous creatures, which made me cry out, "O master!
I am afraid they will kill us and eat us."

"No, no, child," said my master, "they will carry us to Algier and sell us."

---

[9] *master*: captain.
[10] *the western islands*: Ireland.
[11] *at topmast-head*: atop the mast.
[12] *kenning*: perceiving.

The very first words they spake, and the first thing they did, was beating us with ropes, saying, "Into boat, you English dogs!" And without the least opposition, with fear, we tumbled into their boat, we scarce knew how. They having loaden their boat, carried us aboard their ship, and diligent search was made about us for money, but they found none. We were the first prize they had taken for that voyage, and they had been out at sea about six weeks. As for our vessel, after they had taken out of her what they thought fit and necessary for their use, they sunk her, for she being laden with fish, they thought it not worthwhile to carry or send her home to Algier.

About four or five days after our being thus taken, they met with another small English ship which also came from Newfoundland, with five or six men aboard, which was served as ours was. And two or three days after that, they espied another small English vessel with five or six men aboard, laden with fish and coming from New England. This vessel was, at their first view of her, some leagues at windward of them, and there being but little wind and so they being out of hopes of getting up to her, they used this cunning device, viz., they hauled up their sails and hanged out our English king's colors and so, appearing man-of-war-like, decoyed her down[13] and sunk her also.

Two or three days after this, they took a fourth little English ship with four or five men aboard, laden with herrings, of which they took out most part and then sunk the ship.

And last of all they met with a small Dutch ship with seven men, laden partly with pipe staves,[14] which ship also they sunk. This ship was, as the before-mentioned, at a great distance windward from them when first espied, and they used the like stratagem to decoy her down, viz., by putting up Dutch colors. But when the Dutchman came so far as near about half a league from him and perceiving him to be a Turk, he then began to loof up[15] with all his sail, but to no purpose, for ere it was night he was overtaken.

This being a summer's voyage, in which season of the year their ships are usually but very badly manned (the reason is because of their camps being out at this time of the year, of which hereafter), I think the Algerines had not above thirty or forty fighting men aboard, insomuch that there was a great inclination amongst us to rise and venture our lives for our liberty. And we had not small encouragement, considering that we were near thirty new-

---

[13] *decoyed her down*: by raising the false flag, they tricked the English ship into lowering its sails.

[14] *pipe staves*: strips of wood used for making casks or barrels.

[15] *loof up*: bring the head of the ship closer to the wind (so as to increase speed).

taken slaves, besides there were between twenty or thirty old slaves brought with the pirate out of Algier, for such they usually bring to sail the ship and to do all the ship's work for them while the new slaves are put into irons in the hold and for a month's time not able to stand on their legs nor to come upon deck, being confined either to sit or lie down without the least provision of bedding to ease themselves. In this sorrowful case we were, insomuch that we were almost weary of our lives. For you may imagine that the food we had to sustain nature was answerable to the rest of their kindness, and indeed this generally was only a little vinegar (about five or six spoonfuls), half a spoonful of oil, and a few olives, with a small quantity of black biscuit and a pint of water a day.

Well, as I hinted, a platform was laid for our mutinying, and the old English slaves were as fully resolved as the new, the *purtezara* (which is, as we may call him, the boatswain's mate, an Englishman who had the rigging and other ironwork in his disposal) being of the confederacy and to supply all the rest with some weapon or other, and, as I think, the first adviser of an insurrection was one Mr. James Goodridge, now of Exon, who was one of the old slaves and a cabin servant, and in order to it brought down two naked swords and a pair of pincers to loose the iron bar on which we were shackled. All this while, none of the Spaniards or slaves of other nations knew anything of our design. And we so ordered it: for fear we should be discovered by them, only the English and Dutch were privy to it. The night being come when we were resolved to rise and in order thereto had loosened the iron bar on which we were shackled, the heart of the Dutch master flagged, and so a stop was put to our design. Whereas had we been all unanimous, the thing might, and would undoubtedly, have been accomplished with a great deal of honor and profit. For it was in the time of Ramazan[16] (their month of fast, of which hereafter) when they eat meat only by night, and therefore in the morning, somewhat before day came, they would in all likelihood be all fast asleep. This was the time when we designed to put our plot in practice, but the divine providence had further trials for us (especially for me) to undergo, as will appear in the progress of this history.

And now with a fresh westerly wind we entered the Straits[17] by night, which the Algerines seldom attempt to do during the wars with us, fearing our men-of-war. When we came almost in the sight of Algier, the boatswain of the ship was ordered to loose the slaves that were in irons, who coming

[16] *Ramazan*: Ramadan.
[17] *Straits*: the Straits of Gibraltar.

down with a candle and finding that the key that was put into the end of the iron bar was broken: "O ye English dogs," said he, "what, your design was to rise!" And after we were loosed and brought upon deck, he presently told the captain of it, who immediately fell into a very great rage and caused Mr. John Milton of Lymson, our mate (who sat at the end of the bar on which we were shackled and so was suspected to open the key, as indeed he did), to be called forth to the bastinadoes;[18] and he was forthwith laid down on the deck and had his arms turned and held behind him, one man sitting on his legs and another at his head, and in the posture the captain, with a great rope, gave him about an hundred blows on his buttocks, but he would not confess the fact, generously choosing rather to suffer himself than to bring us all under the bastinadoes also. We being now brought into our undesired haven, viz. Algier, were carried ashore to the captain's house and allowed nothing but a little bread and water that night. The next morning (as their custom is) they drove us all to the king's, or dey's, house; where the dey[19] makes his choice and takes the *pengick*, i.e., the eighth part of the slaves, for the public use, as also the eighth part of the cargo. After which, we were all driven from thence to the *battistan*, or marketplace, where Christians are wont to be sold. There we stand from eight of the clock in the morning until two in the afternoon (which is the limited time for the sale of Christians) and have not the least bit of bread allowed us during our stay in the marketplace. Many persons are curious to come and take a view of us while we stand exposed to sale, and others that intend to buy, to see whether we be sound and healthy and fit for service. The taken slaves are sold by way of auction, and the crier endeavors to make the most he can, and when the bidders are at a stand, he makes use of his rhetoric, and saith he, "Behold what a strong man this is! What limbs he has! He is fit for any work. And see what a pretty boy this is! No doubt his parents are very rich and able to redeem him with a great ransom." And with many suchlike fair speeches does he strive to raise the price. After the bidders have done bidding, the slaves are all driven again to the dey's house, where any that have a mind to advance above what was bidden at the battistan may, and whatsoever exceeds the bidding at the battistan belongs not to the picaroons[20] but goes to the dey.

As to the city of Algier, for its situation and building, it is situated on the

---

[18] *bastinadoes*: beatings administered with a stick (usually to the feet).

[19] *dey*: not really a king but rather the governor of Algiers under Ottoman sovereignty.

[20] *picaroons*: pirates.

side of a hill, and its walls are adjoining to the sea. The tops of the houses are all over white, being flat and covered with lime and sand as floors. The upper part of the town is not so broad as the lower part, and therefore at sea it looks just like the topsail of a ship. It is a very strong place and well fortified with castles and guns. There are seven castles without the walls and two tier of guns in most of them. But in the greatest castle, which is on the mole[21] without the gate, there are three tier of guns, many of them of an extraordinary length, carrying forty-, fifty-, sixty-, seventy-, yea, eighty-pound shot. Besides all these castles, there is at the higher end of the town, within the walls, another castle with many guns. And moreover on many places on the walls towards the sea are great guns planted. Algier is well walled and surrounded with a great trench. It hath five gates, and some of these have two, some three, other gates within them, and some of them plated all over with thick iron so that it is made strong and convenient for being what it is, a nest of pirates.

About ten or twelve mile off Algier to the westward is a pretty little town called Blida, accommodated with fine gardens, full of all manner of fruits and plenty of water, insomuch that there are upon the river gristmills, which is such a rarity as I seldom or never saw in any other part of that country. In this town I lived many years with my second patroon.[22] It lies in a spacious and pleasant plain called Mateeja, adjoining to an high mountain, on which live a rude sort of people called Kabyles,[23] who speak a language different from that of the Turks or Moors, of whom I shall speak a little more hereafter.

This town lying so near to Algier and being so exceeding pleasant and delightful, many Turks marry and reside there, so that there is no need of keeping garrison there as they do in most other towns within the territories of Algier. This *mateeja*, or plain, contains about twenty miles in length and six or seven in breadth. It is very fruitful and abounds with many handsome farmhouses. There are several markets weekly kept on this plain. The Turks do frequently (for their diversion) take their muskets and make a progress, two or three in a company, through this plain, for ten or twenty days space, living at free quarter at one farmer's house or other, none daring to refuse them, and many times they abuse their wives, too. These and many more injuries and abuses the poor Moors suffer from the Turks of Algier, which

[21] *mole*: fortified seawall built to protect the harbor.
[22] *patroon*: slave master.
[23] *Kabyles*: Berbers.

makes them very uneasy under their government. Insomuch that I have often heard them say that they wished that the Christians would come and take Algier, assuring themselves that they should have better usage from them.

Farther west, almost a day's journey, is another town, called Miliana. A small but handsome town west of Miliana, about fifteen mile, is another town called Mazouna, where the Turks keep garrison. Farther west, about three or four days' journey, is a town called Mostaganem, where the Turks keep garrison also. And the farthest town in the western territories of Algier is Tlemcen, a town of great note in former days, before Mohammet began his imposture. And indeed, by its strong walls and gates, and the ruins thereof, which I saw, it seemed so to have been. This is a place abounding in all sorts of curious and delicious fruits. And the women and boys here are reputed the fairest and most beautiful in all the Algerine dominions, even to a proverb. Here the Turks keep garrison also. When I went into their great mosque, I admired the great door thereof, which was a folding door and all solid brass, or bell metal,[24] with curious workmanship wrought on it. This great gate, they say, was found by the seaside, supposed to be some wreck, and was brought by a marabout[25] on his shoulders from the seaside to Tlemcen, which is about twenty miles; which marabout lies entombed just before the said great door.

To the northward of Tlemcen, joining to the sea, is a strong fortified town called Oran, held by the Spaniards, of which I shall speak anon.

Eastward of Algier there is scarce a town worth taking notice of (for I have frequently traveled it) till we come to Constantine, which lies above two hundred miles from Algier. This is the greatest and strongest town they have in all the eastern parts of their dominions. It is situated on the top of a great rock so that it needs no walls for its defense. It's difficult for horses to get up to it, the way being steps hewn out in the rock. Here the Turks likewise keep garrison, and the bey[26] hath his dwelling house. The usual way of executing great criminals here at Constantine is pushing them off the clift.[27] About two days' journey east of this place is another town adjoining the sea, called Beladernab[28] by the Moors, but in our maps Bona, a seaport town for small vessels or galleys. 'Tis a walled town, very fruitful, and hath a strong castle built on the top of an hill, in which also the Turks keep garrison.

[24] *bell metal*: an alloy of copper and tin.
[25] *marabout*: a Muslim holy man revered among the Berbers or Moors.
[26] *the bey*: Turkish title for an official of high rank; here referring to the dey of Algiers.
[27] *clift*: cliff.
[28] *Beladernab*: Annaba (or Bone).

A few leagues east of Bona is a little island which is inhabited by the Genoese, whose chief employment is dragging for coral. Both the Algerines and Tunisians claim a right to this island, therefore the Genoese pay tribute to each. I know not certainly how much they pay, but if I mistake not it is an horseload of coral every two months to each. The Turks being unskillful in fishing for this coral, for their profit permit the Genoese to dwell here and have the free enjoyment of their own religion.

Westward of Bona is a little town called Cool.[29] And westward of Cool is another called Bougia, lying also by the seaside, where the Turks likewise keep garrison. Here Sir Edward Sprague, in the year 1670, destroyed several of their ships which were got under the castle for protection, which played briskly on the English with their cannon.[30]

One word or two of the southern part of the Algerine territories.

South, or rather southeast, about three or four days' journey, are two towns, the one called Piscree,[31] the other Zammora,[32] both garrisons. They lie near to the Sahara, or desert, which is all sand and therefore produces no sort of fruit but dates, which always prosper best in sandy countries.

CHAPTER II. CONTAINING AN ACCOUNT HOW THE ALGERINES
BEHAVE THEMSELVES AT SEA, AND THEIR SUPERSTITIOUS
ADDRESSING THE MARABOUTS FOR SUCCESS

In this second chapter, I shall give you some account of the Algerines' manner at sea.

First of all, when any ship comes home from cruising, with all expedition they take all things out, ballast and all, and then careen again and tallow all underwater[33] to the very keel. Having so done, they take in all again as fast as they can, and when they are ready and fit to put to sea, a signal is given for any that will come onboard, and they refuse none that offer themselves, whether they be able or unable, old or young. The gunners have two parts or shares of what is taken; and the soldiers likewise; and the slaves that labor,

[29] *Cool*: Collo.
[30] *Sir Edward Sprague . . . their cannon*: In 1669 war broke out between England and Algiers. In May 1671 the English admiral Spragge burned seven Algerian ships in an attack at Bougia.
[31] *Piscree*: Biskra.
[32] *Zammora*: There is a Djemorah River that flows through Biskra.
[33] *careen again . . . all underwater*: scrape and then reseal the part of the hull that is below the waterline.

4444

4444

some two, some three, and some four, but it goes to their patroons; and all the rest have one part.

The guns being fired, they all take their leave of their friends, saying, "*Allah smorla dick*," i.e., "I leave you with God." Their friends usually return, "*Allah deumlik meara*," i.e., "God give you a good prize." And here it is to be noted that if there be several ships go out together, then the captain which was first registered is admiral of the said several ships, and none can be registered a captain until he can bring in eight Christian slaves, that so the governor may have the *pengick*, i.e., the one-eighth. And every such captain has when he dies, in honor of him, an ancient staff set up at the head of his sepulchre, and every Sabbath day, which with them is the Friday, his surviving relations hang up their flag on it, and this they do for many years after his decease.

At their return from the sea, if they have gotten any prize, then all the slaves and cargo are sold by way of auction; and all sorts of people, whether Turks, Moors, Jews, or Christians, have their liberty to advance in bidding; and after the money is paid which is bid, then every person receiveth his part or parts. The Algerines are a very timorous sort of people, willing to sleep in a whole skin[34] and therefore care not how little they fight but show themselves wondrously valiant upon poor small merchantmen. But many times they have made some attempts on great merchantmen and have come off with shame and broken bones. And this is not much to be admired at because they have no order in their engagements, neither is their any punishment for such of the inferior soldiers as fight not.

They dread much our English men-of-war, for when we have war with them, they will never venture in or out the Strait's mouth[35] by daytime but only in the nighttime, and that when they have a brisk fair wind, and they were more especially afraid to do it while Tangier was ours.[36] But if they have peace with us, though they have war with all Christendom besides, they will then not scruple to pass the strait's mouth by day more than by night.

I have often heard them say that there are none like the English to give them chase, for as for other ships, say they, when they chase us a while and see no great probability of soon overtaking us, they will give over their chase, but as for the English infidels, they will chase three days after they have lost us.

---

[34] *willing to . . . whole skin*: desiring to go to bed at night without being harmed during the day, i.e., wanting to remain uninjured.

[35] *the Strait's mouth*: the Strait of Gibraltar.

[36] *Tangier was ours*: Tangier was occupied by the English from 1661 to 1684.

When they are in the strait's mouth, they make a gathering of small wax candles, which they usually carry with them, and bind them in a bundle, and then together with a pot of oil, throw them overboard as a present to the marabout, or saint, which lies entombed there on the Barbary shore near the sea and hath so done for many scores of years past, as they are taught to believe, not in the least doubting that the present will come safe to the marabout's hands. And if at any time they happen to be in any great strait or distress, as being chased or in a storm, they will gather money and do likewise. When this is done, they all together hold up their hands, begging the marabout's blessing and a prosperous voyage. [Here's true Sergius:[37] this is exactly *ora pro nobis*,[38] and indeed their whole religion is a miscellany of popery, Judaism, and the gentilism of the Arabs, as may by seen in D. Prideaux's excellently written life of Mohammet.][39] When they are in a storm or chased as aforesaid, they usually light up abundance of candles in remembrance of some dead marabout or other, calling upon him with heavy sighs and groans. At such time they gather money and wrap it in a piece of linen cloth and make it fast to the ancient staff [40] of the ship, so dedicating it to some marabout or other, and there it abides till the arrival of the ship, and then they bestow it in candles or oil for to give light or in some ornament to beautify the marabout's sepulchre. For these marabouts have generally a fine room built over their graves, resembling in figure their mosques, or churches, and this little neat room is very nicely cleansed and well looked after. There are several of them about Algier, to which the women on Fridays flock to pay their visits and perform their *salah*, or prayer, begging of the marabout to hear and answer their petitions. Many people there are who will scarce pass by any of them without lifting up of their hands and saying some short prayer. And so great a veneration have they for those marabouts that they will hardly believe one another unless oath be made by one marabout or other.

[37] *Here's true Sergius*: The author sees a similarity between Islamic reverence for the marabouts and the Christian cult of saint worship. Sergius was said to be a Nestorian monk who helped Muhammad to "invent" Islam.

[38] ora pro nobis: Latin, meaning "pray for us." This was the congregation's response in the Latin liturgy's Litany of Saints, and so this refers to the Roman Catholic belief in the efficacy of prayers for a saint's intercession.

[39] *D. Prideaux's . . . life of Mohammet*: Dr. Humphrey Prideaux's *The True Nature of Imposture Fully Display'd in the Life of Mahomet, with a Discourse Annexed for the Vindication of Christianity* was published in London in 1697.

[40] *ancient staff*: flagstaff.

But to return to their custom at sea. If they find no succor from their before-mentioned rites and superstitions, but that the danger rather increases, then they go to sacrificing of a sheep (or two or three upon occasion, as they think needful), which is done after this manner: having cut off the head with a knife, they immediately take out the entrails and throw them and the head overboard, and then with all the speed they can (without skinning), they cut the body in two parts by the middle and then throw one part over the right side of the ship and the other over the left, into the sea, as a kind of propitiation. Thus those blind infidels (as the papists do, to whom they are really something akin in several things) apply themselves to imaginary intercessors instead of the living and true God who alone is able to command the swelling and mounting billows of the sea to be quiet and be still.

As I intimated before, they are wondrously valiant against a weak enemy and vigorous in their chase after small vessels, and so careful are they that nothing may hinder their speed that they will scarce suffer any person in the ship to stir, but all must sit stock still unless necessity otherwise require. And all things that are capable of any motion must be fastened or unhanged (even the smallest weight) lest the pursuit should be something retarded thereby. But as they are eager upon a small ship, so if it happen at any time that they chase a great ship, they'll soon slack their pace as soon as they come near enough to apprehend what he is. Or if at any time they see a ship preparing to fight them, their courage is apt to be very soon daunted. Many ships of twelve, ten, or but eight guns have escaped their hands very manfully, whilst the Turks have come home shattered and with shame. Many instances of this nature might be related, but I will only mention one, which happened not long before I came away out of the country.

There was an Algerine at sea, and he met with a Dutch vessel, which as I well remember had but ten guns and it may be about sixteen men, whereas the Algerine had between twenty and thirty guns and was very well manned. The Dutch vessel by courage got clear, and the cowardly Algerine made haste home much shattered and reported that he had fought with a great Flushing privateer, and it passed all for truth. But it unluckily happened that a few days after the same Dutch merchantman was met by another Algerine of about the same bigness with the former, and the poor Dutchman having lost some of his men, and others wounded, and being much disabled, was at last forced to yield and was brought into Algier, to the great shame of the other Algerine, who was sufficiently checked for his cowardice and had much ado to escape the bastinadoes. So that the Algerines are not in truth such daring sparks as they are thought to be. And I verily believe that many ships, much unequal to them in strength, might escape being taken if they would but appear brave and look them boldly in the face.

CHAPTER III. AN ACCOUNT OF THE TURKS' MANNER OF EATING;
THEY ARE MUCH ADDICTED TO THE CURSED AND UNNATURAL
SIN OF SODOMY

It may not be altogether frivolous or unacceptable to give you a very brief account of the Turks' manner of eating.

Their low round table being placed not above three or four inches above the floor, they all sit down cross-legged, as tailors do when they are at work on their shopboard,[41] and they have a napkin[42] that reaches all round to wipe with. The victuals being put on the table, everyone says his grace (more to my knowledge than thousands of Christians do), and this is "*Be, isme olloh,*" i.e., "in the name of God." The same expression they use in all things they set about, to the shame of those who pretend to more and yet have not God in all their thoughts, as the Psalmist speaks of some wicked men.[43] The meat is always seasoned before it comes to the table, so that they make use of no salt at table. Neither are knives or forks of any use at the table because the flesh which they boil is always cut into pieces while raw (and so is what they roast), and after that they parboil it and then take it out with the liquor[44] and then put in the flesh again with roots or cabbage, or what the season doth afford, cut small, together with a little pepper, herbs, and onions, after which they pour in a small quantity of the liquor again and stew it so long that it is no very hard matter to shake the flesh off the bones: This they call by the name of *terbeea*.

I could here enlarge upon the several sorts of their victuals and their manner of cookery, which I am well acquainted with, but this would eat up too great a part of my little book. As they use no knives or forks at table, so neither do they trenchers, for their tables do serve instead of them. They usually eat quick, and having done, everyone returns thanks, saying, "*el ham do lilloh,*" i.e., "thanks be to God."

The table being removed (before they rise), a slave or servant that stands attending on them with a cup of water to give them a drink steps in the

---

[41] *shopboard*: raised platform on which tailors sit while sewing.
[42] *napkin*: linen tablecloth.
[43] *the Psalmist . . . wicked men*: See Psalm 10:4.
[44] *liquor*: stock or broth.

middle with a basin and a copper pot of water (somewhat like a coffeepot) and a little soap and lets the water run upon their hands one after another, in order as they sit, and they also wash their mouths after eating.

As for their drink, 'tis well know that wine is forbidden by the Mohammetan law (and so is swine's flesh), and beer and cider they are altogether strangers to, so that their common drink is water, except at some certain times they make a sherbet with water and sugar. They are great coffee drinkers, but coffee you know is not to quench thirst. But though wine be forbidden, yet there is no punishment for those that drink it, notwithstanding none use to drink it but the rascality.[45] For a person of figure and reputation will by no means drink wine, because it is contrary to his principles and so is a scandal to his reputation. And as for such as do take to drink wine, they generally drink it so immoderately that they hardly leave off till they are drunk, and then they are extremely abusive and quarrelsome, sometimes even to murder, for they are no good-natured drunkards, as some among us are said to be; but I am of opinion they would be much better natured if they were no drunkards at all.

When their camp is setting forth (of which in the next chapter), then especially they are apt to drink (i.e., the soldiery) and are abominably rude, insomuch that it is very dangerous for any woman to walk in any by-place[46] but more dangerous for boys, for they are extremely given to sodomy, and therefore care is taken that it be cried about the town that all people take care of their wives and children. And yet this horrible sin of sodomy is so far from being punished amongst them that it is part of their ordinary discourse to boast and brag of their detestable actions of that kind. 'Tis common for men to fall in love with boys as 'tis here in England to be in love with women. And I have seen many when they have been drunk that have given themselves deep gashes on their arms with a knife, saying 'tis for the love they bear to such a boy. There are many so addicted to this prodigious sin that they loathe the natural use of the woman (such the Apostle inveighs against, Rom. 1:27).[47] And I assure you that I have seen many that have had their arms full of great cuts, as so many tokens of their love (or rather worse than bestial lust) to such their catamites. But this being so inhumane and unnatural a thing, I

---

[45] *rascality*: rabble.

[46] *by-place*: out-of-the-way area.

[47] *the Apostle . . . Rom. 1:27*: Paul describes how those men who abstained from "natural" intercourse with women "were consumed with passion for one another" and then punished by God for this "error."

profess I am ashamed to enlarge further upon it, as I could. But what I could say on this subject must needs be disgustful to every modest and Christian reader, and therefore, I think, I am obliged to forbear. Only I crave leave to make this reflection, viz., that intemperance in drinking hurries men on to the worst of vices, and though the inclination of these hot people and the countenance that is given to such crimes are too great incentives, yet, avoiding intemperance, they would be less liable to them.

As I have observed before, when their camp is setting out is a sort of licentious time and a rendezvous of all wickedness imaginable, and therefore, I shall now, in the next chapter, give you a true account of the order and management of their camps.

CHAPTER IV. AN ACCOUNT OF THEIR CAMPS, WITH THE REASON
OF THEM; OF THE KABYLES, A RUGGED PEOPLE THAT DWELL IN
THE MOUNTAINS

The Algerines, in the month of April, have three several camps go forth: one to the east, one to the west, and one to the south, of which the first is the greatest and consists of about an hundred tents, each tent containing twenty men. The western camp consists of about seventy or eighty [of] the like tents, and the southern camp but of fifteen. Each of these divisions hath a bey, or general, who give so many thousand pieces of eight monthly for his place to the dey, or governor of Algier, and moreover defrays the whole cost and charges of the camp and is to make due provision of bread, butter, oil, and also wheat to make *burgu*,[48] and likewise flesh for them twice a week, and barley for the horses. It is to be observed that every tent have their allowance, which allowance is far more than they can dispense withal, and therefore they have the liberty to take what they think will serve them and the rest in money, which they divide among themselves.

The bey's tent is pitched in the middle of the camp, and all the tents are pitched so close together that an horse cannot pass, and this is so ordered that there may be but one entrance into the camp, which is directly toward the door of the bey's tent: I suppose for the better security and also to signify that that way they are to take, upon their next removal, to which the door of the bey's tent points. Each bey, or general, may have, as I conjecture, about four or five hundred miles in his circuit, excepting him that leads

---

[48] burgu: in Arabic, *burghul*, a North African staple food made from cracked wheat, called bulgur in English.

the southern camp, for the country is not far inhabited to the southward. Every tent hath sixteen soldiers, one cook, one *otha-bashe* (or sergeant), one *beulick-bashe*, who is above the sergeant, and one *vekil-harg*, or steward (under the *otha-bashe*), who looks after the provision, which amounts, as I said before, to the complement of twenty men to every tent.

At the end of seven years, an *otha-bashe* is preferred to be a *beulick-bashe* and so by degrees to an higher office, till he comes to be an aga, or colonel. And with a great deal of splendor he remains in that post for the space of two months, after which he is not obliged to do any service at all but receives his pay, which is duly brought to him every two months. So that offices of this nature are conferred without respect of persons, in a constant order.

Each tent hath, moreover, three or four horses and two or three camels to carry the provision and baggage, and three or four servants are allowed to drive and look after these beasts. The *vekil-harg*, or steward of every tent, hath an horse to himself which carries the tent. These stewards go before with the servants and baggage, and after them go the cooks with their horses, viz., each cook an horse, carrying the utensils and other things belonging to his profession, which are a very good burden. The cooks go always in order, one close after another, but they always go on foot, being never permitted to ride on their horses because the horses have a sufficient burden without it. When they come to the place where they intend to pitch, as soon as the bey's (or general's) tent is mounted, every cook, with his respective steward, mount their tents all at once. This being done, the cook of every respective tent rides with all convenient speed to fetch water in his goatskins, to dress victuals for the soldiers withal and for them to drink.

The servants belonging to each tent make all the speed they can to get ready provender, etc., for the horses. And the steward of each tent is no less busy to put all things in order before the soldiers arrive, so that when the soldiers come to their tents, they find all things ready and have nothing to do but to take off their accoutrements, to clean their arms from the dust and dispose of them into their proper places, and then, if so it please them, to spread their bedding on the mats and so lie down to take their repose till the steward awakes them to eat, insomuch that I am apt to believe that no soldiers in the whole world take less pains and live more at ease than they do.

In their march they move but two in a breast, each rank keeping at a considerable distance, so that but a thousand men make a great show and a long train. The *cayah-beulick*, or lieutenant, rides in the van of the army with two *hoages*, or clerks, each of them bearing a flag. The sergeants follow on foot, and then comes the aga, or colonel, and him follows the bey, or general, with trumpets, drums, pipes, kettledrums, and suchlike warlike music. They have a pretty odd way of beating their drums, viz., the drummer beats with a drumstick knobbed at the end in his right hand upon the head of the drum, and the bottom of the drum he at the same time strikes with a small wand which he holds in his left hand.

The bey is accompanied with his *spahis*, or troopers, which generally wear a woven crimson cloak and on their head turbants[49] of red silk swathes. Every trooper hath a packhorse to carry his bedding, clothes, and all necessaries, with his servant riding thereon. And every soldier is very neat in keeping his arms and will not suffer the least spot to be upon them.

In their march they are attended with several *sacces*, or water carriers, to supply them with water, which every soldier takes at his pleasure with a copper dish which he hath hanging at his side for that purpose. And as soon as the water is spent, the carriers ride hastily for more.

They do not travel very hard, for they march, in a day, not above eight, ten, or twelve miles, unless it be at the season of their returning home, and then they travel from morning to night.

The eastern camp makes its return from a town called Constantine, about fourteen days' journey from Algier, after having kept out about six months. The western camp stays out about four, and the southern about three month. And as soon as ever the very day of their expedition is expired, the soldiers will return home in spite of the bey's commands or menaces, whether the business and design of it be effected or no. The reason and intent of the Algerines setting forth these camps is to overawe the Moors and to cause them to hasten in their tribute to the bey, which whether they do or no, yet I say the soldiers will not stay in the camp beyond their stated time.

And now, as I did in the second chapter acquaint my countrymen of the cowardice of the Algerines at sea (of which really advantage may be made by those that shall at any time happen to be attacked by them), so I will here give you a little account of their valor by land, which is equivalent with that at sea.

They know then very well that the Moors, their tributaries, are but of small courage and are commonly for a running fight. But if the Moors do happen but to stand, the Turks are easily daunted. But it seldom happens that the Moors do stand their ground, except it be some sort of them, viz., Kabyles, who live (as I said) in mountains and are a very rugged sort of people and care not to pay the tribute demanded from them by the bey, at which

[49] *turbants*: turbans.

the bey is enraged and oftentimes gives toleration for the soldiers to do what mischief they can unto those Kabyles, and to take their cattle, persons, wives, and children, and to gratify their base lusts as they please, and also to destroy their corn, burn their houses, and ruin their vineyards, if in their power so to do. Those Kabyles dwell in little houses (on the mountains) but little better than hog sties, and those Moors in the plains dwell in tents of haircloth.

I do not wonder to see the cruelty and barbarity they often use towards poor Christians, whilst they are so inhumane to those of the Mohammetan religion with themselves as to destroy them and theirs for a small matter. For frequently the cause of falling out between the Moors and the bey is very trivial. It may be for not paying in full to two or three shillings or something as inconsiderable. But after all their resistance and obstinancy, the Moors are (most commonly) so distressed by numbers that they are forced to come and submit themselves to the bey, paying the full sum demanded, and to petition for their wives and children and pay dearly for their ruggedness.

Many of those Moors never knew what a Christian is. I have traveled eastward and westward, to the utmost bounds of their territories, and I remember when I was journeying with my patroon from Bona, which is some hundreds of miles eastward of Algier, we did every night quarter in the Moors' tents, and the Moors, both men, women, and children, would flock to see me, and I was much admired by them for having flaxen hair and being of a ruddy complexion. I heard some of them say, "Behold! What a pretty maid it is!" Others said, "I never saw a Nazarene (i.e., a Christian) before." "I thought they had been," said some, "like unto *hallewfs* (or swine), but I see now that they are *benn Adam* (or children of men)."

The Moors are a people much given to sloth, for after sowing time they have nothing to do, nor betake themselves to anything, but only wait for the harvest. At harvest, their corn being cut and brought all together, they immediately tread it all and winnow it and then put it into great pits in the open field. The mouth of those *mutmors*, or pits, is but small, but within the cavity is much greater, being dug all round and of some depth. They put straw into the bottom and round by the sides of those pits, and then they put in their corn and so cover it over with earth, laid on some sticks and straw upon that, on the mouths of them, which they cause to be even with the surface of the ground. So that by this means their corn is preserved when they are put to flight by the bey, but much damnified,[50] being kept in so damp a place

---

[50] *damnified*: damaged.

instead of a barn. They never dress or dung[51] their ground as we do, and yet they have great plenty, for it is a common thing to see ten, sometimes fifteen, nay twenty stalks, shoot up together. Nay, I have heard told of sixty or more, which is wonderful! This plenty is of wheat and barley, for rye and oats they have none. And truly they have no need of it, for as our country people, many of them feed on rye, so they feed on barley; and as our horses are fed with oats, so theirs with barley.

These Moors are so very lazy that they make their wives saddle their horses while they go to ease themselves, which they are ashamed to do in a plain and open place but go a pretty way off, accounting it a great piece of rudeness to exonerate[52] in the sight of another. And here I may add that as for their wives they are little better than slaves, for they do not only what is properly women's work but grind all the corn used in the house and fetch all the wood and water on their backs, and oftentimes at a considerable distance. They also bake their bread daily on earthen pans and milk their kine and do all other things of the like nature that are to be done. And notwithstanding all this, if they have any vacant time in the day, they employ it in grinding of corn, which they do with such cheerfulness and singing that I have often admired how they could go through so much work without complaining, much more how they could do it with such cheerfulness. The women are not permitted to eat at the table with their husbands but must take what their husbands are pleased to leave them. Their fare is generally bread and milk and *cus ka sue*,[53] which is made of meal and water. They take a little meal and sprinkle water on it in a broad wooden platter and then stir it about with the palm of their hand till it becomes as small seeds or gunpowder, which being done, they put it into a colander and set the colander on the mouth of the pot that is boiling o'er the fire with victuals, etc. In a little time the steam gets up through the *cus ca seu* (in the colander) and it becomes all-together of a lump. Then they turn it out into a platter and beat it abroad and so mix it with butter. And then they turn out of the pot that is boiling, the broth, etc., upon the *cus ka seu* and almost cover it with the liquor, which in a little time it soaks up, and then they eat it with their hands, making use of no spoons, i.e., in the country amongst the boors. Their fare therefore being so mean, and yet the women not being suffered to partake of it with their husbands, one would think it should be but a small encourage-

---

[51] *dress or dung*: fertilize.
[52] *exonerate*: "relieve the bowels" (*O.E.D.*).
[53] cus ka seu: couscous.

ment to marriage. I am sure our country dames would esteem it so (which leads me to give you in the next chapter some account of the Algerines' way of marriage, etc.).

CHAPTER V. OF THE ALGERINES' WAY OF MARRIAGE AND THE
GREAT LAMENTATION THE WOMEN MAKE FOR THEIR DEAD
HUSBANDS; ALSO THEIR WAY OF TEACHING CHILDREN; AND
OF THE ILL USAGE I RECEIVED FROM MUSTAPHA MY FIRST
PATROON, ETC.

There is no such privilege allowed among the Turks as wooing or courting their mistresses. Nay, no person is permitted to speak one word to her whom he intends to make his spouse, nor to have the least glimpse or sight of her till just before such time as he is to go to the nuptial bed with her.

The father of the damosel[54] usually makes up the match, though there are some persons who make it their business to be matchmakers (a dangerous employment in Europe, and too often a curse procurer). When all matters are adjusted and agreed upon, the man to be married, together with some of his intended wife's relations, goes to the *kadi*, or judge or magistrate, and before him draws up some small instrument in writing wherein he promiseth to pay so much to his wife that shall be for her *sadock*, or jointure, and there's an end of the matrimony, without any further ceremony or formality, as of, "I, John, take thee, Joan," etc. The father of the damsel promiseth little or nothing, but it may be he will set forth his daughter with a few fine clothes and bedding or the like, and that's all. The time being come when they are to bed together, they usually make a little feast and invite their friends, who are to depart (i.e., the men) immediately after eating their meat, but the women tarry till they see the bride-folks in bed. After the entertainment is over, the bridegroom is put into the chamber alone with a candle, and after a little time the bride is put in unto the man and the chamberdoor made fast, the women meanwhile waiting without the door. The bride, if a virgin, takes off her drawers which she hath about her and puts under herself to receive the tokens of her virginity.[55] After the bride-folks have known one another as man and wife, the said drawers are thrown out in the chamber, and immediately upon notice the women at the door rush in and catch them up and hold them up to be seen by the whole

[54] *damosel*: young, unmarried woman.
[55] *receive the . . . her virginity*: absorb the blood that will flow when her hymen is penetrated.

company, expressing a great deal of joy, with loud singings, that all the neighborhood can hear it if the bride was found as expected, but if she be found otherwise, she must look to be divorced. But if all things happen well, and the man and wife agree together in love, then the *sadock* before-mentioned is not at all required, for there's no occasion for it, but if things happen ill and a divorce ensues, then the man is liable to pay the woman the said *sadock* and maintain such offspring as shall be begotten by him during their cohabiting.

The parties being thus divorced, they are both free to marry again, whom and when they please, and 'tis a thing very common amongst them so to do, for I have known many that have so done.

It hath been reported that a Mohammetan may have as many wives as he pleaseth, and I believe it is so, yet there is not one in a thousand hath more than one wife, except it be in the country, where some here and there may have two wives, yet I never knew but one which had as many as three wives.

The women (in the country especially) do usually manifest a great deal of sorrow for their deceased relations, peculiarly for their husbands. Some, if they can get their garments dyed black, they will, but at least they will be sure to take a little oil or grease and soot and therewith smut[56] their faces almost all over and make most hideous cries and lamentations, and the neighboring women do use to come and condole, it may be, twenty or thirty of them together, who all place themselves round the woman that hath lost her relation, making so prodigious a noise as may be heard sometimes near half a mile off, all the while scratching down their faces with their nails till they make the blood run down their cheeks.

Thus they continue to do half an hour and more at a time, every day for a considerable space, and afterward once a week, or as the fit shall take the widow, and thus, in and out, it may be for a whole year.

How sincere this their sorrow is, is hard to tell, but if it be no more than that of some of our English widows is, it is wittily and truly described in Sir Roger L'Estrange's fable of the inconsolable widow (*Fab.* 268).[57]

In the country not one among an hundred wears any shoes, but they generally go barefoot and barelegged. The men wear neither shirts nor drawers, and but few of them wear anything on their heads, only a flannen[58] wrapped

---

[56] *smut*: smudge or blacken.

[57] *Sir Roger L'Estrange* . . . Fab. *268*: L'Estrange (1616–1704), a prolific author and translator, published the *Fables of Aesop, and Other Eminent Mythologies: with Morals and Reflections* (London, 1692), the work cited here.

[58] *flannen*: piece of flannel cloth.

about their bodies. Some of the better sort indeed have something like a cloak about them.

And as for the women, they wear a piece of flannen before, down halfway the leg, and so behind, pinning the two ends on their shoulders with skewers or little iron pins, and have a woolen rope about their middle so that a little wind, without care, will soon cause their − to appear.[59]

They have great plenty of camels and sheep, also of corn (as I hinted before), though they bestow no dressing at all.

As for their children, when young they take no pains to bring them to go but leave them to crawl about till they can go of themselves. They teach them to swear by their Maker as soon as they can speak. The female sex are seldom taught to read.

The compendious[60] method which they (i.e., the Moors) take to teach their children to read and write is this, viz., everyone hath a thin board of oak, scoured white, to write on. Their ink is commonly a little burnt wool mixed with water. Their pen is made of a cane, for they hold it to be unlawful to write with a quill, as Christians do. The scholar being thus furnished, after some few directions the master speaks the boy's lesson, which is some of the Alcoran,[61] and the boy writes it and having written it, is not only bound to read it but to learn it without book. And thus he is to do every day till he hath retained a considerable part of the Alcoran in his memory. The boy having learned his day's lesson, rubs it out and then whitens his table again to write down the next day's lesson on.

I have known it to be a common thing (though I must speak it with shame, to consider how the holy Bible, the heavenly oracles, the Word by which we must be judged at the Last Day, is slighted and neglected among us) for traders and shopkeepers and such as have more leisure than many have to set themselves a daily task to recite so much of the Alcoran without book as in thirty days to take up the whole Alcoran. And this many continue to do during their whole life, believing that they merit much by it. (I wish to God that Christians were as diligent in studying the holy scriptures, the Law, and the Gospel, wherein we have eternal life, as those infidels are in poring upon that legend of falsities and abominable follies and absurdities.) At the end of every time they read in order to remember such a part of the Alcoran, they

---

[59] *their -- to appear*: Here and in several other places in the text, the printer discretely omitted words that describe bodily exposure or function.

[60] *compendious*: expeditious and economical.

[61] *Alcoran*: the Qur'an.

hold up their two hands at a little distance from their face, saying some short prayer, begging a blessing on what they have done, and then smooth down their face with their hands, and so much for that time. This many do in their youth and retain what they read to their dying day. They are (for the greater part) illiterate and yet value reading at such an high rate, insomuch that many to my knowledge have begun their *elif, be, te*,[62] i.e., as I may say, their ABC, when they have had gray hairs. And I have heard many say, "*Ocue mok billei dem!*" i.e., "Oh! that I could but read!" lamenting much the squandering of their youth.

The pronunciation of Arabic is very difficult, for every letter must have its proper sound, some are gutturals, and some must be pronounced from the roof of the mouth, and sometimes the mouth must be brought awry to pronounce the word aright. All these things likewise, the scholar must give an account of to his master.[63]

They have a very great veneration for their books, but most especially for the Alcoran, which they call *Calam Allah*, i.e. to say, the Word of God, and on the forrel[64] of it, there is written (commonly in golden letters) "la ta messa ha billa metah heart," i.e., "Touch not without being clean or being washed." (Of their cleansing I shall speak hereafter.) They will never suffer the Alcoran to touch the ground, if they can help it, and if it chance at any time to fall, they check themselves for it, and with haste and concern recover it again and kiss it, and put it to their forehead in token of profound respect. When they hold it in their hands, they'll never hold it below their middle, accounting it too worthy to be touched by any of the lower parts.

If they are going a journey and carry it with them, as usually they do, they will be sure to secure it well in a cerecloth and in a clothbag, hanging it under their armpits. And if at any time they have occasion to go to stool or make water, they must take it off and lay it at a distance from them, at least one fathom,[65] and then wash before they take it in hand again, or if they cannot come by any water, then they must wipe as clean as they can till water may conveniently be had. Or else it suffices to take *abdes*[66] upon a stone (which I call an imaginary *abdes*), i.e., smooth their hands over a stone two or three times and rub them one with the other as if they were washing them with

---

[62] elif, be, te: first three letters of the Arabic alphabet.
[63] *scholar . . . to his master*: the student . . . to his teacher.
[64] *forrel*: case or cover.
[65] *one fathom*: six feet.
[66] abdes: ritual ablutions performed by Muslims.

water. The like *abdes* sufficeth when any are sickly, so that to use water might endanger their life. And after they have so wiped, it is *gaise*, i.e., lawful, to take the book in hand again. But they are still uneasy till they come to water. They think they cannot prize the Alcoran enough and that there cannot be too much care in preserving it. Nay, I have known many that could not read one tittle of it to carry some part of it always about them, esteeming it as a charm to preserve them from hurt and danger. And if any mishap do notwithstanding befall them, they will rather impute it to their own demerit than to any defect of virtue in the part of the Alcoran.

They have so great a veneration and esteem for the Alcoran that they'll not suffer a scrip of clean paper to lie on the ground but to take it up and kiss it and then put it into some hole or cranny or other because on such the name of God is or may be written. I have heard them oftentimes condemn the Christians for the little regard they have to their books: "For," say they, "you'll use the paper of them to burn, or light your pipes, or to – put to the vilest uses."[67]

They have a great veneration for idiots, accounting them no less than inspired, and the reason is because Mohammet, when he devoted himself to a solitary life in the cave near Mecca, by much fasting and an austere life much impaired his health so that he began to talk and behave himself like a natural.[68]

The correction and punishment they give scholars[69] or children at work is beating them on the bare feet. And the punishment inflicted on soldiers is beating them on the buttocks, and that sometimes to that extremity, though the crime be not very great, as to make the blood come out through their drawers, and sometimes the flesh mortifies thereupon, and then they must have their flesh cut off in order to a cure. If they are so rigorous and severe among themselves, well may you think what cruelty they exercise towards the poor captives!

Within eight and forty hours after I was sold, I tasted of their cruelty, for I had my tender feet tied up and beaten twenty or thirty blows for a beginning. And thus was I beaten for a considerable time, every two or three days, besides blows now and then, forty, fifty, sixty at a time. My executioner would fill his pipe and then give me ten or twenty blows and then stop and smoke

---

[67] *to – put to the vilest uses*: a reference to using "toilet paper" for wiping is omitted.

[68] *natural*: born idiot.

[69] *scholars*: schoolchildren.

his pipe for a while, and then he would at me again and when weary stop again, and thus cruelly would he handle me till his pipe was out. At other times he would hang me up neck and heels and then beat me miserably. Sometimes he would hang me up by the armpits, beating me all over my body. And oftentimes hot brine was ordered for me to put my feet in, after they were sore with beating, which put me to intolerable smart. Sometimes I have been beaten on my feet so long, and cruelly, that the blood hath ran down my feet to the ground. I have given an account in another chapter of the cruelties I suffered, and therefore I shall only tell you for the present that I have oftentimes been beaten by my patroon so violently on my breech that it hath been black all over and very much swollen and hard almost as a board, insomuch that I have not been able to sit for a considerable time.

I was sold three times, and my first patroon was called Mustapha, and second Ibrahim, and the third Omar, but must needs acknowledge that with my last patroon I lived very comfortably. But this was not satisfaction: I longed still to be gone out of this country, and my chief reason was that I might worship God as I ought.

As for the Mohammetan worship, I shall give you an immediate and full account of it.

CHAPTER VI. OF THE MOHAMMETAN FAITH: OF THE
PREPARATION THEY MAKE BEFORE THEY GO TO THEIR
WORSHIP IN THE MOSQUES; OF THE MANNER OF THEIR
WORSHIP THERE; OF THEIR HAMMAMS OR BATHING
HOUSES; THE RAMAZAN FAST, ETC.

Though a strict outward devotion be found amongst those Turks, yet almost all manner of wickedness and immorality (except murder and theft) are left unpunished. But as for those that are religious in their way, they'll not live in the neglect of performing their *sallah* or *nomas*, i.e., their worship, might they gain never so much. Nay, there are some among them so zealous that after they are reformed from their former extravagancies, they labor to make up what they have run back in the time of youth by their neglect of *salah*, and in order to fetch up their arrears, they'll be up out of their beds an hour or two before day, and having prepared themselves, they'll be engaged in their devotion till they be quite tired.

Their *salah* is to be performed five times every day at church (or mosque), unless in case of extraordinary business or hindrance. First in the morning when the daylight is broke, before the candles are out, be it winter or

summer; this is called *sobboh-nomas*. The second performance of *salah* is
near about two of the clock in the afternoon, which is called *eule nomas*, or
service. The third is about four o'clock, called *ekinde nomas*. The fourth is
just after candle lighting, called *acsham nomas*. And the last about an hour
and half after night, called *gega* or *el-asheea nomas*.

In all these several times of devotion, they differ as to the number of their
devotions (which are all taken out of the Alcoran) and also the manner of
performing them, in both which they are very exact, as I shall further
acquaint you by and by. And I believe I may be bold to say that hardly any
man hath ever given so full and punctual[70] a description of the manner of
their worship as the sequel contains.

I shall speak, first, of the care and pains they take to prepare themselves,
ere they can set about their devotion. And, next, of their behavior in the performing of it.

First, in the morning as soon as they are up, the first thing they do is going
to the house of office,[71] carrying with them a pot of water, somewhat like a coffeepot, holding about a quart of water, and after they have evacuated, they take
the pot in their right hand and let the water run into the left hand and therewith wash their posteriors and their genitals. (Note that when men make water
they do it in the same posture as women do, for they hold that urine doth defile
as much as ordure.) And thus they keep washing till the pot of water is all
spent, which being done, they take another pot of water, and turning up their
sleeves above the elbow, they therewith wash their hands, first of all, three
times; they fill the right hand full of water and soop[72] it into their mouth and
then with the right thumb rub the right jaws and with the right forefinger rub
the left jaws, which being done three times, they fill the right hand again with
water and snuff it up into their nostrils three times, as often blowing their nose.
After which they wash their face three times, then wash their arms up as far as
the elbow, then wet the right hand and with the left hand take off their cap,
bringing their right hand over their naked head (for they shave their heads
weekly). Then they wet both hands again and poach[73] the two forefingers into
their ears, rubbing the ears behind with the two wet thumbs, and then wet their
neck with the two little fingers. They also wash their feet very well, as far as the
ankles. And in the last place, they wet both hands again and then hold up the

---

[70] *punctual*: precise and accurate.
[71] *house of office*: privy.
[72] *soop*: sweep or scoop.
[73] *poach*: push.

forefinger of the right hand, saying, *"la e la he il allah, Mohammet raseul-allah"* or *"lah illabi, illallah Muhammet resul-allah,"* i.e., "There is but one God and Mohammet the prophet or messenger of God." And the holding up the forefinger when they express these words is made to signify the unity.

I have been very particular in relating these their preparatory ceremonies because they think themselves strictly obliged to be most exact and critical in the observance of them.

After having thus done, they are fit and in a readiness to go to the *geamea*, i.e., the public place of worship, etc., whither they immediately hasten (after the clerk[74] hath called from the top of the tower). But in none of their places of public devotion have they any seats, but only the area is a plain beaten floor, like the floor of a malthouse,[75] spread all over with thin mats of rushes, but near the imam with carpets. Their galleries they have likewise spread with the same. But they have nothing of any fine ornaments in those their *geameas*, mosques or public places of worship, neither any picture, images, or anything of that nature, but the walls are naked white, for they utterly abhor images or anything like them.

When they come to the door of the *geamea*, they slip off their shoes and clap one sole against the other and so go in barefoot and lay their shoes down before them, kneeling down and bringing their back parts on the heels as for a resting place. [There is no such thing as ordination of the imam, as I think or ever heard, but the dey appoints him.] Now, they being all in a readiness, the imam (or priest), being in the front upon equal ground with the congregation and his back towards them, the muezzins, or clerks, are ready to observe his motions, being placed in a little gallery by themselves for that purpose. But before the imam begins, they (i.e., the clerks) stand up and speak out, so loudly that all the congregation may hear them, in a curious tune, *"Allah whyek barrik, allah whyek barrik, ashhaed wa la e la he il allah, ashhaed wa la e la he il allah, ashhaed wa Mohammet raseul allah, ashhaed was Mohammet raseul allah, hy alla sallah, hy alla sallah, hy alla sallah, by alla fellah, hy alfellah, wa ta coum ala sallah, wa ta coum ala sallah, allah whyek barrik, allah whyek barrik, la he la he ill allah,"* etc.[76] (Much the same words they use on the top of the steeple,[77] when they call

---

[74] *clerk*: muezzin.

[75] *malthouse*: a building where malt is prepared and stored, usually for brewing beer and often in the same building as the brewery (thus an irreverent comparison).

[76] Allah whyek . . . allah, *etc.*: the Muslim call to prayer.

[77] *steeple*: minaret.

'em to service, etc.) In the clerk's saying the last words, they all (i.e., the congregation) bring their two thumbs together and kiss them three times, and at
every kiss they touch their forehead with their thumbs, and then rising up all
and standing on their legs, they stand exactly close by one another in rank,
like a company of soldiers at close order.

They all imitate the imam or priest in the front, who as soon as he is upon
his legs, brings his two thumbs to touch the lower part of his ears. At which
the clerk above, having his eyes always fixed upon the priest, cries out, *"Allah
whyek barrik,"* at the hearing of which, they all at once touch their ears as the
priest did, saying the same words privately to themselves; and then they (i.e.,
the Hanafis)[78] put their hands on their belly, one on the other, and the imam
says some short lesson in the Alcoran, which being ended, he bows with his
hands resting upon his knees, at which motion of the priests, the clerk cries
again, *"Allah whyek barrik,"* and when the priest recovers himself upright,
the same expression is used again. It signifies "Great and blessed God!"

Then the priest placeth his hands on his thighs and gently goes down on
his knees and then stretcheth forth his hands on the ground and with the
same brings his forehead to touch the ground, at which ceremony the clerk
repeats again, *"Allah whyek barrik."* Then the imam recovers himself on his
knees, with his hands on his thighs, and the clerk repeats the same expression, *"Allah,"* etc. All which postures and ceremonies the imam or priest performs a second time, and the clerk useth the same words as at first, which
being done, the imam or priest sits still (or rather sits and kneels at the same
time, as I hinted before) about a minute with his hands on his thighs and fixing his eyes upon the ground and saying a short prayer, at the end of which,
he looks about over his right shoulder first and then over his left, saying,
"Salem maelick" at each, i.e., "welcome (viz.) my angels" (for the Turks hold
that everyone hath two angels to attend him, especially at the time of their
service or worship). This is called two *erkaets*,[79] or two messes.[80] You must
observe that everyone in the congregation doth use the very same gestures
with the priest, and that all at once in order, and the clerks speaking loudly
in the audience of them all is a sufficient token when to bow or rise, the clerk

[78] *Hanafis*: one of the four schools of religious law under Sunni Islam. They use a
slightly different set of postures in prayer than the other three schools (the Maliki,
Shafii, and Hanbali). The Turks were Hanafis, unlike the rest of the Muslims in North
Africa (Shafii in Egypt, Maliki in the Mahgreb).

[79] erkaets: literally, Arabic for "prostration."

[80] *messes*: masses.

(as I said) having alway his eye upon the imam or priest, if I may inoffensively call him so. And note that they all stand with their faces one way, i.e., toward the *kiblah*,[81] or the temple at Mecca, in the midst of which is a place called *beat-allah*, or the house of God.

At the conclusion of their service or worship and after all the *erkaets* be over, the imam, who officiates at the very upper end of the mosque, being kneeling in an oval place in the wall and turning his face towards the congregation (and so consequently his back is towards the *kiblah*) who are all upon their knees, and he, all the congregation imitating him, takes out his *tesbea* (or *tesbih*), or beads, which are ninety-nine in number and have a partition between every thirty-three. These they turn over, and for every one of the first thirty-three, they say *"subhan allah,"* i.e., "admire God." For the second thirty-three, they say *"el ham do lilloh,"* i.e., "thanks be to God." And for the third thirty-three, *"Allah whyek barrik."* All which being ended, the imam, with the whole assembly, hold up their hands at a little distance from their faces, putting up their silent orisons, and to conclude all, smooth down their faces with their hands, take up their shoes which lie before them, and so go their way.

This is the manner after which they behave themselves in their public worship, which lasts about a quarter of an hour.

And here I shall give you an account of the number of *erkaets* which they perform at every time of service. And first of all, for the *sobboh-nomas*, or morning service, as soon as they come into the *geamea* they perform two *erkaets* silently by themselves and then wait till the time of service (which is when it is daylight, before the candles are out in the church), and then they perform two more with the imam. At this time of service, the imam speaks aloud so that all the congregation may hear him.

The second time of their service is (as I said) about two of the clock in the afternoon, which they call *eulea nomas*, at which time they hoist up a white flag on a pole on the top of the tower (i.e., about an hour before service begins) to give notice to people that they be in a due preparation. At this second time, when they enter into the *geamea*, or church, they perform four *erkaets* by themselves, four with the imam and four afterwards apart by themselves. At this second time of *sallah-nomas*, or service, the imam speaks so softly that he cannot be heard.

The third time of service, which they call *e kinde nomas*, is about four of the clock in the afternoon and is performed exactly as the second was, excepting performing four *erkeats*, after the imam has done, by themselves.

---

[81] kiblah: direction of Mecca.

Acsham nomas, being the fourth time of service, is a little after sunset, which they perform with candlelight. About a quarter of an hour before it begins, they have a short form of singing with the imam, who reads a sentence, and then he and they sing. They always sing one thing, and one tune goes with it, viz., "*Allah hum salle, wa salem: alla, se ye de na wa moulaw na, Mohammet wa awela, awela, se ye de na Mohammet!*" i.e., "All praise and blessing and thanksgiving be to God and to our master Mohammet!" This singing is not *farz*, i.e., a matter strictly and universally enjoined as a duty by express command, but only *seunet* (or *sunnah*), i.e., a voluntary devotion. At this fourth *nomas*, the *erkaets* which they perform are three with the imam, who now also speaks with an audible voice, and two afterwards by themselves.

The fifth and last time of their service is (as I told you before) about an hour and half after the fourth, the lamps continuing burning in the *geamea* all that while. At their entering into which, they perform four *erkaets* by themselves, four with the imam, who then speaks two with an audible voice and two softly, and five afterwards by themselves. Note that those *erkaets*, or prayers, which they perform before and after the imam, are called (as I said) *seunet*, i.e., voluntary devotions, and those performed with the imam are styled *farz*, i.e., commanded. At every two *erkaets*, they look over their right and left shoulder, as I told you before the imam did, viz., to salute the angels.

They seem to be very devout in the time of their worship, fixing their eyes on the ground just before them, not in the least gadding or wandering with their eyes.

Friday is their sabbath, or *gemahgune*, but yet on that day there is but little difference in their devotion from that of other days, excepting that the *hatteeb*, i.e., a priest which is above the imam, officiates on their sabbath day, and that at one of the clock and for about the space of an hour, after which he mounts a pair of stairs (about six or seven) with a staff in his hand and there makes a sort of a short sermon, about a quarter of an hour or a little more and then performs *sallah* as the imam doth at other times.

But yet at this time of their worship the gates of the city (Algier) are shut, and many shut their shop windows during service, and some that are more zealous will not open their windows all the afternoon but walk and recreate themselves. But after the fourth time of service (which is called, as I said, *acsham nomas*), or rather a little before, both the gates of the town and all the shop windows are shut, and their buying and selling and work are all over for that day. And although the town is very populous, yet seldom anybody is to be seen in the streets after candle lighting, and the shops are seldom opened again till sunrise.

I should have observed to you before that after they have washed, or taken *abdes*, in the morning, it may serve for the whole day after, with this proviso, viz., that they keep themselves clean, i.e., from going to stool and making water and breaking wind backward and from the least sign of blood on any part of their body. For if they discover the smallest speck of blood, it is thought to make them unclean as much as any of the other escapes. And if it be no more than the scratch of a pin, they must wash again after it before they can go to their worship. Or if after they have taken *abdes*, they find the least drop of candlewax on their hand, they must take a fresh *abdes* because the place under the said wax was not wet.

Three times a day at least they take *abdes*, but they must do it five times if they are not satisfied of their being clean. They are so very ceremonious in these matters that they commonly keep the nails of the fingers closely pared because their fingers are always in the victuals when they eat, so that the fat or grease is apt to gather under their nails and so to hinder the water from soaking under their nails when they do take *abdes*, so that to have long nails is not *gays*, i.e., lawful. But yet they say 'tis more lawful for those that live in the country because their food is not so gross as that of those that live in towns and cities is. And besides, seeing their labor is mostly about husbandry, and consequently the earth gathers under their nails, which the water can easily soak through, the country people are not so strict in paring of their nails.

If they chance to sleep between the times of prayers, then they must also take a fresh *abdes*, and the reason is because they are not sure whether they brake wind in their sleep or no.

Nay, I assure you I have seen many go out of the church or mosque in the midst of their devotion to take a fresh *abdes* because the former hath been spoiled some of the forementioned ways or other.

The performance of *sallah* (of which I have given some account before) is incumbent upon the female sex as well as the men, though I think that few of them but live in the neglect of it, for they are never permitted to enter into their mosques or churches. And besides, it is more difficult for the women duly to perform *sallah* upon another account, viz., because they must be very careful to watch their menstrua,[82] for while those are upon them, there is no performing of *sallah*.

Friday being (as I said) their sabbath, the women flock out thousands in

[82] *menstrua*: menstrual cycles.

the morning to visit the sepulchres of their deceased relations, weeping over their graves and petitioning to them, and when they have done they'll carefully weed and cleanse them from stroyl[83] and dirt.

Many people among them have their burying places walled in, with a door to enter in at, which places are very clean and whitened with lime. The women also pay their visits to the marabouts (of whom I gave you some account before, chap. II) which have lain entombed, it may be, some hundred of years before, and to them they petition also, and indeed this is most of the liberty the women have; nay, many of them cannot attain unto this. Though, as I observed before, they are equally obliged to perform *sallah* with the men. And as for their liberty in conversation, it is as little, for though some may pay their visits one to another upon occasion, yet they never unveil themselves till the man of the house (if then present) depart.

If there be two, three, or four families in one house, as many times there happen to be, yet they may live there many years and never see one another's wife. But perhaps you'll say that it is odds but that the women may at some time or other be accidentally seen by the men, coming in or going out. But in answer to that you must know that the men are seldom within doors (especially those of the poorer sort, who often thus live many families under one roof), and when they chance to come home to their houses, before they enter at the door they usually speak aloud these words, viz., "*Ammiltreak,*" i.e., "Make way!" At the hearing of which every woman scuds into her house from the court (for every house hath a court in the middle foursquare, and on every square there is a room, and above there are galleries or balconies all round from whence you may look down into the court). The tops of their houses are all flat beaten floors made with lime and sand.

As for the men, they never visit one another at their houses. Nay, it is not esteemed civil or decent for one married man to inquire for another at his house. Nay, what is more, it is thought a rude thing to ask of any person, "Sir, where is your house?" or "Where do you live?" I myself once spake innocently to one when in Egypt, saying, "Whereabouts is your house in Algier?" and he took me up somewhat roughly and said, "Why do you ask that question? My shop is in such a place of the town." The doors of their houses are always kept fast latched.

The manner of the Turks complimenting, if equals, is putting the right hand on the left breast with a little bow and kissing each other's cheek (though sometimes without kissing). If an inferior comes to pay his respects

[83] *stroyl*: creeping weeds.

to a superior, then he takes his superior's hand and kisses it, afterwards putting it to his forehead. But if the superior be of a condescending temper, he will snatch away his hand as soon as the other hath touched it. Then the inferior puts his own fingers to his lips and afterwards to his forehead, and sometimes the superior will also in return put his hands to his lips. As for the Moors, if they are equal, they'll hold fast each other's hand, striving to kiss it several times, and they'll ask how each other do, but in all their compliments they never ask one the other how their wives and children do. They take care of that[84] for a reason well enough known. They never take off their turbants as we do our hats in complaisance to one another; neither do they stand bare in the greatest presence. Nay, they are never uncovered even in their mosques when they are at their worship but wear their turbants while they are at their prayers.

The women (as I intimated before) wear veils, so that a man's own wife may pass by him in the street and he not have the least knowledge of her. The women will not stop to speak with men, or even their own husbands, in the street. They always go barefooted within doors, except it be wet weather, and then they wear their thin slippers. Some wear silver slippers, and in their chambers they always go barefoot. They keep their houses very clean and wash them so often and well that they may go out of their chambers into the court barefoot without dirting their feet. Their shoes they generally leave in the entry.

The Algerines never take either apprentices or hired servants into their houses because they are a people given so much to jealousy (and truly they have reason enough for it on both sides) that there would be but little love or content under their roof should they take any. And therefore such as have occasion for servants do buy slaves and bring them up to their household work, as our servant maidens are here in England, who as soon as they have done up all their work in the house are usually allowed the liberty to go abroad and visit their countrymen, commonly bearing each a child with them, and if the child be a boy it rides on the slave's shoulders.

Slaves in such places do always strive to get into the children's affections, which if they can they fare much better for the children's sakes, and many faults are connived at and many blows forborne upon the child's account, lest it should grieve too much to see the dear slave punished.

The Turks are but seldom jealous of their slaves, though 'tis thought oftentimes they are made cuckolds by them, and that by the solicitations of the

---

[84] *take care of that*: take care not to mention that (implying both the husbands' jealousy and the prevalence of infidelity mentioned later).

patroonas[85] or mistresses themselves, for it would be dangerous presumption for the slave to dare to make the least item that way without encouragement from his mistress.

I have heard of some who have suffered much like Joseph[86] for refusing to comply with the lascivious desires of their mistresses who, like Potiphar's wife, have forged a quite contrary story to their husbands, which has occasioned the poor slave to be severely beaten and afterwards to be sold.

They have many *hammams*, or washhouses, to bathe themselves in. They go into them almost naked, only with a thin white wrapper on. There are several whose business it is to give attendance, and they are very ready to do it as soon as any person comes in. When any go in, they leave their clothes in an outer room, put on a pair of clogs or pattens,[87] and so walk with their guides into the hot places, where after they have been for a while they grow into a great sweat, and after having continued in it for some space, they have their armpits shaved by their guide and then retire into a private room where they have their pudenda also shaved, accounting it to be very beastly to have it otherwise. After which they lie down on the smooth pavement, and one of the guides or tenders, being ready with a glove stuffed with something for that purpose, rubs their body all over and cleanses it from filth, and I profess I have often wondered to see so much filth come off from a single person, considering how often they use thus to bathe or wash.

Having washed all over, and at last with soap, then the tender for a while leaves every person to himself to throw water on his body, and this they may have from two cocks,[88] one hot, the other cold, which run into an earthen pan or else a great basin of marble, so that they may make the water of what temper of heat or cold they please. Having thus done and taken *abdes*, the tender waits with wrappers, one for the upper and the other for the lower parts of the body, which having put on, the bathed person comes out into a cooler room, and there lies down a while till his sweating is well over, and then puts on his clothes again, and at his going out the tender sprinkles rosewater on his face, and all these refreshing accommodations may be had for three or four pence.

The time of the men's coming in is till one o'clock in the afternoon, and then the women take their turn of bathing till it be candle lighting.

---

[85] *patroonas*: wives of the slave masters.

[86] *like Joseph*: Joseph resists the advances of Potiphar's wife only to have her falsely accuse him of seducing her (Genesis 39:6–20).

[87] *pattens*: sandals.

[88] *cocks*: faucets.

But the women do not use to be shaved as the men, but instead thereof they mix some ingredients together, which used by way of unction on the abovesaid places of the body, causes the hair to fall away and the parts to be as bare as if they were shaved with a razor, but it in a little time grows again.

I mention these *hammams* in this place because they are not only designed for recreation and keeping the body clean but chiefly upon a religious account because upon some occasions they cannot perform *sallah* without thus washing the whole body. As for instance, if they have lain with an whore, or be it with their own wives, or if their nature has gone from them in a dream,[89] then the first thing they do is going to these *hammams* where they wash their body all over and then take *abdes*, and then they are fit for *sallah*.

And I really believe that few or none of them would adventure to perform *sallah*, being in any of the forementioned circumstances, without washing their whole body, might they gain never so much. Nay, the most negligent among them, and such as scarce perform *sallah* through the whole year, will be sure, if in any of such circumstances, to wash themselves and take *abdes* and then perform a few *erkaets*.

Now the great and fundamental article of the Mohammetan faith, which chiefly makes them Mussulmans or believers, consists in these words, viz., "*La he, la he, ill allah Mohammet, rasaul allah*," i.e., "There is but one God and Mohammet his prophet, or the messenger of God."

For the saying of these words, be it but once in a man's whole life, all his debaucheries and sins (they say) shall be forgiven, and he shall assuredly get to heaven, though for some time he may lie in hell till his sins are burnt away.

[This is very much like the Romish purgatory, which among the papists is an invention to get money by. 'Tis a plain cheat, to any observing man. And for ought I know a doctrine of the most damnable consequences of any in their whole religion, and we may challenge the consistory of cardinals[90] to produce one place of scripture which in the sense of any rational man can be supposed to prove it. I don't find the Turks make the use the papists do of it.]

But as for a Christian, they have no charity, for they say that let him live never so well all his days, yet all's in vain, so that without believing in Mohammet there is no salvation. I remember a story that was told me, not foreign to the matter in hand, and I believe the tale was true. A Turk and a

---

[89] *their nature . . . dream*: they have ejaculated while sleeping.

[90] *consistory of cardinals*: ecclesiastical senate, presided over by the pope, that decides matters of church doctrine and practice.

Greek were in company together, and the Greek had with him his sister, which was a very beautiful woman.

The Turk, among other talk, said, "That's a very pretty woman, why dost thou not lie with her?"

"She is my sister," replied the Greek.

"What then," quoth the Turk, "thou wilt never go to hell the sooner, for to hell thou wilt go, whether thou liest with her or no."

The Mohammetans hold the doctrine of the blessed trinity to be the greatest blasphemy imaginable. For most profanely, say they, "Was God ever married to beget a son?" They will not hear of the son of God with any patience. 'Tis true, they own Christ to be a great prophet and born of the Virgin Mary; so they have it in their Alcoran very often hinted, *Eusa Ebn Mirriam*, i.e., Jesus, the son of Mary. And they do also acknowledge him to be one of the greatest prophets that ever has been on earth, but they never own him to be the son of God (as some have related) or acknowledge his doctrine as the last will and word of God and his apostles as the ministers of it, for all these things they utterly deny, though some have asserted that they believe the Old and the New Testament, the Law and the Gospel. Yet I say, how can it be? For, as for the Law, 'tis true they do pick some things out of it but yet not in any due order or as it is there set down.

For circumcision they observe not on the eighth day, as the Jews, but when they please, sometimes when the child is two, three, four, or five years old. So do they vary from the Old Law[91] about payments tithes, sacrifices, etc.

And as for the Gospel, it is what I cannot but admire at, that any writers, especially learned men, should affirm they believe, since they do expressly deny Christ to be the Savior of the world. And therefore they who do assert that Mohammet believed all the articles of the Christian faith must needs be in the wrong. And they will hardly bear to hear of those miracles which were done by our Lord and his apostles.

Now, besides the great and fundamental article of the Mohammetan faith but now mentioned, there are six things which they are all bound to believe, the disbelieving of one of which will exclude a person from being a true Mussulman:

1. The first of these six things is, viz., *Aman to billohhe*, i.e., To believe in God.

---

[91] *Old Law*: Judaic law set forth in the Hebrew scriptures.

2. *Wa malaic kat he*, i.e., And his angels.
3. *Wa keu tu be he*, i.e., And in his written Word.
4. *Wa raseu ule he*, i.e., And in his prophets.
5. *Wa yow mila beree*; i.e., And of the Last Day.
6. *Wa bilcoder hirebe wa sherrehe min ollo he taallah*, i.e., And that all things that happen, whether good or evil, are disposed by the providence of God.

These several points the Turks do assent to, which is more than most men (as I am apt to think) do imagine the Turks do know or give any credit to.

But besides the one great fundamental article of their faith and these six credenda, there are several practical duties enjoined them, and which many of them do indifferently well observe. As:

1. *Shahedet cala mace gettermeck*, i.e., often to repeat the following words, in which (as I told you) is contained the prime and fundamental article of their faith, viz., "*La he, la he, il allah ashhad Mohammet raseul allah.*"
2. *Wa obtas [abdes] olmok*, i.e., to wash before *sallah*.
3. *Wa nomas culmok*, i.e., duly to perform *salleh*, or prayers.
4. *Wa zekaet wearmok*, i.e., and to give such a part (if I mistake not, the fortieth part) of their gettings[92] to the poor, but this command but few perform aright.
5. *Wa caeba warmok*, i.e., and to go on pilgrimage to Mecca (*scit.*) if health and ability permit.
6. *Wa orouch dootmok*, i.e., and to keep the fast Ramazan.

All which injunctions many among them do strictly and conscientiously observe, which with their abstaining from certain things which they account sins, viz., smoking tobacco, eating swine's flesh, drinking of wine, etc., makes them to be looked on very much. And yet (which is strange) there is no punishment for those that do what is forbidden by the Mohammetan law or neglect what is commanded. For as I observed before, there is scarce any sin punished among them except murder and theft. As for drinking of wine, it is flatly forbidden, yet but few of them in their youth refrain it, nay, the excess of it. But indeed, when they begin to grow old, then they usually fall in love with money which bars other extravagancies.

[92] *gettings*: income.

And as I also hinted before, those which take to drink wine do usually drink it to excess. And though it be altogether as strictly forbidden as swine's flesh, yet those who drink wine do seem to loathe and abhor the thoughts of pork. And yet, on the other hand, I have heard many to say that it is more lawful to eat pig than to drink wine, and they give this good reason for it: that the former doth satisfy hunger and nourish the body, but the latter doth intoxicate so as to breed quarreling and oftentimes murder.

But to return to the six points of practical duty, the two last of which I shall insist on, and begin with the sixth, viz., the fast of Ramazan, which I mentioned (chap. 2), and the other, viz., going on pilgrimage to Mecca, I shall reserve to a distinct chapter.

As Christians date by the month, so the Turks date by the moon, so that this month of Ramazan, or month of fast, doth every year fall back ten or eleven days, so that this month in the space of thirty years or thereabouts goes round the whole year. And here the reader may be pleased to note that they are altogether ignorant of astronomy and hold it to be a great piece of arrogance and profaneness for any to dive into these things which belong to that science. And they moreover say that no man in the world knows when the new moon is but God alone knows. And they say that none but Christians will presume to inquire into such hidden and abstruse matters. And therefore many will not believe there is a new moon till they see it, so that they begin their fast the next day after the moon appears and fast till they see the next moon. Unless it so happen that the weather hinder the sight of the moon, and then they complete thirty days' fast after they have seen the Ramazan moon.

As soon as they see the new moon in seaport towns, they fire a cannon gun to give notice when they are to begin the fast, upon which signal, they'll immediately make provision for the night, and rise every morning about two or three o'clock (which I reckon the night) to eat and drink, and then continue without meat or drink, smoking or chewing tobacco, or taking snuff (which three things are much in use amongst them) till it be half an hour after sunset. Nay, there are some so scrupulous that they question whether it be lawful for them to go into the room where there is a gristmill lest the flour get into their throats and through their nostrils. Others have been afraid to wash their bodies lest water should soak into their belly through the navel.

It was in this month of Ramazan, they say (though I can't imagine how they can make it out) that the angel Gabriel dictated to Mohammet the Alcoran, in the cave which is by the town of Mecca, on the top of a little hill from whence you have a prospect of the town and of the Kaaba, or Temple of

Mecca, of which (and their pilgrimage thither) I shall give you a true and faithful account in the following chapter.

CHAPTER VII. CONTAINING AN ACCOUNT OF THE MOHAMMETANS' PILGRIMAGE TO MECCA: THEIR MANNER OF DEVOTION THERE; OF SOME OF THE MOST CONSIDERABLE PLACES BETWEEN MECCA AND ALGIER, AS ALEXANDRIA, GRAND CAIRO, ETC.

Going on pilgrimage to Mecca is (as I informed you before) a duty incumbent on every Mussulman, if in a capacity of health and purse, but yet a great many that are in a capacity live in the final neglect of it.

There are four caravans which come to Mecca every year with great numbers of people in each.

There is first the Maghreb caravan, which comes from the west, from the emperor of Fez's country, and toucheth at Egypt, where they take in what provision will serve to Mecca, and back again to Egypt. Note that the *emir hagge*,[93] or chief leader of the caravan, makes a stop at every town he passeth through, that so all such persons as are desirous to go to Mecca that year may, if they please, go in company with him.

This *emir hagge*, into whatsoever town he comes, is received with a great deal of joy because he is going about so religious a work, and it is who can have the favor and honor of kissing his hand or but his garment. He goes attended in much pomp, with flags, kettledrums, etc., and loud acclamations rend the skies, and the very women get upon the tops of the houses to view the parade.

The second caravan goes from *Misseer* (or *Messe*), i.e., Grand Cairo in Egypt, which is joined by great multitudes because this caravan is better armed, and so they go with more safety under its protection. And it is also more pleasant because they go everyone in order, and each knows his place, so that there arise no quarrels or disputes at all on the road about precedency.

With this caravan is sent the covering of the *beat-allah*, or House of God, of which I shall give a description by and by.

The third caravan is called *Shamcarawan*, which brings those that come from Tartary and parts thereabout, and also from all Turkey, Natolia,[94] and the Land of Canaan,[95] without touching at Egypt.

[93] *emir hagge*: *Emir* is Arabic for "commander," and *hagge* is a title of respect identifying a Muslim who makes the *hajj*, or pilgrimage to Mecca. Thus *emir hagge* refers to the commander of the pilgrimage caravan.

[94] *Natolia*: Anatolia.

[95] *Land of Canaan*: Palestine.

The fourth is called *Hind carawan*, which comes from the East Indies and brings many rich and choice goods which are sold to all sorts of persons who resort to Mecca.

These four caravans do even jump all into Mecca together, there being not above three or four days' difference in their arrival, which usually is about six or seven days before the *curbane byram*.[96]

But it may asked, perhaps by some who know or at least have heard or read of the town of Mecca, how such great numbers of people can possibly have lodging and entertainment for themselves and beasts in such a little ragged town as Mecca is?

I answer, as for house room,[97] the inhabitants do straiten themselves very much in order, at this time, to make their market. And indeed, they make the *hages*, or pilgrims, pay for their house room during their stay there (which is generally only about sixteen or seventeen days) more than the rent of a whole year amounts to. And as for such as come last, after the town is filled, they pitch their tents without the town, and there abide till they remove towards home. As for provision, they all bring sufficient with them, except it be of flesh, which they may have at Mecca, but as for all other provisions, as butter, honey, oil, olives, rice, biscuit, etc., they bring with them as much as will last through the wilderness, forward and backward. And so for their camels they bring store of provender, etc., with them and besides meet with some small refreshments on the road.

[I had the curiosity to look upon the great and worthy Mr. Collier's *Dictionary*[98] to see what was there said of Mecca and Medina, and I find his author very much out[99] in both. And Davity,[100] he saith, was a late[101] writer, for Davity describes Mecca to be a very large place and that the constant inhabitants make up about six thousand families, whereas it indeed is nothing near so pop-

---

[96] *curbane byram*: the annual Feast of the Sacrifice, a Muslim holiday commemorating Abraham's sacrifice of Isaac.

[97] *house room*: lodging.

[98] *Collier's* Dictionary: Jeremy Collier (1650–1726) is best known today for his attack on the "immorality" of the Restoration stage. He is the editor of *The Great Historical, Geographical, Genealogical and Poetical Dictionary* (volumes 1 and 2 published in 1701 and 1705), the text of which is taken primarily from French sources.

[99] *very much out*: quite wrong.

[100] *Davity*: Pierre d'Avity (1573–1635) was a geographical writer and publisher of atlases. He is cited as the author of the articles on Mecca and Medina in Collier's *Dictionary*.

[101] *late*: recent.

ulous, and the buildings are very mean and ordinary. And as for Medina, Davity saith 'tis but four, I say about ten days', journey from Mecca. He saith likewise that the pillars of the mosque of Medina are charged[102] with three thousand silver lamps, whereas in truth there are but few lamps and almost all of glass. He saith moreover that Mohammet's tomb is richly adorned with plates of silver and covered with cloth of gold, which is not so, but I suppose he mistakes this covering for that of the *beat-allah*, of which I have given an account. There are no lamps lighted about Mohammet's tomb by day. All Turks are not absolutely bound to visit the tomb at Medina.]

When a ship is going for Alexandria, it is cried about the town of Algier, where I lived, that she will sail such a day, and then everyone that hath designed for[103] Mecca that year joyfully embraces the opportunity of going so far by sea because they thereby save both a great deal of trouble and cost which they must sustain if they were forced to go by land.

That year I went from Algier to Mecca, we arrived at Alexandria in between thirty and forty days, which is reckoned to be a very good passage.

At Alexandria we tarried about twenty days. Historians, no doubt, have given a far more satisfactory account of Alexandria than I can pretend to give, but yet I hope my observations may be accepted.

No doubt this was a very famous city in time and celebrated for its greatness and neatness, for the very ruins thereof leave an image of magnificence in a man's mind. In my walks about it I saw many curious[104] pieces of archwork underground. It is accommodated with a small branch or cut of Nilus, which fills their wells, and to these wells New Alexandria and all the ships that thither resort are beholden for fresh water. The mouths of these wells are entire stones of marble.

Great part of the walls of this city are yet standing with firm iron gates. I think all the walls, unless some part of the upperwork be fallen.

There are two churches in Alexandria, one of which is called by the name of *Bing-Beer Drake*, i.e., a Thousand and One Pillars, for so many they say it hath. There are several pillars in the ruins of Old Alexandria of a vast bigness and heighth; one especially I did much admire, for it is as big about as three or four men can fathom and higher than I could mount a stone. It shines like glass, and the color of it is much like Porphyrian marble. 'Tis all one entire piece with some curious stonework on the top of it.

---

[102] *charged*: hung.
[103] *designed for*: intended to go to.
[104] *curious*: intricate.

The city of Alexandria is situated about two bow shoots[105] from the seaside, and the New Alexandria joins to the sea.

Here is not such a plenty at all times to be had, as further up in the country, and the reason is because abundance of ships of all nations do continually resort hither and take off such supplies as they want.

Having tarried here at Alexandria about twenty days, we embarked for a place called *Roseet* (or Rosetta), which is about two leagues, as I guess, up in the River Nilus, which river they call also *Bahor el Nile*, i.e., the sea of Nilus.

I think we sailed from Alexandria about five or six leagues eastward of it before we come to the open mouth of the famous River Nile where it emptieth itself into the Mediterranean and with its muddy color threatening as if it would change the whole Mediterranean into its own color and sweetness. For I drank of its water a considerable way off at sea and found that it was no way salt,[106] to my great satisfaction and the truth of what I heard of it.

This river is not only famous, among other things, for depth but also for breadth. I cannot give an exact account of the breadth of it, but I well remember it is so broad that I could scarce distinguish a man's from a woman's habit on the other side. As for its depth, you may guess 'tis very considerable because there are many of the Turks' merchantmen, navigated by Greeks, which are called by the name of *shykes*, somewhat like our English ketches, of two or three hundred ton, which come up to *Roseet*, and from thence it is navigable up to *Boelock* (or Bulaq) by great boats or barges deeply laden, and how much further up I know not.

Roseet is the place where all the boats unload which come from Cairo and Alexandria, for the boats which come from Cairo are not fit to sail down for Alexandria; neither are the Alexandrian big boats fit to sail up to Cairo, for want of sufficient depth of water.

The mouth of Nilus is oftentimes very dangerous, and vessels are cast away there by reason of its being choked up with sands, and many times vessels are forced to wait ten or twelve days for a clear mouth.

This river is known by many and famous over the world.

It hath another great mouth, where it empties itself also, some leagues eastward of the former, which is called by the natives *Dimyot*.[107] Some have written of several more mouths, but if there be any such, they must be small

---

[105] *bow shoots*: bow shots' distance.
[106] *no way salt*: not salty at all.
[107] *Dimyot*: Damietta.

streams which I never observed or heard of from the natives. I am sure of this, viz., that these two I have mentioned are the great ones and navigable.

I was not in Egypt but at Mecca at the time of the Nile's overflowing, but they say it comes gradually and gently, not at all damnifying[108] the inhabitants, who receive it with a great deal of joy, and it remains about forty days on the land. And when it is gone off, they make very great feasting and rejoicing, and good reason for't, for they have a mighty dependence on the overflowing of this river, for were it not for it, Egypt would be a very barren country, they having little or no rain. After Nilus hath left the land, then is their time of tilling and sowing. After their seed is into ground, they are not much solicitous whether it rain or not, hardly reckoning themselves obliged to the showers of heaven.

They have a particular mark[109] when the flood is at its heighth. And they say that if it rise a finger's breadth above the mark, it is a sign of plenty, but if it come so much short of it, 'tis a sign of scarcity,

The river of Nile affords plenty of fish and fowl, as wild ducks, geese, etc.

I was credibly informed of a pretty way they have there to take wild ducks, viz., someone that can swim and dive very well takes the head of a dead duck and swims with it in his hand, and when he comes pretty near the ducks, he dives, holding the duck's head just above the surface of the water till he comes to the ducks, and then he takes hold of them by the legs and so catches them.

I have seen and handled a bird taken on this river, about the bigness of a heron, which hath under his throat a bag of skin with the mouth of it towards the beak.

This bird they call *sacca cush*, i.e., bird water carrier, and like dotterels[110] they say that when Abraham built the temple at Mecca,[111] these birds supplied him with water.

And I remember that when we were sailing up the River Nilus towards Cairo, one of our company shot one of these water carriers, thinking it to be a wild goose, but when it was known what it was, it was much lamented, even with tears, that such a creature should be so killed.

[108] *damnifying*: harming.

[109] *particular mark*: mark indicated on the Nilometer, a pillar used as a gauge to indicate the level of the Nile's floodwaters.

[110] *dotterels*: birds (particularly plovers) that are easily caught, thus implying dupes or credulous fools.

[111] *Abraham built . . . at Mecca*: A Muslim tradition states that Abraham built a place of worship in Mecca that is now the site of the Kaaba.

As for crocodiles here, I saw none.

The river of Nile is not clear of robbers, which rob in boats.

There are towns all along its banks, insomuch that you are no sooner out of the sight of one but in sight of two or three more.

They say it is above 250 miles up from *Rosset* to the country where the famous city of Cairo stands, and in all this way, scarce an hill as big as an house to be seen.

About four or five miles on this side Cairo, this river parts and betakes itself into two streams; the one runs to *Rosset*, the other to *Dimyott*.

The inhabitants of Egypt are a mixture of Moors, Turks, Jews, Greeks, and Copties,[112] which last I understand to be the race of the ancient Egyptians.

The chief commodities in this country are rice, flax, most sorts of grain, sugar, lin-cloth[113] in abundance, hides in abundance, especially of buffles,[114] balsams, etc.

As for their fruits, they have but little tree fruit but abundance of other sorts such as melons, watermelons, etc.

Here is also great plenty of East India commodities, as silks, muslins, callicoes, spices, coffee, etc.

Likewise here is great plenty of milk, butter, cheese, oil, olives, etc.

The habits of the Moors and Egyptians or Copties (Coptics) differ only in their turbans, the Moors' turbants being all white and the Copties' white striped with blue.

They speak all one language and generally wear a long black, loose frock sown together all down before.

The Jews wear a frock of the same fashion but of broadcloth, but their caps are of an odd figure, being somewhat like the poll of a man's hat case covered with broadcloth.

And as for the Jewish women, they wear a long sort of headdress which is like one of our women's steeple-crowned hats, but not quite so taper at the top yet of a greater length, jutting out behind at the poll, in which they look very awkward indeed.

The Greeks differ but little from the Turks in their habit, except it be in their turbants and caps.

There is in no part of the world, I am apt to think, greater encouragement given to whoredom than in Egypt. It is impossible for me to give you a full

[112] *Copties*: Copts, or Christian Egyptians.
[113] *lin-cloth*: linen cloth.
[114] *buffles*: water buffaloes.

account of their licentiousness of this kind, and which is tolerated, too. But yet I cannot forbear speaking something of it, hoping it may be a motive to cause my countrymen to make a good use of it and to bless God that we have such punishment by the laws to be inflicted in order to the suppression of this soul-destroying sin.

In Egypt then, they have distinct streets and places, which are all full of lewd-houses,[115] into any of which none of repute will enter but upon absolutely necessary occasions.

The whores used to sit at the door or walk in the streets unveiled.

They are commonly very rich in their clothes, some having their shifts and drawers of silk, with silk coats like unto men's (as for petticoats, they never wear any in this country) and a silk swash[116] about their middle (as indeed all others in these parts do, both men, women, and children) with a knife tucked in at their girdle, the sheath of which is commonly silver.

These courtesans, or ladies of pleasure, as well as other women, have their broad velvet caps on their heads beautified with abundance of pearls and other costly and gaudy ornaments, and they wear their hair in tresses behind, reaching down to their very heels, with little bells or some such things at the end, which swing against their heels and make a tinkling sound as they go.

They also wear nose jewels, and therefore 'tis not altogether improbable that these, or some like them, were the vanities of bewitching apparel which the prophet exclaims against (Isaiah 3:16).

These sparks[117] go along the streets smoking their pipes of four or five foot long, and when they sit at their doors, a man can scarce pass by but they will endeavor to decoy him in.

I have often wondered how these creatures can maintain themselves at the rate they do, seeing, I am told, that for three or four *parrahs*, i.e., pence, any man may gratify his lust upon them.

But they are so cunning that they will not encourage any man to stay longer with them than in the fact and payment for it because they will be ready for a fresh gallant.

And now to speak something more of Grand Cairo, a place eminent in history.

In this place they have wells in most of their churches into which water is by an aqueduct conveyed at the time of the overflowing of Nilus, and there

---

[115] *lewd-houses*: whorehouses.
[116] *swash*: sash.
[117] *sparks*: well-dressed, attractive women.

are men appointed who stand at the windows of several of their churches to give cups of water to all such as pass by.

If I mistake not, it is reported that in this city there are five or six thousand public and private mosques or churches. [Not six thousand public mosques and twenty thousand particular ones, as I find in the worthy Mr. Collier's great *Dictionary* from his author. I am positive it cannot be near the number. Nor three and twenty thousand, as Monsieur de Thevenot[118] hath it (part I, page 129), though I honor that author, for he is as exact in the Turkish history as any that ever I yet saw. I speak of what I know and have seen.] Among which, some are very large and stately, with curiously wrought fronts and gates, as likewise high round minarets, or towers; and some of the said minarets have several balconies round them, some two, some three; which balconies during the time of Ramazan are illuminated with abundance of lamps, glorious to behold!

Many miles before we come to Cairo, the two pyramids, which are many miles beyond it, discover themselves. They are of a prodigious height and in the form of a sugarloaf.

There is a town joining to the river of Nile, about a mile and half before we come to Cairo, called *Bolock* (or Bulaq), where resort many hundred of barks laden with corn, etc.

Here we hire asses or camels to carry our things to Cairo where, notwithstanding the resort of strangers and merchants and all the fame that this city Cairo hath in history, all the entertainment for strangers is a naked room or chamber without the least furniture.

In this city are said to be spoken no less than seventy-two languages.

As for the buildings here, they are but very ordinary and no more than two or three stories high; except some *hawns*, i.e., public houses of entertainment,[119] which are three or four stories high. These *hawns* are built after the same figure with their other houses, viz., foursquare with a court in the middle, and some of them are so large that they have three or four score rooms in them.

There are several hundred of these *hawns* in this city, which have in the midst of their several courts little mosques or churches built. Considering which, and the great houses with the large courts that every man of note

[118] *Thevenot*: Jean de Thévenot's *Relation d'un voyage fait au Levant* (Paris, 1665) was translated and printed as *The Travels of Monsieur de Thevenot into the Levant* (London, 1686).

[119] *public houses of entertainment*: inns.

hath, you must needs think it to be a very fair and magnificent city, to take a distant prospect of it. But yet the streets are very narrow, which (it being very populous) is an inconvenience, for people frequently are very much thronged[120] as they pass the streets and sometimes lose their slippers off their feet.

The people here usually ride on asses if they go but a mile or two in the city (and call for an ass as they call for a coach in London), and the women ride astride as the men do. Those asses pace as fast as any horse, and for one *parrach*, i.e., one penny, you may ride a mile. The owner of the ass drives the ass, and the drivers as they go are bound to call out to any on the way, lest any hurt be done by sudden meeting or turning, so that all day long is heard a great noise caused by the ass drivers, who are continually crying either *"wuggick"* or *"thorick*," or *"shemalick"* or *"yeamejenick*," i.e., "Have a care of your face or back, or left side or right side."

Twice a day they generally water their streets because of the excessive heat. And there are many that get a livelihood by carrying of water in goatskins, with two or three brass cups in which they offer water to drink to those that pass by, for which some give them to the value of half a farthing.

As for the plenty which abounds here, 'tis wonderful. You may have twenty, nay five and twenty, eggs for one *parrah*, or penny.

And you may also have about fourteen or sixteen little cakes of bread (each of which is very near as big as an halfpenny loaf with us) for one *parrah*, and all other things are here proportionably cheap.

The water which they have in this city is very brackish, and therefore most of the water which they make use of is brought on camels from the River Nile, and many hundreds get their living by bringing of it. This water hath such a quality in it that it usually purges[121] strangers at first.

Here is great scarcity of wood. 'Tis brought from the Black Sea and sold as coal is with us, only the wood is sold by weight as sea coal[122] by measure. Wood is so scarce that they heat their ovens commonly with horse or cow dung, or dirt of the streets.

There's but little fruit here, as I said, except it be melons, watermelons, cucumbers, and the like. No such thing (that I know) as apples, pears, cherries, or such sorts of tree fruit.

There are daily brought into this city large herds of goats, and if any be

---

[120] *thronged*: densely packed together.
[121] *purges*: causes a person to empty the bowels.
[122] *sea coal*: mineral coal.

minded to buy any of their milk, they milk it for them before their faces that they may be satisfied it is good and new. Indeed most of common necessaries are brought about to their doors to be sold, except it be flesh.

They have a very pretty way in hatching chickens hereabout (it's possible some may think what I am going to tell you a fable, but I declare I have seen it and aver it to be true), viz., they have a place underground (not unlike to an oven) the bottom of which is spread all over with straw on which they lay some thousands of eggs, close one by the other, which without the warmth of the hens or any other prolific heat but that of the sun, dung, and such ignite[123] particles as the earth may afford, are brought to life. When the chickens are thus hatched, they sell them to poor people by the measure, and when they are full grown up and fat, the value of them is no more than two or three *parrahs* (pence) apiece.

In this city of Grand Cairo there is a particular place of market which is held twice a week for the selling of Christian slaves which are brought by merchants from Turkey and were taken mostly by the Tartars and for most part are only women and children, for the men slaves are generally kept in Turkey for the service of the galleys.

These slaves brought here to be sold are most of them Muscovites and Russians and from those parts and some of the emperor of Germany's country.[124] They are curiously decked and set out with fine clothes when they are exposed to sale, that they may carry the better price.

And although the women and maidens are veiled, yet the chapmen have liberty to view their faces and to put their fingers into their mouths to feel their teeth and also to feel their breasts. And further, as I have been informed, they are sometimes permitted by the sellers (in a modest way) to be searched whether they are virgins or no.

It hath been affirmed by some that the slaves that are sold in this country are never compelled to turn to the Mohammetan religion.

In Algier I confess it is not common (though I myself suffered enough from them, God knows), but in Egypt and Turkey, I affirm, it is otherwise.

The younger sort that are sold slaves are immediately put to school to learn to read, for they are very poor ignorant creatures. And indeed, after they have turned they fare very well in those parts, almost as well as their patroon's children, if they are any way ingenious.

---

[123] *ignite*: combustible.
[124] *emperor of Germany's country*: areas under the rule of the Austrian Hapsburg monarch (including Hungary).

They say that these renegadoes have a greater blessing than the natural Turks, for that they commonly become great men and bear sway. And it is observed by them that the children of those Turks that marry here in Egypt seldom live to men's estate but that the offspring of those renegadoes live as long as the natives do and that they have a blessing on the account of Joseph's being sold into Egypt.[125]

Here are no Turks, you must know, but what come from Turkey, and they are all *yeane-sherres*, or janizaries, i.e., soldiers.

The people of this country (and particularly of this city of Cairo) are very rugged and much given to passion. They'll scold like whores but seldom care to fight, and when they do, they strike with the palm of their hand and not with the fist.

They are extremely addicted to cozening and cheating, especially of strangers who are not well acquainted with their coin and their manner of buying and selling.

They are also very abusive to strangers, insomuch that it is dangerous for any stranger to be in the street after candle lighting. Nay, I have known them to fall on a stranger at midday and rob him and beat him to that degree that it hath cost him his life.

The porters in this place are very strong men to bear burdens. They'll bear three hundred pound weight or more on their backs at once. And if I mistake not, none can be admitted into their company unless he can carry five hundred weight such a length.

But though they love cheating of strangers so well, as I have told you, yet they are strict in punishing a false balance. And therefore the bakers' bread is examined into, and if it prove less than the just and legal weight, they take it away and give it to the poor and punish the offending baker with many hard blows on the bare feet. For fear of which, many times such as know their bread to be less than the standard weight run away and leave their bread to be seized on, thereby to avoid corporal punishment.

There are abundance of buffles in the country. They are somewhat bigger than our oxen but not quite so hairy. They hold their noses much forward, with their horns pointing backward. The people use them for the same purposes as oxen are used with us.

I need not tell you of the abundance of rice here, for this is known to be the chief country for rice in the whole world. But notwithstanding the great

---

[125] *Joseph's being . . . into Egypt*: After Joseph was sold into slavery by his brothers, he prospered in the service of his Egyptian master (Genesis 39:1–6).

plenty which this country abounds with, in all my life I never saw the like multitude of beggars as here. For it's a common thing to see ten, twelve, or more of them in a company together, and especially Thursday evening, which is the evening before their sabbath. At which time if there be any charity going, it is shown.

People in this country are much afflicted with sore eyes and swollen legs, and such as are porters have their privy members also commonly very much swollen by bearing of extraordinary heavy burdens.

They have a saying that "God hath such a love for this city that he casts his eye upon it seven times a day to behold it with complacency."[126]

Most of the gentry of this country keep eunuchs or gelt negroes in their houses, with whom they entrust their wives, and wheresoever they go, be it to the bathing houses or elsewhere, these eunuchs go with them and make way for them with a long staff in their hand. Their masters, indeed, entrust them with all, in a manner, and have a great esteem for them, insomuch that they call them masters. The reason, no doubt, is because they would engage them to be faithful in the trust of their wives.

These eunuchs cost a considerable price because they are young when they are castrated, and several die to one that lives. They usually grow to a great stature, and they have an effeminate voice and never have any hair grow on their faces.

There is a well in this city of Cairo of a very considerable depth and about twenty foot square. There is a way to go down halfway, dug round about it, to which light is given from the top of the well, through great holes dug in the sides of it. If I mistake not, there are about three hundred broad steps down to the halfway, where there is a stable in which oxen are kept to draw the water from the bottom, and there is a great cistern where the water is emptied, from whence it is drawn by other oxen, after the same manner, to the top.

The manner of drawing it up is thus: viz., they have a wheel somewhat like a millwheel; on this wheel are two ropes, and between the two ropes are fastened little earthen pots to both of the ropes, about four foot distance one from the other. As the ox goes round, so the wheel goes round and brings the pots up full, which empty themselves into the cistern and so go down empty with their mouths downward to take in more water.

The contrivance is for their baths and watering of gardens, etc. But it is not so much for the sake of this machine that I mention this well, as for

[126] *complacency*: contentment.

another reason, viz., because this is affirmed by them to be the well in which Joseph was kept a prisoner by Potiphar.

But I am afraid I have held the reader too long in suspense before we come to Mecca. I shall beg his patience but a little further.

From Cairo we proceeded on in our journey towards Mecca, and at the bottom or utmost bounds of the Red Sea, we came to a town called *Sweis* (or Suez), which is about a day's journey from Cairo and hath a port where do anchor the ships that use the Mecca voyage. They are an odd sort of ships, having no decks, and are deeply laden, altogether with provision for Mecca.

In this town of *Sweis* (or Suez) we paid a groat or sixpence a gallon for fresh water. And having furnished ourselves at Cairo with three or four months' provision, enough to serve us back again into Egypt, and having intelligence that the ships are ready, we hire camels and away from Cairo to this town of *Sweis* (or Suez).

'Tis but a few miles after we come out of Egypt before we enter into the wildernesses.

After we had sailed about two or three days from *Sweis*, or Suez, we anchored at *Toor*, or Tor, or el-Tor, a very small town and port, where we refreshed ourselves with water, for every passenger carries his own water. We had also here plenty of apricots and other fruit, which were brought from Mount Sinai, which is called by them *Toor-Dog*, i.e., Law Mountain, because the moral law was there given.

After we had sailed a little further, we were showed the place where (they say) the children of Israel passed through the Red Sea, which they term by the name of *Kilt el-Pharown*, i.e., the well or pit of Pharaoh, meaning where he and all his host were drowned in their pursuit after the Israelites.

They report that in this place is much danger without a fresh gale of wind because it is a kind of vortex, the water running whirling round, and is apt to swallow down a ship.

I guess that the breadth to the Red Sea in this place where the Israelites are said to have passed through is about six or seven leagues.[127]

There is no safe sailing in this sea by night, unless it be in one place of about two nights' sail, because of the multitude of rocks (though I don't observe that the maps describe those rocks), which are so thick that we were always in sight of some or other of them, and sometimes in the midst of a great many of them, and sometimes so near as to be able to throw a stone to them.

---

[127] *six or seven leagues*: about twenty miles.

Some of these rocks are much bigger than others; some look like little islands; others just appear above water; and some are to be seen a little underwater; so that every evening we came to an anchor to the leeward of one rock or other.

Their sailors are prisoners of their own and, I think, are used as bad (if not worse) as any galley slaves in the world.

At the hithermost bounds of the Red Sea, i.e., at *Sweis* (as I said before), where we took shipping, it's but of a little breadth. For the space of four or five days' sail from Tor, we keep near the side of the wilderness on the left hand, and after that we lose sight of the shore on the right hand.

This sea, i.e., the Red Sea, is much salter hereabout than in other parts, insomuch that when they took *abdes* with this water (for none did otherwise because of the scarcity of fresh water) it made their bums exceedingly to smart.

We were on this sea about thirty days, and after we had sailed from *Sweis* about twenty days, we came to a place where was buried ashore a marabout, i.e., (as you have heard) a saint or one reputed eminently devout and religious, and perhaps some hundreds of years are passed over since he was here interred. When, I say, we came to this place, one of the ship's crew (with the consent of the rest) makes a little ship, about two foot in length, and goes to every one of the *hagges* or pilgrims, desiring them to bestow their charity in honor of the said marabout which lies there interred on the shore, and at such a time they liberally bestow some piece of money to the said end. Then they take some small wax candles, with a little bottle of oil, and put them into the ship together with the money they have received of well-inclined people, as they say, but I am apt to think they put in but a very small part of the money, if any at all, but keep it to themselves. This being done (as I told you, chap. 2), they all hold up their hands begging the marabout's blessing and praying that they may have a good voyage. And then they put the ship overboard into the sea, not in the least doubting of its safe arrival to the marabout, for the benefit of his sepulchre, though it be a desolate place and not at all inhabited where he is said to lie interred.

Poor ignorant creatures!

This marabout, they have a tradition, died in his voyage towards Mecca, and therefore his memory is most highly esteemed and venerated by them.

Note that if any die before they come to Mecca, yet they are ever after termed by the honorable name of *hagge*.

I should have told you that the veneration they have for these marabouts is so great that if any person that hath committed murder flies to one of the little houses (which, as I informed you, are built upon their sepulchres) for sanctuary, he's as safe as if he were in a convent, for none durst touch him in order to fetch him thence.

A few days after this, we came to a place called *Rabbock*,[128] about four days' sail on this side Mecca, where all the *hagges* (excepting those of the female sex) do enter into *hirawem*, or *ihram*, i.e., they take off all their clothes, covering themselves with two *hirrawems*, or large white cotton wrappers. One they put about their middle, which reaches down to their ankles; the other they cover the upper part of the body with, except the head, and they wear no other thing on their bodies but these wrappers, only a pair of *gimgameea*, i.e., thin-soled shoes like sandals, the overleather of which covers only the toes, their inchsteps[129] being all naked. In this manner like humble penitentiaries they go from *Rabbock* till they come to Mecca to approach the temple, many times enduring the scorching heat of the sun till their very skin is burnt off their backs and arms and their heads swollen to a prodigious size. Yet when any man's health is by such austerities in danger and like to be impaired, they may lawfully put on their clothes, on condition still that when they come to Mecca they sacrifice a sheep and give it to the poor. During the time of their wearing this mortifying habit, which is about the space of seven days, it is held unlawful for them so much as to cut their nails or to kill a louse or a flea, though they see them sucking their blood. But yet if they are so troublesome that they cannot well endure it longer, 'tis thought lawful for them to remove them from one place of the body to another.

During this time they are very watchful over their tempers and keep a jealous eye upon their passions and observe a strict government of their tongues, making continual use of a form of devout expressions. And they will also be careful to be reconciled and at peace with all such as they had any difference with, accounting it a very sinful and shameful thing to bear the least malice against any. They do not shave themselves during this time.

Now we come to Jedda, the nearest seaport town to Mecca, not quite one day's journey from it, where the ships disburthen themselves. Here we are met by *dilleels*, i.e., certain persons that come from Mecca on purpose to instruct the *hagges*, or pilgrims, in the ceremonies (most of them being ignorant of them) which are to be used in their worship at this *beat-olloh*,

---

[128] *Rabbock*: Rabigh, about one hundred miles north of Jedda, on the Red Sea coast.

[129] *inchsteps*: insteps.

or temple, which they call the House of God and say that Abraham built it, to which I give no credit.

As soon as we come to the town of Mecca, the *dilleel*, or guide, carries us into the great street which is in the midst of the town and to which the temple joins, and after the camels are laid down, he first directs us to the fountains, there to take *abdes*, which being done, he brings us to the temple, into which (having left our shoes with one who constantly attends to receive them) we enter at the door called *Bab-el-Salem*, i.e., the Welcome Gate. After a few paces' entrance, the *dilleel* makes a stand and holds up his hands towards the *beat-olloh* (it being in the middle of the temple or mosque), the *hagges* imitating him and speaking after him the same words. At the very first sight of the *beat-olloh* the *hagges* melt into tears. Then we are led up to it, still speaking after the *dilleel*. Then we are led round the *beat-olloh* seven times and then make two *erkaets*. This being done, we are led out into the street again, where we are sometimes to run and sometimes to walk very quick with the *dilleel* from one place of the street to the other, about a bow shoot. And I profess I could not choose but admire to see those poor creatures so extraordinary devout and affectionate when they were about these superstitions and with what awe and trembling they were possessed. Insomuch that I could scarce forbear shedding of tears to see their zeal, though blind and idolatrous. After all this is done, we return to the place in the street where we left our camels with our provision and necessaries and then look out for lodgings, where, when we come, we disrobe and take off our *hirrawems* and put on our ordinary clothes again.

All the pilgrims hold it to be their great duty well to improve their time whilst they are at Mecca, and not only to do their accustomed duty and devotion in the temple but to spend all their leisure time there, and as far as strength will permit, to continue at *tawoaf*, i.e., to walk round the *beat-olla*, which is about four and twenty paces square. At one corner of the *beat* there is a black stone fastened, and framed in with silver plate, and every time they come to that corner they kiss the stone, and having gone round seven times they perform (as I told you) two *erkaets-nomas*, or prayers.

This place is so much frequented by people going round it that the place of *towoaf*, i.e., the circuit which they take in going round it, is seldom void of people at any time of the day or night. Many have waited several weeks, nay months, for the opportunity of finding it void of people. For they say that if any person is blessed with such an opportunity, that for his or her zeal in keeping up the honor of *towoaf*, let them petition what they will at the *beat-ollah*, they shall be answered. Many will walk round till they are quite weary, then rest and at it again, and at the end of every seventh time they perform two *erkaets*, then at it again. This *beat* is in effect the object of their devotion, the idol which they adore, for let them be never so far distant from it, east, west, north, or south of it, they'll be sure to bow down towards it, but when they are at the *beat*, they may go on which side they please and pay their *sallah* towards it. Sometimes there are several hundreds at *towoaf* at once, especially after *acsham-nomas*, or fourth time of service, which is after candle lighting (as you heard before), and those both men and women, but the women walk outside the men, and the men nearest to the *beat*. In so great a resort as this, it is not to be supposed that every individual person can come to kiss the stone aforementioned. Therefore in such a case the lifting up the hands towards it, smoothing down their faces, and using a short expression of devotion, as "*Olloh-whyick barrick*" (or "*Allah ekber*"), i.e., "blessed God" or some such like, and so passing by it till opportunity of kissing it offers, is thought sufficient. But when there are but few men at *towoaf*, then the women get opportunity to kiss the said stone, and when they have gotten it, they close in with it as they come round and walk round as quick as they can to come to it again and so keep possession of it for a considerable time. The men, when they see that the women have got the place, they'll be so civil as to pass by and give the women leave to take their fill, as I may say, in their *towoaf*, or walking round, during which they are using some formal expressions. When the women are at the stone, then it's esteemed a very rude and abominable thing to go near them, respecting the time and place.

I shall now give you a more particular description of Mecca and the temple.

First, as to Mecca. It is a town situate in a barren place (about one day's journey from the Red Sea) in a valley, or rather in the midst of many little hills. 'Tis a town of no force, wanting both walls and gates. Its building is (as I said before) very ordinary, insomuch that it would be a place of no tolerable entertainment, were it not for the anniversary resort of so many thousand *hagges*, or pilgrims, on whose coming the whole dependence of the town (in a manner) is, for many shops are scarcely open all the year besides. The inhabitants (as I hinted before) will be sure to make more of one or two rooms to the *hagges* than will pay the year's rent for the whole house.

The people here, I observed, are a poor sort of people, very thin, lean, and swarthy. This town is (as was intimated) surrounded with many thousands of little hills, for many miles, and those hills are very near one to the other. I have been on the top of some of them near Mecca and have been able to see some miles about but yet not able to see the farthest of the hills. These hills

are all stony rock and blackish, and all near of a bigness and appear at a distance like pooks[130] of hay, but all pointing towards Mecca. Some of them are
half a mile in circumference, etc., but all near of one height. As to these hills,
the people here have an odd and foolish sort of tradition, viz., that when
Abraham went about building the *beat-olloh*, God by his wonderful providence did so order it that every mountain in the world should contribute
something to the building thereof, and accordingly every mountain did send
its proportion. Between these hills is good and plain traveling, though they
stand near one to another.

There is upon the top of one of these hills a cave, which they term *Hira*,
i.e., "blessing." Into this cave (they say) Mohammet did usually retire for his
solitary devotion, meditations, and fastings; and here they believe he had a
great part of the Alcoran brought him by the angel Gabriel. I have been in
this cave and observed that it is not at all beautified, at which I admired.

About half a mile out of Mecca is a very steep hill, and there are stairs
made to go to the top of it, where is a cupola under which is a cloven rock
into which, they say, Mohammet, when very young, was carried by the angel
Gabriel, who dissected his breast and took out his heart, and from thence
picked some black blood specks, which was his original corruption, and
afterward closed up the part again, and that during this operation Mohammet felt no pain.

Into this very place I myself went (because the rest of my company did so)
and performed some *erkaets* as they did.

This town, Mecca, hath its plenty of water, but few herbs notwithstanding, unless in some particular places. Here are yet several sorts of
good fruits to be had, viz., grapes, melons, watermelons, cucumbers,
pumpkins, and the like, but these are brought two or three days' journey
off, where there is a place of very great plenty called, if I mistake not,
Habbash. Likewise, sheep are brought hither and sold. So that as to
Mecca itself, it affords little or nothing of comfortable provisions. It's situate in a very hot country, insomuch that people run from one side of the
streets to the other to get into the shadow as the motion of the sun causes
it. The inhabitants, especially men, do usually sleep on the tops of the
houses for the air or in the streets before their doors. Some lay the small
bedding they have on a thin mat on the ground; others have a slight frame
made much like a gibb[131] on which we place barrels, standing on four legs,

[130] *pooks*: heaps.
[131] *gibb*: platform?

corded with palm cordage[132] on which they put their bedding. Before they bring out their bedding, they sweep the streets and water them. As for my own part, I usually lay open without any bedcovering; only I took a linen cloth and dipped in the water, and after I had wrung it, I covered myself with it in the night, and when I awoke I should find it dry; then I would wet it again; and thus I did two or three times a night.

Secondly, the temple of Mecca hath about forty-two doors to enter into it, not so much, I think, for necessity as figure,[133] for in some places they are close by one another. The form of it is much resembling that of the Exchange[134] in London, but I believe it's near ten times bigger. 'Tis all open and graveled in the midst, except some paths that come from certain doors which lead to the *beat-ollah* (which, as I said, stands in the midst of the temple) and are paved with broad stones. The walks or cloisters all round are arched overhead and paved beneath with fine, broad stone and all round are little rooms or cells where such dwell as give themselves up to reading, studying, and a devout life, which are much akin to their dervishes or hermites.[135]

The dervishes are most commonly such as live an eremitic[136] life, traveling up and down the country like mendicants, living on the charity of others, wearing a white woolen garment and a long white woolen cap (much like some of the orders of friars in the Romish church) with a sheep- or goatskin on their back to lie on, with a long staff in their hand. When they read they commonly sit down, putting their legs across and keeping their knees above the ground. They usually carry their beads about their arms or necks, whereas others carry them in their pockets. Many Turks, when they reform, give themselves up to a dervish sort of life. And for an instance, my second patroon had a younger brother who had lived a very debauched life, but on a sudden a great change seemed to be wrought upon him, insomuch that he let his beard grow, never shaving it, and put on his great green turbant, which none presume to wear but such as are of the blood and race of Mohammet, and betook himself to the learning his *elif be te*, i.e., as ABC, and in a little time attained to read very well and spent a great part of his time in reading. Some of his old jolly companions would joke at him for it, but he still kept on this strict way of living, not regarding their gibing.

[132] *palm cordage*: cord made from the fibers of palm trees.

[133] *as figure*: as for decoration or form.

[134] *the Exchange*: The new Royal Exchange, a square building with an arcaded courtyard plan, was completed in 1671.

[135] *dervishes or hermites*: Muslim ascetics.

[136] *eremitic*: ascetic.

The *beat-olloh*, I have already told you, stands in the middle of the temple and is foursquare, about twenty-four paces each square, and near twenty-four foot in height. 'Tis built with great stone, all smooth and plain, without the least bit of carved work on it. 'Tis covered all over from top to bottom with a thick sort of silk. Above the middle part of the covering are embroidered all round letters of gold, the meaning of which I cannot well recall to mind, but, as I think, they were some devout expressions, each letter being near two foot in length and two inches broad. Near the lower end of this *beat* are great brass rings fastened into it through which passeth a great cotton rope to which the lower end of the covering is tacked. The threshold of the door that belongs to the *beat* is as high as a man can reach, and therefore when any person enters into it, a sort of ladder-stairs are brought for that purpose. The door is plated all over with silver, and there's a covering which hangs all over it and reaches to the ground, which is kept turned up all the week except Thursday night and Friday, which is their sabbath. The said covering of the door is very thick embroidered with gold, insomuch that it weighs several score pounds' weight. The top of this *beat* is flat, beaten with lime and sand, and there is a long gutter to carry off the water when it rains, at which time the people will run, throng, and struggle to get under the said gutter, that so the water that comes off from the *beat* may fall upon them, accounting it as the dew of heaven and looking on it as a great happiness to have it drop upon them. But if they can recover some of such water to drink, they esteem it to be yet a much greater happiness. Many poor people make it their endeavor to get some of this water and present it to the *hagges*, for which they are well rewarded.

In this town of Mecca there are thousands of blue pigeons which none will affright or abuse, much less kill them, which therefore are so very tame that they'll pick meat[137] out of one's hand. I myself have often fed them in the house where I resided while at Mecca. These pigeons come in great flocks to the temple, where they are usually fed by the *hagges*, for the poor people of Mecca come to the *hagges* with a little sort of a dish made with rushes with some corn on it, begging the *hagges* to bestow something on *hammamet metta nabee*, i.e., the pigeons of the Prophet. I have heard some say that in their flight they'll never fly over the *beat-olloh*, as if they knew it to be the house of God. But it is a very great mistake, for I have seen them to fly oftentimes over the *beat-olloh*.

---

[137] *meat*: food.

As I mentioned before, in one corner of this *beat* is a black stone fastened in with a plate of silver, which stone, they say, was formerly white, and then it was called *haggor essaed*, i.e., the white stone, but by reason of the sins of the multitude of people that kiss it, it is become black and is now called *haggor eswaed*, or black stone.

This *beat-olloh* is opened but two days in the space of six weeks, viz., one day for the men and the next day for the women. I, tarrying at Mecca about four months, had the opportunity of entering into it twice, a reputed advantage which many thousands of the *hagges* have not met with, for those that come by land make no longer stay at Mecca than sixteen or seventeen days. When any enter into the *beat*, all that they have to do is to perform two *erkaets* on each side, with the holding up the two hands and petitioning at the conclusion of each two *erkaets*. And they are so very reverent and devout in this doing that they will not suffer their eyes to wander and gaze about, for they account it very sinful so to do. Nay, they say that one was smitten blind for gazing about when in the *beat*, as the reward of his vain and unlawful curiosity. I could not, for my part, give any credit to this story but looked on it as a legendary relation and therefore was resolved, if I could, to take my view of it. I mean, not to continue gazing about it but now and then to cast an observing eye. And, I profess, I found nothing worth seeing in it: only two wooden pillars in the midst to keep up the roof and a bar of iron fastened to them on which hanged three or four silver lamps (which are, I suppose, but seldom if ever lighted). The floor of the *beat* is marble and so is the inside of the walls, on which there is written something of Arabic, which I had not time to read. The walls, though inside of marble, are yet hung all over with silk which is pulled off before they enter. Those that go into the *beat* tarry there but a very little while (viz., scarce so much as half a quarter of an hour) because others wait for the same privilege, and while some go in, others are going out. After all is over, and all that will have done this, the sultan of Mecca, who is a *sherif*, i.e., one of the race of Mohammet, accounts himself not too good to cleanse the *beat*, who with some of his favorites doth wash it and cleanse it. And first of all they wash it with the holy water, *zem zem*, and after that with sweet water. The stairs which were brought for to enter in at the door of the *beat* being removed, the people crowd under the door to receive on them the sweeping of the said water. And the besoms[138] wherewith the *beat* is cleansed are broken in pieces and thrown out amongst the mob, and he that gets a small stick or twig of it keeps it as a sacred relic.

---

[138] *besoms*: brooms.

Every year (I mentioned before) the covering of this *beat-olloh* is renewed in Grand Cairo in Egypt, by the order of the Grand Seigneur,[139] and when the caravan goes with the *hagges* to Mecca, then is the new covering carried upon two camels, and those two camels do no other work all the year long. It is sent out of Egypt with a great deal of rejoicing, and so it is received into Mecca with wonderful joy, many people even weeping for joy and some kissing the very camels that carry it, bidding welcome again and again, reaching their hands up to the covering and then smoothing down their faces. This and a great deal more they do, showing what great veneration they have for this new covering, though not yet put on about the *beat*. Well may you think then what esteem they have for the *beat-olloh* itself.

When the old covering, or *hirrawem*, or *irham* (for so the name of it is), is taken down, the new one is put up by the sultan *sherif* of Mecca, with some to assist him. The old covering the sultan takes into his custody, for it properly belongs to him, and cuts it in pieces and sells them to the *hagges*, who care not almost how much they give for a piece of it. They being so eager after these screeds,[140] a piece of the bigness of about a sheet of paper will cost a *sultane*, i.e., nine or ten shillings. Yea, the very cotton rope to which the lower part of the covering (as I told you) was fastened is also cut into pieces and untwisted and sold. Many buy a piece of the covering of the *beat* on purpose to have it laid on their breast when they are dead and be buried with them. They carry it always with them, esteeming it as an excellent amulet to preserve them from all manner of hurt and danger. I am apt to believe that the sultan *sherif* makes as much money of the old covering as the new may cost, although they say that the work that is in it is alone the employment of many people for a whole year's space.

But to speak something further of the temple of Mecca (for I am willing to be very particular in matters about this, though in so being, I should, it may be, speak of some things that may be thought trivial): the compass of ground round the *beat* (where, as you have heard, the people exercise themselves in the duty of *towoaf*) is paved with marble, and round this marble pavement stand pillars of brass about fifteen foot high and twenty foot distance from each other, above the middle part of which iron bars are fastened, reaching from one to the other, and several lamps made of glass are hanged to each of the said bars to give light in the night season, for they pay their devotions at the *beat-ollah* as much by night as by day during the *hagges*' stay in Mecca.

[139] *Grand Seigneur*: Ottoman sultan.
[140] *screeds*: shreds.

On each of the four squares of the *beat* is a little room built, over each of which is a little chamber with windows all round it, in which chambers the imam (together with the muezzin) performs *sallah* in the audience of all the people which are below. These four chambers are built one at each square of the *beat*, by reason that there are four sorts of Mohammetans. The first are called Hanafi: most of them are Turks. The second is called Shafii, whose manners and ways the Arabians follow. The third is Hanbali, of which are but few. The fourth is Malaki, of which are those that live westward of Egypt, even to the emperor of Morocco's country. These all agree in fundamentals; only there is some small difference between them in the ceremonial part.

As for instance, the Hanafis, when they stand at their devotion, having touched the lower part of their ears with their two thumbs, they place their hands on their bellies, the right hand on the left, intimating that they stand bound, in the presence of God, to live well. The Malakis and Shafiis lift up their hands in a sort of careless manner and then let them fall down and hang by their sides, which intimates (as they say) a reverence for the divine majesty.

As for the Hanbalis, they differ but little from the Hanafis, but of all these four sorts, the Hanafis seem to be the most serious, devout and deliberate in their worship and other preparatories. All Mussulmans are bound to believe in all Mohammet's apostles (as they call them), especially those four, viz., Abu Bakr, Ali, Osman, Omar, which were the great and principal sticklers[141] for the religion of Mohammet after his death. But one of these four sorts, i.e., the Hanbalis, do not own Ali[142] to be one of Mohammet's apostles, upon which account they are looked on by the rest as heretical.

But to return to the *beat*: a little from which (about twelve paces) is (as they say) the sepulchre of Abraham who by God's immediate command built this *beat-olloh*, or temple, which sepulchre is enclosed within iron grates. A small distance from the said sepulchre, on the left hand, is a well which they call *Beer el Zem Zem*, the water whereof they call holy water and as superstitiously esteem it as the papists do their holy water. In the month of Ramazan they'll be sure to break their fast with it. They report that it is as sweet as milk, but for my part, I could perceive no other taste in it than in common water, except that it tasted somewhat brackish. The *hagges*, when they come first to Mecca, drink of it unreasonably, by which means they are not only much purged but their flesh breaks out all in pimples, and this they

[141] *sticklers*: strong advocates; active supporters.
[142] *Ali*: son-in-law of the prophet Muhammad.

call the purging of their spiritual corruptions. There are hundreds of pitchers which belong to the temple, which in the month of Ramazan are filled with the said water and placed all along before the people (with cups to drink) as they are kneeling and waiting for *acsham nomas*, or evening service, and as soon as the muezzins (or *mezuims*), or clerks, on the tops of the steeples, or minarets, begin their bawling to call them to *nomas*, then they fall a-drinking (before they begin their devotions) thereof. This *beer*, or well, of *Zem Zem* is in the midst of one of these little rooms before-mentioned to be at each square of the *beat*, distant about twelve or fourteen paces from the *beat-olloh*, out of which four men are employed to draw water, without any pay or reward, for any that shall desire it. Each of these men have two leather buckets tied to a rope on a small wheel, one of which comes up full, while the other goes down empty. They do not only drink this water but oftentimes bathe themselves with it, at which time they take off their cloths, only covering their lower parts with a thin wrapper, and one of the drawers pours on each person's head five or six buckets of water. The person bathing may lawfully wash himself therewith above the middle but not his lower parts, they accounting them not worthy, only letting the water take its way downwards. In short, they make use of this water only to drink and take *abdes* and bathing; neither may they take *abdes* with it unless they before cleanse the privy parts with other common water. Yea, such an high esteem they have for it, that many *hagges* carry it home to their respective countries in little latten[143] pots and present it to their friends, half a spoonful, it may be, to each, who receive it in the hollow of their hand with great care and abundance of thanks, sipping a little of it and bestowing the rest on their faces and naked heads, withal holding up their hands and desiring of God that they also may be so happy and prosperous as to go on pilgrimage to Mecca.

[The worthy Monsieur Thevenot saith that the waters of Mecca are bitter, but I never found them so but as sweet and as good as any others, for ought as I could perceive.]

I come now to tell you how, when, and where they receive this honorable title of *hagges* for which they are at all this pains and expense.

The *curbaen byram*, or the Feast of Sacrifice, follows two months and ten days after the Ramazan. The eighth day after the said two months, they all enter into *hirrawem* again (which *hirrawem*, or *irham*, I have already given you an account of) and in that manner go to a certain hill called *Gibbel el orphat* (or el-Arafat), i.e., the Mountain of Knowledge. For there, they say,

---

[143] *latten*: made of a mixed metal of yellow color that resembles brass.

Adam first found and knew his wife, Eve. And they likewise say that she was buried at Jedda near the Red Sea, at whose sepulchre all the *hagges* that come to Mecca by way of the Red Sea perform two *erkaets nomas* and, I think, no more. I could not but smile to hear this their ridiculous tradition, for so I must pronounce it. When I observed the marks which were set, the one at the head and the other at the foot of the grave, I guessed them about a bow-shot distance from each other. On the middle of her supposed grave is a little mosque built where the *hagges* pay (as I just now told you) their religious respect.

This *gibbel*, or hill, is not so big as to contain the vast multitudes that resort thither, for 'tis said by them that there meet no less than seventy thousand souls every year on the ninth day after the two months after the Ramazan. And if it happen that in any year there be wanting some of that number, God will supply the deficiency by so many angels.

I do confess the number of *hagges* I saw at this mountain was very great; nevertheless, I could not think they could amount to so many as seventy thousand. There are certain bound-stones[144] placed round the *gibbel*, or mountain, in the plain, to show how far the sacred ground (as they esteem it) extends. And many are so zealous as to come and pitch their tents within these bounds some time before the hour of paying their devotion here comes, waiting for it. But why they so solemnly approach this mountain beyond any other place and receive from hence the title of *hagges*, I confess I do not more fully understand than what I have already said, giving but little heed to these delusions. I observed nothing worth a seeing on this hill, for there was only a small cupulo[145] atop of it. Neither are there any inhabitants nearer to it than Mecca. About one or two of the clock (which is the time of *eulea nomas*), they having washed themselves and made themselves ready to perform it, perform that, and at the same time they perform *ekhinde* (or *quinde*) *nomas*, which they never do at one time but upon this occasion because at the time when *ekinde nomas*, or *sallah*, should be performed in the accustomed order, viz., about four o'clock in the afternoon, they are then imploring pardon for their sins and receiving the imam's benediction.

It was a sight indeed able to pierce one's heart to behold so many thousands in their garments of humility and mortification with their naked heads and cheeks watered with tears and to hear their grievous sighs and sobs, they begging earnestly for the remission of their sins and promising newness of life

[144] *bound-stones*: stone boundary markers.
[145] *cupulo*: cupola.

using a form of penitential expressions and thus continuing for the space of four or five hours, viz., until the time of *acsham nomas*, which is performed (as I said before) about half an hour after sunset. (It is matter of sorrowful reflection to compare the indifference of many Christians with this zeal of those poor blind Mohammetans, who will—'tis to be feared—rise up in judgment against them and condemn them.) After their solemn performance of their devotions thus at the *gibbel*, they all at once receive that honorable title of *hagge* from the imam, *emaum*, or priest, and are so styled to their dying day. Immediately upon their receiving this name, the trumpet is sounded, and they all leave the hill and return for Mecca, and being gone two or three miles on their way, they there rest for the night, but after *nomas*, before they rest, each person gathers nine and forty small stones about the bigness of an hazelnut, the meaning of which I shall acquaint you with presently.

The next morning they move to a place called *Meena*, or *Muna* (the place, as they say, where Abraham went to offer up his son, Isaac, and therefore in this place they sacrifice their sheep), about two or three miles from Mecca, where they all pitch their tents (it being in a spacious plain) and spend the time of *curbaen byram*, viz., three days. As soon as their tents are pitched and all things orderly disposed of, every individual *hagge*, the first day, goes and throws seven of the small stones, which (as I said just now) they gathered, against a small pillar or little square stone building. Which action of theirs is intended to testify their defiance of the Devil and his deeds. And there are two other of the like pillars which are situate near one the other, at each of which, the second day, they throw seven stones; and the same they do the third day. As I was going to perform this ceremony of throwing the stones, a facetious *hagge* met me; saith he, "You may save your labor at present, if you please, for I have hit out the Devil's eyes already."

[Monsieur de Thevenot saith that they throw these stones at the *gibbel*, or mount, but indeed it is otherwise, though I must needs say he is very exact in almost everything of Turkish matters, and I pay much deference to that great author.]

You may note that after they have thrown the seven stones on the first day (the country people having brought great flocks of sheep to be sold) everyone buys a sheep and sacrifices it (some of which they give to their friends, some to the poor which come out of Mecca and the country adjacent, very ragged poor, and the rest they eat themselves), after which they shave their heads, throw off *hirrawem*, and put on other clothes, and then salute one the other with a kiss, saying, "Byram mabarick ela," i.e., "The feast be a blessing to you."

These three days of *Byram* they spend festivally, rejoicing with abundance of illuminations all night, shooting of guns, and fireworks flying in the air, for they reckon that all their sins are now done away, and they shall when they die go directly to heaven, and that for the future, if they keep their vow and do well, God will set down for every good action ten, but if they do ill, God will likewise reckon every evil action ten. And any person that after having received the title of *hagge* shall fall back to his vicious course of life is esteemed to be very vile and infamous by them.

Some have written that many of the *hagges*, or pilgrims, after they have returned home have been so austere to themselves as to pore a long time over red-hot bricks or ingots of iron, and by that means they willingly lose their sight, desiring to see nothing evil or profane after so sacred a sight as the temple at Mecca, but I never knew any such thing done.

During their three days stay at *Meena*, or *Muna*, scarce any *hagge* (unless impotent) but thinks it his duty to pay his visit, once at least, to the temple at Mecca. They scarce cease running all the way thitherward, showing their vehement desire to have a fresh sight of the *beat-olloh*, which as soon as ever they come in sight of, they burst into tears for joy, and after having performed *towoaf* for a while and a few *erkaets*, they return again to *Meena*. And when the three days of *Byram* are expired, they all with their tents, etc., come back again to Mecca.

They say that after the *hagges* are gone from *Meena* to Mecca, God doth usually send a good shower of rain to wash away the filth and dung of the sacrifices there slain. And also they say further that those vast numbers of little stones which I told you the *hagges* throw in defiance of the Devil are all carried away by the angels before the year comes about again. Notwithstanding, I am sure I saw vast numbers of them that were thrown the year before lie upon the ground. After they are returned from *Meena* to Mecca, they can tarry no longer than the stated time, which is about ten or twelve days, and no more, during which time there is a great fair held, where are sold all manner of East India goods and abundance of fine stones for rings and bracelets, etc., brought from Yemen; also of chinaware and musk and variety of other curiosities. Now is the time in which the *hagges* are busily employed in buying, for they do not think it lawful to buy anything till they have received the title of *hagge*. The evening before they leave Mecca, everyone must go to take their solemn leave of the *beat*, entering in at the gate called *Babe el Salem*, i.e., Welcome Gate, and having continued at *towoaf* as long as they please (and many do till they are quite tired). It being the last time of their paying their devotions to it, they do it with floods of tears, as

being extremely loath to part and bid farewell, and having drank their fill of
the water *zem zem*, they go to one side of the *beat*, their backs being towards
the door called by the name of *Babe el Weedoh*, i.e., the Farewell Door,
which is opposite to the Welcome Door, where they having performed two
or three *erkaets*, they get upon their legs and hold up their hands towards the
beat, making earnest petitions, and then keep going backward till they come
to the abovesaid Farewell Gate, being guided by some or other, for they
account it a very irreverent thing to turn their backs towards the *beat* when
they take leave of it. All the way as they retreat, I say, they continue petitioning, holding up their hands with their eyes fixed upon the *beat* till they
are out of sight of it, and so go to their lodgings weeping.

Ere I leave Mecca, I shall acquaint you with one passage of a Turk to me
in the temple cloister (for, as I said, the temple is much of the figure of the
Royal Exchange, with cloisters or piazzas, and the *beat* stands in the midst
of the court) in the nighttime, between *acsham nomas* and *gegee nomas*, i.e.,
between the evening and the night services. The *hagges* do usually spend that
time or good part of it (which is about an hour and half) at *towoaf* and then
sit down on the mats and rest themselves. This I did and, after I had sat a
while and for my more ease, at last was lying on my back with my feet
towards the *beat*, but at a distance, as many others did, a Turk which sat by
me asked me what countryman I was.

"A Maghrebi," said I (i.e., one of the west).

"Pray," quoth he, "how far west did you come?"

I told him, "From *Gazair*," i.e., Algier.

"Ah!" replied he, "Have you taken so much pains, and been at so much
cost, and now be guilty of this irreverent posture before the *beat-olloh*, or
House of God?"

Here are many Moors who get a beggarly livelihood by selling the models
of the temple unto strangers and in being serviceable to the pilgrims. Here
are also several effendis,[146] or masters of learning, who daily expound out of
the Alcoran, sitting in high chairs, and some of the learned pilgrims whilst
they are here do undertake the same.

Under the room of the Hanafis beforementioned, people do usually gather
together (between the hours of devotion) and sitting round cross-legged, it may
be, twenty or thirty of them, they have a very large pair of *tesbeehs*, or beads,
each bead near as big as a man's fist, and so they keep passing them round,
bead after bead, one to the other, all the time, using some devout expressions.

[146] *effendis*: masters (a Turkish title of respect).

Here are likewise some dervishes that get money as well as at other places by burning of incense, swinging their censers as they go along before the people that are sitting, and this they do commonly Fridays, which is their sabbath. In all other *gamiler*, mosques, or churches, when the *hattib*[147] is preaching and the people all sitting still (as you have heard) at their devotion, they are all in ranks, so that the dervish, without the least disturbance to any, walks between every rank with his censer in one hand. With the other hand he takes his powdered incense out of a little pouch that hangs by his side.

I shall now entertain you with a story or two, which may be of use.

The first of a certain beggar at Mecca which would use no other expression to excite the people to charity towards him than this: "*Her ne yapparsen gendinga*," i.e., "Whatsoever thou dost, thou dost it to thy self," implying the reward that will hereafter be conferred on the charitable man. And there passed by one of his neighbors (none of the best men to be sure, but why he did attempt such a desperate thing against the poor beggar, I can't give an account), who thought with himself he'd try whether this saying of the beggar were true or not, and so goes and makes a cake of bread and mixes poison with it and then gave it as an alms to the beggar. He puts it thankfully up into his bag, the other the meanwhile thinking in a little time to hear of his death. But the beggar's saying proved true at length, and that unfortunately for the man that so gave him the poisoned cake, for it happened that a child of his being at play and seeing the beggar mumping,[148] asked him for a piece of bread, and he very innocently gave the child the very same he had received from his father, who [ate] it and died. I have reason to believe this story, and if so, it is a wonderful argument to encourage charity to the poor.

One story more of a beggar, who would always use this expression in begging, viz., "*Her ne wearersen elingla, O gidder senne la*," i.e., "Whatsoever thou givest with thy hand, that will go with thee," implying after death, which shows also that even these blind Mohammetans do believe a reward reserved hereafter for the noble virtue of charity.

Once more I crave leave, before I part from Mecca, to acquaint the reader that the reason of the Mohammetans esteeming the water of *Beer el Zem Zem* holy water is because, as they say, it was the place where Ishmael[149] was laid by his mother, Hagar. I have heard them tell the story exactly as it is

---

[147] *hattib*: Arabic *khatib*, meaning "preacher."

[148] *mumping*: begging.

[149] *Ishmael*: the son of Abraham and according to Muslim tradition the progenitor of the Arab peoples.

recorded in Genesis 21. And they say that in the very place where the child spuddled[150] with his feet, the water flowed out. But although this place, Mecca, is esteemed so holy, yet it comes short of no place for lewdness and debauchery. As for uncleanness, 'tis equal to Grand Cairo, and they'll also thieve and steal, even in the temple itself.

Now to what I have related concerning the Mohammetans' great veneration for the Alcoran and way of worship in their mosques, together with their pilgrimage to Mecca and manner of devotion there, I shall only add that I was lately perusing an English Alcoran,[151] where I find in the preface that the translator saith that the vulgar are not permitted to read the Alcoran but (as the poor Romanists) to live and die in an implicit faith of what they are taught by their priests. This I utterly deny, for it is not only permitted and allowed of, but it is (as I intimated before) looked on as very commendable in any person to be diligent in the reading of it.

The Alcoran amongst the Turks is strictly forbidden to be translated into any other than the Arabian language.

CHAPTER VIII. THE PILGRIMS' RETURN FROM MECCA: OF THEIR
VISIT MADE AT MEDINA, WHERE IS THE TOMB OF MOHAMMET.
OF THE MIGHTY WELCOME THE HAGGES RECEIVE AT THEIR
RETURN HOME AND THE GREAT REJOICING MADE ON THAT
OCCASION. OF A DREADFUL PLAGUE AT GRAND CAIRO, ETC.

Having thus given you an account of the Turks' pilgrimage to Mecca and of their worship there (the manner and circumstances of which I have faithfully and punctually related and may challenge the world to convict me of a known falsehood, though errors will slip through the most skillful fingers), I now come to take leave of the temple and town of Mecca.

Having hired camels of the carriers, we set out. We give as much for the hire of a camel from Mecca to Egypt, which is about forty days' journey, as the real worth of it is, viz., about five or six pounds sterling. And if it happen that the camel dies by the way, the carrier is to supply us with another. And therefore these carriers, who come from Egypt to Mecca with the caravan, bring with them several spare camels, for there is hardly a night passeth but many camels die upon the road. For if a camel should chance to fall, 'tis sel-

---

[150] *spuddled*: paddled.
[151] *English Alcoran*: English translation of the Qur'an, possibly that of Alexander Ross, first published in 1649 as *The Alcoran of Mahomet*.

dom known that it is able to rise again, and therefore 'tis a common thing when a camel once falls to take off his burden and put it on another camel and then kill the fallen camel, which the poorer sort of the company eat. I myself have eaten of camel's flesh, and 'tis very sweet and nourishing. If a camel tires they e'en leave him upon the place.

The first day we set out of Mecca it is without any order at all, all hurly-burly, but the next day everyone labors to get forward, and in order to it, there is many times much quarreling and fighting. But after everyone hath taken his place in the caravan, they orderly and peaceably keep the same place till they come to Grand Cairo. They travel four camels in breast, and the camels are all tied one after the other, like as in teams. The whole company is called a caravan, which is divided into several *cottors*.[152] Each *cottor* hath its name and consists, it may be, of several thousand camels, and they move one *cottor* after another like distinct troops. In the head of each *cottor* is some great gentleman or officer who is carried in a thing like an horse litter, borne by two camels, one before and the other behind, which is covered all over with cerecloth, and over that again with green broadcloth, and set forth very handsomely. If the said gentleman or officer hath a wife with him, she is carried in another of the same. In the head of every *cottor* there goes likewise a sumpter[153] camel, which carries the said gentleman's treasure, etc. This camel hath two bells hanging one on each side, the sound of which may be heard a great way off. Some other of the camels have bells about their necks, some about their legs, which makes a pleasant noise and makes the journey pass away delightfully. Thus they travel in good order every day till they come to Grand Cairo, and were it not for this order, you may guess what confusion would be amongst such a vast multitude.

They have lamps to give light by night belonging to each *cottor*, which are carried on the tops of high poles to direct the *hagges* in their march. These lamps are differently figured and numbered, so that every one knows by the lamps which *cottor* he belongs to. These lamps are also carried by day, not lighted, but yet by the figure and number of them the *hagges* are directed to what *cottor* they belong, as soldiers are by their colors where to rendezvous. And without such directions it would be impossible to avoid confusion in such a vast number of people.

Every day they pitch their tents and rest a while, and about four o'clock in the afternoon the trumpet is sounded, which gives notice to everyone to

[152] cottors: Arabic, meaning "units."
[153] *sumpter*: pack.

take down their tents, pack up their things, and load their camels in order to proceed on their journey. It takes up about two hours' time ere they are all in their places again. At the time of *acsham nomas*, and also *geagee nomas*, they make a halt and perform their *salah* (so punctual are they in their worship), and then they travel till next morning. As for provisions, we bring enough out of Egypt to suffice us till we return thither again. At Mecca we compute how much provision will serve us for one day, and consequently for the forty days' journey to Egypt, and if we find we have more than we m[ay] well guess will suffice us for so long a time, we sell the overplus at Mecca. There is a charity maintained by the Grand Seigneur for water to refresh the poor which travel on foot all the way. For there are many poor people which undertake this journey (or pilgrimage) without any money, relying on the charity of the *hagges* for subsistence, knowing that they largely extend their charity at such a time.

Every *hagge* carries his provision, water, bedding, etc., with him, and usually three or four diet together and sometimes discharge a poor man's expenses the whole journey for his attendance on them. Now there was an Irish renegado who was taken very young, insomuch that he had not only lost his Christian religion but his native language also. This renegado had endured thirty years of slavery in Spain and in the French galleys but was afterwards redeemed and came home to Algier. He was looked upon as a very pious man and a great zealot by the Mohammetans for his not turning from the Mohammetan faith, notwithstanding the great temptations he had so to do. Some of my neighbors who intended for Mecca the same year I went with my patroon thither offered this renegado that if he would serve them on this journey they would defray his charges throughout. He gladly embraced the offer, and I remember when we arrived at Mecca, he passionately told me that God had delivered him out of an hell upon earth (meaning his former slavery in France and Spain) and that God had brought him into an heaven upon earth, viz., Mecca. I admired much his zeal but did pity his condition.

Their water they carry in goatskins which they fasten to one side of their camels. It sometimes happens that no water is to be met with for two, three, or more days, but yet it is well known that a camel is a creature that can live long without drinking (God in his wise providence so ordering it; otherwise it would be hard traveling through the parched deserts of Arabia). Every tent's company have their convenient place for easing nature, viz., four long poles, fixed square, about three or four foot distance from each other, which is clothed round with canvas, because (as I said before) the Mohammetans esteem it very odious to be seen while they are exonerating. And besides, otherwise, if they should go too far they would hardly be able to find the way to their tent again.

In this our journey, many times the skulking thievish Arabs[154] do much mischief to some of the *hagges*. For in the nighttime they'll steal upon them (especially such as are outside of the caravan), and being taken to be some of the servants that belong to the carriers or owners of the camels, they are not suspected. When they see an *hagge* fast asleep (for it is usual for them to sleep on the road), they loose a camel before and behind, and one of the thieves leads away the camel with the *hagge* upon his back asleep. And another of the thieves meanwhile pulls on the next camel to tie it to the camel from whence the halter of the other was cut, for if that camel be not fastened again to the leading camel, it will stop and all that are behind will then stop or course, which might be an occasion to discover those robbers. When they have gotten the stolen camel with his rider at a convenient distance from the caravan and think themselves out of danger, then they awake the *hagge* and sometimes destroy him immediately, and at some other times, being a little more inclined to mercy, they strip him naked and let him return to the caravan.

About the tenth easy day's journey after we come out of Mecca, we enter into Medina, the place where Mohammet lies entombed. Although it be (as I take it) two or three days' journey out of the direct way from Mecca to Egypt, yet the *hagges* pay their visit there for the space of two days and come away the third.

Medina is but a little town and poor, yet it is walled round and hath in it a great mosque, but nothing near so big as the temple at Mecca. In one corner of the mosque is a place built about fourteen or fifteen paces square. About this place are great windows fenced with brass grates. In the inside it is decked with some lamps and ornaments. It is arched all over head. (I find some relate that there are no less than three thousand lamps about Mohammet's tomb, but it is a mistake, for there are not, as I verily believe, an hundred lamps, and I speak what I know and have been an eyewitness of.) In the middle of this place is the tomb of Mohammet, where the corpse of that bloody impostor is laid, which hath silk curtains all around it like a bed. The curtains are not costly nor beautiful. There is nothing of his tomb to be seen by any, by reason of the curtains round it, nor are any of the *hagges* permitted to enter there. None go in but the eunuchs who keep watch over it, and

---

[154] *Arabs*: Here, "Arabs" refers specifically to the bedouin tribes of Arabia.

they go in only to light the lamps burning there by night and to sweep and cleanse the place. All the privilege that the *hagges* have is only to thrust in their hands at the windows between the brass grates and to petition the dead juggler,[155] which they do with a wonderful deal of reverence, affection, and zeal. It is storied by some that the coffin of Mohammet hangs up by the attractive virtue of a lodestone[156] to the roof of the mosque, but believe me 'tis a false story. On the outside of this place, where Mohammet's tomb is, are some sepulchres of their reputed saints, among which is prepared a sepulchre for Christ Jesus, when He shall come again personally into the world (for they hold that Christ will come again in the flesh, forty years before the end of the world, to confirm the Mohammetan faith). They do say, and hold likewise, that our Savior was not crucified in person, but in effigy, or one like him.

Medina is much supplied by the opposite Abyssine country,[157] which is on the other side of the Red Sea. From thence they have corn and necessaries brought in ships, and odd sort of ships as ever I saw, their sails being made of matting, such as they use in their houses and mosques to tread upon.

We having taken our leave of Medina the third day and having traveled about ten days more, we were met by a great many Arabians who brought abundance of fruit to us, particularly raisins, but from whence I cannot tell. When we came within fifteen days' journey of Grand Cairo, we were met by many people who came from Cairo with their camels laden with presents for the *hagges* sent from their friends and relations, as sweetmeats, etc.

When we come within seven days' journey of Cairo, we are met by abundance more. And when within three days' journey of it, we have many camel loads of the water of Nile brought us to drink. But the day and the night before we come to Cairo, thousands come out to meet us with extraordinary rejoicing. 'Tis thirty-seven days' journey from Mecca to Cairo, and three days we tarry by the way, which together make up (as I said) forty days' journey. And in all this way there is scarce any green thing to be seen; neither beast or fowl to be seen or heard; nothing but sand and stones excepting one place which we rid by[158] by night. I suppose it was some village where were some trees and, as we thought, gardens. We traveled through a certain valley which is called by the name of *Attash el Wait*, i.e., the River of Fire, the vale being

---

[155] *juggler*: fraud who uses trickery to deceive.
[156] *virtue of a lodestone*: power of a magnet.
[157] *Abyssine country*: Ethiopia.
[158] *rid by*: rode past.

so intensely hot that the very water in their goatskins hath sometimes been dried up with the gloomy,[159] scorching heat. But we had the good fortune to pass through this valley when it rained, so that there the fervent heat was much allayed thereby, which the *hagges* looked on as a great blessing and did not a little praise God for it. When we came into Cairo the plague was very hot there, insomuch that it was reported there died sixty thousand within a fortnight's time, wherefore we hastened away to *Roseet* and from thence to Alexandria, where in a little time there was a ship of Algier ready to transport us thither.

After we came to Alexandria, I was walking with the Irish renegado I spake of but now (who was maintained in his pilgrimage to Mecca for his service and attendance, etc.) on the key,[160] and there was an English boat with a man in it. The said renegado was very earnest for me to speak to the man in the boat. I would have done it without a request, had I thought it safe or convenient. But the more importunate he was, the more shy I seemed for I feared some ill consequence of it. However, watching an opportunity, I spake to the Englishman in the boat and asked of him from whence his ship.

He looked intently in my face and said, "From Topsham," at which words my heart smote me.

I asked him further who was the master.

He replied, "Mr. Bear of Topsham." He then asked me where I learned my English.

I told him, "In England."

"Are you an Englishman, then?" quoth he.

I told him, "Yes."

"Of what part of England?" continued he.

"Of Exeter," said I.

I told him also by whom I was taken and other circumstances but did not think fit to hold any long discourse with him and so passed from him. It happened that there was at this time onboard Mr. Bear,[161] one John Cleak of Lymson, whom I very well knew when we were boys together. He, hearing of what had passed, came ashore next day with the said man, who spying me walking, told Cleak I was the man, whereupon he came running to me and hugged me in his arms, saying, "So. I'm glad to see thee with all my heart!" I did not know him at first. He told me again who he was. I called him to mind

---

[159] *gloomy*: excessively hot from the sun's rays.
[160] *key*: quay.
[161] *Mr. Bear*: Mr. Bear's ship.

but was afraid to hold any discourse with him though very desirous to have farther talk with him. He desired to drink a glass of wine with me. I refused, alleging that I was newly come from Mecca and therefore it would be much taken notice of. He then invited me to the coffeehouse with him, but I told him it would not be convenient for me to go with him thither neither because the house was full of Turks. So we did not go together. But I inquired of my father's and friends' healths, and he told me he saw my father but a little before he came away. I desired him to carry a letter for me; he told me he would (the letter you have inserted hereafter). But truly I was troubled that I could not conveniently have had some conversation with my old acquaintance. This was no small renewal of my trouble and affliction, and when I thought upon the circumstances I was then in, my heart did bleed.

You may remember that in our journey to Mecca, when we came to this city of Alexandria, I spake of a vast high pillar of marble which I now well remember to be called by the name of Pompey's Pillar.

The plague was hot here in Alexandria at this time, and some persons infected with the plague being taken onboard our ship, the plague reigned in the ship, insomuch that besides those that recovered, we threw twenty persons overboard, who died of the plague. And truly I was not a little afraid of the distemper[162] and wished I were safe at Algier, hoping that if I were got there I should escape the plague. But I was not sooner got ashore there but was taken down in the plague, but through the divine goodness I escaped death. It rose under my arm, and the boil which usually accompanies the plague rose on my leg. After it was much swollen, I was desirous to have it lanced, but my patroon told me it was not soft enough. There was a neighbor, a Spaniard slave, who advised me to roast an onion and to apply a piece of it, dipped in oil, to the swelling, to mollify it, which accordingly I did, and the next day it became soft, and then my patroon had it lanced, and through the blessing of my good God, I recovered. Such a signal mercy I hope I shall never forget, a mercy so circumstantiated, considering everything, that my soul shall thankfully call to mind as long as I have any being. For I was just returned from Mecca when this mercy was dispensed to me. I do observe the divine providence plainly in it and hope ever to make the best use of it.

We are now arrived back again at Algier from our long pilgrimage. And being so, I shall take this occasion of acquainting you with some of my observations which I have hitherto omitted. The women of Algier look on it as

---

[162] *distemper*: disease.

very ornamental to wear great rings, almost like gyves,[163] about their legs and also their armwrists. Some wear them of gold, others of silver, others of brass, and some of horn (i.e., in the country). And if the countrywomen can get a few ordinary stones and a few cloves to string up and make a bracelet with, they think themselves very fine indeed. And the women here commonly paint their hands and feet with a certain plant[164] dried and beaten to powder, which they moisten with water and so use it, and it in a month's time or thereabout makes the part of a deep saffron color. The like is often done to their horses if white, i.e., they dye their feet, tail and mane, and under the saddle the said color.

I should have told you before, when I was speaking of the situation of Algier and the places adjacent (chap. I), that a little westward of Algier, viz., about two or three leagues, is a tower of considerable bigness about. I was never so near it as to be able to give an exact description of it, but I was informed that it was an entire stone, and they have a tradition that a Christian woman was enchanted there, and therefore they call it to this day *Cub el-Romeea*, i.e., the cupola of a Christian woman.

I should have told you likewise that in our voyage from Algier to Alexandria, in order to go to Mecca, we espied a small vessel in the morning, which we chased till it was almost night. We hung out French colors, and the chased vessel did the like but still shunned us, which made us continue our chase. And near night we came up with him and found the men to be all Turks and Moors, in a French vessel, who it seems were brought from Malta to be carried and sold at Leghorn, who told us that that very morning they were at an anchor at a certain place, and some of the French crew went ashore in their boat and left only two men and a boy aboard whereupon the slaves arose and killed the two French men and so became masters of the ship. And therefore, upon our hanging out French colors at the first, they were in a great consternation, but when they knew that we were Turks, they as much rejoiced as they feared before. Some of them—men, women, and children—came onboard of us and would by no means return to the French vessel again. They steered directly for Tunis, where we heard they safely arrived.

A few years before I came out of Algier, there happened a terrible fire among their ships in the mole, a little before candle lighting. Several of their fine ships were burnt, among which was one which was reputed the biggest that ever was built in Algier. This noble ship was just finished and fit for a

---

[163] *gyves*: shackles.
[164] *a certain plant*: henna.

voyage, able to carry sixty guns, when this fire broke out. Besides, several prizes were burnt, in all about sixteen sail, and there was much ado to save their three galleys. And had the wind been harder, the fire must have burnt their ships on the stocks and all the timber that lay by. Their castle on the mole was likewise in danger, they much fearing that the powder magazines would take fire. It was a most dreadful fire. Notwithstanding, methought I could not be much concerned for the sufferers.

I call to mind also that while I was at Algier there was a prize brought in thither by a *frigatto* as they call it (i.e., a long sort of vessel, with eleven or twelve oars on each side, and with sails galleylike, fit only for the summer's expeditions). These are generally manned with Moors, well armed with small arms, having five or six *pattareroes*.[165] And they get over to the Spanish shore, but mostly about Majorca and Minorca, and there skulk about the creeks and wait to snap[166] small coasters. And where they know is an house, they'll land and carry off the whole family. When this *frigatto* came to Algier, it was reported by the *frigattogees*[167] that the Christians who were in the taken ship ran ashore and that the said prize was found, without a soul therein, on the seas, which to some seemed very strange because the boat was all this while in the prize[168] and to be sure they could not fly to the shore. It was the general suspicion therefore that they had barbarously thrown the poor men of the ship overboard. And a little time after, I myself was credibly informed that one of the *frigatogees* was heard, on a time, to say that nothing grieved him so much as to see such a pretty boy thrown overboard. And it was in all likelihood an English ship, of about thirty or forty ton, richly laden, which, probably, was the occasion of this barbarity, for it was in a time when the English had peace with the Turks. And I must tell you 'tis not the first time, by a great many, that when we have had peace with them they have turned *isbandote*, i.e., buccaneers or robbers, or perfidious villains—or what you'll call them—and have taken our ships and sold ship, men, cargo, and all to those that have at the same time been at war with us also. I must confess this treachery is not allowed of in Algier, but yet, after some time, a sum of money to the dey makes up all, and 'tis all connived at and in a little time quite forgotten.

I have only one thing more to recollect relating to Algier and the places

---

[165] *pattareroes*: pedreros, or small cannons.

[166] *snap*: capture.

[167] *frigattogees*: crew of the *frigatto*.

[168] *in the prize*: onboard the ship that was captured by the Algerians.

adjacent, and that is that in Algier, as well as in other places, on Friday, which is their sabbath, in the afternoon they generally take their recreation. And amongst their several sports and recreations, they have a comical sort of wrestling which is performed about a quarter of a mile outside the gate called *Bab el wait* which is the western gate. There's a plain just by the seaside where, when the people are gathered together, they make a ring, all sitting on the ground expecting the combatants. Anon, there comes one boldly in and strips all to his drawers. Having done this, he turns his back to the ring and his face is towards his clothes on the ground. He then pitcheth on his right knee and then throws abroad his arms three times, slapping his hands together as often, just above the ground, which having done, he puts the back-side of his hand to the ground and then kisseth his fingers and puts them to his forehead, then makes two or three good springs into the middle of the ring, and there he stands with his left hand to his left ear and his right hand to his left elbow. In this posture the challenger stands, not looking about, till some-one comes into the ring to take him up, and he that comes to take him up does the very same postures and then stands by the side of him in the manner aforesaid. Then the tryer of the play[169] comes behind the *pilewans* (for so the wrestlers are termed by them) and covers their naked backs and heads, and makes a little harangue to the spectators. After which the *pilewans* face each other, and then both at once slap their hands on their thighs, then slap them together, and then lift up their hands as high as their shoulders and cause the palms of their hands to meet, and with the same, dash their heads one against another three times, so hard that many times the blood runs down. This being done, they walk off from one another and traverse their ground, eyeing each other like two gamecocks. If either of them find his hands moist, he rubs them on the ground for the better holdfast;[170] and they will make an offer of closing twice or thrice before they close. They'll come as often within five or six yards one of the other, and clap their hands to each other, and then put forward the left leg, bowing their body and leaning with the left elbow on the left knee for a little while, looking one in the other (as I said) just like two fighting cocks. Then they walk a turn again. Then at it they go, and they being naked to the middle and so there being but little holdfast, there's much ado before one hath a fair cast on his back, they having none of our Devonshire or Cornish skill. He that throws the other goes round the ring, taking money of many that give it him, which is but a small matter, it may be a farthing and halfpenny or a

---

[169] *tryer of the play*: referee.
[170] *holdfast*: grip.

penny of a person, which is much. Having gone the round, he goes to the tryer and delivers him the money so collected, who in a short time returns it again to the conqueror and makes a short speech of thanks. And it may be while this is doing, other two shall come into the ring to wrestle.

But at their *Byrams*,[171] those which are the most famous *pilewans*, or wrestlers, come in to show their parts before the dey, eight or ten together. And these do anoint themselves all over with oil, having nothing on their bodies but a pair of leathern drawers which are well oiled, too. These stand in the street near *Bab el Wait* (the abovesaid gate, withoutside which are all their sports held) spreading out their arms as if they would oil people's fine clothes unless they give them some money, which many do to carry on the humor. The *pilewans*, as I said, are the choice of all the stout wrestlers, and they wrestle before the dey, who sits on a carpet spread on the ground, looking on. And after the sport is over, he gives, it may be, two or three dollars to each. And then the dey with the basha[172] mount their horses, and several *spahis*[173] ride one after another, throwing sticks made like lances at each other, and the dey rides after one or other of them who is his favorite and throws his wooden lance at him, and if he fortune to hit him, the *spahi* comes off his horse to the dey, who gives him money. After all which diversions, they ride to the place where the dey hath a tent pitched, and there they spend the afternoon in eating and drinking of coffee and pleasant talk, but no wine. The dey usually appears in no great splendor at Algier. For I have seen him oftentimes ride into the town from his garden in a morning on a mule, attended only by a slave or another mule.

Being thus, as I have told you, returned to Algier from Mecca, the first camp I made after I returned from Mecca to Algier was, as I remember, against Oran, a Spanish garrison on the Barbary shore within the territories of Algier, which is a great eyesore to the Algerines and proves oftentimes a great damage to the country about them.

When these Spaniards of Oran have war with the neighboring Moors, they often make incursions and do great spoil among the Moors and bring them slaves into Oran and from thence send them into Spain. But as it commonly happens that private and intestine[174] quarrels and dissensions do more mischief to a people than the force of a foreign enemy, so many times the

[171] *Byrams*: feast days.
[172] *basha*: the Turkish viceroy appointed by the Ottoman sultan as regent in Algiers (as opposed to the dey who heads the council, or "diwan").
[173] *spahis*: members of the corps of Turkish cavalry.
[174] *intestine*: internal.

Moors fall out between themselves, and the consequence is that some or other of them, to be revenged, steals away by night and gets to Oran, and there agrees for a sum of money with the marquess, or governor, to discover and lead him to such or such a village that he may pillage it. The Spaniard, glad of the bargain, goes forth by night, and falls upon the said village by surprise, and takes and carries away men, women, children, cattle, and all. This hath been often done. But then let the traitor look to it, for there's no more coming back into his country without certain death. But he must stay all his life time with the Spaniards, and if occasion be, fight for them, but he's allowed to retain the Mohammetan religion.

The advantage the Spanish king hath by keeping this garrison, one would think, should be inconsiderable. I know it to be some advantage to the Spaniards in keeping it that when the Moors adjacent have peace with Oran, as they mostly have, they bring a great many necessaries into their market to sell, and the country affords great plenty, as wheat, barley, butter, honey, sheep, wax, etc., which the Spaniards buy and carry in ships into Spain.

As I was speaking, the first camp I made was against this Oran. The dey was in person there with about three or four thousand men, which is there reckoned a great force, and also with bombs and several pieces of canon. We laid siege against it about three months, plying sometimes our cannon and sometimes our bombs,[175] but all that we did signified not much, for the Turks in Algier are nothing expert in firing their bombs. The Spaniards, on the other side, had orders not to sally out but to be upon the defensive. The Algerines had not courage enough to come very near the town. Whilst we were besieging Oran, the French came a third time to bombard Algier,[176] *anno* 1688 (when that tragedy happened which you'll hear of hereafter), and there happened some bombs to fall on the *hazna*, i.e., the treasury or place where the money was kept that was to pay off the soldiers, immediately upon which there was an express dispatched to the dey as he lay before Oran signifying the absolute necessity of his presence at Algier. He forthwith rode post to Algier and having pacified matters, as 'twas thought, and secured the *haznah* in a little time, returned to the camp. But soon after this there was a plot hatching to take away this dey's life. This dey's name was Ibrahim (i.e., Abraham) Hogea (i.e., Scribe) because he was, before he came to be dey, but an ordinary man, though indifferently well skilled in letters.

---

[175] *bombs*: mortar shells.

[176] *the French . . . bombard Algier*: In 1688 the French were at war with Algiers, and in June a French fleet under Admiral Jean d'Estrées bombarded the city.

The nature of the plot was this. Ibrahim Hogea was *cayah*, or deputy, to Hagge Heusin, or Medio-Morto (who, as you'll find, succeeded him in the deyship, though he was dey before him, too). This Medio-Morto, being a politic man and well knowing what a ticklish, though splendid, place he was in when first dey, weighed what interest he could, privately, to be advanced to be a basha, for then he knew he should be safe from all evil designs that otherwise might be laid against him. For the basha of Algier is no way concerned in the government but only represents the state of the Grand Seigneur and hath allowance sufficient to maintain it.

Now Medio-Morto's design was not only to be made a basha but so to work matters as to be called home to Turkey by the Grand Signor and so to be quite out of fear of danger. For 'tis customary, upon reasons of state, to remand one basha and send another in his room. This policy Medio-Morto soon accomplished. And then Ibrahim became dey in his room, and all things seemed to be very quiet and serene. According to Medio-Morto's design, a ship came from Constantinople to Algier with a new basha and to carry the old basha, viz., Medio-Morto, to Turkey. At this very time (as I was speaking) we were besieging Oran, where came an express to acquaint the dey of the arrival of the ship to fetch Medio-Morto. The dey immediately sent back an express to tell him that if he went from Algier he should go as he came, viz., with just nothing. For the dey had entrusted Medio-Morto in his absence with the *hazna*, or treasury, and so was afraid lest he should have gone off with good part of the riches. Medio-Morto being thus disappointed excused himself from going to Constantinople and remained still in Algier, where he made it his business to gain a party to himself in order, if an occasion did offer, to set himself up for dey again in revenge to Ibrahim for his ill treatment shown him. Accordingly, he carried on his plot so successfully that the conspiracy grew to such a head that an express came to our camp before Oran to arrest the dey, viz., Ibrahim. The express came to the aga[177] of our camp, and the letter was directed to him, and the dey happened to be in the aga's tent at the very same time the express came to him, and so took the letter first into his own hand, and running it over to himself, went immediately to his own tent and took what light treasure he could and with two or three friends made his escape. Presently the rumor went through the camp, and it was all in a confusion. So that had the Spaniards nicked[178] that opportunity and made a sally upon us, they might have done great execution. But they did

---

[177] *aga*: commanding military officer.
[178] *nicked*: taken advantage of.

not, and the next day we drew off our forces and marched back to Algier again. The said dey never appeared more in Algier after this. So that Hagge Heusin succeeded him in the deyship (though he had been dey before) who was nicknamed by the Christians Medio-Morto, i.e., half-dead, because he was a very weak and a sickly man.

This dey was also, a little time after he came to his new honor, forced to fly for it, or else he had lost his life, for becoming dey again, he ceased to be a basha. And indeed it's a rare thing for a dey of Algier to die a natural death. It was but a few years before I was taken, Hagge Ali, who was dey, was murdered. And some years after I had been there, Baba Hassen, i.e., Father Hassen, was also slain.[179]

The year after this, the Moors belonging to the emperor of Morocco[180] broke their bounds and damaged the Moors within the territories of Algier, westward of *Tillimsan*.[181] The Algerine Turks which kept garrison in *Tillimsan* sallied out to assist the Moors of their side but lost most of their men in the action. The dey of Algier being enraged at this forthwith caused a great camp to march forth of Algier, with cannon and bombs, in order to be revenged on the emperor of Morocco. We were in all about three thousand foot and two thousand horse of Turks and about three thousand horse of Moors. We marched into the emperor of Morocco's country, and all the inhabitants as we went declared for the dey. At length we came within half a day's journey of the enemy's camp, which consisted, as 'twas supposed, of thirty thousand men; notwithstanding, we thought they would not have faced us. When we came within five or six miles of the enemy, we called a council of war, at which time notice is always given to all the soldiers to draw near to the dey's tent where the council of war is held. In the conclusion it was resolved to attack the enemy, and in doing this 'twas ordered that half the infantry and half the horse should march before with the baggage and the rest were to come behind. It was my place to be in the rear, but being desirous to see the beginning of it, I offered to exchange places with one of the tent wherein I was, who gladly accepted it. Coming forth from between two mountains, at the bottom of the hill we saw the enemy before us, their tents being all pitched on the further side of the river called

---

[179] *Baba Hassen . . . also slain*: Baba Hassan was acting dey in 1682 during another French bombardment of Algiers. He was assassinated after giving up 570 captives to the French and was immediately succeeded by Medio-Morto.

[180] *emperor of Morocco*: Mulay Ismail (ruled 1672–1727).

[181] *Tillimsan*: Tlemcen.

Melweea[182] (in the map it may be seen). Here we were at a stand, for positive orders were given that no man should fire a piece till our camp was pitched. But however, we had not patience very long but ran down the hill to the riverside, and at it we went. After we had been engaged about half an hour, the enemy, seeing we were but few in number in comparison of them, made an attempt to pass the river, but we hindered them. This attempt of theirs was a discovery to us where the river was passable, which we knew not before, being altogether strangers, and in most places the river was very deep. After we had been engaged about an hour or somewhat more, our party which was in the rear came up with us, and then the enemies' hearts began to flag. Then we plied them with our artillery and bombs so that in a very short time they fled and left to us their tents and baggage. We soon passed the river, and our *spahis*, which were about three thousand, pursued their horse; their foot took to the mountains. But at length the enemy's horse, perceiving themselves to exceed ours in number, wheeled about towards us, which made our horse wheel towards our foot, at which time was the greatest of our loss. But the enemy were afraid to come near our foot and so wheeled about again and marched off. After we had buried our dead and tarried two or three days by the river, we marched forward three or four days' march, intending to storm Fez, and we advanced so far as within one day's journey of it, where the whole body of the enemy lay. The emperor of Morocco, hearing that his son (the general in the late engagement) was defeated, came against us in person with what forces he could make. We pitched within two or three miles of him, in a vast plain, in sight of each other. After we had looked on one another for about an hour or two, the emperor sent an ambassador to our dey to treat of peace, who after he had tarried with the dey about an hour returned with an ambassador of ours to his master.

Upon his having audience of the emperor, it was concluded that the next day the emperor and the dey were to meet on horseback in the middle way between the two camps, each with fifty horse to attend him. When they came near one another, the rest of the horse halted, and the emperor and the dey, with a servant each, went to meet and salute one another, and after high compliments on both sides, a carpet was spread on the ground, and down they sat. In two or three hours' time, all matters were adjusted. The emperor promised to give satisfaction for the charges the dey had been at, urging this

[182] *river called Melweea*: probably the Moulouya River, which runs down to the sea between Fez and Tlemcen.

as an argument of accommodation: viz., our principles are to fight against the Christians and weaken their interest, and not to worry one another. Upon this easy agreement, the emperor presented our dey with his saddle which was all of beaten gold, and the next day we marched back again for Algier and thus ended the campaign. After this campaign was over and all matters accommodated between the two potentates, at the time appointed in the treaty, the emperor of Morocco sent his son to Algier with treasure sufficient to pay for the damage done the Algerines and with many rich presents. In a few days after the prince of Morocco came to Algier, it happened to be *Byram*, and it being a time of more leisure than ordinary, thousands of country Moors flocked thither to see him and to behold the sports and entertainments that were prepared for him without the gate *Bab el Wait*, which is (I said) the place where they have all their diversions and exercises. At the time of these sports, there happened a quarrel betwixt a Turk and some Moors, whereupon the Turks all began to cry out that the Moors had a design to mutiny and rebel, which took the more easily with the Turks' mob because the prince of Morocco happened to be there at that very juncture. And therefore they all ran into the city of Algier and betook themselves to arms and would suffer no Moor to enter the gate without examination. In this fray there were, in the several quarters of the town, about three or four score innocent Moors killed, for the outcry of the Turks was altogether groundless and a false alarum.[183] Yet this tragedy dashed all their sports and recreations. And the prince himself was put into a great concern and much feared what the event of it would prove.

CHAPTER IX. AN ACCOUNT OF THE AUTHOR'S TURNING MOHAMMETAN THROUGH THE BARBAROUS CRUELTIES AND TORTURES WHICH HE SUFFERED; OF THE CONCERN AND REMORSE HE HAD THEREUPON; A LETTER FROM HIS FATHER; A LETTER FROM HIM TO HIS FATHER; A CONSPIRACY CONTRIVED BY HIS SECOND PATROON TO BE DEY OF ALGIER

The reader, I suppose, will expect an account how I became qualified to write such a history as this (though it may be guessed at by what has gone before) and how I was let into the secrets of the Mohammetan religion, so as to be able to give such an exact description, as is herein published, of their religion, particularly of that at Mecca. Why truly, I will not dissemble but (undervalu-

[183] *alarum*: alarm.

ing all the censures of the world) freely and particularly declare the whole
matter, and herein I will deliver nothing but naked truth, as I protest I have
hitherto done (i.e., what I speak of as my own knowledge) in this whole relation.

I spake something before of the cruelties exercised upon me by the Turks
but now shall give a more particular account of them, which were so many
and so great that I being but young, too, could no longer endure them and
therefore turned Turk to avoid them.

GOD BE MERCIFUL TO ME A SINNER!

It is usually reported among us here in England that when any Christians
are taken by the Algerines, they are put to the extremest tortures that so they
may be thereby brought over to the Mohammetan faith, and, I doubt not,
many who have been slaves in the Turks' country and come home again have
asserted so much out of a vanity to be thought to relate something very affecting to those that are strangers to that country. But I do assure the reader it is
a very false report, for they never, or at least very seldom, use any such sever-
ities on such an account, though it was my hard fortune to be so unmercifully
dealt with. They do not use to force any Christian to renounce his religion.

Indeed in the Grand Turk's country,[184] in Egypt, and the parts thereabout
where those sorts of Christians are which are taken by the Tartars, coming
out of the country of the Russians, Georgees,[185] Circassians, etc. These, I say,
being a very ignorant sort of Christians, and especially the younger sort of
them, are no sooner taken slaves and sold, but they are immediately clothed
with the Turkish habit, put to school, and brought up in the Mohammetan
way. But in Algier, I aver 'tis otherwise, for I have known some Turks in
Algier, when they have perceived their slaves inclinable to turn Turks, they
have forthwith sold them, though by some of them this is looked on as very
odd and to savor too much of want of religion. But the truth is they are more
in love with their money than they are with the welfare of their slaves. And
you must know that when a Christian slave turns Mohammetan, there can
be no ransom for him, but yet it is looked on as an infamous thing for any
patroon, in some few years' time, to deny them their liberty and to refuse to
set them out handsomely into the world.

'Tis an error among some, too (I find), that as soon as ever a Christian
turns Turk, he is emancipated or become free (and so some think of Turks
that become Christians, that they also are freemen), but as for those Chris-

---

[184] *the Grand Turk's country*: Turkey.
[185] *Georgees*: natives of Georgia in Transcaucasia.

tians that turn Turks, it is not so, but it lies wholly in the patroon's breast to dispose of them as he pleaseth.

I have known some that have continued slaves many years after they have turned Turks, nay, some even to their dying day. And many, I know, have been as little respected by their patroons after the changing of their religion (or less) as before. For my part, I remained several years a slave after my defection, and suffered a great deal of cruel usage, and then was sold again.

My first patroon would (when exercising his barbarous cruelty upon me) press me to turn Mussulman, but all this while I did not believe that he was really willing I should so do, but only he might think that he discharged his duty in importuning me thereunto. And my reason why I thought so is because I knew at that time he could badly sustain such a loss. For a little before, he bought a little boy of Dover which soon renounced his holy religion and died in some years after. This my first patroon, a cruel man, I lived with about two or three months, and then he sent me to sea in one of the ships to attend upon the *toepgee bashe*, or the head gunner. We made (as they said) but a very ordinary voyage, for we took but one ship, and that a Portuguese, with eighteen slaves. We were out about two months, to my great ease and content, but when we were returning to Algier, and I out of hopes of being retaken for that time, my heart began to be heavy with the thoughts of entering again into my former misery. But there was no remedy but patience; into the hands of the tyrant I must fall again. But blessed be God, within a few days I was sold again and so out of the possession of that inhuman wretch.

While I lived with my second patroon in the country, who was called by the name of *Dilberre Ibrahim*, i.e., Handsome Abraham (For note that the Turks are mostly nicknamed, especially those that are soldiers. If a man be blind in one eye, they use to call him Blind Hugh, or what his name is. If tall, long such an one. If short, short such an one. If fat, fat such an one. If lean, lean such an one. If in his younger days given to much drinking, *sorhowsh*, or drunken such an one. If black-browed, then black-browed such an one, which is esteemed the greatest beauty among them, etc. Besides this way of nicknaming they often use another manner of distinction, calling men by the name of their country, as Exeter John, Welsh Tom, or the like. But all this by the by.), and who had several slaves, both Christians and Negroes, I fortuned to lose a shirt, which indeed was scarce worth looking after, and it seems one of the Negroes had stolen it. I had it again, and said but little about the matter. But some time after this I happened to lose my jacket, whereupon I made my complaint to my patroon, and my patroon told me he would beat all the slaves round[186] but he would find out the thief. Upon which threatening of my patroon's, one of the Negro slaves stood up and said, "Sir, there is no reason that all should suffer for one, and therefore, if I may presume so far, there is at Blida (a place about three miles from our country house) a black woman who can, as they say, tell fortunes and inform people where their lost goods are." Upon which my patroon appointed two Negroes to go with me to the said cunning woman.[187] When we came into her house, I told her that we come to be informed of something by her. Upon which she took a thing like a dish and put meal into it, and after she had smoothed over the meal and made it plain, she bid me put my hand on it and withal to think within myself what I would be informed of. Accordingly I did, and my thought was to know where my jacket was. In two or three minutes' time she told me that I had some time before lost a white thing. I told her I had so, which I understood to be my shirt. She then assured me that the same person who stole my shirt had stolen my jacket, which proved to be the Negro aforesaid, by his own confession. I was much surprised at this discovery but repent my folly in going to such persons on any such account.

My second patroon, whose name, as I told you, was Ibrahim, had two brothers in Algier and a third in Tunis. The middle brother had designed to make a voyage to Tunis to see his brother there, and it seems I was bought in order to be given as a present to him. I was then clothed very fine, that I might be the better accepted. The ship being ready, we put to sea, and in about fourteen or fifteen days' time we arrived at Tunis and went forthwith to my patroon's brother's house, which brother had two wives who lived each in a house distant from one another. The next day my patroon's brother['s] son, taking a pride to have a Christian to wait upon him, made me walk after him. I was ready and glad to do it because I was desirous to see the city. As I was attending upon my new master through the streets, I met with a gentleman habited like a Christian, not knowing him to be an Englishman as he was. He looked earnestly upon me and asked me whether I were not an Englishman.

I answered him, "Yea."

"How came you hither?" said he.

I told him I came with my patroon.

"What, are you a slave?" said he.

I replied, "Yes."

---

[186] *round*: severely.

[187] *cunning woman*: female fortune-teller or conjurer.

"To what place do you belong?" continues he.

"To Algier," quoth I.

But he was loath to enter into any further discourse with me in the public street and therefore desired of the young man on whom I waited that he would please, at such an hour of the day, to bring me to his house, with a promise of an hearty welcome. The young man assured him he would, for being a drinker of wine and knowing the plenty of it in the said gentleman's house, he was the rather willing to go. After the gentleman was gone from us, my young new master told me that he whom we talked with was the English consul, which I was glad to hear. We went as appointed to the consul's house, where, when we came, I was directed up to his chamber. He asked me many questions about my country, parentage, etc. And withal asked me whether I could write and understood arithmetic. I told him I could do both tolerably. Then he asked me what I thought was the inducement for my patroon to buy me. I told him he designed me for a present to his brother here at Tunis. Upon the whole, the consul kindly told me if I were left in Tunis, he would order matters to my satisfaction, but if my patroon designed to carry me back again to Algier, I should acquaint him with it in season, and in the meantime, he bid me, if I had so much liberty, to come every day to his house, where I should be welcome.

After I had been in Tunis about thirty days, I understood that my patroon's brother cared not to accept of me and that therefore I was to return to Algier. This very much troubled me, upon which I went to the consul and acquainted him with it. The consul told me that he and other two merchants (there being no more English merchants in the town) would the next day come and talk with my patroon about me. Accordingly they did, with their interpreter, and asked him whether he was willing to sell me. He told them he was, upon terms. They asked him what price he put upon me. He told them five hundred dollars, which was, I suppose, three hundred more than he bought me for. They offered two hundred. He made a slight of that and laughed at them. They advanced to two hundred and fifty dollars. He still made a pish of[188] it. They at length came up to three hundred dollars, which is near sixty pounds sterling, but my patroon plainly told them he would not abate one asper[189] of his demands. At which the consul told me that I must have patience, for an hundred pounds was a considerable sum to be contributed by three only and providence might work some other way. Upon

---

[188] *made a pish of*: expressed contempt for.

[189] *asper*: a small silver coin from Turkey or Egypt, worth only a few pence.

hearing this, I burst into tears, notwithstanding returning them a thousand thanks for their generous goodwill. The consul laid his hand on my head and bid me serve God and be cheerful and promised me that as soon as he returned to England he would prefer a petition to the king for me, and so he parted from me.

My hopes were thus all dashed, which was no small trouble to me, but patience overcomes all disappointments and afflictions.

My patroon now carried me onboard in order to go back again for Algier. The vessel in which we went was bound no further than Bona, which is near about halfway to Algier, so that at Bona my patroon hired two mules on which we came by land to Algier, which is about two hundred and fifty miles.

[Some years after this, when I had my freedom and went to camp, I somewhere about this part of the country passed through a a river, the water of which was so hot, I could scarce suffer it. And I was credibly informed that a little further up in the river the water was hot enough to boil an egg.]

About two months after this, my chief patroon, being captain of a troop of horse, was sent to Tunis by land, and about twenty *spahis* with him, who carried me with him also, so that I was not wanting from Tunis above four months before my second coming thither. The next day after we came now to Tunis I was sent out on an errand and accidentally met with the worthy consul again, whose name, I should have told you, was Baker, I think Charles Baker, brother to Thomas Baker, consul in Algier. When he saw me again, "What, my boy," said he, "art thou come again?" "Yes, sir," said I, "I came now with my chief patroon." "While you were absent," said he, "I bought a young man for my purpose for considerably less than I offered for you, but however you may tell this your patroon: that if he be disposed to sell you, I will still stand to my proposal." I gave him many thanks and went immediately and told my patroon of it, who surlily answered me, "*Seu le mang keu pek*," i.e., "Hold your peace, you dog!" I saw that there was no good to be done with him and therefore desisted.

We returned back to Algier in some small time, and a little after that he carried me into camp with him, and so it was that his two brothers, being *spahis*, or troopers, were with him in one and the same tent. His younger brother would be frequently (behind his brother's back and sometimes before his face) persuading me to turn Mohammetan and to gain me he made me large offers, but I little regarded them. And I can truly appeal to almighty God that it was not out of choice, or inclination, or persuasion, or any temporal advantage that I became a Mohammetan, for I abhorred the thoughts of such an apostasy.

The eldest brother, who was my chief patron, I found was not very fond of my turning, for he would often threaten me that if I did turn Turk and not learn my book well, he would beat me soundly. But his younger brother, who as I said had been so often tampering with me, saw that no arguments nor offers would prevail with me. He then began to lie very close to[190] his brother to force me to turn and as an argument would often tell him that he had been a profligate and debauched man in his time, and a murderer, and that the proselyting [of] me would be some sort of a proper atonement for his past impieties, and flatly told him that otherwise he would never go to heaven. Whereupon (as guilty men are willing to lay hold on every pretense to happiness, though never so slight and groundless) his brother endeavored to persuade me, and finding that would not do, he threatened to send me hundreds of miles off into the country where I should never see the face of any Christian. But finding all these methods to be ineffectual to the end they drove at, the two brothers consulted together and resolved upon cruelty and violence, to see what that would do. Accordingly, on a certain day, when my patroon's barber came to trim him, I being there to give attendance, my patroon bid me kneel down before him, which I did. He then ordered the barber to cut off my hair with his scissors, but I mistrusting somewhat of their design, struggled with them, but by stronger force my hair was cut off, and then the barber went about to shave my head, my patroon all the while holding my hands. I kept shaking my head, and my patroon kept striking me in the face. After my head, with much ado, was shaved, my patroon would have me take off my clothes and put on the Turkish habit. I told him plainly I would not. Whereupon I was forthwith haled[191] away to another tent, in which we kept our provision, where were two men, viz., the cook and the steward, one of the which held me while the other stripped me and put on me the Turkish garb. I all this while kept crying and weeping, and told my patroon that although he had changed my habit, yet he could never change my heart. The night following, before he lay down to sleep, he called me and bid me kneel down by his bedside and then used entreaties that I would gratify him in renouncing my religion. I told him it was against my conscience and withal desired him to sell me and buy another boy who perhaps might more easily be won, but as for my part, I was afraid I should be everlastingly damned if I complied with his request. He told me he would pawn his soul for mine, and many other importunate expressions did he use. At length I desired him to

---

[190] *lie very close to*: put pressure on.
[191] *haled*: dragged forcibly.

let me go to bed, and I would pray to God, and if I found any better reasons suggested to my mind (than what I then had) to turn by the next morning, I did not know what I might do, but if I continued in the same mind I was, I desired him to say no more to me on that subject. This he agreed to, and so I went to bed. But my patroon (whatever ailed him) having not patience to stay till the morning for my answer, he awoke me in the night and asked me what my sentiments now were. I told him they were the same as before. Then he took me by the right hand and endeavored to make me hold up the fore-finger, as they usually do when they speak those words, viz., "la illahi illallah Mohammet resul allah," which initiates them Turks (as I have related before), but I did with all my might bend it down so that he saw nothing was to be done with me without violence, upon which he presently called two of his servants and commanded them to tie up my feet with rope to the post of the tent, and when they had so done, he with a great cudgel fell a-beating of me upon my bare feet. He being a very strong man and full of passion, his blows fell heavy indeed, and the more he beat me, the more chafed and enraged he was, and declared that in short if I would not turn, he would beat me to death. I roared out to feel the pain of his cruel strokes, but the more I cried, the more furiously he laid on upon me, and to stop the noise of my crying, he would stamp with his feet on my mouth, at which I begged him to dispatch me out of the way, but he continued beating me. After I had endured this merciless usage so long, till I was ready to faint and die under it, and saw him as mad and implacable as ever, I begged him to forbear and I would turn. And breathing awhile but still hanging by the feet, he urged me again to speak the words. Yet loath I was and held him in suspense awhile and at length told him that I could not speak the words, at which he was more enraged than before and fell at me again in a most barbarous manner. After I had received a great many blows a second time, I beseeched him again to hold his hand and gave him fresh hopes of my turning Mohammetan, and after I had taken a little more breath, I told him as before, I could not do what he desired. And thus I held him in suspense three or four times, but at last, seeing his cruelty towards me insatiable unless I did turn Mohammetan, through terror I did it and spake the words as usual, holding up the forefin-ger of my right hand, and presently I was had away to a fire and care was taken to heal my feet (for they were so beaten that I was not able to go upon them for several days), and so I was put to bed.

   All the ceremony that any person that turns Mohammetan by compulsion useth is only holding up the forefinger of the right hand and pronouncing these words: "La illahi ill alla Mohammet resullallah." But when any person voluntarily turns from his religion to the Mohammetan, then there is a great deal of formality used. Many there are that do so turn, out of choice, without any terror or severity shown them. Sometimes in a mad or drunken humor, sometimes to avoid the punishment due to some great crime committed by them, as murder or the like, they become Mohammetans, being afraid to return into their own country again.

Now when any person so turns Mohammetan, he goes to the court where the dey and divan (i.e., his council) sits, and there he declares his willingness to be a Mohammetan, upon which he is immediately accepted without demanding of him any reason for his so doing. After which, the apostate is to get on horseback, on a stately steed, with a rich saddle and fine trappings. He is also richly habited and hath a turbant on his head (but to be sure, not of a green color, for none durst wear their turbants of that color but such as are of Mohammet's blood). But nothing of this is to be called his own, but only there is given him about two or three yards of broadcloth which is laid before him on the saddle. The horse, with him on his back, is led all round the city, and he carries an arrow in his right hand, holding it straight up and thereby supporting the forefinger of his right hand, which he holds up against it. This he doth all the while he is riding round the city, which he is several hours in doing. But if he happen to be tired with long holding up his forefinger against the arrow, then he may now and then take it off for a moment and then up with it again in the said posture. The apostate is attended with drums and other music, and twenty or thirty *vekil-harges*, or stewards, who (as I told you, chapter four) are under the *otho-bashees*, or sergeants, who march in order by each side of the horse, with naked swords in their hands, intimating thereby (as I was informed) that if he should repent, and show the least inclination of retracting what he had declared before the dey and divan, that he deserved to be cut in pieces, and the *vekil-harges* would accordingly cut him in pieces. There are likewise two persons who stand one on each side of the street as he marcheth through, to gather what people are pleased to give by way of encouragement to the new convert (as they call him), and it may be one here and there drops a farthing or halfpenny. 'Tis much if any be so zealous as to give a penny. After this show and ceremony is over, he is immediately entered into pay[192] and directed to the place where he shall quarter with some of his fellow soldiers. And within a few days the *seunet gee* of the town, i.e., the circumciser, comes and performs the ceremony of circumcision. And then he is a Turk to all intents and purposes. It is reported by some that when

---

[192] *entered into pay*: placed on the payroll of the local Turkish garrison.

any thus voluntarily turns Mohammetan, he throws a dart to the picture of Jesus Christ in token of his disowning him as the savior of the world and preferring Mohammet before him, but there is no such usage, and they who relate such things do deceive the world. I am sure I have reason (God pardon me!) to know everything in use among them of this nature, and I assure the reader there is never any such thing done.

The crier goes before with a loud voice giving thanks to God for the proselyte that is made, and at some particular place of the city, especially in the *casharees*, or the places where many of the soldiers dwell together, the multitude hold up their hands, giving thanks to God.

I was very much concerned for one of our countrymen who had endured many years of slavery and after he was ransomed and went home to his own country, came again to Algier and voluntarily, without the least force used towards him, became a Mohammetan.

Another Englishman I knew, who was bred to the trade of a gunsmith, who after he was ransomed and only waited for his passage, reneged and chose rather to be a Mohammetan than to return to his own country.

About two or three months, as near as I can guess, after I was taken a slave, I writ a letter to my father, giving him an account of my misfortune, to which letter I did receive from my father a kind and affectionate answer. A copy of the letter I have not by me, but I well remember that therein he gave me very good counsel, viz., to have a care and keep close to God and to be sure never, by any methods of cruelty that could be used towards me, to deny my blessed Savior. And that he had rather hear of my death than of my being a Mohammetan. But this first letter from my father came not to my hands till some days after I had, through my patroon's barbarity to me, turned from my religion. Which after, through extreme torture, and out of love to a temporal life, I had done, I became very sad and melancholy, considering the danger my poor soul was in. The said letter was taken up in Algier by my master George Taylor of Lymson, who sent it to the camp and directed to an English lad, one of the bey's, or general's, slaves, who being afraid to deliver me the letter openly, slid it into my hand as he passed by me. As soon as I cast my eye upon the superscription, I knew it to be my father's hand and in a great deal of sorrow made what haste I could out of the camp, as pretending to go to ease myself, to read the letter, but when I had opened it could scarce read a word for weeping. And I am apt to think that if the letter had come to my hands before I had turned Turk that my patroon would rather have accepted of the promised ransom for me than that I should become a Mohammetan. After I had read some part of the letter (for I could not read it through at once, for fear my patroon should find me wanting) I was ready to sink. I put up the letter therefore, intending to read the whole another time, and returned to our tent with a more dejected heart and countenance than before, insomuch that my patroon perceiving it, asked me whether I had been weeping. I replied, "Sir, you don't see me weep." Many other angry words he had with me, and at length truly my heart was so big that I could not contain any longer but fell into tears and at the same time produced him the letter which I received from my father and told him that my father would ransom me, and, said I, "I am no Turk, but a Christian." My patroon answered me with, "Hold your tongue, you dog, for if you speak such a word again, I'll have a great fire made and therein burn thee immediately," at which I was forced to be silent.

In two or three days after this, I writ my father a second letter, which I was forced to do by piecemeals, in a great deal of danger and fear, in which I gave him a perfect account of the whole matter and told him the naked truth lest he should have thought that what I did, I did voluntarily and without any coercion. And in order thereunto, I privately desired the aforesaid English lad, a servant to the bey, to lend me pen, ink, and paper, and took an occasion to go outside the camp, and there in fear writ two or three lines at a time, as I could, without discovery, till I had finished my epistle.

The substance of my letter was that though I was forced by that cruelty that was exercised upon me to turn Turk, yet I was really a Christian in my heart (some may term me hypocrite for so doing, but I'll not reply any more than this: that I speak it not to extenuate my sin but to set the matter in a true light, how I turned and the reasons of my so doing). And withal, I assured my father and mother that I would, as soon as ever I could find an opportunity, endeavor to make my escape and therefore entreated them to be as contented as they could under their great trouble and affliction and expect what time would produce.

Sometime after my father received this my second letter, he sent me another, which was directed (as the former) to my master Taylor in Algier, and he sent it forward and directed it to an Englishman at Blida, where I then lived, of whom I received it, and I look upon it as a signal providence, for there was but that one Englishman then living in the town. The substance of the letter is as followeth, viz.: "Yet I cannot choose but call thee dear and loving son, although thou hast denied thy Redeemer that bought thee, especially considering the tenderness of thy age, the cruelty of thy usage and the strength of thy temptations. I confess, when I first heard of it, I thought it would have overwhelmed my spirits. And had it not been for divine supports, it had been a burden too, too, unsupportable for my weak

shoulders to have crippled[193] under, especially considering the loss of thy
soul." But withal, my father in his letter comforted me with telling me that
he had been with several ministers who unanimously concurred in their
opinion that I had not sinned the unpardonable sin. And therefore he goes
on to comfort me:

> Truly child, I do believe that what thou hast done with thy mouth
> was not with thy heart and that it was contrary to thy conscience. Take
> heed of being hardened in thine iniquity; give not way to despondency,
> nor to desperation. Remember that Peter had not so many temptations
> to deny his lord and master as those hast had, and yet he obtained
> mercy,[194] and so mayst thou. Yet the door of grace and mercy is open
> for thee. I can hardly write to thee for weeping, and my time is but
> short, and what shall I say to thee more, my poor child? I will pawn
> the loss of my soul upon the salvation of thine, that if thou dost but
> duly and daily repent of this thy horrid iniquity, that the blood of that
> Jesus whom thou hast denied, there is sufficient satisfaction in Him to
> save thee to the utmost or otherwise let me perish. I will promise thee
> as welcome to me upon thy return and repentance as though thou
> hadst never done it. And if there be such bowels[195] of pity in an earthly
> parent, which is but drops to the ocean, what dost thou think of the
> boundless mercies of God, whose compassions are like to himself, infi-
> nite? I confess it's something difficult for thee to make thy escape, but
> yet I am confident that if thou dost keep close to God, notwithstand-
> ing this thy miscarriage, that infinite wisdom and power will be set at
> work to find out ways, in such untrodden paths that I cannot imagine,
> for thy relief. Which is the daily prayer of thy
>
>   affectionate father,
>   John Pitts.

It pleased God that this my father's second letter, though cause of many
sorrowful reflections in me, did yet administer great support and comfort to

---

[193] *crippled*: hobbled.

[194] *Peter had . . . obtained mercy*: The apostle Peter denied Christ three times
(Matthew 26:69–75) but went on to witness the Transfiguration and helped to lead the
early Christian community.

[195] *bowels*: inner depths (the "bowels," or inside of the body, were believed to be
the seat of sympathetic emotions).

me, and I would often go into some by-corner[196] or under some hedge of a garden to read it.

The reader may easily think that one under my circumstances could have but very few opportunities of writing home to his parents and friends, which was the reason why I writ no oftener.

In my return from Mecca to Algier, at Alexandria I accidentally met with John Cleak of Lymson, who belonged to Captain Bear's ship of Topsham (as I related to you before, p. 113),[197] in whom, being my old acquaintance, I could put confidence, and so desired him to carry a letter for me, which he readily granted me. But since I came home to Exon, he (the said Cleak) told me that he was under great fear and concern lest the Turks' officers onboard (who are much like our tidesmen[198]) should, when searching their chests, etc., find the letter in his custody, to prevent which, he hung it inside the ceiling of the ship. The reader will excuse my not dating the letter when I tell him that truly then I forgot the month and the year because the Turks reckon after a different manner from us, and therefore I did not only omit the date of the letter but sent it also unsealed, as the manner of sending letters is there. For indeed they are very illiterate, not one in an hundred being able to read, and therefore they run no great risk in sending their letters unsealed.

> Honored and dear Father and Mother,
>
> It is not the want of duty or love which makes me negligent of writing to you, but 'tis chiefly the consideration of the little comfort you can take in hearing from me, having been a great grief and heartbreaking to you.
>
> Dear Father and Mother, how often have I wished that I had departed the world when I hung upon your breasts, that I might not have been the bringer of your gray hairs with sorrow to the ground. Therefore, if you would be an ease to my grief, I desire you to wait God's leisure.
>
> Your grief, though great, is but little in comparison of mine. Put it to the worst, you have lost but a son, but I for my part have lost both a dear father and mother, brothers, relations, friends, acquaintance, and all! But my greatest sorrow is that God hath deprived me of His holy

---

[196] *by-corner*: out-of-the-way place.
[197] *p. 113*: See p. 295.
[198] *tidesmen*: customs officials.

scriptures, of any good counsel or discourse, for I see nothing but wickedness before mine eyes.

The Lord of heaven reward you for your endeavors to bring me up in the ways of Jesus Christ, for the bad improvement of which privilege I now here find and suffer the want of it.[199] I am in great fears, and great hazards do I run, in writing these few lines. About fourteen months I have been wanting from Algier, for I have been with my patroon to Mecca, where is, they say, the house of God, and after they have been to pay their devotions thither, they do account that all their sins are forgiven.

Mecca is about forty days' travel beyond Grand Cairo. Being now therefore in my way back again to Algier (as far as Alexandria), I embrace this opportunity of sending to you from hence. With my kind love to all my brothers, relations, friends, and neighbors, desiring yours and the prayers of all good people to God for me, I rest,

> your dutiful son till death,
> Joseph Pitts.

I lived still a miserable life with this my patroon and was oftentimes so beaten by him that my blood ran down upon the ground. After I had thus turned Turk, he had rather less kindness for me than before, and one reason truly was because he thought that I was no true Mussulman in my heart, for he observed me to be far from being zealous in the Mohammetan way. (And I must declare that oftentimes I would go to mosque without ever taking any *abdes* at all, which none of the thorough-paced[200] Mohammetans would do, might they gain ever so much.) For which I fared (many ways) much worse than my fellow slaves which had not turned and did lie with them in a stable and also eat with them. And indeed our victuals were very coarse and ordinary, viz., mostly barley bread, with sour milk. But if a sheep did chance to die, the flesh would come for our share, and many joyful and hearty good meals should we make of it.

This my patroon was a married man, and being wanting about fourteen months from his wife upon a stretch, in which interval she was delivered of bastard twins, he turned her away and in a little time married another who

---

[199] *for the bad . . . want of it*: Meaning "I have been unable to live as a proper Christian because Christianity is lacking here."
[200] *thorough-paced*: thoroughly trained.

was a great fortune to him. He having got great riches, and being a man full of ambition, had a great tooth[201] for the deyship of Algier and to compass his design had (by large promises of promoting them) corrupted many among the soldiers, who declared they were resolved to stand by him. The dey, whose name was Hassan (whom they also called Baba Hassan, i.e., Father Hassan), having had some private information of this my patroon's design, banished him. Now the way of banishment is thus: viz., the crier cries it about the town and proclaims the exiled person and offers a great reward to any person that shall discover him from that time.

My patroon, notwithstanding, left not his country nor his country house but kept himself very private all day and lay in the fields by night with me and others of his slaves. At length, search was made for him and his two brothers, and the troopers would come sometimes and beset his country house for to take him. He finding himself no longer safe in those parts betook himself to the mountains of the Kabyles who, as I told you before, are a rugged sort of people, refusing oftentimes to be tributary to the dey of Algier. I, with two or three more of his slaves and his two brothers, were with him in the mountains, where he, by his plausible[202] tongue, at length got into the favor and esteem of the Kabyles, so that they resolved to stand by him.

Now it happened that at this very juncture the French came and bombarded Algier because their demands of the French slaves there were not answered. Upon which, all being in great confusion by the bombs, the dey's wife set herself to persuade her husband to release the slaves. He was accordingly prevailed upon and yielded up the said slaves to the French then before the town, at which the soldiers began to express their dissatisfaction that he had not consulted with them about it and were somewhat turbulent, saying one among another, "We are brought to a brave pass now, to become tributary to the French!" And in a little time the jealousies against him grew so high that they slew him in the night time without the mole-gate.[203]

A third time the French came, with a squadron under the command of Maréchal d'Estrée, who fired 10,000 bombs into the town, as also abundance of carkashes,[204] which are fired as a bomb is, but a bomb is filled only with powder, but this is filled with several combustibles and hath holes all round,

[201] *tooth*: taste or desire.
[202] *plausible*: ingratiating.
[203] *without the mole-gate*: outside the gate leading to the mole or harbor.
[204] *carkashes*: round iron shells or firebombs filled with combustible material and pierced with holes to emit flames.

and in every hole something like the barrel of a pistol, laden with several shot therein. These break not all at once, as the bombs; these were designed for the ships that were in the mole, but they did no great execution upon them, for to the best of my remembrance, they lost not one privateer, only some prizes which lay then in the harbor. For the Algerines themselves sunk their privateers before the French began to fire their bombs.

'Tis true the city was so much beaten down that you could not distinguish one street or lane from another, and 'twas several years before the damage was quite repaired. The French fleet anchored out of gunshot of the town but the bomb-vessels were within gunshot, at which the Turks plied their cannon very briskly. But they saw no good was to be done, for the shot could not pierce the sides of the French ships but fell into the sea. The French therefore were in no fear of their cannon. The Turks at length thought it their wisest way to save their ammunition.

There were (as I remember) nine bomb-vessels, each having two mortars, which kept firing day and night, insomuch that there would be five or six bombs flying in the air at once, which was a terrible sight to behold. At this the Algerines were horribly enraged and to be revenged fired away from the mouth of their cannon about forty French slaves, and finding that would not do but d'Estrée was rather the more enraged, they sent for the French consul, intending to serve him the same sauce. He pleaded his character and that he hoped they would not use a person of his post and figure[205] so barbarously, that 'twas against the law of nations, etc. They answered they were resolved, and all these compliments would not serve his turn. At which he desired a day or two's respite till he could dispatch a letter to the admiral, which was granted him, and a boat was sent out with a white flag. But after the admiral had perused and considered the consul's letter, he bid the messenger return this answer: viz., that his commission was to throw 10,000 bombs into the town, and he would do it—to the very last. And that as for the consul, if he died, he could not die better than for his prince. This was bad news, you may imagine, to the consul and highly provoked the Algerines, who immediately, upon this message, caused the consul to be brought down and placed him before the mouth of a canon and fired him off also. This was very dreadful to behold.

The French bombarded Algier three times while I was there. The first time, as I remember, was because the Turks would not yield up the French slaves that they had. They then threw but few bombs into the town, and that

---

[205] *post and figure*: position and importance.

by night. Nevertheless, the inhabitants were so surprised and terrified at it, being unacquainted with bombs, that they threw open the gates of the city, and men, women, and children left the town. Whereupon the French had their countrymen that were slaves for nothing. In a little after, the French came again to Algier, upon other demands, and then, as I have related, by the persuasion of his wife, the dey surrendered up all the French slaves, which proved the said dey's ruin. And then (as I have also told) they came a third time and fired many thousands of bombs into the town, notwithstanding the dey stood his ground and would not yield up one slave without an equivalent. So that the French brought ashore thirty or forty Turks or Moors in their boat and had as many of their own countrymen that were slaves in exchange for them.

Immediately upon the death of Baba Hassan, some of my patroon's friends took horse and came posthaste to acquaint him of this seemingly favorable event. He instantly equips for Algier, which being a day's journey, there was a new dey elected before he could arrive thither, whereas if he could have come sooner than he did, 'twas the general notion that he would have been dey. But though he came too late to be dey, yet all former matters were accommodated, and he, in all appearance, in favor with the present dey. But however it was, in a few days this dey became incensed against him, whereupon he was a second time banished. My patroon, at this being very much puzzled what to do or where to go, at length went to a marabout to crave his advice, what he was best to do in this exigence. The marabout told him that he should distribute fifty dollars to the poor, kill four sheep and give [them] to the poor, and after he had so done go back to Algier, not doubting success in his enterprises there. He took his leave of the marabout, having received of him his old patched cloak, which he looked on as a mighty preservative from all manner of danger. And according to the marabout's advice, he, with his two brothers and two other Turks of their acquaintance, being well armed with small arms under their cloaks, mounted their horses and posted[206] to Algier and were at the gate as soon, almost, as it was open. They left their horses at the gate and went directly to the house where the dey sat with the divan, or council. At the gate of the dey's house the aga, with other officers, sits, and there usually complaints are made. To him therefore my patroon makes his complaint, telling him that he was not conscious of any harm that he had done against the government and that therefore he was unjustly banished and that if there could anything be proved against him that

---

[206] *posted*: traveled at top speed.

deserved it, he was come presently ready to suffer death. The aga having received his complaint sends for one of the seven *chiauxes*, or *chiaous*, who are equal to our sergeants and bid him go in and acquaint the dey with it. When the dey heard they were without, he immediately ordered the *chiauxes* to apprehend them, for fear what the consequence of any delays might prove. The *chiauxes* therefore running upon them to seize them, my patroon and his company drew their swords and defied them, at which the *chiauxes* were afraid and fell back, and my patroon and his accomplices made to a *casherea*, i.e., a sort of a guardhouse, where were many soldiers, and with large promises engaged them to stand by him, and so they shut the gate of the *casherea*, making it a sort of garrison. But in a little time the town was up in arms, and the soldiers beset the place and demanded the gate to be opened, which was done, and my patroon with his forlorn[207] were seized, and they had all their heads cut off.

Thus my patroon miscarried in a seemingly rash attempt, though it was certainly the general opinion that if, instead of complaining to the aga, he had gone right into the room where the dey was (as he might) and have killed him, he would infallibly have obtained his end.

The next day after this tragedy, the soldiers were sent out to his country house, and all he had was seized on and brought to Algier. And I was called before the dey to witness what I could, but he only asked me whether my patroon had any children. I told him yes, whereupon all his seized goods were restored again for the good of his family, which were now in most dismal lamentations, those of the male sex not shaving their heads for near the space of two months, which with them is a token of extraordinary mourning.

I was in hopes that my patroona, or mistress, would now have given me my freedom, but she would not but intended to sell me there in the country. But I earnestly desired that I might be sold in Algier, which at length she granted, and according to custom I was carried three days (by the crier) about the streets and was bought the third time by an old bachelor. My work with him was to look after his house, to dress his meat, to wash the clothes, and in short to do all these things that are looked on as a servant maid's work in England.

I must own I wanted nothing with him: meat, drink, clothes, and money, I had enough. After I had lived with him about a year, he made his pilgrimage to Mecca and carried me with him. (About the pilgrimage to Mecca, I have related before, chap. 7.) But before we came to Alexandria my patroon

---

[207] *forlorn*: group of soldiers who risked their lives.

was taken sick, and thinking verily he should die, he having a woven girdle about his middle under his swash (which they usually wear) in which was much gold and also my letter of freedom (which he intended to give me when at Mecca), he took it off and bid me put it on about me and took my girdle and put it on himself, and withal told me that if he died on the way, I should be sure to perform the *al-hage*,[208] or *el-Hagge*, not doubting that there would be sufficient care besides taken to bear my charges. This was argument enough how much he loved me. But it pleased God that he recovered, and one thing I observed in him was that he was before a great smoker of tobacco but after that sickness never smoked at all, which was looked on as a token of his repentance, for though abundance of tobacco be smoked among the Turks, yet it is accounted a sin to smoke it.

I have given an account of the pilgrimage to Mecca (chap. 7) but forgot to tell you that at Mecca every *hagge*, almost, buys of those that come from the East Indies a *caffin*, i.e., a shroud of fine linen cloth, to be buried in (for they never use coffins for that purpose), which *caffin* might have been bought in Algier at a much cheaper rate, but they choose to buy it here at Mecca because they have the advantage of dipping it in the holy water *zem zem*. They'll be sure to carry the said *caffin* wherever they travel, by sea or land, that they may be sure to be buried therein.

And I forgot also to tell you that just before I went to Mecca, being newly come to this my last patroon, we living in a court,[209] or *funduck*, as they term it, where lived none but bachelors, everyone had his slave to do the like service with him, as I did with my patroon, among which slaves there was one James Grey, an Englishman of Weymouth, with whom I became very intimate, insomuch that I communicated my greatest secrets to him and particularly how I came to turn Mohammetan and how uneasy I was upon it, and withal I told him I had thoughts to go to the dey and tell him that I was forced to turn and that I hoped he would let me be at my choice, for I would be no Mohammetan, and desired this Grey's opinion, whether I were best so to do. He answered I should by no means do it, for it would make the worse for me and endanger my life. He told me also that 'twould not be long before my patroon would go to Mecca, and there in all likelihood give me my liberty, and after that I might find some way or other to escape. Well, I hearkened to his advice, but afterwards I had cause to repent of making him so much my confidant. For when I returned from Mecca to Algier, I found this James

---

[208] al-hage: pilgrimage to Mecca.
[209] *court*: a group of dwellings issuing onto a common courtyard.

Grey himself very much inclined to turn Mohammetan. I was with my heart
willing to discourage him from it and to lay the horrid evil of it before him,
but I was afraid lest he should betray me. One day particularly, he came and
asked my advice whether he was best to turn or not. I thought him perfidious and therefore told him he should use his own mind; I would use no
arguments with him pro or con. For, said I, if I should persuade you to turn,
and your patroon should not be so kind to you as you expect, viz., to give you
your liberty, then you'd lay the blame on me. But in a little time this Grey did
turn Turk, and that without the least temptation, his patroon no way desiring him so to do. I guessed him to be about thirty years of age when he
turned.

About a year afterwards, his patroon gave him his liberty, and he entered
into pay. He became very diligent in learning to read the Alcoran and very
forward to perform *sallah*, so that he was looked on as a zealot. He would
often correct me for my backwardness to go to mosque and for my intimacy
with the neighboring slaves, insomuch that I was afraid to oppose or contra-
dict him in anything.

But it pleased God that in a little time this Grey died and that in a very
dismal manner, for he pined away after a strange rate[210] and before his death
became a very miserable object indeed. And without breach of charity, I was
not sorry for his death.

I suppose this Grey had some expectations of great matters which made
him turn, but he found himself disappointed. I am sure 'twas not from any
such inducements that I became a Mohammetan but through my patroon's
cruel and merciless usage to me, and yet I fared rather worse with him than
before. Though sometimes they show themselves partial enough to those of
the Mohammetan religion with themselves, an instance of which I shall not
easily forget: viz., while I was in Algier, there were two Negro slaves belonging to a Tagarene, or Andalusian, one of which was a Mohammetan and the
other a Portuguese and a Christian. It seems that these two slaves, while they
were at their work in their patroon's garden, having some old grudge, conspired to take away his life and rob him of his money. Accordingly, on a certain day they understood that their patroon was to go to Algier with a considerable sum of money with him, and most of it in gold, and they waylaid
him and murdered him.

This barbarous fact was not presently discovered, but at length these
Negroes forsooth must go and enjoy themselves and in order thereunto went

---

[210] *after a strange rate*: in a strange way.

to the moneychangers to change some pieces of gold, by which means they were suspected and apprehended and upon a strict examination into the matter were found guilty and both executed. He that was a Mussulman had a great deal more favor shown him than the other, for he was fairly hanged, the manner of which in Algier is thus: viz., they have a hole made in a wall, just up to the top, through which one end of the rope is put and fastened on the other side the wall, and the other about the criminal's neck, he sitting upon the wall, and after he hath spoken what he will, he is pushed off the top of the wall and so is hanged. But the poor Portuguese was stripped naked to the middle and had his hands tied behind him and a hole made in the heel of each hand, into which were put wax candles burning. The same was done in both his shoulders, and in this manner was he led along the streets with the crier of the town before him publishing his crime. I thought they intended to have burnt him alive and therefore went out of the gate to see him executed, but they cut off his head first and then burnt his body to ashes.

There was a Spaniard that killed a Moor and was therefore condemned to be burnt, but to escape the fire, if not save his life, he turned Mohammetan. But this would not save his life, yet it gained him the favor, instead of being burnt, to be pushed off the wall at the gate *Bab el zoon*, which is the common place of execution.

The Turks and renegadoes of Algier have that privilege above the *cull ougles*, that is, the sons of the *yenesherres*, or soldiers, of being aga, which none of the said *cull ougles* can be, for when any of them becomes a *kaya*, which is under the aga, he is forthwith made *mazel-aga* and has his pay, not being in the least obliged to perform any duty and so can advance no further. And the reason of this difference made between the Turks, renegadoes, and the *cull ougles* is this: viz., some scores of years past, the abovesaid *cull ougles* had conspired together to murder the Algerine Turks in general, which was a dreadful design, but it took no effect, and many of the *cull ougles* lost their lives, great heaps of whose heads are at this day to be seen on the walls of Algier over the gate *Bab el-Zoon*, or Eastern Gate. Notwithstanding, the *cull ougles* will upon the least provocation twit the renegadoes with words like these: *"Eir youle bullerfen catcherfen,"* i.e., "Thou wilt run away, if thou knewest how." And at other times they will jeer the renegadoes with *"Domus eate, the hoe dishing dader,"* i.e., "There is yet swine's flesh in thy teeth" (meaning they have still a tang of Christianity), and especially when any renegado runs away, the rest shall be thus jeered by them.

And now I am speaking of renegadoes running away, I can't well omit this story, which is not foreign to the matter in hand.

Ibrahim Hogea, the dey of Algier, had several Christian slaves and also several renegadoes, and he would distinguish the renegadoes and prefer them when anything offered, and particularly I remember there was a Spaniard renegado whom I knew, which the dey had preferred to be a captain of a privateer. This renegado, after he had made two or three voyages, had got together onboard him a parcel of renegadoes who were entirely devoted to his will and would comply with anything he proposed to them. It happened that coming near Tetouan, a Moor's town near the Strait's mouth, they sent, as usually, their boat ashore to take in wood for their cruising voyage. The Turks were all willing to go ashore and did so, whereupon the renegadoes, being all agreed, as soon as the boat was gone ashore hoisted up their sails and stood over for the Spanish shore, where in a few hours they safely arrived, and there they sold ships and slaves and reembraced their former religion.

This did not a little nettle the Turks. And therefore they would cast it in the teeth of almost every renegado they met, but my patroon would not open his mouth against me, unless when in a passion, but would speak upon occasion in my behalf, saying *"Ben ebn, ouglanem eumra catch mes,"* i.e., "My son will never run away."

CHAPTER X. AN ACCOUNT OF THE AUTHOR'S ESCAPE AT SMYRNA. OF HIS BEING ROBBED. OF MANY OTHER OCCURRENCES ON HIS JOURNEY HOME TO EXETER

I being now at liberty from my patroon (who gave me my letter of freedom at Mecca) and entered into pay but living still with him (because he had a great kindness for me, not doubting that I was a true Mussulman), I was of the mind to use the seas and did two or three voyages, hoping to be retaken or some way or other to make my escape, but providence did not order it that way. It happened at length that there came a messenger from the Grand Turk[211] to Algier to bespeak some of the Algerines' ships to assist him, which was granted. I was in good hopes it would fall to my lot to go in one of the ships, intending, if I could, to make my escape at Smyrna, but it fell to my turn to go to the camp that year. But, however, I made an exchange with one who agreed to go in my room to the camp, and I was to go in his in the ship, which I was earnestly desirous of, because I was acquainted with one Mr. Butler, a merchant in Algier who lived with the consul, who (as it will here-

---

[211] *Grand Turk*: Ottoman sultan.

after appear) was my great friend in facilitating my escape. In order to give you an account of which, it will be convenient to inform you how I came acquainted with that honest and worthy gentleman, Mr. Butler.

Some few months before I came away from Algier, I was afflicted with a very sore eye, insomuch that I was in danger of losing my sight, and understanding that there was an English doctor (a slave for whom I knew Mr. Butler had a kindness and paid his patroon so much a month) whom he had taken into his house, I went to Mr. Butler's to advise with the said doctor for a cure of my eye. He undertook the cure, and so I usually went twice or thrice a day to his house where sometimes I would take a Bible in my hand and read, for I thought myself out of the danger of any Turks seeing me. And it happened that once Mr. Butler came in while I was reading in the Bible. He seemed to wonder at it and asked me why I did so (for he knew that persons under my circumstances would not venture to do so). I answered him I had no hatred to the Bible, which was the most I durst say for that time, but by frequent coming to his house to be dressed[212] by the doctor, in a little time I grew better acquainted with him, insomuch that he invited me on a day to dine with him. I did, and then he told me that if I would dine with him the next day he would entertain me with a curious dish (a great rarity indeed in that country), which was, as I remember, a piece of bacon, with other things. He did this, I suppose, to try me whether I would eat swine's flesh or not (for the Mohammetans strictly abstain from swine's flesh; nay, they have such an aversion to it that if any chance to kill a wild pig—for tame they have none— they look on the merit of it to be almost equivalent to the killing a Christian in fight) that he might be confirmed in his opinion of me, for he truly suspected that I was no real Turk. Nevertheless, I refused to eat of it, fearing what the event of eating might prove. But at length, once being made merry by him, he told me that he wondered why I would tarry here in this country and said he wished that I were in England. I smiled but withal desired him to forbear such discourse. But still, every now and then, he would drop a word or two about the same matter and at length went so far as to assure me that if I were resolved to make my escape, he would assist me all that lay in his power. To which I replied, "Sir, shall I be plain with you?" "Prithee be," said he, "and I will be your bosom friend." This engaged me to open my sentiments to him, and I freely told him, viz., that I once little thought to be in this condition and, while I was in it, was never in the least inclined to Mohammetanism but that it was through the cruel usage that I suffered at

---

[212] *dressed*: treated.

their hands that I was forced to do what I did (a particular account of which their cruelties I gave him), which made him sympathize with me, and not only did he do that, but he projected a way for my escape, which was this: viz., that when our English men-of-war came to Algier to renew the peace (which they usually did once in two or three years) he did not doubt but to get me safe on board one of them. But I did not approve of that way, acknowledging, notwithstanding, all obligations to the gentleman for his kind proposal. I told him I had thought of another way, which I imagined might be more feasible, viz., that I was going with the ships of Algier up to the Levant and that then I designed, if possible, to make my escape and that if he could do me any good that way, I should be very thankful to him. He answered me that he would acquaint Mr. Baker, the consul in Algier, of it and confer with him about it.

When the time came that within a few days we were to sail, I went and asked of him whether he had been pleased to acquaint the consul with my business. He told me he had and desired me to walk out to the consul's garden, about a mile from Algier, where he kept his summer seat; accordingly, I did, though I had never the honor before of being known to the consul. When I came before him, I asked him whether Mr. Butler had told him anything concerning me. He said he had and made me very welcome. After I had been there some time, he discoursed me at large about my design to escape, and upon the whole, finding me to be real in the matter (for if I had been otherwise, so as to discover anything of what passed between us, it would infallibly have cost him his life, and therefore he sifted me narrowly),[213] he told me that he would give me a letter of recommendation to Mr. Ray, who was then the English consul in Smyrna, in which he requested him to assist me in my design, for he read it to me before he sealed it and charged me to keep it very safe and if at any time before my getting to Smyrna I should be sick or any way in danger of death or discovery, I should convey it overboard for his safety. Upon which I thankfully took my leave of him, this being the only time of my having any discourse with him.

Being got about thirty days' voyage towards Smyrna, where I designed to make my escape, and being a little off of one part of the Morea,[214] we espied seven or eight Venetian galleys at anchor under the shore. The Turks had a great tooth for those galleys but knew not how to come at them, not being able to adventure so far as galleys safely may. At length they consulted,

[213] *sifted me narrowly*: questioned me carefully.
[214] *Morea*: peninsula forming the south part of the mainland of Greece.

being fifteen ships in number, to hoist up French colors if peradventure any of them might be decoyed out; having done this, we hauled up our sails and brought to, pretending as if we were desirous of some news from the Levant. They, at this thinking we were French men-of-war, sent out two of their galleys, upon which the Turks were ordered to lie close and not to stir, for fear of showing their turbants, and such officers or others that were obliged to be moving took off their turbants to avoid discovery and put on a hat or cap instead thereof, but the slaves were all ordered to be upon deck to color the matter[215] and make us look more like Christians. At length, one of the galleys being within musketshot, we fired upon him and soon made him strike. The other seeing that, who was also under gunshot, turns and rows with all his might and main to get ashore, the Algerines all the while making what sail they could after him, but 'twas in vain, for the Venetian got clear, the wind being off the shore just in our mouth.[216] In that galley which we took, there were near four hundred Christians and some few Turks that were slaves.

The Turks, to show what an exploit they had done in taking this vessel, took the trouble to tow the prize up to Turkey, where they were received with an universal *housh-galding*, i.e., welcome.

When we came to Scio,[217] we were met and joined with ten sail of the Grand Turk's ships, carrying seventy or eighty brass cannon guns each. And being now twenty-five in number, we had the courage to cruise about the islands of the archipelago, which looks in them a pretty bold attempt,[218] though it be in their own country. For 'twas but a year or two before this that thirteen sail of the Venetians, with one fireship, put thirty sail of their ships to flight, some being of Tripoli, and some of Tunis, and some of the Grand Turk's ships, together with thirty Turkish galleys, which run some into one harbor, some into another, as they could.

We being now, as I said, five and twenty sail, as we were cruising we espied a ship at an anchor at the leeward of an island, who suspecting what we were slipped his cable[219] and made all the sail he could to fly from us. He being to the windward of us and coming clear of the island, the wind was very hard, insomuch that his mainmast was carried by the board,[220] where-

[215] *color the matter*: conceal their true purpose.
[216] *just in our mouth*: directly against us.
[217] *Scio*: Chios.
[218] *looks in . . . old attempt*: was for them a great display of boldness.
[219] *slipped his cable*: untied the rope attached to the anchor.
[220] *by the board*: overboard.

upon he was forced to bear away before[221] the wind and so unavoidably must fall in amongst us. Notwithstanding, he was resolved to fight his way through and held it stoutly a considerable time, but unfortunately for him his fore-topmast by a shot was carried by the board also and so, being disabled, was forced to yield but politicly yielded by the side of the admiral of Algier,[222] choosing rather to be carried to Algier than to Constantinople, knowing that at the latter place no money would prevail for his ransom, as it would at the former. But after a long contest between the Grand Turk's admiral and the Algerines' admiral [over] who should have the captain of this prize, the admiral of the Grand Turk's had him, rendering the Algerine admiral many of the taken slaves in lieu of him, and carried him to Constantinople, whence he was never to be redeemed.[223] This captain was a Leghornese and styled Captain Paul, whose name rung among them, for he had been in his time a great plague to them both by sea and land. His ship carried about forty guns and an hundred men. But though he had been such a scourge to them for many years, yet the slaves which were at any time taken by him were kindly treated, insomuch that when we came to an anchor at some places, the inhabitants would bring him fruits and wine, etc., onboard as presents, espe-cially in the island called Eustanchue, or Long Island, near Scio. In this island, and in the principal town thereof (by the way), is a tree of a prodi-gious bigness, so big that I question whether there be another like it for big-ness in the whole world. Under which are several coffeehouses, barber's shops, and other shops and several fountains of water, wherewith to take *abdes*, and if I mistake not, there are five and thirty, or seven and thirty, pil-lars, some of which are marble and some of timber, to support the branches thereof. This tree is famous, to a proverb, all over Turkey.

Some time after we arrived at Scio, an island since taken by the Venetians, inhabited by the Greeks, but governed by the Turks, about fifteen leagues on this side Smyrna. The Turks had liberty, for one month's time, to go home to visit the respective places of their nativity.

I went to Smyrna and hired a chamber there. And after I knew where the consul's house was, I went thither and inquired of the *yenecherres* (or janizaries), i.e., Turkish soldiers, which kept guard at this door, whether the consul was at home. They then directed me to one of his three interpreters, who brought me to the consul. The consul, not knowing who I was, compli-

---

[221] *bear away before*: turn and go in the direction of.
[222] *admiral of Algier*: Algerine flagship.
[223] *redeemed*: ransomed.

mented me much because I was handsomely appareled, and I returned the compliment to him after the Turkish manner and then delivered him my letter of recommendation. The consul having perused the letter, he bid the interpreter to withdraw because he should not understand anything of the matter. After the interpreter was gone, the consul asked me whether I was the man mentioned in the letter. I told him I was. He said the design was very dangerous and that if it should be known to the Turks that he was any way concerned in it, it was as much as his life and his all was worth. But after he had discoursed me further and found that I was fully resolved in the matter, he told me that truly, were it not upon Mr. Baker's request, he would not meddle in such a dangerous attempt, but for the friendship and respect he bore to him would do me all the kindness he could, which put life into me.

We had no English nor Dutch ships at Smyrna then but daily expected some, and he told me I must wait till they came and withal cautioned me not to frequent his house, unless upon some more then ordinary business. A day or two after this, I was sitting in a barber's shop, who was an Armenian, where both Christians and Turks did trim,[224] and there was a-trimming then an Englishman, whose name was George Grunsell, of Deptford. He knew me not otherwise than a Turk, but when I heard him speak English I asked him in English whether he knew any of the west parts of England to be in Smyrna. He told me of one who he thought was an Exeter man, which when I heard, I was glad at heart. I desired him to show me his house, which he very kindly did, but when I came to speak with Mr. Elliott, for so was his name, I found him to be one of Cornwall who had served some part of his apprenticeship in Exon with Mr. Henry Cudmore, a merchant. He was very glad to see me for country's sake. After some discourse, I communicated to him my design and how I had been with the consul. He was very glad to hear of it and promised to assist me and told me that I need not run the hazard of going to the consul's house but that if I had anything of moment to impart to him, he would do it for me. I thought it good to follow his friendly advice.

In a month's time it was cried about the city of Smyrna that all Algerines should repair to their ships, which lay then at Rhodes (another island inhabited by Greeks, as Scio, and governed by the Turks).

You must observe that no Algerine is forced to return to Algier again, but they may discharge themselves when they please.

All this while, no English or Dutch ships came to Smyrna. The consul and Mr. Elliot therefore consulted which was my best way to take. To tarry in

---

[224] *trim*: have their hair and beards trimmed or shaved.

Smyrna after all the Algerines were gone would look suspiciously, and therefore they advised me not to tarry in Smyrna but either to go to Scio with the Algerines, which is part of our way back to Rhodes, or else to go up to Constantinople and when I were there to write to the said Mr. Elliot to acquaint him where I was and to stay there till I had directions from them to return to Smyrna or what else to do.

I pursued their advice and went with some of the Algerines to Scio, and there I made a stop till all the Algerines were gone from thence and writ Mr. Elliot where I was. A short time after, he writ me that he was very glad that I was where I was but withal gave a damp to²²⁵ my spirits with the bad news that our Smryna fleet were said to be intercepted by the French, with the cold reserve of comfort that it wanted confirmation and that they hoped it was not true.

Now the Devil was very busy with me, tempting me to lay aside all thoughts of escaping and to return to Algier and continue a Mussulman. What with the temptation, and what with the disappointment, I was very melancholy. But here the goodness of God was manifested to me in such a measure that I at last surmounted all the temptations and fears that so furiously beset me, which were indeed very great, for it was suggested to me, first, that it was a very difficult, if not a desperate, attempt to endeavor to make my escape and that if I were discovered in it, I should be put to death after the most cruel and exemplary manner. And also, in the next place, the loss that I should sustain thereby, in several respects, viz., the loss of the profitable returns which I might make of what money I had to Algier and the loss of receiving eight months' pay due to me in Algier and the frustrating my hopes and expectation which I had from my patron, who made me large promises of leaving me considerable substance at his death, and I believe he meant as he promised, for I must acknowledge he was like a father to me.

After I had my liberty to go from him or live with him, I chose to live with him, and he was so willing of it that he gave me my meat, coffee, washing, lodging, and clothes freely and in short loved me as if I had been his own child, which made me sincerely to love him, I do acknowledge. This was also a great temptation for me to return to Algier.

In the midst of all, I would pray to God for His assistance and found it. For I bless God that after all my acquaintance were gone from Scio to Rhodes, I grew daily better and better satisfied, though my fears were still very great, you must imagine, and I was indeed afraid everybody I met did

---

²²⁵ *gave a damp to*: depressed.

suspect my design. And I can truly say that I would not go through such a labyrinth of sorrows and troubles again might I gain a kingdom. For at this very hour, when I reflect upon my danger, my concern revives, and my very flesh trembles.

While I was in Scio, I wrote, as I said, a letter to our English consul, Mr. Ray, and to Mr. Elliot, acquainting them with what strong temptations I was assaulted. They answered me with very kind and comfortable lines, which gave great life to my drooping spirits.

The first letter that Mr. Elliot sent me while I was at Scio, he directed to a Greek of Scio who did business for the consul of Smyrna, to be delivered to me, naming me by my Turkish name. I was altogether unknown to the Greek, so that he was forced to inquire among the Algerines for one of that name, and indeed there were one or two more of the same name with myself, but by good hap they were gone from Scio to Rhodes, otherwise 'tis odds but[226] the letter had come to the hands of one of them, and then my design had been discovered, and I should undoubtedly have been put to death there at Scio or secured in the Algerine ships, and my dreadful punishment would have been reserved till I had been carried back to Algier, there to be made a public example for all renegadoes to take warning by for the future. For 'tis certain death for all in the like circumstances with me who endeavor to make their escape, if it be known. And I have seen some executed at Algier for so doing. But the good providence of God towards me ordered it better for me.

Upon this I wrote to Mr. Elliot, earnestly desiring him to direct to me after another manner, which he was so kind as to do after this.

When I first came to Scio from Smyrna according to the advice of these my true friends, the consul and Mr. Elliot, as I have told you, I happened to take up my lodging at a *hawn*, or inn, adjoining to the harbor, where were two Algerines that were Spanish renegadoes. I had no acquaintance with them at all, for they belonged not to the same ship that I did, nor do I remember that I had ever seen them before, but we being all Algerines soon became familiarly acquainted, insomuch that they would fain have me lodge in the same room with them. Accordingly I did, but the next day I better considered on't and thought it not convenient to be so near the harbor because the Algerines would be often asking of me when I would return to Algier, and laying matters together,[227] I thought likewise that I were better break off society with those two fellows, which I did and removed to one end of the town

---

[226] *odds but*: likely that.
[227] *laying matters together*: considering the circumstances.

to a Greek's house where I hired a room. The two said renegadoes found me out and were still very desirous to be with me, to which I at length consented. And when I better knew them, their company pleased me because I could not observe any of the Mohammetan religion in them; neither would they at any time talk of going to Rhodes, where our ships lay, which made me, at length, to suspect that they were of my mind, designing to make their escape. And what somewhat confirmed me in this suspicion was this: the younger of them would sometimes speak slightly of Mohammet, calling him *sabbatero*, i.e., shoemaker, and the other would seem sometimes faintly to reprove him for it, and I also would seem to show my dislike of it though I was truly pleased to hear it. But it seems this was all to try me. And indeed I would sometimes try them, too, and therefore would take an Arabic Alcoran in my hand to read, of which they were both wholly ignorant, and they would both laugh at me and at last came to pop the Alcoran out of my hand and blow out the candle and tell me I should read no more. At length we came to know one another's mind, and I found that they applied themselves to some French priests in Smyrna to make their escape, as I did to the consul and Mr. Elliot.

About this time I received another letter from Mr. Elliot, in which he informed me that the reported bad news concerning our ships being intercepted by the French was true but that he and the consul had conferred that day what was best to be done for my safety and upon due consideration were of opinion that it would be in vain for me to wait for any English ships, for it might be a long time before any came, and it would be charge and loss of time for me to stay for them. And therefore they advised me to go off in a French ship, though somewhat more expensive, and in order thereunto to hasten back again to Smyrna in the first boat that came.

Accordingly, I came to Smyrna again and went immediately to Mr. Grunsell's house, who received me gladly, for he, with my other friends, was afraid that I had gone back to Algier.

I lodged at Mr. Grunsell's house and kept myself very private for the space of twenty days till the French ship was ready to sail, where I was visited daily by Mr. Elliot, who (I thank him) did always administer comfort to me under my fears, which were not small, particularly because I had heard how an Englishman was served who turned Turk in Algier and made his escape and afterward, using the seas, made a voyage to Smyrna. The Algerines happened to be there at that time, and he being in a barber's shop, some of the Algerines passing by seemed to remember him. He, suspecting it, went away immediately. The Turks followed him, and he, perceiving it, made the more haste, at which the Turks pursued him the more closely, and he, to avoid them, ran into an English factor's house. But the Turks were so close upon him that he had not power to make fast the door after him, so that they cut him in pieces. This was but a few years before I came away, which (together with my being acquainted too well with their cruelty, which they glory in when it is, as they think it, for the cause of religion) filled me with great fears and dreadful apprehensions.

Now the French ship in which I was to make my escape was intended to sail the next day, and therefore in the evening I went to go onboard, appareled as an Englishman, with my beard shaven, a campaign periwig,[228] and a cane in my hand, accompanied with three or four of my friends in the boat. The boat was brought just to the house where I lodged, and as we were going into the boat there were some Turks of Smyrna walking by, but they smelt nothing of the matter. My good friend Mr. Elliot had agreed with the captain of the ship to pay four pounds for my passage to Leghorn, but neither the captain nor any of the Frenchmen knew who I was. My friends, after they brought me safe aboard, took their leave of me and told me that if the ship did not sail the next morning they would visit me again, which accordingly they did, the ship not sailing, and brought wine and victuals aboard, upon which they were very merry, but for my part I was very uneasy till the ship had made sail. I pretended myself ignorant of all foreign languages because I would not be known to the French, who (if we had met with any Algerines) I was afraid would be so far from showing me any favor so as to conceal me that they would readily discover me.

We had a month's passage from Smyrna to Leghorn, and I was never at rest in my mind till we came to Leghorn, where as soon as ever I came ashore I prostrated myself and kissed the earth, blessing almighty God for his undeserved mercy and goodness to me that I once more set footing on the European, Christian part of the world. The custom of Leghorn (as well as of some other parts) is, when any ships come from Turkey or Barbary, not to suffer the men (straightway) to come ashore, fearing least their country should be infected with the plague, because the Turk's and Moor's country is seldom entirely void of the plague. Therefore, I say, they will not permit any to come ashore, but they and their cargo are put on an island, and there they are to perform their quarantine, i.e., to stay forty days, after which every man of them is searched by the physician, and if they find no infection upon any of

---

[228] *campaign periwig*: The *O.E.D.* cites R. Holme's *Armoury* (1688) 2.18.118: "A campaign wig hath knots or bobs (or a dildo on each side) with a curled forehead, a traveling wig."

them, they are admitted ashore, but still, if any one of them should chance to die within forty days, then they must begin the quarantine again. But when we came out of Smyrna, it was pretty free from the plague, which they having intelligence of, they ordered us to remain on the said island only five and twenty days, during which time, every day, necessaries are brought to be sold, but the sellers keep themselves at a distance from us, laying down their provisions and telling aloud the price, and then we that buy put the price of them into a vessel of water, placed there on purpose, and afterwards they come and take out the money.

It happened a few days after I had been upon the lazaret,[229] i.e., the said island, that there came a French vessel from Algier, in which were some redeemed slaves, amongst which were some Dutchmen, and one of them was a nigh neighbor of mine in Algier who was mightily surprised but very glad to see me and said that he, with the rest of his countrymen, would be glad of my company homeward, for that they had rather travel home by land than by sea. I was no less glad of their company than they of mine, and therefore after being permitted to go ashore and tarrying in Leghorn one night, the next day we went on our journey. It was about Christmastime, when there was very frosty weather, and great snows fell so that we traveled twenty days in the snow. The first day we set out from Leghorn we came to Pisa; from thence to Florence; from thence to Bologna; and so onward. We had a note of all cities and towns we were to pass through, as far as to Augsburg. After I had traveled with my company about two hundred miles in Italy and was just entering into Germany, my left leg failed me so that I was not able to hold on with them, whereupon they went away and left me, fearing their money would fall short if they should stay for me.

After I was left behind, I was much troubled, but it pleased God to mitigate my pains, and the next day I followed them but never could overtake them, they being always a day's journey before me.

After I had traveled those two hundred miles with them, I was forced to travel five hundred miles (as they told me it was) on foot afterwards in Germany till I came to Frankfort. I fell into some misfortunes in traveling through Germany, and among them this was one: viz., one day I had traveled through a great wood, and as I came out of it, I met with four or five German soldiers who bid me stand. I did. They examined me, and I gave them an account of myself. They made me go back with them, saying I was a Frenchman come as a spy into their country. I earnestly begged of them to

[229] *lazaret*: place of quarantine, formerly the site of a leper colony.

let me go. They would not but carried me back into the wood again and brought me to a by-place, which made me very much afraid they would take away my life, and there they robbed me of my money, as much as they could find, then beat me and bid me be gone, but as divine providence ordered it, they did not strip me, for if they had, they would have found more money about me.

When I came to Augsburg (which was the last place on the note of directions given us, of which I took a copy when my company left me) I thought the river Rhine had come up so far but was mistaken, for I was informed that I must travel farther, as far as Frankfort, which was off about an hundred and fifty miles more. No remedy or help there was, but put to it I must. Having therefore got directions for as far as Frankfort, I trotted on many a weary step till I came thither. When I came to Frankfort, the gates of the city were just ready to be shut, and I offering to go into the city, the sentinel who stood at the gate (they then had war with France) demanded of me who I was. I told them I was an Englishman. They asked me from whence I came. I told them, but they would not believe me, that I came from Leghorn. They bid me show my passport, but I had none, which truly was the occasion of many troubles to me in my travels. I having therefore no pass, they would not let me into the city but told me that I should go such a way, about a mile and half off, and there I should find a village, for there was not so much as one house without the gates of Frankfort. I desired them to have some compassion on my condition and told them that I knew not the way to the said village and that it was almost dark and also that I was very weary and faint. All would not prevail, and so the gate was shut. I sat down upon the ground and wept, bewailing my hard fortune and their unkindness, having not a bit of bread to eat nor fire to warm myself in the extreme cold season which then was, though God be thanked I had a little money. But there being just outside the gate a little hut or tent where the soldiers kept guard, the corporal, seeing me in such a condition as I was, called me in, where they had a good fire, and after I had warmed myself he gave me some of his victuals, for which reasonable kindness I gave him some money to fetch us some good liquor. And I told the corporal if he would get me into the city the next day, I would requite him for it. Accordingly he did. I thought indeed there had been some English merchants in the city and desired him to conduct me to one of them, but he could find none. At length he brought me to a Frenchman's house, who had a son that lived in England some time and was lately come home again, who made me very welcome. He asked me what my business was. I told him 'twas to get a pass to go safe down the river (for they are so strict there in time of war that they'll examine even their own countrymen) and withal desired him to change a pistole[230] for me and to give me instead of it such money as would pass current down the river. For (as I told him) I have sometimes changed a pistole, and before the exchange of it hath been expended in my travels, some of the money would not pass current. He changed my pistole for me and told me what money would pass in such a place and what in such a place and what I should reserve last to pass in Holland. And he was moreover so civil as to go to the public office and obtain a pass for me. After which he brought me to his house again and caused one of his servants to direct me to an inn the next door where I should quarter and bid me come again to him the next morning, when he sent his servant to call me and also to pay off my host, but I had paid him before, for which he showed his dislike. After all which, he conducted me to the river's side where was a boat full of passengers ready to go to Mentz.[231] This obliging gentleman (whose name was Mr. Van der Lah'r) told the master of the boat that he would satisfy him for my passage to Mentz. And moreover desired an acquaintance of his in the boat to take care of me and, when at Mentz, to direct me to such a merchant, for whom he gave me a letter and therewith a piece of money to drink his health.

When we came to Mentz, we were every man to produce his passport, and as the passes were looking over, the person in the boat who was desired to take care of me sent a boy to call the merchant to whom I was to deliver the letter, who immediately came and after he had perused the letter invited me to his house.

It happened that this gentleman was a slave in Algier at the same time I was. He inquired of me about his patroon, whom I knew very well, and we talked about many other things relating to Algier. I received much kindness and hospitality from this gentleman; he paid off my quarters[232] for that night and also gave me victuals and money and paid for my passage from Mentz to Cologne and moreover sent by me a letter of recommendation to his correspondent there.

At Cologne I received the like kindness and had my passage paid for to Rotterdam, and if I would, I might have had a letter of recommendation to

---

[230] *pistole*: A term used to denote various gold coins; in Pitts's day, usually a Spanish coin worth about eighteen shillings.
[231] *Mentz*: Mainz.
[232] *paid off my quarters*: paid for my lodging.

some gentlemen there, too, but I refused it (with hearty thanks for the offer), being loath to be too troublesome to my friends and their interest.

I found great kindness at Rotterdam and Helversluyce, whither our English packet boats arrive. But when I came into England, my own native country, here I was very badly treated, for the very first night that I lay in England, I was impressed[233] for to go in the king's service. And notwithstanding that I made known my condition and used many arguments for my liberty, with tears, yet all this would not prevail, but away I must and was carried to Colchester prison where I lay some days. While I was there in prison, I writ a letter to Sir William Falkener, one of the Smyrna Company in London, on whom I had a bill[234] for a little money. He immediately got a protection for me and sent it me, which was not only my present discharge but prevented all further trouble to me on the road homeward, which otherwise I must unavoidably have met with.

When I came from Colchester to London, I made it my business, as in duty bound, to go and pay my thanks to that honorable gentleman from whom I received fresh kindness. After this I made what haste I could home to dear Exeter, where I safely came, to the great joy of my friends and relations, who had buried me in their thoughts long before.

I was in Algier above fifteen years. After I went out of Topsham, it was about half a year before I was taken a slave. And after I came out of Algier, it was well nigh twelve months ere I could reach home.

Thus have I briefly given the world an account of my travels and misfortunes and of the good providences of almighty God towards me, which if it may do any manner of good, in any respect, to any individual person, I shall reckon it a great happiness.

And as to my own part, I hope I shall never forget the wonderful goodness of the Lord towards me, whose blessed name I desire to glorify in the sight of all men.

To Him therefore, Father, Son, and Holy Ghost, be all worship, honor, and thanksgiving, forever and ever! Amen.

O merciful God who hast made all men and hatest nothing that Thou hast made nor wouldest[235] the death of a sinner but rather that he should be converted and live, have mercy upon all Jews, Turks, infidels, and heretics, and

---

[233] *impressed*: forced into public service (in the navy).

[234] *on whom I had a bill*: for whom I had a bill of credit (authorizing a payment from Falkener to Pitts).

[235] *wouldest*: would want.

take from them all ignorance, hardness of heart, and contempt of thy Word, and so fetch them home, blessed Lord, to Thy flock, that they may be saved among the remnant of the true Israelites and be made one fold, under one shepherd, Jesus Christ our Lord, who liveth and reigneth with Thee and the Holy Spirit, one God, world without end. Amen.

FINIS

TWO BALLADS

The Algerian Slave's Releasement; or,
The Unchangeable Boatswain[1]

No prison like the Jail of Love,
  Nor no such torments found,
To those that loyal mean to prove,
  Whose loves are firm and sound;

This loyal person ne'er would change,
  Like a true lover he
Endured his fetters and his chains,
  And Betty's captive be.
  (To the tune of "Awake, Oh my Cloris")

Of a constant young seaman
A story I'll tell
That I hope all true lovers
Will please very well.
All his cry was still, "Though
I continue a slave,
Yet the want of my dear,
Is far worse than a grave."

---

[1] From *A Century of Ballads*, ed. John Ashton (London: Elliot Stock, 1887), 221–24. No date given, but the publisher who issued this ballad, J. Deacon, was active circa 1684–95, according to Ashton.

"All the tedious long night
In close prison I lie,
But methinks I behold
My dear love lying by.
In the midst of my pains,
This doth still give me ease;
That is pleasant to me
Which some call a disease.

Sometimes to the galleys
I am forced to go,
Though amongst all my fellows,
like a slave I do row;
And when I am spent
With this labor and pain,
The thought of my love
Doth revive me again.

And when with strappadoes
Sometimes I do meet,
I find little pain
If I think on my sweet.
Thus 'twixt pleasure and pain
My time I do spend,
Yet vow to be constant
Unto my life's end.

No torture nor prison
Shall make me forsake,
Nor fly from my reason,
For my Betty's sake.
I do slight all the torments
Bestowed by the Turk,
When I think on my dear,
And in galleys do work.

But a renegado
To make me they strive.
I'll never consent to't,
whilst I am alive,

But will a courageous
True Protestant be.
I'll be true to my faith
And be constant to thee.

Ah Betty, when billows
Do rage and do roar,
For want of thy sight
I am troubled sore.
Whist others are troubled
With terror and fear,
Yet I am cheered up
With the thoughts of my dear.

No prison is like
To the want of thy sight,
Which locks up my bliss,
For thou art my delight.
Though distant I am,
Therefore only oppressed,
Yet still my dear Betty
doth lodge in my breast.

In the midst of my sorrows,
Whilst others do mourn,
'Tis the want of my love
that doth make me forlorn;
Yet would not enjoy thee
In this cursed place,
Though for want of thy love
My tears trickle apace.

But be of good cheer,
For everyone knows,
'Tis an ill wind indeed
That no comfort blows.
And again I do hope
thee in England to see:
Then who'll be so happy
as Betty and me?

And now, through providence,
I am returned
By shipwrack I 'scaped,
For our ship it was burned.
No torment like mine was
When I was a slave,
For the want of my Betty
Was worse than a grave."

                    Printed for I. Deacon at the Rainbow near
                         [David's] Inn in Holborn.

*The Lamentable Cries of at Least 1500 Christians: Most of
Them Being Englishmen (Now Prisoners in Argiers Under
the Turks) Begging at God's Hand That He Would Open the
Eyes of All Christian Kings and Princes to Commiserate the
Wretched Estate of So Many Captives: and Withal to Free
Them from That Turkish Slavery, in Which Both Bodies and
Souls Are in Danger: with a Petition to the King's Most
Excellent Majesty and All Christian Princes*[2]

Not many moons have from their silver bows
Shot light through all the world, since those sworn foes
To God and all good men . . . that hell-born crew
Of pirates (to whom there's no villainies new),
Those half-Turks and half-Christians, who now ride
Like sea gods (on rough billows in their pride),
Those renegadoes, who (their Christ denying)
Are worse than Turks, Turks them in heart defying;
These, these are they that have from Christians torn
Of ships sixscore but one, and the men borne
(To th'number of a thousand) to th'Turks' shore,
All they being slaves now tugging at the oar.

---

[2] From C. H. Firth, *Naval Songs and Ballads* (London: Navy Records Society,
1908), 31–33. The text is taken from a manuscript in the Bodleian Library (MS Rawlin-
son Poet. Clii. f. 36). Originally printed in 1624.

Count from what time the worthy Mansfield[3] came
From that devil's den (Argiers). . . . Just since that flame
Of war went out at sea, in that short space
From thence till now these thieves have held in chase
All ships which passed the Straits of Gibraltar,
To rob or sink them, were they men-of-war,
Merchants, or others; and when worst they thrive
And nothing get, yet get they men alive.
O wretched state of Christian souls so taken!
To look upon whose torments would awaken
Tyrants to thrust their arms up, through their graves,
To guard from blows these Christian galley slaves.
They that could safely stand but on the shore
To view a sea fight, hear the cannons roar,
See Turks board English ships whilst Englishmen
Like lions fight and fling them o'er. . . . But when
Numbers of big-boned runnagates so swarm
That not one man of ours dare lift an arm
At a Turk's head, the ship with blood embrued,[4]
And overmastered with damned multitude,
Should any stand so and get off unwounded,
They would, to see this, be with grief confounded.
But on those following lines fasten your eyes;
Yourselves may draw forth all their miseries.
Being boarded so, and robbed, then are they tied
On chains, and dragged t'Argiers to feed the pride
Of a Mahumetan dog (eight in a row).
Each eighth man to the Argier king must go
And th'eighth part of what's ta'en is still his prize;
What men he leaves are anyone's who buys
And bids for them, for they then are led
To market and like beasts sold by the head,
Their masters having liberty by law
To strike, kick, starve them, yet make them draw
In yokes, like oxen, and if dead they beat them.

---

[3] *what time the worthy Mansfield*: alternative spelling of "Mansell." Refers to Sir
Robert Mansell's expeditions against Algiers in 1620 and 1621.
[4] *embrued*: stained.

Out are they thrown for beasts and ravens to eat them.
He that's condemned to th'oar hath first his face,
Eyebrows and head closeshaven (for more disgrace
Cannot betide a Christian). Then, being stripped
To th'girdle (as when rogues are to be whipped),
Chained are they to the seats where they sit rowing
Five in a row together, a Turk going
On a large plank between them; and though their eyes
Are ready to start out with pulling, he cries,
"Work, work, you Christian curs," and though none needs
One blow for loitering, yet his bare back bleeds
And riseth up in bunches, which the Turk
With a bull's pizzle gives him, crying still, "Work,
Work, dog," whilst some so faint, at th'oar th[e]y die,
Being cast (like dogs) overboard presently.
Their slavery done at sea, then are they laid
In dungeons worse than jails, poorly arrayed,
Fed with coarse horse-bread,[5] water for their drink,
And such sometimes puddles cannot worser stink.
Then if upon a Turkish rogue they frown,
Or give him a cross word, held are they down
O' th'ground upon their backs, whilst on the rim
Of their bare bellies they are forced from him
To bear four hundred blows: their soles o' th'feet
And shins like payment now and then do meet.
Why are the Turks thus cruel but to draw
Christians from Christ to their Mahumetan law?
You, who at home in golden pleasures dance,
Wasting both noons and night in dalliance,
O when these groans of Christians pierce our ears,
To free them, give your charity, and your tears,
Whilst you that are our Christian princes styled
(All jars amongst yourselves being reconciled)
Into the field with one knit army come
To kill this lion that thus tears Christendom.

[5] *horse-bread*: "bread made from beans, bran, etc. for the food of horses" (*O.E.D.*).

APPENDIX 2

LETTERS FROM CAPTIVES TO THEIR
FAMILIES IN ENGLAND

Samuel Harres to His Father[1]

Laus deo[2] the 16th of July 1610 from Tripelo in Barbere[3]

Loving and kind father, my duty being remembered to you and your health in the Lord, these are to certify you that the 15th day, being off Cape Spartimint,[4] there rowed up to us two galleys of Tripolo and a frigate which when our master[5] perceived they were Turks demanded of us what we were willing to do. The most part of us would have fought, but some would not, for fear we should be made slaves; so the master commanded to strike our sails, and then they came aboard and fetched all but six aboard the galleys, whereof I was one. So they sent the ship for Tripolo, and we went for the Gulf,[6] making attempt to go for Valona, but we met with the wind at the norwest so we were fain to go for provese[7] to the norward of Sufelane,[8] and there we found five

---

[1] Manuscript. Trinity House Transactions, 1609–35, 13 [f.7].

[2] Laus deo: Latin, meaning "Praise be to God."

[3] *Tripelo in Barbere*: Tripoli in Barbary.

[4] *Cape Spartemint*: Cape Spartimento, now Palinuro or Spartivento.

[5] *master*: commanding officer on the ship.

[6] *the Gulf*: either the Gulf of Taranto or the Adriatic Sea (the latter was sometimes called the Gulf of Venice).

[7] *provese*: provisions.

[8] *Sufelane*: Perhaps Sazan, a town in Albania on an island in the Strait of Otranto.

galliots[9] of Bizerte. So they consorted[10] together, and when we put to
sea we met with the wind at south, so we bore up for Valona; but when
we came thwart[11] of Cape Lugo,[12] we met with five Venetian galleys
which gave us chase, but our consort being hindermost was taken
wherein were six of our men; but we rowed away from them, and that
night we took a ship of Ragusa that was bound for Venice and laded at
Corfu. The men they took but let the ship go. So we went for Tripelo,
where we found our ship and our men. I was afraid I should have been
made a slave, for when I was in the galley I was chained to a bank[13]
and made to row naked and beaten, and then I took such a cold, which
brought me to a bloody flux,[14] and as yet I am not well; and here they
keep us perforce and will make us to serve them for a voyage or two,
and then they say they will let us go, but I believe them not. Wherefore
I pray, father, if it be possible, to get me clear. Let me hear from you if
you be at Lant, for this life is odious to me. I pray comfort my mother
concerning me and do my duty to her; and for my portion, when it is
due I pray pay it to my mother or else to employ it to myself. I pray if
you think it will be some danger for me to come home, I pray do what
you may to work my peace, for I must go perforce, and about two
months hence we make attempt to go forth some four sails. Our ship is
the best of them. We go to the westward, as far as I know. I pray commend me to my brother William and Richard, and to my sisters and
William Bull with the rest of our friends and quaintance.[15] Thus I end,
praying to God to keep you all in health, and so send us a good and a
joyful meeting to His glory and our comfort. Randall Jesson[16] com-
mending him to you and to my brother William and to Phillip.

> Your loving and obedient son,
> Samuel Harres

---

[9] *galliots*: small galleys, propelled by both sails and oars.
[10] *They consorted*: the Tripolitan galleys joined together with the galliots from Bizerte.
[11] *thwart*: next to.
[12] *Cape Lugo*: Perhaps Kep-i-Lagit, on the Albanian coast.
[13] *bank*: (rowing) bench.
[14] *bloody flux*: dysentery.
[15] *quaintance*: people well known to us.
[16] *Randall Jesson*: someone known to Harres's family, possibly because he was
taken captive at the same time as Harres.

Robert Adams to Captain Robert Adams[17]

To his most loving father, Captain Robert Adams, at his house, in Ratcliff, give this—I pray you pay the post—from a poor captive in Salley. [written on the back of the letter in a different hand:]

4 November 1625.

—From Robert Adams, a poor captive at Salley, to his father.
—For the King.
[in the margin:] I pray let me hear an answer from you, soon as possible you can.

From Salley, this 4th of November, anno 1625.

Loving and kind Father and Mother, my humble duty remembered unto you, both praying to God continually for your health as my own.

You may please to understand that I am here in Salley, in most miserable captivity, under the hands of most cruel tyrants. For after I was sold, my patroon[18] made me work at a mill like a horse, from morning until night, with chains upon my legs, of 36 pounds weights apiece, my meat nothing but a little coarse bread and water, my lodging in a dungeon underground, where some 150 or 200 of us lay altogether, having no comfort of the light but a little hole, and being so full of vermin for want of shift[19] and not being allowed time for to pick myself that I am almost eaten up with them, and every day beaten to make me either turn Turk or come to my ransom. For our master's boy had told my patroons that I was the owner's son of the ship and you were able to ransom home forty such as I was, which was not sooner known but they forced me to come to my ransom and agree to them, though I always pleaded poverty. For then they made me grind more then I did formerly, and continually beat me, and almost starved me. So, though unwilling, I agreed at 730 ducats of Barbary, for I was forced to it, being brought so low for want of sustenance that I could not go without a staff.

---

[17] In Le Comte Henry de Castries, ed., *Les Sources Inédites de l'Histoire du Maroc—Archives et Bibliothèques d'Angleterre*, premiere série—dynasty Sa'dienne, vol. 2 (Paris: Paul Geuthner, 1936), 591–92.

[18] *patroon*: slave master.

[19] *shift*: change of clothing.

So I have six months' time for my ransom to come, whereof three months are gone, and if it come not, then I must arm myself to endure the most misery of any creature in the world. Therefore I humbly desire you on my bended knees, and with sighs from the bottom of my hart, to commiserate my poor distressed estate and seek some means for my delivery out of this miserable slavery. For here are some 1500 Englishmen here in as bad case as myself, though something better used, for they misuse none but such as are able to pay their ransom. And, dear father, I humbly beseech you, for Christ Jesus' sake, to take some course for my deliverance, for if neither the king take no course, nor my ransom come, I am out of all hope ever to behold my country again.

> Thus ceasing to trouble you, I rest
> Your most dutiful and obedient
> son till death,
> Robert Adams.

Mr. Legg is here at ransom for 730 Barbary ducats likewise. I have sent three or four letters before this by several men and never heard from you.

Thomas Sweet and Richard Robinson, Published by Parliament[20]

Dear Friends,

It is now about six years since I was most unfortunately taken, by a Turk's man-of-war on the coasts of Barbary, captive into Argier, since which time I have written oft to London to Master Southwood of the upper ground, to Richard Barnard of Duke's Place, Richard Coote of the Bankside, to Master Linger, a haberdasher in Crooked Lane; and in that to Master Southwood I sent an enclosed to my father, if living, and other letters to my brothers and friends, if not dead. I could never hear whether any of you were alive or dead, which makes me think the letters are either miscarried or all of you deceased or gone to other places, or else I know you are so much Christians and friends that you would have looked upon me in such a condition. O!

[20] Manuscript. Thomason 669.f.11[3]. British Library.

my friends, once more I tell you: I, a miserable captive in Argier, taken by a Flemish vessel two years after I left the wars in Gilderland.[21] My patroon[22] is one Baron, a French renegado that lives in the country but hires me and another Protestant captive (one Master Robinson, a Norfolk man) out in Argier for this time, and if we go up to the country, you may never hear of us again. Our misery is that the price of our redemption will be no less than 250 pounds because we are thought to have good friends in England, and we must both go off together. Master Robinson hath written to his friends, and we have deeply bound ourselves to each other that we will engage our friends to us both equally. Ah! Father, brother, friends, and acquaintance, use some speedy means for our redemption. Many hundred slaves have been redeemed from their misery since we came hither, which makes us hope still we may be the next, and then the next, but still our hopes are deceived. We do pray you therefore, for the Lord Christ's sake that redeemed you, that you would use all possible means for our redemption. There is now a party in England[23] renowned over the Christian world for their piety this way. O! make your address to those noble worthies in the name of Christ for whose sake we suffer. We did never so well understand the meaning of that psalm[24] penned by those captive Jews held in Babylonish captivity as now: "By the waters of Babylon we sat down and wept when we remembered thee, O! Sion," when we remembered thee, O! England. O! good friends, we hope these our sighs will come to your ears and move pity and compassion. We are told there is a merchant in London, one Mr. Stanner of St. Mary's Axe, that hath a factor in Leghorn and one Mr. Hodges and Mr. Mico, Londoners that are dealers there, who are able to direct you in the readiest way for our redemption. Deny us not your prayers if you can do nothing else. It will be some comfort to hear from friends. There is a post in London that conveys letters into all parts, and you may have

[21] *wars in Gilderland*: perhaps a reference to the Thirty Years' War, where Robinson, as a Protestant, might have served in the Low Countries (Gilderland?) against Spain and her allies.

[22] *patroon*: slave master.

[23] *a party in England*: The First Civil War in England had ended in June 1646, leaving the puritan, parliamentary "party" in control.

[24] *that psalm*: Psalm 137.

an opportunity of letting us hear from you, if you please, within a
month or six weeks. The Lord direct your thoughts with ways of love
and strengthen us with faith and patience.

> Your sorrowful friend and brother in Christ,
> Thomas Sweet.
> There subscribes to these besides:
> Richard Robinson.

From Barbary: September 29, 1646.

Sithence our last sent you in September, Master Cason,[25] the Parliament's agent, and the basha[26] here concluded a peace, and it is
agreed that all English captives (not turned renegadoes) shall be
redeemed at the price they were first sold in the market for, which our
patron, understanding before the agreement, made us over by bill[27] to
a Moor in Tunis being a merchant of his acquaintance, the place being
under another government, and swore we should not be redeemed till
the last man there, unless we could procure the sum first demanded,
which is 250 pounds. I do keep his books of accompts[28] and merchandise, and that keeps me here in misery when others that are illiterate
go off upon easy terms for cloth,[29] so that my breeding is my undoing
unless pity be shown.

> Thomas Sweet

November 26.

The long and lamentable bondage of Thomas Sweet and Richard
Robinson, our neighbor Englishmen (and good Protestants), being

---

[25] *Master Cason*: Edmund Casson, author of *A Relation of the Whole Proceedings
Concerning the Redemption of the Captives in Argier and Tunis* (London, 1647), was
one of the charter members of the Barbary Company. In September 1646 he arrived in
Algiers and succeeded in ransoming 244 English subjects. He would serve as English
consul in Algiers from 1653 to 1654, the last two years of his life.

[26] *basha*: governor of Algiers, under Ottoman sovereignty.

[27] *made us over by bill*: sold us by a bill of credit.

[28] *accompts*: accounts.

[29] *go off . . . for cloth*: are ransomed cheaply, in exchange for a certain amount of
cloth.

cleared unto us by the testimony and recommendation of divers godly ministers of the Assembly,[30] and of this city of London, upon the desire of their friends, we can do no less than recommend the sad condition of these men to your godly consideration and Christian charity, heartily wishing and desiring you would yield your utmost and most speedy furtherance that they may be redeemed with the first.

Richard Price, Baronet,
And seven others, members of the honorable House of Commons.
Published by authority [April 16, 1647].

[30] *the Assembly*: the Westminster Assembly of Divines.

APPENDIX 3

LETTER AND DEPOSITIONS DESCRIBING "TURKISH" CORSAIR
RAIDS ON THE WEST COUNTRY SENT BY THOMAS CEELY TO
THE PRIVY COUNCIL (1625)[1]

Letter to the Privy Council

To the right honorable Lords of his Majesty's most honorable Privy
Council. Haste, haste, posthaste.
Plymouth, the eighteenth of April,
eight in the evening.
–Thomas Ceely, Mayor.
[on the reverse side, in another hand:]
For his Majesty's service
–18 April 1625.
–From the Mayor of Plymouth.

Right Honorable,
My duty in all humbleness remembered,

   –May it please your honors to be advertised that this day I heard
of certain Turks, Moors, and Dutchmen of Sally in Barbary, which lie
on our coasts spoiling[2] divers such as they are able to master, as by
the examination of one William Knight (which your honors shall

---

[1] In Le Comte Henry de Castries, ed., *Les Sources Inédites de l'Histoire du Maroc–
Archives et Bibliothèques d'Angleterre*, premiere série–dynasty Sa'dienne, vol. 2 (Paris:
Paul Geuthner, 1936), 558–63.
[2] *spoiling*: plundering.

here enclosed receive) may appear, whose report I am induced the rather to believe, because two fisherboats mentioned in his examination were very lately found floating on the seas, having neither man nor any tackle in them; as also because, by the examination of one William Draper of Plymouth, some part of the said Knight's examination is confirmed (which examination is also here enclosed sent your honors).

And may your honors be pleased farther to be advertised that I am credibly informed that one Pethericke Honicombe, an English captive in Sally, hath lately written a letter, dated the fifth of March last, to his wife dwelling in Stonehouse near Plymouth, wherein, among other things, he advises her that there were thirty sail of ships at Sally now preparing to come for the coasts of England in the beginning of the summer, and if there were not speedy course taken to prevent it, they would do much mischief. The letter itself I cannot by any means get but have received these instructions from an honest, understanding neighbor which read the letter. Hereof I thought it my duty to inform your honors.

> And so I rest,
> Your honors' in all duty bounden,[3]
> Thomas Ceely, Mayor.
> Plymouth, the 18th of April 1625.

Deposition of William Knight

THE EXAMINATION OF WILLIAM KNIGHT, OF ST. BUTOCKES,[4] TAKEN BEFORE THOMAS CEELY, MERCHANT, MAYOR OF THE BOROUGH OF PLYMOUTH, THE 18TH DAY OF APRIL, ANNO DOMINI 1625.

This examinate saith that the fifteenth day of this instant[5] month of April, he this examinate,[6] coming out of the river of Yalme[7] near Plymouth in a

---

[3] *bounden*: held under obligation (to you).
[4] *St. Butockes*: Saint-Budeaux, located four miles northwest of Plymouth.
[5] *instant*: present.
[6] *examinate*: person under examination (as a witness).
[7] *Yalme*: estuary and port located six miles southeast of Plymouth.

barge loaden with sand, he met with a fisherboat of Yalme which then came from a ship of Salcombe[8] bound for Newfoundland, which was, as they of the said boat told him, taken the twelfth of this instant April by a ship of Sally of thirty tons or thereabouts, wherein were nine Dutchmen, six Turks, and three Moors, and one of them a black Moor. And also said that there was one other pink[9] in company with the said ship of Sally that bore towards Looe in Cornwall, which he thought was in consort with the said ship of Sally.

And this examinate farther saith that one which was in the said fisherboat, whose name he remembereth not, told this examinate that he, being in a boat of Looe aforesaid, in company with one other boat a-fishing, were both taken the 11th of this month near Eddystone, in sight of the harbor of Plymouth, by the said ship of Sally. And they did take all the men out of the said two boats of Looe, being in number twelve, and cut off the tackle of the said boats and after left them fleeting[10] on the stream.

And this examinate also saith that the said party told him he escaped out of the said ship of Sally after he was taken, in this manner: to weet,[11] being bound in the said ship of Sally with the others which were taken with him, a black Moor of the said bark of Sally unloosed his bands, and after he was unbound, he crept out through a porthole of the said ship of Salcombe, lying near the said bark of Sally.

And lastly saith that the said party which so hardly[12] escaped from the said bark of Sally told this examinate that there were eleven persons taken out of the said ship of Salcombe, and so much provision as was worth a hundred fifty-one pounds, and so cast off the said ship. And the said examinate saith that he took the said party out of the said boat of Yalme into his barge and landed him at Crymmell Passage, near Plymouth, the day of this his examination.

---

[8] *Salcombe*: port in the county of Devon, located nineteen miles southeast of Plymouth.

[9] *pink*: small sailing vessel.

[10] *fleeting*: drifting.

[11] *to weet*: namely.

[12] *so hardly*: with great difficulty.

Deposition of William Draper

THE EXAMINATION OF WILLIAM DRAPER OF PLYMOUTH, TAKEN
BEFORE THOMAS CEELY, MERCHANT, MAYOR OF THE BOROUGH
OF PLYMOUTH AFORESAID, THE 18ᵀᴴ DAY OF APRIL 1625.

He saith that eighteen days sithence[13] he was at Flushing and there did see a
bark of French built[14] of twenty-five tons or thereabouts, with nine Turks and
divers other Dutch and one black Moor in her, and as they of Flushing
reported, they were bound for Sally hauled out their bark and began their
voyage about eighteen days sithence, but what is become of her sithence, he
knoweth not but verily believeth that this was the bark that robbed the ship
of Salcombe and fisherboats of Looe.
William Draper.

Deposition of William Court

THE EXAMINATION OF WILLIAM COURT, OF PLYMOUTH,
SHIPWRIGHT, AGED TWENTY-THREE YEARS, TAKEN BEFORE
THOMAS CEELY, MERCHANT, MAYOR OF PLYMOUTH
AFORESAID, THE 7TH OF MAY 1625.

The said examinate saith that, about a year sithence, he went from the port
of Plymouth in a ship of Amsterdam called the [*Fortune*], of the burden of
two hundred tons, in a merchant voyage for Portugal, of which ship one
William Thomas was master, and that within six days after their departure
from Plymouth, they were surprised by a Turkish pirate of Sally, and that the
said pirate took out of the said ship, the [*Fortune*], this examinate and four
other Englishmen, and the rest of the company being Flemings, they did not
meddle with but suffered them to proceed with their said ship, the [*Fortune*],
in their intended voyage but carried away this examinate and the other four
English to Sally, where this examinate ever sithence hath remained as a slave.
    And farther saith that, about eight weeks sithence, he came out of Sally in
a Turkish ship of Sally, in company with five other Turkish ships of the same
place, who did bend their course for the coasts of England, and by the way,

---

[13] *sithence*: since; previously.
[14] *bark of French built*: French-built ship.

to weet,[15] about a month sithence, one of the said six Turkish ships took a ship of London of three score tons or thereabouts in the Norther Cape, and took out of her eleven men and their ordinance, and after sunk the said ship. And about six days after, they did take six French barks, a little off from Scilly,[16] and six score men which were in the said barks, all which men the said pirates took into their ships and chained them and left the barks fleeting on the stream.

And farther saith that, about twelve days sithence, the Turkish pirate wherein this examinate was did, a little off from Scilly, take a ship of Plymouth of the burden of three score tons, bound for the Newfoundland in a fishing voyage, wherein one William Legg[17] was master, and did take out of her the said master and seventeen others of her choicest men, all which also they chained, leaving in the said ship of Plymouth six of her worst men, and put this examinate also therein, and so cast off the said ship of Plymouth, which, about five days sithence, came into St. Ives in Cornwall.

And this examinate verily believeth that the said five other Turkish ships have done great spoil sithence the taking of the said six French barks, but what spoil they have done he certainly knoweth not.

And lastly saith that one Cooper was captain of the said Turkish ship wherein this examinate was, and four other English, and five Flemish runnegadoes,[18] besides thirty Turks and Moors, and that he hath heard the English and Flemish runnegadoes often say that they would fetch the Christians from the shore.

Tho. Ceely, Mayor

[On the reverse side, in another hand:]

The examination of William Court, of Plymouth, shipwright, 7 May 1625.

–Received 23 May.

[15] *to weet*: it is to be noted.
[16] *Scilly*: the Scilly Isles, a group of small islands off the coast of Cornwall.
[17] *William Legg*: also mentioned at the end of Robert Adams's letter (see p. 350).
[18] *runnegadoes*: variant spelling of *renegadoes*.

APPENDIX 4

PETITION SENT BY ENGLISH CAPTIVES IN
MOROCCO TO KING CHARLES I (1632)[1]

To the King's most excellent Majesty,

This humble petition of thirty-eight of Your Majesty's poor, distressed subjects, captives here in Barbary, under the king of Morocus,[2] whose names are hereunto annexed.

May it please Your Majesty of your gracious goodness and princely compassion to commiserate and think so upon the distressed estate of us, Your Majesty's poor subjects, slaves under the king of Morocus, who have lived here some twenty years, some sixteen, some twelve, and he that hath been least, seven years in most miserable bondage, without any succor from friends or country. Besides some, through the extreme want and servitude which we daily endure, have turned Moors,[3] and some have endured intolerable torment for Christ His sake. And still are living in hope that Your Majesty will be pleased to redeem them from this miserable slavery and to hasten Your Majesty's servant Mr. John Harryson's[4] dispatch back again with Your Majesty's letter, whereupon our liberty dependeth, who can further relate unto

---

[1] In Le Comte Henry de Castries, ed., *Les Sources Inédites de l'Histoire du Maroc–Archives et Bibliothèques d'Angleterre*, premiere série–dynasty Sa'dienne, vol. 3 (Paris: Paul Geuthner, 1936), 179–81.

[2] *king of Morocus*: The king of Morocco at this time was Mulay al-Walid.

[3] *turned Moors*: converted to Islam.

[4] *John Harryson's*: John Harrison was an English factor in Morocco who acted as royal agent to the Moroccan court under James I and then Charles I. As such, he was involved in negotiations to ransom enslaved Englishmen in Morocco.

Your Majesty our grievances and the occasions whereupon all this while we have been detained here, which we hope Your Majesty and honorable council will take into your royal considerations and not respect the private benefit of a few merchants[5] before the lives and liberties of so many of your poor, distressed subjects

And we all, as in duty are bound, shall not cease night and day to pray for Your Majesty's long and happy reign.

The names of the English captives under the king of Morocus, besides what are in Salley some seven or eight and in other places we know not how many.

Thomas Lambe	John Harnyman
William Shilton	Thomas Merrick
John Shilton	James Saunderson
William Headlye	Richard Griffin
Samuell Rosse	John Thomas
Josias Martine	Rening Shorte
John Tapley	Hercules Cooshine
Robert Weekes	Christopher Willson
Mathew Downe	Andrew Tape
Robert Cabell	Lewis Smith
George Pepperell	Teige Oswillivant
William Tovie	Garrett Barrye
Owin Mathew	William White
Richard Burrell	Morrice Bryan
Thomas Dixson	Nicholas Skinner
David Oliver	Edmund Hore
Thomas Tovie	Laurence Pessettgarnse
Nathaniell Fullthorne	William Collye
John Wright	John Daniell

Richard Martin out of a Dutch ship, a smith.

[Written at Marrakesh, probably between November 16, 1631, and February 1632.]

[5] *private benefit . . . few merchants*: Merchants may have opposed the ransom of certain English captives for one of two reasons at this time: either they did not want seamen who had been pirates, rather than legitimate merchantmen, to go free; or they did not want to stimulate the trade in bodies because the payment of ransom would strengthen the power and increase the resources of the Barbary corsairs, which would in turn make it more difficult for English merchant vessels to conduct trade in the Mediterranean without being attacked by those corsairs.

APPENDIX 5

LAUDIAN RITE FOR RETURNED RENEGADES (1637)

A Form of Penance and Reconciliation of a Renegado or Apostate from the Christian Religion to Turkism[1]

I. Let the offender's conviction[2] be first judicially had before the bishop of the diocese, that so there may stand, *apud acta*,[3] his detection or confession and that thereupon an excommunication be decreed and denounced[4] both in the cathedral and the parish church where he lives, yet so as that upon his submission there in court, he may be absolved *in diem*,[5] and the form of his penance enjoined him in manner following.

II. Let the minister of the place have frequent conference with the party in private; lay open and aggravate[6] the heinousness of his sin both in respect of God, the Church, and his own soul; and see whether his conscience be troubled with any other grievous crime, that so he may be the better fitted for absolution of all together.

III. Let there be an order decreed in court, referring him to the minister of the place, to see his penance performed accordingly and to reconcile him

---

[1] Reprinted in *The Works of the Most Reverend Father in God, William Laud, D. D., Sometime Lord Archbishop of Canterbury* (Oxford: John Henry Parker, 1853): 5.2.372–76.

[2] *offender's conviction*: Before undergoing the rites of penance and reconciliation, the offender had to be formally convicted of apostasy by an ecclesiastical court.

[3] apud acta: Latin, meaning "in the presence of his public acts."

[4] *denounced*: formally and officially proclaimed.

[5] in diem: Latin, meaning "before God."

[6] *aggravate*: add weight to.

to the Church, and let that order be published in the parish church on a Sunday at morning prayer, next before the communion service.

IV. The next Sunday following, let the offender be appointed to stand, all the time of divine service and sermon in the forenoon, in the porch of the church (order must be taken that boys and idle people flock not about him) if it have any, if none, yet without[7] the church door, if extremity of weather hinder not, in a penitent fashion in a white sheet and with a white wand in his hand, his head uncovered, his countenance dejected, not taking particular notice of any person that passeth by him; and when the people come in and go out of the church, let him upon his knees humbly crave their prayers and acknowledge his offence in this form: "Good Christians, remember in your prayers a poor, wretched apostate or renegado."

V. The second Sunday, let him stand in the church porch and in his penitential habit as before, and then, after the *Te Deum*[8] [is] ended, let him be brought in by one of the churchwardens so far as to the west side of the font of the said church. There let him penitently kneel till the second lesson be ended; then let him make his submission and ask mercy of God in the form following:

O Lord God of heaven and earth, be merciful unto me most wretched sinner. I confess, O Lord, I have justly deserved to be utterly renounced by Thee because I have yielded to renounce my Savior and that holy profession which I had formerly made of His name, whereby I was received into Thy Church. O God, forgive me this heinous and horrible sin, with all other my grievous sins against Thee, and let me, upon Thy gracious pardon and infinite mercy, be restored to the sight and benefit of this blessed sacrament, which I have so wickedly abjured, and be received (though most unworthy) into Thy gracious favor and the communion of Thy faithful people, even for Thy great mercy's sake in Jesus Christ, my blessed Lord and Savior.

(This said, let him smite his breast three times.)

Which done, let him, in an humble and devout manner, kiss the bottom stone of the font, strike his breast, and presently depart into the church porch as before.

[7] *without*: outside.

[8] Te Deum: The *Te Deum laudamus* (Latin, meaning "We praise thee, O God") is a chant sung during the traditional service of the Church of England.

VI. The third Sunday, let him at the beginning of divine service be brought into the body of the church and be placed near unto the minister's pew, and there let him stand in his penitential habit during the time of divine service, where the minister, immediately before the Apostles' Creed,[9] shall publicly put the offender in mind of the foulness of his sin and stir him up to a serious repentance, advising him that a slight and ordinary sorrow is not enough for so grievous an offence.

Which done, the minister shall ask the penitent publicly whether he hath found a true and earnest remorse in his soul for his sin, and whether he hath thoroughly humbled himself before God for it, and whether he doth desire that the whole congregation should take notice of his humiliation and unfeigned repentance.

In signification whereof, the offender shall say these words, or to the like effect, after the minister (let him name here himself both by his Christian and his surname):

I do here in the presence of almighty God and before you His faithful people humbly and penitently confess that I have grievously offended the majesty of God and deeply wounded my own soul in that I so far yielded to the weakness of my sinful flesh, as that I suffered myself through the cruelty of God's enemies to be miscarried to the renouncing of my dear Savior and the true Christian religion wherein I was brought up. I do well know what I have deserved, both at the hands of God and of His Church, for this wicked and graceless act, and now, as I have often betwixt God and my own soul washed this sin with my tears and craved His merciful forgiveness, so I beseech you all to take knowledge of this my public sorrow and humiliation and both to pardon and forgive that just offense[10] which I have herein given to you also, and the whole Church of Christ, and also to join with me in humble and hearty prayers to almighty God, that He will be pleased to seal unto my soul the full pardon and remission of this my grievous sin, even for the sake of His dear Son, my blessed Savior and Redeemer. In whose name and words I desire you to accompany these my prayers, saying with me, "Our Father, etc."

After this, the minister shall speak to the congregation to this effect:

[9] *Apostles' Creed*: a statement of belief in the basic Christian doctrines, ascribed to the Apostles. It begins, "I believe in God, the Father Almighty."

[10] *just offense*: a crime of which the renegade has been justly found to be guilty.

Seeing now, dear Christian brethren, that this offender hath given so good and full testimony of his true repentance and hath so humbly and fervently craved the forgiveness of God and His Church, I shall not need to use many words in persuading you how ready you ought to be both to conceive full hope of God's gracious pardon of him (as who is always ready to prevent and meet us in our turning to Him) and also to profess your forgiveness of him for so much as concerneth has offense towards you, and charitably to embrace him with the arms of tender pity and compassion as a true Christian convert to His Savior, and gladly to welcome him into that holy communion which his sinful fear and frailty caused him to forsake. Now therefore I do earnestly beseech you, in the bowels[11] of Christ Jesus our blessed Savior, to pass by the great offense of this sorrowful penitent, as well considering the weakness of our frail nature, when it is overpressed with violence and extremity of torments, and both to commiserate his fearful apostasy and to encourage and comfort him in this happy return to Christ and His Church.

VII. Here let the penitent kneel again eastward, and bowing to the very pavement, let him say thus, either by himself, if he be able to read it, or else after the minister:

O my soul, bless the Lord! Blessed be the Father of mercies and the God of all consolation; blessed be the Lord Jesus the Son of God, the Savior of the world; blessed be the Holy Spirit, God the Holy Ghost; blessed be the Holy Trinity, one God everlasting; blessed be the holy Catholic Church, and all you the servants of the Lord Jesus Christ; the name of God be blessed evermore for the assembly of His saints, and of the divine ordinances of His holy word and sacraments, and of His heavenly power committed to His holy priests in His Church, for the reconciliation of sinners unto Himself, and the absolving of them from all their iniquity. So here I, upon the bended knees of my body and soul, most humbly beg the assistance of all your Christian prayers and the benefit of that His holy ordinance; and I meekly beseech you, sir, as my ghostly[12] father, a priest of God, and the Church's deputy, to receive me into that grace and into the bosom of the Church and by loosing me from the bands of my grievous sins to make me partaker of that ines-

[11] *bowels*: merciful spirit.
[12] *ghostly*: spiritual.

timable benefit and so to reconcile me unto the mystical body of Christ Jesus, my Lord and Savior.

Then let the priest come forth to him and stand over him and, laying his hand on his head, say, as is prescribed in the Book of Common Prayer, thus:

The Lord Jesus Christ, who hath left power to His Church to absolve all sinners which truly repent and believe in Him, of His great mercy forgive thee thine offences; and by His authority committed to me, I absolve thee from this thy heinous crime of renegation[13] and from all other thy sins, in the name of the Father, of the Son, and of the Holy Ghost. Amen.

Then let the priest, turning himself eastward, kneel down in the same place, the penitent kneeling behind him, and say the collect which stands after the absolution in the Visitation of the Sick, but changing the later part of it thus:

O most merciful God, which according to the multitude of Thy mercies dost so put away the sins of those which truly repent that Thou rememberest them no more, open Thy eye of mercy upon this Thy servant, who most earnestly desireth pardon and forgiveness; renew in him, most loving Father, whatsoever hath been decayed by the fraud and malice of the Devil or by his own carnal will and frailness; preserve and continue him in the unity of the Church; consider his contrition and accept his humiliation; and forasmuch as he putteth his full trust only in Thy mercy, impute not unto him his former abnegation of Thee, but receive him into Thy favor, through the merits of Thy most dearly beloved Son, Jesus Christ our Savior. Amen.

After that, let the minister take him up and take away his white sheet and wand and, taking him by the hand, say unto him,

Dear brother (for so we all now acknowledge you to be), let me here advise you with what care and diligence every day of your life you ought to consider how much you are bound to the infinite goodness of God, who hath called you out of that woeful condition whereinto you had cast yourself, and how much it concerneth you ever hereafter to walk worthy of so

---

[13] *renegation*: apostasy.

great a mercy, being so much more careful to approve yourself in all holy
obedience to God by how much you have more dishonored and provoked
Him by this your shameful revolt from Him, which the same God, the
Father of mercies, vouchsafe to enable you unto, for the sake of the dear
Son of His love, Jesus Christ the righteous. Amen.

After this, let him be openly promised that upon any communion day following he shall be admitted to the holy sacrament, for which let him be
directed to prepare himself, and when he receives, let him make a solemn
oblation according to his ability, after the order set down in the service book.

APPENDIX 6

PARLIAMENTARY ORDINANCE FOR COLLECTIONS
TO BE MADE FOR THE RELIEF OF CAPTIVES IN ALGIERS
(ISSUED APRIL 25, 1643[1])

Upon the humble petition of Elizabeth Chickley, Susan Robinson, Mary Savage, Katherine Swanton, Mary Taylor, Julian Morris, and Lucie Michell, on the behalf of themselves and many others, setting forth,

That their husbands and others were taken by Turkish pirates, carried to Algier, and there now remain in miserable captivity, having great fines imposed on them for their ransoms; and that the petitioners have endeavored (by sale of their goods and help of their friends) to raise what part they can of the said fines but, being very poor and having great charge of children, are no ways able to make up the said fines without with some other relief, so that their said husbands (with the other captives and themselves), for want thereof, are like to perish; for relief wherein, the petitioners humbly implore the aid of this Parliament, as by the said petition may appear. And whereas the Parliament did heretofore take course for the setting forth of a fleet of ships for the suppressing of those pirates and deliverance of those poor captives, which hath not taken that success which could be wished, in respect of the rebellion in Ireland and distempers in this kingdom,[2] the safety of both which kingdoms have enforced

---

[1] In C. H. Firth and R. S. Rait, ed. *Acts and Ordinances of the Interregnum, 1642–1660*, 3 vols. (London, 1911), 1:134–35.

[2] *distempers in this kingdom*: The English civil war had broken out during the previous year.

the Parliament to employ several fleets of ships for the defense, preservation, and safety of His Majesty's dominions and clearing the seas of pirates
and other enemies to the state nearer home. It is therefore thought fit, and
so ordered by the Lords and Commons in Parliament, that collections be
made in the several[3] churches within the City of London and Westminster
and the borough of Southwark, and the suburbs and liberties of the said
cities, of the charitable benevolences of well-disposed Christians for and
towards the relief of the said captives; and the monies then collected to be
returned and paid by the churchwardens and collectors into the hands of
the commissioners of the navy appointed by both houses of Parliament,
who are to take care of the distribution and employment thereof, for and
towards the redemption of the said captives; the Lords and Commons not
doubting of a free and liberal contribution of all His Majesty's people to
so good and pious a work, the great pressures being upon the state at
present disabling or not permitting them to afford them any other relief.
The collection to last two months and to be but once made in any parish.

[3] *several*: various.

APPENDIX 7

LETTER FROM PHILIP LLOYD, THE ENGLISH
FACTOR IN TUNIS, TO KING CHARLES II (1680)[1]

24 Jan 1680
. . . It is more for the honor of Your Majesty's service, as well for the safety and ease of your trading subjects, that the same form of passes be now used which hath been formerly used in execution of the treaties with Argiers[2] and is at present in course and execution of the treaties with Tunis and Tripoli[3] and that the transmitting to the outports[4] blank passes signed and sealed may be of dangerous consequence to the peace and give occasion to slanderous reports of our negligence in committing to others the care and trust reposed in us and expected from us by the Argierines in pursuance of their treaty.

[1] Manuscript. Additional MSS 46412 [f.18]. British Library.
[2] *treaties with Argiers*: A treaty, negotiated by Admiral John Lawson, was signed by England and Algiers in 1662. It created an elaborate system of passes to be carried by both English and Algerian ships and presented as evidence of official government sponsorship. Algerian privateers were allowed to send two men to board and inspect the cargo and passenger lists of English vessels carrying passes. The passes were engraved on parchment and ornamented with the image of a ship or of sea gods. Scolloped indentures were then cut through the engraved images, and the top portion of a pass was sent to the authorities in Algiers, who were instructed to permit all ships producing passes that fitted these tops to travel freely. After a period of renewed conflict between England and Algiers, a new peace treaty was negotiated by Sir Edward Spragge in 1671 and yet another agreement was reached in 1676.
[3] *treaties with Tunis and Tripoli*: Treaties quite similar to those concluded with Algiers were also made with Tunis and Tripoli in 1662.
[4] *outports*: all English ports other than London.

And further we most humbly propose to Your Majesty to send order to Admiral Herbert[5] to go to Argiers and to acquaint that governor that the form of the passes hereunto annexed, which is the same used for Tunis and Tripoli, is that which Your Majesty hath directed us to make use of, and that he negotiate their acquiescing therein. . . .

[The following form of pass is given in the letter:]

Suffer the ship _____

to pass with her company, passengers, goods, merchandizes without any let, hindrance, seizure, or molestation. The said ship appearing unto me (or us) by good testimony to belong to the subjects of our sovereign lord the King and to no foreigner. Given under my hand (or our hands) and the seal of my (or our) office of Admiral at _____ the _____ day of _____ in the year of our Lord one thousand six hundred eighty.

To all persons whom these may concern,

By command of _____

[5] *Admiral Herbert*: Admiral Arthur Herbert took command of the English Mediterranean fleet in 1680.

BIBLIOGRAPHY OF ENGLISH CAPTIVITY NARRATIVES FROM THE SIXTEENTH AND SEVENTEENTH CENTURIES

This bibliography includes only accounts by English captives who were enslaved or held for ransom under Muslim masters. Not included here are the other early modern captivity narratives describing Englishmen who were held captive or enslaved by the Spanish or by sub-Saharan African tribes or held as galley slaves in France, Italy, and other Christian principalities.

Brooks, Francis. *Barbarian Cruelty. Being a True History of the Distressed Condition of the Christian Captives under the Tyranny of Mully Ishmael Emperor of Morocco, and King of Fez and Macqueness in Barbary. In which is likewise given a particular Account of his late Wars with the Algerines. The manner of his Pirates taking the Christians and Others. His breach of faith with Christian princes. A Description of his Castles and Guards, and the Places where he keeps his Women, his Slaves and Negroes. With a particular Relation of the dangerous Escape of the Author, and two English Men more from thence, after a miserable Slavery of ten Years*. London, 1693. Reprint, Boston, 1700.

Browne, Abraham. Manuscript. Massachusetts Historical Society. "A Book of Remembrance of God's Provydences towards me, A. B., throughout the cours of my Life, written for my own medytacion in New Engl." [The portion of this biographical narrative describing Browne's captivity in Salé is printed as part of an article titled "Abraham Browne's Captivity by the Barbary Pirates, 1655," in *Seafaring in Colonial Massachusetts*, ed. Stephen T. Riley (Boston: Colonial Society of Massachusetts, 1980).]

Coxere, Edward. Manuscript. *A Relation of the Several Adventures by Sea with the Dangers, difficulties and Hardships I Met for Several years as also the Deliverances and Escapes through them for which I Have Cause to Give the Glory to God For Ever.* Printed as *Adventures by Sea of Edward Coxere.* Ed. E. H. W. Meyerstein. Oxford: Oxford University Press, Clarendon, 1945. [This life narrative includes the description of Coxere's capture and imprisonment by the Turks in 1657–58 (pp. 53–80). The text as a whole is a kind of spiritual biography, documenting Coxere's conversion to Quakerism.]

Deane, James. "A Further Narrative of James Deane and others," in William Okeley, *Eben-ezer; or, A Small Monument of Great Mercy Appearing in the Miraculous Deliverance of William Okeley, John Anthony, William Adams, John Jephs, John -- Carpenter, From the Miserable Slavery of Algiers,* 2d ed. (London, 1684), 86–100. [Deane sailed for Barbados in 1679, when he was captured by Algerian corsairs. He lived as a slave in Algiers for two and a half years before being ransomed.]

Elliot, Adam. *A Modest Vindication of Titus Oates the Salamanca-Doctor from Perjury; or, An Essay to Demonstrate Him only Forsworn in several Instances.* London, 1682. [Includes "A Narrative of My Travails, Captivity and Escape from Salle, in the Kingdom of Fez." Elliot was captured around 1670.]

Ellyatt, Robert. Ms Parm. 988. Biblioteca Palatina di Parma. "All' Ill[ustrissimo] et R[everendissi]mo Sig[no]re mio Colend[issimo] Il Sig[no]re Cardinale Farnese per Il Capitan' Roberto Elliata, Gentilhuomo Inglese di Roma alli 12. d'Agosto 1615." [Written in Italian by an English soldier and Roman Catholic who was captured and brought to Tunis. Reprinted in *Les Cahiers de Tunisie*, ed. Jean Pignon (1961), 33:119–63.]

Fox, John. "The woorthie enterprise of John Foxe, in delivering 266. Christians out of the captivitie of the Turkes at Alexandria," in Richard Hakluyt, *The Principall Navigations, Voiages, and Discoveries of the English Nation Made by Sea or Over-land to the most Remote and Farthest Distant Quarters of the Earth at any time within the compasse of these 1600 Yeeres* (London, 1589), 131–56. [Another version of this narrative appeared as Anthony Munday, *The Admirable Deliverance of 266 Christians by John Reynard Englishman from the captivitie of the Turkes, who had been Gally slaves many yeares in Alexandria* (London, 1608).]

Gee, Joshua. Manuscript. Wadsworth Atheneum. Printed as the *Narrative of Joshua Gee of Boston, Mass., while he was captive in Algeria of the Barbary States, 1680–1687.* Ed. Albert C. Bates. Hartford, 1943.

Hasleton, Richard. *Strange and Wonderfull Things Happened to Richard Hasleton, borne at Braintree in Essex, in his ten yeares travailes in many forraine countries. Penned as he delivered it from his own mouth.* London, 1595. [Reprinted in *An English Garner: Voyages and Travels*, ed. E. R. Beazley (New York: Cooper Square, 1964), 2:151 ff.]

Johnson, Richard, et al. "The casting away of the *Toby* near Cape Espartel, without the strait of Gibraltar on the coast of Barbary, 1593," in Richard Hakluyt, *The Principal Navigations, Voyages, Traffiques and Discoveries of the English Nation*, 2d ed., 3 vols. (London, 1598–1600), 2:201–2. [A very brief narrative describing the shipwreck and capture of an English ship and crew on the coast of Morocco. Ten members of the crew were soon ransomed and lived to return to England.]

Knight, Francis. *A Relation of Seven Yeares Slaverie Under the Turkes of Argeire, suffered by an English Captive Merchant. Wherein is also conteined all memorable Passages, Fights, and Accidents, which happined in that Citie, and at Sea with their Shippes and Gallies during that time. Together with a description of the sufferings of the miserable captives under that mercilesse tyrannie. Whereunto is added a second Booke conteining a description of Argeire, with its originall manner of Government, increase and present flourishing estate.* London, 1640. Two printings.

Middleton, Henry. "The sixth Voyage, set forth by the East-Indian Company in three Shippes; the *Trades Increase*, of one thousand Tunnes, and in her the Generall Sir Henry Middleton, Admirall; the *Pepper-Corne* of two hundred and fiftie, Vice-Admirall, the Captaine Nicholas Dounton: and the *Darling* of ninetie. The Barke *Samuel* Followed as a Victualler of burthen one hundred and eightie," in Samuel Purchas, *Purchas his Pilgrimes* (London, 1625), 247–66. [Reprinted as "An Account of the Captivity of Sir Henry Middleton By the Turks at Moka, or Mokha; and of his journey from thence, with thirty four Englishmen more, to the Basha at Zenan, or Sanaa: With a Description of the Country, and a Journal of their Travels to that City, and back again," in Jean de Laroque, *A Voyage to Arabia Foelix through the Eastern Ocean and the streights of the Red-Sea, being the first made by the French in the years 1708, 1709, and 1710 . . . To which is added an account of the captivity of Sir Henry Middleton at Mokha, by the Turks, in the year 1612* (London, 1732).]

Newes from Sally: Of a Strange Delivery of Foure English Captives from the Slavery of the Turkes. London, 1642.

Nixon, Anthony. *The Three English Brothers. Sir Thomas Sherley his travels, with his three yeares imprisonment in Turkie: his inlargement by his Majesties letters to the great turke: and lastly, his safe returne into england this present yeare, 1607.* London, 1607.

Okeley, William. *Eben-ezer; or, A Small Monument of Great Mercy Appear-*

ing in the Miraculous Deliverance of William Okeley, John Anthony, William Adams, John Jephs, John -- Carpenter, From the Miserable Slavery of Algiers, with the wonderful Means of their Escape in a Boat of Canvas; the great Distress, and utmost Extremities which they endured at Sea for Six Days and Nights; their safe Arrival at Mayork: With several Matters of Remarque during their long Captivity, and the following Providences of God which brought them safe to England. London, 1675. Reprint, 1676. 2d ed., 1684. 3d ed., 1764.

Phelps, Thomas. *A true account of the captivity of Thomas Phelps, at Machaness in Barbary, and of his strange escape in Company of Edmund Baxter and others, as also of the burning two of the greatest pirat-ships belonging to that kingdom, in the River of Mamora; upon the thirteenth day of June 1685.* London, 1685.

Pitts, Joseph. *A True and Faithful Account of the Religion and Manners of the Mohammetans. In which is a particular Relation of their Pilgrimage to Mecca, The Place of Mohammet's birth; And a description of Medina, and of his Tomb there. As likewise of Algier, and the Country adjacent: And of Alexandria, Grand-Cairo, &c. With an Account of the Author's being taken Captive, the Turks Cruelty to him, and of his Escape. In which are many things never Publish'd by any Historian before.* Exeter, 1704. Reprint, Exeter, 1717. 2d ed., London, 1719. 3d ed., London, 1731 (with additions, titled *A Faithful Account*). Reprint, London, 1738.

Rawlins, John. *The Famous and Wonderfull Recovery of a Ship of Bristoll, called the Exchange, From the Turkish Pirates of Argier. With the Unmatchable attempts and good successe of John Rawlins, Pilot in her, and other slaves; who in the end wiuth the slaughter of about 40 of the Turkes and Moores, brought the Ship into Plimouth the 13 of February last; with the Captaine a Renegado and 5 Turkes more, besides the resemption of 24 men, and one boy, from Turkish slaverie.* London, 1622. [Reprinted in vol. 7 of Edward Arber, *An English Garner*, 8 vols. (1877–90); and in *An English Garner: Stuart Tracts, 1603–1693*, ed. and intro. C. H. Firth (New York: Cooper Square, 1964), 247–74.]

A Relation Strange and True, of a Ship of Bristol named the Jacob, of 120 tunnes, which was about the end of Octob. last 1621 taken by the Turkish pirats of Argier. And how within five dayes after, foure English youths did valiantly overcome 13 of the said Turks, and brought the ship to S. Lucas in Spaine, where they sold nine of the Turks for gally-slaves. London, 1622.

Saunders, Thomas. *A true discription and breefe discourse, of a most lamentable voiage, made lately to Tripolie in Barbarie, in a ship named the Jesus: wherein is not only shewed the great miserie, that then happened the aucthor hereof and his whole companie, as well the marchants as the marriners in that voiage, according to the curssed custome of those bar-*

barous and cruell tyrants, in their terrible usage of Christian captives: but also, the great unfaithfulnesse of those heathnish infidels, in not regarding their promise. Together, with the most wonderfull judgement of God, upon the king of Tripolie and his sonne, and a great number of his people, being all the tormentors of those English captives. London, 1587. [Another version appears in Richard Hakluyt, *The Principal Navigations, Voyages, Traffiques and Discoveries of the English Nation*, 2d ed., 3 vols. (London, 1598–1600), 2:184–91, as "The voyage made to Tripolis in Barbarie, in the yeere 1583, with a ship called the *Jesus*, wherein the adventures and distresses of some Englishmen are truly reported...."]

Smith, John. *The True Travels, Adventures, and Observations of Captaine John Smith, In Europe, Asia, Affrica, and America, from Anno Domini 1593 to 1629.* London, 1630. [In chapters II through 17 Smith tells the story of his capture by Turks at the battle of Rottenton, his subsequent captivity among the Turks, and his escape.]

S[mith], T[homas]. *The Adventures of (Mr. T. S.) An English Merchant, Taken Prisoner by the Turks of Argiers and carried into the Inland Countries of Africa: With a Description of the Kingdom of Argiers, of all the Towns and Places of Note thereabouts. Whereunto is added a Relation of the Chief Commodities of the Countrey, and of the Actions and Manners of the People. Written first by the Author, and fitted for the Publick view by A. Roberts. Whereunto is annex'd an Observation of the Tide, and how to turn a Ship out of the Straights Mouth the Wind being Westerly; By Richard Norris.* London, 1670.

Spratt, Devereux. Manuscript. [First published as "The Capture of a Protestant Divine, by an Algerine Corsair, in the Seventeenth Century," in T. A. B. Spratt, *Travels and Researches in Crete*, 2 vols. (1865; reprint, Amsterdam: Adolf M. Hakkert, 1984), 1:384–87.]

A True and Perfect Account of the Examination, Confession, and Execution of Joan Perry and her two sons ... for the supposed murder of Wm. Harrison [incl.] Mr. Harrison's own account, how he was conveyed into Turkey, and there made a slave for above two years ... how he made his escape. London, 1676.

Wadsworth, James. *The English Spanish Pilgrime; or, A new discoverie of Spanish popery and jesuitical strategems.* London, 1629. Reprint, 1630. [Chapter 5 describes his experiences as a slave in Morocco.]

Webbe, Edward. *The Rare and most wonderful thinges which Edward Webbe an Englishman borne, hathe seene and passed in his troublesome travailes, in the Cities of Jerusalem, Dammasko, Bethelem and Galely: and in the Landes of Jewrie, Egipt, G[r]ecia, Russia, and in the Land of Prester John. Wherein is set foorth his extreame slaverie sustained many yeres togither, in the Gallies and wars of the Great Turk against the Lan-*

des of Persia, Tartaria, Spaine, and Portugall, with the manner of his releasement, and coming into Englande in May last. London, 1590. [This edition was "printed by Ralph Blower, for Thomas Pavier." A "newly enlarged and corrected edition" appeared in the same year, printed for William Wright.] Reprint, 1592 and 1600. [The text was edited by Edward Arber and included in his English Reprints series (London: Murray, 1868). It was also in a version edited by Edmund Goldsmid (Edinburgh: privately printed, 1885).]

Whitehead, John. Ms. Sloane 90. British Library. "John Whitehead his relation of Barbary." [The author was taken by Moroccan corsairs in 1691 and brought to Meknes, where he remained until at least 1697. The manuscript is incomplete and does not include an account of his return to England.]